BACK TO SHARED PROSPERITY

BACK TO SHARED PROSPERITY

The Growing Inequality of Wealth and Income in America

Ray Marshall

editor

M.E. Sharpe
Armonk, New York
London, England

Library of Congress Cataloging-in-Publication Data

Back to shared prosperity : the growing inequality of wealth and
income in America / Ray Marshall, editor.
p.   cm.
Includes bibliographical references and index.
ISBN 0-7656-0424-8 (hardcover : alk. paper).—ISBN 0-7656-0425-6 (pbk. : alk. paper)
1. United States—Economic conditions—1981–   2. United States—
Social conditions—1981–   3. Income distribution—United States.
4. United States—Economic policy—1993–   I. Marshall, Ray F.
HC106.82.B33   2000
399.2′0973—dc21   99-11649
CIP

Printed in the United States of America

The paper used in this publication meets the minimum requirements of
American National Standard for Information Sciences—
Permanence of Paper for Printed Library Materials,
ANSI Z 39.48-1984.

BM (c)   10   9   8   7   6   5   4   3   2   1
BM (p)   10   9   8   7   6   5   4   3   2   1

Contents

List of Tables and Figures

Tables

Figures

Preface

Restoring Broadly Shared Prosperity

The essays in this volume were prepared for the Restoring Broadly Shared Prosperity Project (RBSP), which was initiated by David Hamburg, former president of the Carnegie Corporation of New York. The main questions David asked us to examine were: (1) To what extent are major social and political problems caused by basic income and employment trends? and (2) Is it possible to restore the kind of broadly shared prosperity the United States experienced in the decades before the early 1970s? In keeping with David Hamburg's approach to the many important issues the Carnegie Corporation addressed during his presidency, we sought essayists who could synthesize the very best research to answer these questions. Although these essays were prepared by people from different disciplines and perspectives, there is general agreement that most serious social and political problems are rooted in such fundamental economic trends as stagnant growth in productivity and output, growing inequality of wealth and income, and declining opportunity for many Americans. Broadly shared prosperity is assumed to be in the public interest because, despite a strong economy and low levels of unemployment, the growing inequality of wealth and income we have experienced since the early 1970s poses serious threats to our political, so-cial, and economic well-being. There also is agreement that while some problems might be self-correcting, the most basic economic trends are very powerful and will not be reversed without the kinds of public and private policies suggested in this volume. These essays concentrate on various social and economic problems plaguing the United States and therefore do not stress the fact that the United States remains the world's strongest economy with very high average levels of living. We also have a very dynamic and entrepreneurial business sector, which is at the cutting edge of technological innovation, especially in information and communications technologies. Moreover, relative to Europe,[1] the United States has had strong job creation and low unemployment in the 1990s and provides more room for individual freedom and initiative than any other major industrial economy.

It would be a mistake, however, to allow hubris to cloud our vision about our problems or the sources of our strength. Unemployment is low in the United States despite anemic growth in productivity and output, in part because of slower growth in the workforce than in the 1960s and 1970s. Moreover, the United States has many problems, including relatively low levels of saving and investment; high levels of debt; very large trade deficits; probably the worst K–12 public school system among the major industrialized democracies; high levels of poverty, especially among children; growing numbers of people who remain largely disconnected from the economic mainstream, even in an expanding economy; and more inequality than most other industrialized countries or than we had before the 1980s, as well as stagnant or declining incomes for most Americans. Additionally, American workers have weaker voices in the society and at work than their counterparts in Europe.

Thus, despite our many strengths, the United States is not the model for the world as some argue. Indeed, history and recent experiences in Japan and Asia teach us that countries can learn from the experiences of others, but that no country has found the answers for all others. The essays in this volume are based on the assumptions that our successes give us the resources to address our problems and a failure to develop the appropriate policies and institutions would make our prosperity unsustainable.

The underlying assumption of the RBSP project is that shared prosperity is the key to economic sustainability, social stability, and stronger democratic institutions. Moreover, halting or slowing the growing inequality of wealth and income is a major precondition for shared prosperity. It would be naive to assume that we can achieve equal opportunity anytime soon, but the *trend* should be toward more equality of opportunity, not less.

Widening income and wealth gaps would be less problematic if all Americans had an equal opportunity to attain the highest incomes and if all incomes were rising. Unfortunately, in the United States most incomes are stagnant or falling. The main determinants of opportunity are family background, innate ability, luck, economic growth, and the opportunity structures confronting individuals and groups. Family background has become somewhat less important to economic mobility, but is still the most important factor. While innate ability undoubtedly is a factor in opportunity, there is, however, considerable evidence that public policies can counteract the influence of family background and enable people to prosper according to their abilities and aspirations. Sufficient economic growth is the most important of these conditions, but opportunity is influenced by other factors as well, especially the access individuals and groups have to quality education and rewarding careers. Shared prosperity therefore requires sufficient economic growth to provide jobs for new entrants to the workforce and those displaced by economic and technological change and improvements in opportunity structures. These are the main subjects addressed by this overview and the essays in this volume.

Note

1. The United States experienced a faster rate of job growth than Europe as a whole, but slower growth than many other developed countries. Between 1989 and 1994, the annual rate of job creation in the United States was 1.6 percent, compared with 5.3 percent for Japan, 2.5 percent for West Germany, 2.4 percent for Australia, 6.4 percent for Canada, and 5.9 percent for the Netherlands (Larry Mishel, Jared Bernstein, and Jay Schmitt, *State of Working America 1996–97* (Armonk, NY: M.E. Sharpe, 1997, ch. 4).

Acknowledgments

I am grateful for the many people who made this volume possible. Even though the essayists are among the best and busiest people in their fields, they all responded with enthusiasm to this project. I also want to thank David Hamburg for his leadership and insight during the eight years I served on Carnegie Corporation's board of trustees, but also for initiating and supporting this project. Geri Mannion, the Carnegie program officer responsible for this project, also provided helpful guidance and support. Jeff Faux and his colleagues at the Economic Policy Institute not only contributed a number of excellent essays, but also helped organize a valuable conference at which some of the essays were presented and debated before being assembled with others in this volume. I am especially indebted to Cheryl McVay for her dedicated and very competent assistance with every aspect of this project.

I want to pay special tribute to Robert Eisner, whose recent death deprives us of one of our best and most respected economists. Bob's essay for this volume reflects his insistence that economic policy be based on sound theory, accurate measurement, and clear thinking. I am grateful to Bob's daughter, Mary Eisner Eccles, for her final editing of his essay.

BACK TO SHARED PROSPERITY

Overview

Back to Shared Prosperity:
The Growing Inequality of Wealth and Income in America

Ray Marshall

I. Introduction

Many of America's most serious social problems either are caused or exacerbated by some fundamental economic trends. The most basic forces for change are technology, especially information and communications technology (ICT); some significant demographic and labor market trends; and the intensification of competition, resulting from ICT and the globalization of markets. These changes have eroded the effectiveness of the policies, institutions, and economic arrangements that were responsible for America's enormous industrial strength in the first two-thirds of this century as well as for the longest period of shared prosperity in history—from the 1940s into the 1970s. During this period, Americans with limited formal education who were willing to work hard could earn middle-class incomes and provide better futures for their families.

The global problems exacerbated by the energy price shocks of the 1970s reversed the economic fortunes of most Americans and dampened the expectation that succeeding generations would be better off.[1] Some of the most serious problems since the early 1970s include much slower growth in productivity and output; a rise in long-term joblessness; lower or stag-

nant real wages for all but the top 25 percent of wage earners, but especially for those with high school educations or less; growing inequalities in wealth and income; the need to work longer hours to sustain family incomes as most men's real wages fall; rising poverty levels; and the declining power of employees to participate in workplace and governmental decisions. One of the most important indicators of our economic problems is slower productivity growth (to only about a third as high as between 1945 and 1965 and less than half of the 1870–1970 trend of 2.3 percent). As a result, about three times as much labor is required to get the same increase in output as between 1945 and 1965; between 1990 and 1996, total output (GDP) grew at an annual rate of only 2 percent, compared with 5 percent in the 1960s, 3.6 percent in the 1970s, and 2.8 percent in the 1980s. Indeed, the expansion that began in 1991 is the slowest of any since World War II.

Despite these problems—and others explored in Part I—the American economy is basically strong and could, as some analysts predict, be poised for strong growth in productivity and output without igniting unacceptable levels of inflation. Unfortunately, however, while some demographic and labor market changes could moderate growing economic disparities, without

3

positive interventions the most powerful trends probably will continue to perpetuate inequality.

The widening income and wealth gaps would be less problematic if they were offset by greater upward mobility. In that case, as some analysts argue, inequality would serve socially useful incentive purposes. But the evidence presented in Dan McMurrer and Isabel Sawhill's RBSP essay shows that mobility has not increased to offset growing inequality. As a consequence, opportunity is declining for many Americans.

Edith Rasell, Barry Bluestone, and Lawrence Mishel's work at the Economic Policy Institute for the RBSP project documents the growing inequality of wealth and income and the declining living standards since the early 1970s for most Americans.[2] Their data show that problems are most severe for the 40 percent of families with the lowest incomes. They also reveal that workers with the least education have experienced the largest wage reductions, but that wage losses have spread up the education ladder, so that even men with college degrees had lower real wages in 1997 than in 1973. Between 1989 and 1997 the median real incomes of college graduates with one to five years of experience fell by 7.4 percent for men and 6.1 percent for women. In the previous decade (1979 to 1989), by contrast, the median real incomes of women with one to five years of experience rose by 11.2 percent while that of young men fell by 10.7 percent.[3] There has, in addition, been an increase in poverty among workers employed full time, year round.[4]

Thus, the economic expansion that began in the early 1990s did little to reverse the trend toward growing inequality and declining wages for those in low-paid jobs. Data from the Bureau of Labor Statistics show that the median real wage for workers with high school diplomas fell 6 percent between 1980 and 1996, while wages for college graduates rose 12 per-

cent. Contrary to the assumption that fringe benefits tend to equalize wages, these gaps were even wider for total compensation, which includes government-mandated benefits like Social Security and unemployment insurance and company benefits like health insurance and pensions.[5]

Data for 1997 show that seven years into the recovery that started in 1991, wages and incomes for most workers had not been restored to their pre-recession levels, which were much lower than they were at the beginning of the 1970s. In 1996 and 1997, with tight labor markets, low inflation, and higher minimum wages, real wages for the typical worker rose at an annual rate of 2.6 percent, and even faster for the lowest-wage jobs.[6] Nevertheless, median earnings, adjusted for inflation, were 3.1 percent lower in 1997 than in 1989, during which time real hourly wages stagnated or fell for the bottom 60 percent of workers. Wages for the bottom 80 percent of men were lower in 1997 than in 1989, during which time the median real wage for males fell 6.7 percent. Median wages for women continued to rise, but at an annual rate of only 0.8 percent compared to 5.7 percent in the 1980s.

Income growth for families was slower in the 1990s than in previous decades. Median family income was 2.3 percent ($1,000) less than in 1996 (the most recent year for which data are available) than in 1989, despite the fact that the typical married-couple family worked 247 more hours (over six weeks) in 1996 than they did in 1989.

Jobs also became less secure in the 1990s as the percentage of workers in jobs that last at least ten years fell from 41 in 1979 to 35.4 in 1996. Most of the deterioration in job security has been since the late 1980s.

Income inequality continued to grow rapidly in the 1990s, though at a somewhat slower rate than in the 1980s. Additionally, the typical middle-class family had nearly 3 percent less wealth in 1997 than in 1989, despite the stock market boom. The richest 10 percent of American households reaped 85.8 percent of the growth in the stock market between 1989 and 1997. In 1995, less than one-third of U.S. households held more than $5,000 in stock, 90 percent of which was owned by the wealthiest 10 percent of households; 60 percent of households owned no stock in any form. Economic Policy Institute projections show that the share of wealth held by the top 1 percent of households grew from 37.4 percent in 1989 to 39.1 percent in 1997, while the share of wealth held by the middle fifth of families fell from 4.8 percent to 4.4 percent.

Despite relatively faster growth in wages of the lowest-paid workers as the recovery expanded into its sixth year, the poverty rate in 1996 (13.7 percent) was actually higher than it was in 1989 (12.8 percent). Poverty among children was 20.5 percent in 1996, 19.6 percent in 1989, and 16.4 percent in 1979. A much larger percentage of American children are poor than in any other major industrial country.

According to Rasell, Bluestone, and Mishel, the basic reasons for rising income inequality are the slowdown in economic growth and the absorption of a larger share of that growth by higher income families and business profits than was the case between 1952 and the mid-1980s. These analysts attribute the economic slowdown mainly to slower productivity growth, decreased public and private investment, the shift of jobs to lower-productivity service sectors, American businesses' focus on short-term profits, high real interest rates, and rising joblessness (i.e., unemployment and underemployment). The principal causes of declining real wages, according to these analysts, were: declining manufacturing employment, more intensive international competition, the declining real value of the minimum wage, decreased collective bargaining coverage, and deregulation.

Wealth, according to Ed Wolff in his RBSP essay, has become even more unequally distributed than income. The wealthiest 20 percent of households had 84 percent of the nation's marketable wealth in 1992 and received 99 percent of the increase in wealth between 1983 and 1989. The share of wealth owned by the bottom 80 percent of households fell from 19 to 16 percent between 1982–92 and they received only 1 percent of the increase in wealth between 1983–89.

One of the most important consequences of low levels of wealth for middle- and low-income families is to weaken the "cushion" for families when they are without income. The average American family had accumulated only enough wealth in 1989 to sustain its normal consumption for 3.6 months; the second quintile of households had only enough wealth to sustain consumption for about one month, and the bottom 20 percent had no cushion at all.

The income and wealth gaps are not just relative—they are absolute. In terms of average real wages, most workers are worse off than they were in 1970. The absolute problem is that most families have barely enough income to maintain their living conditions, despite working more and incurring larger debts. These families are disturbed not only because they often face time constraints and perceive fewer opportunities for their children, but also because nobody has developed a credible policy paradigm to deal with U.S. and global economic problems. The paradigm that served the United States and other industrial countries so well in the 1950s and 1960s became much less effective in the early 1970s.

Some insights can be gained into what might be done to restore shared prosperity by examining the forces that contributed to broader participation in economic progress from the end of the Great Depression until the early 1970s— sometimes referred to as America's Golden Era.

America's Golden Era

The economy that evolved in the United States during the first two-thirds of the twentieth century had three distinguishing characteristics: a heavy natural resource orientation; supporting policies and institutions, especially pragmatic public–private partnerships to build the education, transportation, and other infrastructures that facilitated rapid economic growth and revived the system during the 1930s when private demand faltered; and the mass production system, made possible by a large and growing internal market for standardized products. The system's main economic advantage was its ability to achieve very high productivity levels through economies of scale with a combination of relatively high fixed capital costs, a few highly educated and skilled workers, and a heavy reliance on front-line workers who needed little more than basic literacy and math skills. The advantages of the mass production system caused its management practices to be widely emulated in governments and schools as well as in industry.

The mass production organization of work was rationalized by Frederick Taylor's scientific management system, which primarily sought to give management almost complete control by modeling the "one best" method for performing a task and transferring ideas, skills, and knowledge to management and machines. Only managerial, professional, and technical workers needed higher-order thinking skills.

Most workers could perform the "one best" method with routine work skills and very basic academic training. Management's control of the work was facilitated by detailed instructions and regulations enforced by layers of supervisors and inspectors.

Despite its productivity, the mass production system faced a number of very serious problems by the end of the 1940s. During the 1930s, the United States and other industrialized countries addressed the most critical of these problems, periodic recessions and depressions, through "Keynesian" policies designed to reduce unemployment by stimulating aggregate demand. Many analysts thought that U.S. performance during World War II demonstrated the efficacy of these policies. Despite the heavy human and material costs of the war, the average American was better off in material terms after the war than when it started. Indeed, it is no exaggeration to say that the 1940–73 period was dominated by the war, from which the United States emerged as the only intact major power. The Keynesian demand-enhancing policies also justified unions and collective bargaining and such income support systems as unemployment compensation, pensions, and agricultural price supports.

Another major problem for the mass production system was how to structure the relationships between workers and managers in systems where institutions and public policies gave employers overwhelming power relative to workers. In every industrial democracy, these relationships were worked out in industrial relations systems. At their peak in the 1950s and 1960s, American unions, though never as politically powerful as their European counterparts, nevertheless enrolled about a third of the workforce, strongly influenced wages and working conditions in non-union companies, and had considerable power to represent workers' interests in the workplace as well as in the polity and society.

Although these policies and institutions contributed to the longest period of shared prosperity in history, we should note that the distribution of income, wealth, and opportunity remained very unequal and not all major groups shared equitably in the nation's prosperity. Women and minorities, especially blacks and Mexican-Americans, continued to be disadvantaged by overt and institutional discrimination. Nevertheless, prosperity contributed to a weakening of discrimination as well as to the increased power of women and minorities to combat discrimination. And, as Heidi Hartmann demonstrates in her RBSP essay, even though the gender gap remains, it has narrowed and women continued their economic progress into the 1980s, when men's real wages were declining. Unfortunately, as noted earlier, the wages of men and women fell during the late 1980s and early 1990s.

The New Economy: Global Competition and Knowledge-Intensive Work

Toward the end of the 1960s there were growing signs that America's economic system was in trouble. The main forces for change were technology and increased international competition, which together weakened the mass production system and its supporting institutions. In a more competitive world dominated by knowledge-intensive technology, the keys to economic success became human resources and more effective production systems, not natural resources and traditional mass production economies of scale. Economies of scale are still very important, but they now must be considered in a global context and are called upon to recoup much more extensive research-and-development costs than before.

Although no consensus has formed for a new economic policy model, two things are reasonably clear: the policies that supported the old economy have become less effective and the development of human capital is necessary, though not sufficient, for success in the new economy.

The Basic Choice: High Value Added or Low Wages

It also is clear that with the internationalization of markets, countries, companies, and people can thrive only if they yield to the imperatives of global competition. The most basic of these imperatives is that we can compete in only two ways: reduce wages and income or increase value added (or productivity and quality), sometimes referred to as the "high road." Germany, Japan, and most other industrialized countries have rejected the low-wage, or "low-road," option because they see that lower and more unequal incomes would threaten their political, social, and economic health. They also realize that the only way for the low-wage option to improve incomes is through the use of more labor and physical resources to produce a given output, which clearly limits economic progress. The high-value-added option, by contrast, could create very steep learning and earning curves and therefore holds great promise for personal, organizational, and national advancement. A production system based on ideas, skills, and knowledge clearly is less restrictive than one based on manual work and physical resources. However, since under present institutional arrangements in the United States market forces tend to lower wages for most workers, the high-road outcome will require positive interventions. Such a system is examined in Part III of this overview.

How Are We Doing?

The essays in this volume document several important social problems associated with joblessness, growing inequality, and fundamental structural changes in the American economy since the 1970s.

Opportunity in America

One of the most serious consequences of growing inequality and the slowdown in economic growth has been declining opportunities for many, if not most, Americans. These include poor children, especially minorities; young males, especially blacks; workers with high school educations or less; many children at all income levels whose parents have less time for them because they must work longer hours in order to maintain family incomes; and residents of depressed urban and rural areas. Altogether these groups constitute a majority of the American people.

The essays in this volume, particularly those by Ahituv, Tienda, and Hotz; Wilson; and Dymski, show motivations and aspirations to be very similar across income, racial, and ethnic groups; however, lifetime outcomes not only have declined for many people since the 1970s, but also are widely different because opportunity structures vary greatly. This is an especially important subject for the United States, where "equal opportunity for all" has been a major part of the national credo. Indeed, many conservatives argue that growing inequality is actually a good thing because it creates "an incentive for people to invest in self-improvement."[7] This proposition is valid only if opportunity structures permit people to move up by working hard and investing in themselves. Few would argue that opportunities for the children of the non-working poor that Bill Wilson studied in Chicago either have improved or are anywhere nearly equal to those of the children living in more affluent Chicago suburbs.

Dan McMurrer and Isabel Sawhill conclude that although there is considerable opportunity in America, it has declined since the 1970s because mobility has not increased to offset rising wage disparities. These analysts find that upward mobility is determined mainly by two factors: the extent to which people can improve their incomes independent of family origins and economic growth. McMurrer and Sawhill find that the ability of Americans to advance regardless of their origins has improved, but that less-skilled men are faring poorly because of slower economic growth (56 percent) and rising inequality (44 percent). In 1995, for example, the average annual entry-level income of high school educated males was $15,766. If inequality had not increased, these males would have earned $28,000; if, in addition, growth between 1973 and 1995 had continued at the 1960–73 rate, earnings would have been $42,000, well over twice what they actually were.

McMurrer and Sawhill conclude, however, that education could more than offset the strong effects of family origins on upward mobility. And improvements for low-income families could be achieved through policies that enable them to sustain their incomes and provide better education and health care for their children. These analysts therefore are concerned about the dangers to opportunity from recent reductions in support services for poor families.

In other work at the Urban Institute, Sawhill and her colleagues demonstrate that opportunities not only have declined, but are no higher in

America than in other countries, where inequality is less than it is in the United States. They also note that studies showing substantial upward mobility either used biased data that only included people who had income throughout the analyzed period (and therefore excluded those who were without income at any time during the period) or incorporated such fundamental technical flaws as failing to account for the normal improvements in income as young people age.

Weaker Voice for Workers

The declining voice for employees in the workplace and in the society has been a major factor reducing support for policies to maintain shared prosperity. Technological change and global competition have weakened unions, which are major advocates of shared prosperity, especially for production and service workers. Except for the older craft unions, U.S. union strength was concentrated mainly in oligopolies and regulated industries, which became less viable in a more competitive global economy. Similarly, technological change and more intensive competition weakened unions by reducing the size of firms, dispersing employment to non-union areas, and shifting the composition of employment away from highly unionized blue-collar industrial employment toward relatively unorganized white-collar and service work. Moreover, global job shortages and highly mobile capital and technology greatly strengthened the power of corporations relative to unions. The reduced power of unions has contributed both to growing inequality and a weaker voice for workers on the job and in national economic policy-making.

In their essays, Paula Voos and Tom Kochan note the importance of a stronger voice for workers for improving economic performance and restoring shared prosperity. Teresa Ghilarducci shows that declining union strength has contributed to reduced health care and pension coverage for production workers.

Access to Health Care

Health influences opportunity in many ways. There are well-documented relationships, for example, between the health of women and the mental and physical development of their children. And children's health affects their ability to learn, just as the health of workers and their families strongly influences productivity. Indeed, differences in health conditions are major factors in the degree of labor force participation across population groups. As Karen Davis notes in her essay, poor health has been an especially important cause of joblessness among minority males. Mary Merva and Richard Fowles find statistically significant correlations between poverty and income inequality, mortality, suicide, homicide, aggravated assault, and rape.

Karen Davis also shows that access to health care has deteriorated along with declining incomes and slower economic growth. Since health benefits are closely related to wage levels, low-wage workers are less likely to have health insurance. And the desire to retain health benefits leads many workers to accept lower wages than they would if, like most other advanced countries, the United States had a national system that did not make health insurance dependent upon employment.

Davis also documents the extent to which public support for greater access to medical benefits for low-income people and the elderly narrowed the health care gap during the 1960s and 1970s. According to Davis, "As a direct consequence [of Medicare and Medicaid], differentials in access to health care and health outcomes across different income groups narrowed markedly in the 10 years from 1965 to 1974." However, political and economic changes in the American economy since 1975 have undercut these gains. The proportion of Americans without health insurance fell from one-third in 1965 to 11 percent in 1976, but has subsequently increased to 15 percent. Consequently, employment-based health insurance has eroded; quality of care for middle- and low-income people has deteriorated; and the direct costs to workers have increased. There has been an even greater deterioration in health insurance for retirees. Davis notes, moreover: "These forces are segmenting the health care of different groups of Americans. Those who are uninsured are most at risk—for failure to receive needed care, risk to their health and productivity, and financial ruin that major illness or injury can bring."

In an effort to contain health care costs, companies and governments are relying increasingly on managed care. According to Davis, however:

> Relying on market forces to foster competition through managed care plans without quality and performance standards and governmental oversight runs the risk of widening the gaps among different groups of Americans. Lower-income and minority Americans, especially low-wage workers and their families, run the risk of falling outside the health care safety net, with serious health, social, and economic consequences for the entire society.

Davis shows that the "consequences of being uninsured include failure to get preventive care, inadequate maintenance of chronic conditions, and adverse health outcomes." She also notes important economic as well as personal consequences from inadequate health care, preventable disease, and poor health.

Urban Isolation

Some of America's most intractable problems are associated with the growing isolation of inner-city urban residents, whose welfare has become uncoupled both from major improvements in the overall economy and the experiences of more affluent suburban residents. Elliott Sclar discusses the extent to which public policies are responsible for these developments. He first demonstrates that federal policies have contributed to the isolation of seriously disadvantaged populations in central cities. The policies responsible for this condition are subsidies for middle- and high-income people, not welfare, as some commentators argue. The federal government has, for example, heavily subsidized automobiles and suburban housing at the expense of urban housing and transportation systems. Sclar argues that these and other subsidies accelerated both the creation of suburbs and the depopulation of central cities. Indeed, the suburbanization that resulted in the shift of whites out of ghettos and minorities into them was one of the most important population redistributions in the post-war period. These population shifts had economic causes—especially the decline of manufacturing employment—but were accelerated by public policies. This separation of population by race, class, and geography causes higher-income suburbanites, who constitute half of the national population and a larger proportion of voters, to support public policies that perpetuate their subsidies and favor the wealthy at the expense of lower-income residents in central cities and older urban rings. Political polarization also makes it more difficult for governments to generate support for the resources needed to address critical urban problems. And the heavily subsidized suburbs contribute significantly to traffic congestion and environmental pollution. Both Sclar and William J. Wilson stress the problems caused for cities because of the mismatch between social problems and the geographic scope of taxing authorities.

Second, while the separation of suburbs from cities often is attributed to natural market forces, Sclar contends that these outcomes are due mainly to the "uneven playing field" created by federal policies, not to natural market forces. Indeed, he points out that the United States alone among the industrialized countries has subsidized suburbanization and the depopulation of its cities. Sclar notes, in addition, that contrary to popular myth cities have important competitive advantages in both the high-wage manufacturing and business service sectors in which the United States has significant comparative advantages. He believes, moreover, that "as international competition becomes keener, the economic dysfunctionality of the policy will become increasingly apparent." The economic advantages of central cities are due to the efficiencies they create for the information technologies upon which twenty-first century economies will be based. Sclar argues that these industries are far less footloose than commonly assumed.

The structural shifts over the past twenty years also have contributed to growing inequality by causing poor communities to have fewer and more expensive financial services absolutely and relative to more affluent communities. Access to credit and financial services is particularly important for poor people, who, as Ed Wolff stresses, have few assets to tide them over incomeless periods. Gary Dymski shows that recent shifts in the U.S. economy have had very different effects in suburbs and inner cities. In the early post-war economy, most inner cities were integrated into primary production

activities, which were highly cyclical. However, a number of developments have reduced the sensitivity of inner-city communities to business cycles. These include the decline of manufacturing employment and residential desegregation, which have dispersed minority communities geographically. These communities are still sensitive to economy-wide movements but "the stimulus required to lift the inner-city economy out of stagnation is much greater than in the past."

Deregulation has caused financial institutions to be guided mainly by market forces and profit opportunities, which are much better in affluent areas than in poor communities. As a consequence,

> Lower-income and minority communities experience spillover losses due to redlining and discrimination, branch closures, bank consolidation, and securitization. Externalities in local credit markets lead to the erosion of economic development possibilities in communities populated by critical masses of the unbanked, even as financial infrastructures blossom in communities populated by the wealthy.

Declining work opportunities are a fundamental cause of the diminished fortunes of inner-city residents. From his intensive work in the Black Belt of Chicago, Wilson documents the rise of joblessness for most adults since the 1950s when "a substantial portion of the urban black population was poor but working." However, he determined that "in many inner-city ghetto neighborhoods in 1990, most adults were not working in a typical week."

He shows, in addition, that the conditions of the working poor are very different from those of the non-working poor. Work in the formal economy "provides a framework for daily behavior because of the discipline and regularity that it imposes." This is very important because "a youngster who grows up in a family with a steady breadwinner and in a neighborhood in which most of the adults are employed will tend to develop some of the disciplined habits associated with stable or steady employment." By contrast:

> In the absence of regular employment, a person lacks not only a place in which to work and the receipt of regular income, but also a coherent organization of the present—that is, a system of concrete expectations and goals. . . . In the absence of regular employment, life, including family life, becomes less coherent.

The forces responsible for growing joblessness in inner-city communities include: the interaction of racial with other social and economic changes, the "nationwide decline in the fortunes of low-skilled workers," skill-based technological change, the internationalization of economic activity, the "suburbanization of jobs," the out-migration of working and middle-class families from inner-city areas, and the reluctance of employers to hire blacks from inner-city ghettos. All of these factors generate crime, family disintegration, dysfunctional schools, and a life-destroying emptiness and isolation that create degenerating conditions that will not yield easily to traditional macroeconomic, welfare, or superficial remedies.

Urban Schools

Among the most serious of America's problems is the very poor conditions of urban schools, which are exacerbated by all of the other problems afflicting urban communities. As Marc Tucker observes in his essay, most American schools are geared to the educational needs of a mass production system, not to the realities of a much more competitive information economy. The problem is not so much that our schools have deteriorated as that we need entirely new kinds of schools such as those proposed by Tucker. However, as wide as the gap is between most American schools and the kind needed to enable children to succeed, most urban schools are in even worse condition. Because the needs of these schools are so much greater than those of more affluent suburbs, the huge differences in resources available to them cause the education gaps to be an even more serious cause of inequality. As Marc Tucker observes, money alone will not solve urban education problems, but we are not likely to improve those schools very much without better teachers, facilities, and other resources. It would be hard to imagine a more important challenge to America's future.

Young Black Men

Harry Holzer shows that young black men (YBM), perhaps the most disadvantaged group in our society, experienced rapidly increasing real wages during the 1940s and the 1960s, when civil rights measures and tight labor markets combined to improve employment opportunities. By the 1980s, however, roughly a third of all out-of-school YBM were jobless at any given time. Moreover, the black-white wage gap, controlling for education and other factors, rose to 20 percent or more by the end of the 1980s after having fallen to 10 percent by the mid-1970s. As Holzer shows, these trends clearly have serious long-term social implications. The deteriorating employment and earnings prospects of YBM will limit their lifetime opportunities.

Holzer speculates that the problem of low

wages for unskilled workers relative to more-skilled workers could be self-correcting by providing incentives for the unskilled to acquire more education, but unfortunately there are strong barriers to this self-improvement process, especially faster increases in the demand for skills than YBM can acquire them, the rising cost of education, the wide gap that remains between black and white education achievement, and the hurdles YBM face growing up in poor single-parent families, low-quality schools, dangerous neighborhoods, and social isolation from successful role models.

Latinos

Jorge Chapa shows that the rapidly growing Latino population has not shared equitably in American prosperity. The reasons for this include: the fact that many Latinos entered the United States after the slowdown in the growth of shared prosperity in the early 1970s, the persistent education gap between Latino and Anglo populations, Latinos' relative youth, and the proximity of the United States to Mexico and other places of origin for immigrants which provides a large population that maintains cultural and linguistic continuity with those countries and therefore slows Latino assimilation into the U.S. economy, polity, and society. Chapa demonstrates that since the 1970s Latino employment conditions have converged downward with those of African-Americans.

Crime

Crime is a major problem for the whole country, especially for inner-city neighborhoods. Crime contributes to a deterioration of property values, business conditions, and schools. It is extremely difficult to promote the economic de-velopment of crime-infested neighborhoods. There is, however, some strong evidence that the incidence of crime is closely related to economic opportunities. From his detailed analysis of data for a group of Austin, Texas neighborhoods, for example, William Spelman found that unemployment and poverty were the most important indicators of crime rates over time. In addition, Spelman concluded that studies of such broad areas as states, nations, and metropolitan areas often have failed to detect a relationship between crime and unemployment, poverty, and other economic factors because these factors are closely related in neighborhoods, making this a more appropriate unit of analysis.

Women

In some ways, the economic fortunes of women continued to improve during the 1980s, while those of men were declining. For example, Heidi Hartmann notes that the workforce participation of women has increased, while that of men has fallen at every age; women's earnings have risen relative to men's; and women have entered a broader range of occupations and share greater financial responsibility for families. Moreover, women have increased their proportion of union membership and have slightly reduced their share of contingent work.

A number of factors account for this progress: women have increased their education levels relative to men, have entered higher-paying non-traditional professions, and are heavily concentrated in some rapidly growing occupations. Hartmann believes these trends will continue because they are based on the preferences of women and their families for the higher standards of living and more acceptable lifestyles afforded by women's incomes. She disputes "the notion that women have mainly been forced to work by men's falling wages."

Hartmann notes, however, that despite considerable progress, women still have a number of economic and quality-of-life disadvantages that she expects to diminish over time as women continue to improve their educational and economic positions.

Rural Areas

William Galston shows that opportunity also has diminished for most rural residents. American agriculture benefited greatly from New Deal policies, which were considered to be in the national interest when the New Deal paradigm was viable and the economy experienced rapid and shared growth. Unfortunately for rural non-farm people, political and economic power in these places was heavily concentrated in one industry—commercial agriculture— which has become a dwindling component of the economy. The larger non-farm rural sector has had little political influence and has lacked either the cohesion or the leadership to fashion strong rural development strategies.

Rural areas have experienced the basic consequences of globalization and technological change. With global integration, agricultural products are forced to compete in international markets with lower-priced products from other countries. Moreover, agriculture has experienced large increases in productivity with a consequent massive displacement of labor. As in the case of inner cities, dislocation also was accelerated by federal policies that subsidized land and capital and therefore displaced people. In the 1950s and 1960s many dislocated rural people became the urban working poor; their children and grandchildren have become the non-working poor discussed by Wilson. During the period of faster and more equitably shared growth before 1970, people could be more easily absorbed by urban and rural non-farm labor markets. By contrast, slower growth and reduced demand for unskilled labor have caused rural and urban workers to suffer rising joblessness and declining real wages.

During the initial phases of deeper globalization in the 1960s and 1970s, cheap labor and state and local subsidies induced many manufacturing industries to locate in rural areas. With more deeply integrated global markets, however, low-wage competitiveness strategies are not likely to be viable in a high-wage country. Thus, much rural industry attracted by this strategy was and is on its way to the third world.

The surge in rural growth during the 1970s consequently was reversed during the 1980s, reflecting the vast structural shifts in the American and global economies. There appears to have been a slowdown in rural decline after 1990, when areas with recreation and retirement developments had strong population surges while areas adjacent to large metropolitan places continued their slow population increases and farming-dependent counties continued to lose population. Despite these overall gains, rural workers continue to suffer lower real wages absolutely and relative to those in urban areas.

II. Forces for Change: Technology, Demographics, and Globalization

Some of the forces that have combined to produce the structural changes in the American and world economies mentioned earlier have had sufficiently ubiquitous and powerful impacts to justify the term "universal imperatives." The most important of these, as discussed in Part II, are technology, demographics, and globalization.

Technology

Technology is perhaps the most basic and pervasive of these imperatives. The best definition of technology is how to do things. The essence of technological and economic progress is the use of more ideas, skills, and knowledge in the production process and less manual labor and physical resources, thus improving productivity, the ultimate source of real incomes.

There are several ways technology influences economic growth, incomes, and employment. First, technology can increase productivity, simultaneously displacing labor and providing the means to improve the incomes of those who remain employed. By improving productivity, technology lowers costs in the affected industry and throughout the economy. Through this process, technology can expand markets and produce a higher rate of growth in output and employment, which could have the net effect of increasing both income and employment. In the long run, this "virtuous circle" has been the main outcome of technological innovations. Many observers believe, moreover, that under the right conditions, new information and communication technologies (ICT), along with others such as biogenetics, could form the basis for another Golden Era of economic growth. Some analysts believe that prosperity caused by a more knowledge-intensive economy could be even better and more equitably shared than it was between 1945 and 1973, when it was fueled by the civilian applications of technology developed for military purposes, supportive macroeconomic policies, massive improvements in higher education because of the GI Bill, and strong domestic and global demand.

In the short and intermediate time periods, technology increases the level and duration of unemployment. The short-term effects on unemployment are less troublesome because most displaced workers will find new jobs, depending on their age, education, and skills as well as the demand for labor. The demand for labor, in turn, depends on the relative rates of growth in employment and the labor force.

Long-term structural unemployment due to a mismatch between the skills in demand and those possessed by the unemployed is a much more serious problem and is the type of unemployment that is both most intractable and highly correlated with social pathologies.

There also is evidence that the duration of unemployment is related to the rate of technological change. William Baumol and Edward Wolff, for example, conclude that an increase in the rate of technological change increases the rate and average duration of unemployment. They state that the "mean duration of unemployment approximately doubled in the United States between the early 1950s and the mid-1990s, with most of the increase since the early 1970s."[8] These analysts postulate that the main reason for the rising duration of joblessness in the United States and other industrialized countries is the replacement of older and less-skilled workers with younger and better-educated employees as the pace of technological change accelerates. Firms do not believe it is cost-effective to retrain these workers "either because the retraining costs are higher or because the workers will not be on the job long enough or will not be productive enough for firms to recoup the cost of retraining."[9] Lower average rates of unemployment between the 1970s and the early 1990s masked the dramatic increase of an additional three to four weeks in the mean duration of unemployment. Though this distinction often is ignored, long-term unemployment undoubtedly has much stronger negative impacts than short-term unemployment. Baumol and Wolff cite evidence[10] that "joblessness has a variety of consequences, such as increased suicide, divorce, psychosomatic illness, and criminal activity, whose social cost must surely be added to the foregone output that results from unemployment."[11]

Baumol and Wolff believe two changes in unemployment insurance (UI) could help the long-term unemployed: (1) increasing the twenty-six week cap on benefits to thirty-nine weeks or a year and (2) changing the compensation formula to provide higher real benefit levels. These analysts note that the UI earnings replacement rate was only 36.5 percent in 1995, the same as it was in 1970. They disagree with those economists who believe that raising UI benefits would create an incentive for beneficiaries to remain unemployed longer; as evidence for their position, they note that the duration of unemployment has been rising while the replacement rate has been flat. Baumol and Wolff agree with the UI system's founders that adequate benefits enable the unemployed to "select a job more compatible with their skills and interests."[12]

A second aspect of technology, many economists believe, is that it influences labor markets by reducing the demand for unskilled labor and increasing the demand for skills. This factor is thought by some to be mainly responsible for lower real wages for relatively uneducated workers and for the widening college–high school earnings gap. However, careful analysis suggests that this explanation is too simple. Technology causes both an increase and a decrease in skill levels. A much more important factor probably is the increased knowledge base of the whole economy brought about by the new technology. For example, knowing what to do with all of the information made available by computers is more important than the simple ability to use computers. Similarly, the organization of work within and between companies and countries requires new kinds of skills, especially quantitative, abstract learning, interpersonal, communicating, and problem-solving abilities that put a premium on the knowledge and skills needed to most effectively adapt and use advanced technology.

Technology has, in addition, contributed to growing inequality within and between countries. The rapid diffusion of ICT has bypassed large parts of the global labor force who lack the necessary skills. The demand for skills is likely to intensify as economic processes become more competitive and knowledge intensive.

A third effect of technology has been to alter the organization of production, especially by facilitating globalization, which enabled companies to shift work to low-wage places, hastened the integration of financial markets, and accelerated the growth of both portfolio and direct foreign investment. In addition, technology changes the optimal size and structure as well as the location of production systems. ICT tends to flatten management structures and decentralize decisions to front-line workers, especially where employers adopt high-value-added competitiveness strategies. The development and use of leading-edge technologies is a distinguishing characteristic of high-performance work organizations. By facilitating economies of scale and scope, ICT enables smaller enterprises, and associations of small enterprises, to be internationally competitive.

Finally, technology alters economic performance in ways that are as yet unknown, although some effects are fairly clear. For example, by making more information available to buyers and sellers, ICT clearly intensifies competition and could moderate business cycles by shortening product cycles and better matching demand and supply. These technological changes therefore could improve the ability of macroeconomic policies to achieve non-inflationary growth at lower levels of unemployment.

In their RBSP essay, Robert White and Richard White conclude that technology results in "social and economic transformations on a grand scale." They note, in addition: "There is general agreement that the impacts are positive over the long term, but leave in their wake winners and losers." They conclude that "the race between job creation and displacement from technological advance has always been close, but from a historical perspective, technology has been a net job creator."

In his RBSP essay, Dan Burton discusses the revolutionary implications of the emerging networked economy. This technology was pioneered by the United States, giving American companies enormous advantages over their competitors in Japan and Europe. The networked economy combines computing and telecommunications to enable consumers and businesses "to communicate, transfer, store, and access" vast amounts of information instantly. Networking already has revolutionized traditional American manufacturing and routine service industries, laying the "groundwork for whole new markets."

The networked economy has its own internal logic for optimal development and use. First, networks thrive on openness; in Burton's view, its openness gives the United States significant advantages over relatively closed economies such as that of the Japanese. Second, networks value content, or the flow of information and entertainment of all kinds. Content, in turn, depends heavily on creativity and research and development to produce new knowledge, technologies, and products, as well as on the protection of intellectual property rights to encourage the continuous production and dissemination of innovations. The declining costs of physical resources means that "soft" assets or skills (such as the ability to manage information, relate to people, innovate, solve problems, and learn) become more important for economic success. Third, networks are most effectively developed by market forces. Fourth, networks are lean, in the sense that they tend to eliminate unnecessary structures, resources, and people. Thus, the core characteristics of networked economies are "decentralized decision-making, entrepreneurial risk-taking, and open markets."

Demographics

Population changes also are universal imperatives with very important implications for the ability to restore shared prosperity. Indeed, a preoccupation with short-term economic policies and market forces causes many analysts and policy-makers to neglect the long-term economic consequences of population changes. As Robert Eisner notes, for instance, despite fears that we are burdening future generations, even the most pessimistic forecasts of changes in the GDP/population ratio project much higher per capita income levels in the future. And the age composition of the population will affect future living conditions by determining both the ratio of economically active people to dependents and basic macroeconomic activities such as consumption and savings. For example, savings rates are expected to increase as the huge (78 million, born between 1945 and 1965) baby-boom generation prepares for retirement.

The baby boom was followed by the 1965–79 baby bust. The entry of this relatively small cohort into labor markets during the 1980s and 1990s contributed to the slowdown in the growth of the workforce, which helped reduce unemployment in the 1990s despite slower GDP growth than in previous decades. Many believe the health care and retirement requirements of the baby boomers will create intolerable drains on Social Security funds in the twenty-first century, a proposition disputed in the RBSP essays by Robert Eisner, Dean Baker, and others.

The relative size of a cohort into which people are born affects their life chances as well as general levels of income and employment. In her RBSP essay, for example, Diane Macunovich demonstrates that since 1970, relative cohort size (the ratio of population aged 20–22 to those aged 45–49) and the age composition of the population have had significant effects on the structure of American wages. Macunovich's cohort models "are able to explain 99 percent of the longer-term variation in male relative earnings over the past twenty-five years, 90 to 91 percent of the longer-term variation in the general male unemployment rate over the past 42 years, and 95 to 98 percent of the longer-term variation in men's and women's returns to a college education over the past 31 years." She concludes that her results "constitute strong evidence that cohort-size effects since 1985 have become once again the most important factor in determining the labor market outcomes of young men and women, and are showing signs of becoming even stronger."

The racial, ethnic, and socioeconomic composition of the population has important social as well as economic implications. According to the U.S. Census Bureau, "minorities" will become a majority of the U.S. population by 2050. Minority and low-income children are now the fastest growing components of America's school population. These children have greater education needs but they attend schools with far fewer resources than children from more affluent families. These population changes therefore could exacerbate race and ethnic relations and widen wealth and income gaps in the more competitive knowledge-intensive society of the twenty-first century.

Population shifts within the country also have profound economic, political, and social consequences. For example, the movement of manufacturing and higher-income populations (mostly white) out of central cities has been a major cause of the marginalization of low-income minorities, immigrants, and the non-working poor studied by Wilson, who were unable to leave those areas. As Elliot Sclar notes, public policies either have caused or accelerated these population shifts; they are not due entirely to market forces.

One of the most important and contentious aspects of population growth is immigration. In his essay, for example, Michael Teitelbaum argues that immigrants have contributed to inequality in the United States because they tend to depress wages and employment conditions in low-wage labor markets. Teitelbaum finds the impacts of immigration in the aggregate to be real, but very small, although such impacts are surely more substantial within certain regions, industries, and occupations. And, as discussed earlier, Jorge Chapa noted that Latino immigrants' life chances are diminished by the fact that many of them entered the United States at a time when opportunities for workers with less than college educations have worsened.

Globalization of Markets

The third universal imperative, the globalization of markets, means different things to different people, as does the related concept of "competitiveness." Some economists consider the impact of globalization to be greatly exaggerated. In this view, "globalization" refers only to international trade, which accounts for a relatively small part of GDP, depending on whether both exports and imports are included.[13] However, as Dan Burton observes, although a lot of attention has focused on trade, the competitiveness agenda goes much further, to such areas as technology, education, and investment. Moreover, competitiveness is very much concerned with productivity as a way to improve living standards. The three key elements in the globalization process are: (1) the rapid growth in international trade and investment and a worldwide trend toward trade liberalization, (2) the proliferation of global production systems controlled by variable configurations of transnational business alliances, and (3) the internationalization of financial markets.

Globalization thus means the integration of all markets, foreign and domestic, not just foreign trade. Opening domestic markets causes a fundamental change in national, social, and economic institutions, not just markets. The magnitude of these changes increases as the global integration of domestic markets deepens. In this sense, globalization changes the rules for economic success for countries as well as for individuals and firms. The main significance of international transactions is that they are beyond the control of national governments or processes such as collective bargaining and pricing by national oligopolies. Moreover, the ability to shift production to other countries or freely import high-quality products made by lower-paid workers causes the impact of globalization to be much greater than suggested by the volume of international transactions. Because many of these realities cannot be easily measured, they cause inferential problems for those who believe that useful knowledge comes solely from quantitative analyses.

As noted earlier, globalization also played an important role in undermining New Deal policies, which formed a national economic paradigm based to a significant degree on limited price competition; fixed exchange rates; large oligopolistic firms in most basic industries; collective bargaining, mainly with oligopolies and regulated monopolies; regulated labor, transportation, financial and utility markets; and social safety nets. At the macroeconomic level, the New Deal paradigm used monetary and fiscal policies to keep the mass production system operating at near capacity or "full employment."

As Jane D'Arista demonstrates in her RBSP essay, globalization led to the deregulation of financial markets, which made it more difficult for the Federal Reserve Board (FRB) to control money supplies. Similarly, the ability to stimulate the economy through fiscal policy has been modified by flexible exchange rates, the enhanced ability of imports to absorb part of the increased demand from fiscal stimulus and for exchange rates to rise with interest rates, thus stimulating imports of goods and money and reducing exports.

III. Policies to Restore Shared Prosperity

The essays in Part III are based on the assumption that policies to restore shared prosperity in a more global and knowledge-intensive economy must be comprehensive in the sense of integrating the best factual and analytical insights from a number of academic disciplines and levels of analysis—community, local, national, and international. These essays also assume that public-private cooperation will be necessary to restore shared prosperity because market forces alone will perpetuate inequality. It is, moreover, well established that markets alone cannot generate technology, basic research and development, or human capital formation, all of which are prerequisites to high-value-added economic growth. The challenge, of course, is to develop public, private, and public-private organizations compatible with the requirements for success in a much more global, competitive, and knowledge-intensive society. The essays reviewed in this part reflect these assumptions.

Macroeconomic Policy

Macroeconomic policies are extremely important because of their ubiquitous influence on the economy, especially on its growth, an important determinant of prosperity. McMurrer and Sawhill demonstrate, for example, that slow growth during the 1980s limited upward economic mobility for American workers. In addition, growth is required to prevent rising joblessness as productivity improvements displace workers. And, as noted earlier, monetary-fiscal policies contributed significantly to America's long period of shared prosperity in the decades before the early 1970s. In that period, full employment was the basic economic objective of the United States and most other industrialized democracies. These policies and World War II, the dominant influence on the American economy in the 1940–73 period, did much to create steady employment and income for workers. A problem for the United States in the 1990s is the fact that the New Deal macroeconomic policies are no longer adequate. Moreover, the political movement for a balanced budget limits the use of countercyclical fiscal measures. And monetary policy, like fiscal policy, not only has been weakened by globalization, but as the current Asian crises show, is a very weak instrument to address either structural problems or a failure of aggregate demand. The idea that flexible prices and free market forces could prevent a global recession is as questionable now as it was in the 1920s, when almost all mainstream economists asserted, with great confidence, that a general depression was impossible.

But perhaps the greatest conceptual barrier to using macroeconomic policy to achieve faster growth is the belief that the level of growth is restrained by a relatively high (5–6 percent) non-accelerating inflation rate of unemployment (NAIRU). This idea gained some credibility from the failure of most industrialized market-economy countries to prevent inflation at low levels of unemployment during the 1970s. Most RBSP essayists are critical of the NAIRU concept; they concede that there is a tradeoff between inflation and unemployment, but contend that it is not fixed and that the proper set of policies could achieve faster growth without inflation. These critics also point out that U.S. inflation in the 1970s was caused primarily by external commodity (mainly energy) price shocks, which are not likely to reoccur anytime soon. These analysts also doubt that inflation is as much of a problem in a more open and competitive global economy as NAIRU advocates believe. According to this view, expressed by economics Nobel laureate Robert Solow in his RBSP essay, the risks of overshooting inflation targets are small and the resulting inflation could easily be reversed.

Because of their labor market and social policies and higher rates of productivity growth, Germany and other European countries have avoided the reductions in real wages experienced by American workers. Germany also has had higher unemployment in the 1990s than the United States, but has had smaller price increases. Some analysts contend that more flexible, deregulated labor markets would reduce unemployment in Europe as they have in the United States. Others, by contrast, argue that the high levels of European unemployment and lower wages for most U.S. workers are different aspects of slow growth and result more from macroeconomic policies than from rigidities in labor markets or other presumed causes. These analysts point out that, despite a high degree of market regulation and strong social safety nets, German unemployment rates were lower than those in the United States before German unification in the early 1990s. Robert Solow, for example, has argued that it is not clear how much of Europe's unemployment is due to social policy. However, he proposes:

> a concerted steady expansion of aggregate demand in Europe, aimed at eliminating a substantial margin of unemployment, perhaps as much as 5 or 6 percentage points. In the course of this exploration, we would no doubt discover just how big that margin actually is. Europeans would then be in a better position to think intelligently about the proper scope for the welfare state for guarantees of job security.[14]

Solow adds, "The ... belief that the only good labor market is a dog-eat-dog jungle strikes me as both socially wrong and economically unproductive."

This is an extremely important debate, with more than academic significance. We therefore should examine carefully the question of whether full employment and high value added should be our primary policy objectives. One justification for focusing policy on these outcomes is that there is no inflation problem, but if it did occur it could be effectively countered with a combination of monetary and anti-inflation policies targeted to supply bottlenecks or particular labor market rigidities. Second, the preoccupation with anti-inflation strategies imposes much greater long-term human and material costs than is justified by either the

theoretical or empirical support for that strategy or the damage that might be done by the likely increase in inflation from gradually raising the level of economic growth. However, in his RBSP essay, Solow cautions against ignoring inflationary dangers. While he notes the lack of congruity between NAIRU theory and the facts, and believes NAIRU "gets more respect than it deserves," concerns about inflation should be taken seriously, even though he rejects the "European" view that the absence of inflation is sufficient for sustained prosperity. Solow likewise opposes preemptive strikes to prevent inflation as "unnecessary and self-confirming."

Solow believes macro-policy to be necessary, but not sufficient for shared prosperity—it must be complemented by selective policies, especially labor market and human resource development. He concludes that "good macro-policy can do definite but limited good for the goal of shared prosperity, but bad macro-policy can do unlimited harm." Solow's advice for Europe would appear to be as valid for the United States. We should move cautiously to restore a higher level of economic growth while simultaneously adopting the kind of targeted anti-inflation, structural adjustment, and human resource development policies suggested by several of the RBSP papers.

Public Expenditures and Investments

Budgets and Taxes

In his RBSP essay, Robert Eisner argues that the United States has been prevented from using fiscal policy to restore shared prosperity because "economic policy has been paralyzed by a combination of outworn economic dogmas and strident political ideology ... tied to faulty measures and uncertain theory that defy the accumulating weight of evidence."

Moreover:

> Possible reforms have been distorted by the fairly transparent efforts by many to focus on changes in the system that would be of overwhelming benefit to the richest, least deserving, and least needy ... to the detriment of almost everybody else. And generally emasculating macroeconomic policy has been acceptance of the dogma that fiscal and monetary policies cannot affect the level of employment; demand-side efforts to get and hold unemployment below its "natural" ... rate ... can only doom us to ever-increasing inflation.

Eisner calls the NAIRU limitations on macroeconomic policy "one of the more dismal dogmas of our dismal science."

He also believes that policy-makers engage in much faulty analysis because of poor federal budget practices, which treat capital investments as current expenditures; the belief that we are burdening future generations with national debt, even though this liability to the government is an asset to individuals and incomes are growing much faster than the population; at less than full employment, a budget deficit is not a drag on the economy, but a budget surplus would be; and there is no convincing evidence that federal deficits "crowd out" private investments. Eisner concludes, "Prudent deficits, then, can be good for us." His rule of thumb for "prudent" is a constant debt-to-GDP ratio. The 1996 debt ratio was about 2.5 percent of GDP, or $188 billion, well above the 1996 deficit.

Social Security

The debate over Social Security has enormous implications for our ability to restore shared prosperity. As noted earlier, Social Security was an important component of the New Deal policies contributing to a broader sharing of prosperity. Many of the proposed reforms, by contrast, would accelerate the growth of inequality and could have profound impacts on financial and labor markets. Some of these proposals also are based on highly questionable assumptions. Eisner, for example, disagrees with those who contend there is a crisis in the Social Security system. He believes these proposals to be based either on ignorance or a desire to weaken the system's essential social insurance character that redistributes benefits to low-income and elderly families. Eisner does not believe it is necessary to raise payroll taxes, reduce benefits, or privatize the system. The Social Security trust funds are projected to exhaust their balance by 2032. Thereafter, projected payments into the funds would cover only about 75 percent of the payouts. Eisner points out, however, that this problem could easily be fixed by several measures, including converting the balances into marketable U.S. Treasury securities administered independently from the Treasury, allowing shortfalls to be covered by the sale of securities, and having the Treasury begin issuing securities now to cover the projected shortfall in 2029. The only effect of this process would be to transform the Treasury's "contingent liability" into "gross federal debt." These changes could make the trust funds solvent indefinitely. It would be better for Social Security and national well-being, Eisner believes, to invest projected federal budget surpluses in education and health to improve productivity than to use them to solve an imaginary Social Security problem.[15]

Dean Baker agrees with Eisner's assessment and adds that the Social Security system has been a "remarkable success story," moderating income inequality by providing retirement and disability payments for 35 million people and reducing poverty among the elderly. Contrary to much of the criticism of government, and in contrast to the high administrative costs of private insurance, the Social Security system is a model of efficiency. It also promotes equality by doing more for low-income than for high-income participants.

Baker also sharply challenges arguments for privatizing the Social Security system. He notes that privatization would not increase net saving but would merely substitute private for government saving. Baker believes, in addition, that the privatization of Social Security could very well increase government involvement in the economy and would greatly increase administrative costs, noting that the cost of operating the current Social Security system is less than 0.8 percent of annual benefits, compared with 2.7 percent for private life insurance companies and 15 to 20 percent for the privatized Chilean pension system used as a model by many privatization proponents. The administrative costs of having 100 million individual savings accounts would probably aggregate to 25 percent of the funds' value. There also is a serious question of whether many low-wage earners would in fact save the money diverted from the Social Security Fund. If part of Social Security funds were invested in security markets, it would make more sense to have these investments made by independent trustees insulated from politics.

Baker concludes:

> It makes sense to have a market where people can voluntarily choose the amount to put aside in savings and the assets in which they will place their money. It does not make sense to have a market where the government already made these choices for individuals. . . . The market is prevented from performing any use-

ful function in this situation; it simply wastes resources.

Private Pensions

The macroeconomic and distributional effects of Social Security reforms should be considered in conjunction with private pensions, the growth of which owes much to collective bargaining and federal tax exemptions. In a basic sense, private pension funds are deferred wages and taxes. Thus, as Teresa Ghilarducci shows, private pension policies have important implications for shared prosperity. These policies influence workers' living conditions in their retirement years, as well as our ability to achieve greater labor market flexibility. Pension fund assets are, in addition, the chief external source of equity capital and have been major factors in the globalization of financial markets, the short-term-decision orientation of financial markets, and as a source of funds in corporate takeovers. Unlike Social Security, private pensions have increased inequality because they are available mainly to higher-income workers, though unions have caused pensions to be available for most unionized blue-collar workers. The weakening of unions and traditional pension plans therefore has contributed to the growing inequality of wealth. Ghilarducci points out that pensions were part of the compensation system that resulted from New Deal policies. And, like other parts of that paradigm, pensions are under stress because of the cost-cutting effects of competition, lower collective bargaining coverage, and slower economic growth. The role of private pensions has fallen relative to Social Security, which provided 57 percent of the retirement of middle-income retirees in 1991, up from 47 percent in 1980. The bottom fifth of income recipients receives 80 percent of their retirement income from Social Security. Instead of privatizing Social Security, as some propose, it would be better to extend private supplemental pensions to lower-income people.

Ironically, while pension benefits and coverage have been declining, pension fund assets have grown because of booming securities markets, which escalated the value of financial assets absolutely and relative to wages. One reason for the disjuncture between fund assets and benefits is the fact that the "Wall Street" gains in corporate pension plans, 90 percent of all funds, have primarily benefited companies, not beneficiaries. By contrast, pension plans jointly trusteed by workers and companies have used these gains to improve benefits. Since most experts consider pensions to be deferred compensation, there is some question about the propriety of allowing "reversions" of these gains to company treasuries. The superior performance of jointly trusteed funds, as well as the belief that beneficiaries are the true owners of pension funds, "have led to proposals that all funds be jointly trusteed."

Public Investments

Jeff Faux examines the importance of public investments for restoring shared prosperity. These investments always have enhanced equity and general prosperity by improving productivity and the returns on private investment. Public investments also help equalize opportunity because they are available to everybody and therefore offset the tendency of market forces to widen inequalities in wealth and income. The equalizing effects of public investment are most obvious in the case of education, but they are just as real in the case of transportation, communications, labor market systems, and other public facilities.

The decline in public investments, documented by Faux, therefore contributed to the slowdown in the growth in productivity and output since the 1960s. Faux discusses many arguments advanced for reducing the rate of public investment, but contends that all are based on faulty economic and accounting principles and combine to contribute to very poor economic policy. Most of these reasons relate to ideological opposition to government, though others are due to budget constraints caused by slow growth and the fact that it is easy for the political system to defer capital investments. Opposition to government leads to the absurd idea that all private investments are superior to those in the public sector.

Faux provides some suggestions for reversing the neglect of public investments, as well as where to find the money for those investments. He notes, in addition, that modernizing critical public infrastructures would be a source of direct job creation and have major multiplier effects on the economy.

International Economic Policies and Institutions

The globalization of markets which, as noted earlier, includes more than international transactions, has been one of the universal imperatives undermining the effectiveness of the policies and institutions associated with shared prosperity before the 1970s. Most economists accept the idea that an open and expanding global economy could be an important element in a constellation of policies to restore shared global prosperity. With their multiplier effects on domestic markets, for example, global markets could contribute to a virtuous circle created by new technologies that could generate new markets, investment opportunities, increased productivity, and higher levels of growth and employment. Because of their scale effects, such technology-induced virtuous circles could be most effective in a global context.

There is agreement, however, that even though the basic determinants of economic outcomes are still mainly domestic, globalization has undermined the effectiveness of New Deal economic policies and institutions. The expansion of the international economy also diminishes the effectiveness of previous international as well as domestic policies and institutions and calls for an entirely new conceptual underpinning. In the static theoretical short-term world of comparative advantage and shallow integration of domestic and global economies, there are only winners from trade; in the dynamic, real long-term world of competitive advantage, deep global and domestic market integration, given that almost all international financial flows are highly speculative, there can be losers as well as winners. Clearly, deeper international integration necessitates new rules, policies, and institutions in order to ensure a more equitable sharing of the benefits and costs of change. Indeed, the global economic problems of the 1980s and 1990s make it very clear that unfettered market forces can cause great damage to domestic economies.

There are, however, strong obstacles to establishing the new international economic rules needed to achieve a stable and growing international system. One of these is the lack of consensus about how international economic policy relates to domestic objectives. A second is the absence of international consensus for new policies and institutions. And a third major obstacle to an open global system could be growing resistance to further trade liberalization as a result of the losses and disruptions many people have experienced from more competitive markets.

These losses could be minimized by economic growth and positive adjustment programs to facilitate the shift of labor and other resources from non-competitive to competitive activities.

Most economists and many business and political leaders believe that the gains from a more open trading system would far outweigh the costs. But a majority of Americans doubt this conclusion. A major problem is that the gains are widely dispersed and the pain is inflicted on middle- and low-income workers, the same people who are the principal losers from most other demographic, economic, and technological changes. It is not very comforting for these victims to be told that even though trade has negative outcomes for them, other changes cause them even greater losses. Some international trade specialists who consider "free trade" to be mutually beneficial to all countries nevertheless warn of a political backlash and social disintegration if economists continue both to trivialize the negative consequences of trade and other economic trends for workers and fail to support adequate measures to soften these impacts. And most analysts agree that competitive markets alone will exacerbate growing economic inequality within and between countries. The challenge, of course, is to build support for efficient safety nets and positive adjustment processes while minimizing the negative impacts on the most vulnerable members of society.

Fred Bergsten notes that the movement toward free trade or "competitive liberalization" is driven by a combination of the mobility of capital and the political power of those who gain from trade, especially exporters and importers.[16] However, he also acknowledges that the losers—environmentalists, companies and workers in regulated or non-competitive industries and those who compete with imports—

have mounted fierce opposition to further trade liberalization. Bergsten notes, in addition, that 10 to 20 percent or even more of the stagnation of real wages in the United States is related to globalization.

However, he believes a strong case can be made for continued trade liberalization. First, while there has been substantial liberalization since World War II, this process cannot stand still or it will fall sideways or backward. Second, further liberalization could help improve U.S. wage stagnation by shifting labor and other resources from lower wage service and import-substitution sectors to export industries, where wages are 15 to 20 percent higher. Since service wages are even lower than those in import-substitution industries, a shift from services into export activities would have an even greater positive impact on wages.

Of course, the main reasons for higher wages and productivity in export sectors are their exposure to more vigorous competition and the economies of scale made possible by globalization. Global markets are important, even where companies originate in large domestic markets such as the United States. Bergsten notes, in addition, that 70 percent of U.S. foreign sales are by small and medium-sized companies.

Finally, the United States would gain by further liberalization, according to Bergsten, because American markets already are more open than those of most other countries. This is a crucial factor because access to the U.S. market can be an important bargaining chip and because restrictions on American exports are major causes of large U.S. trade deficits. It is estimated, for example, that reducing the U.S. trade deficit with Japan by $20 billion would create 400,000 export jobs. The trade deficit—which was $166 billion in 1997—reflects U.S. competitiveness directly (i.e., our inability to

produce quality products at competitive costs) and indirectly because the importation of foreign capital necessitated by trade deficits raises the value of the dollar, thus restricting the competitiveness of U.S. companies both here and abroad.

In her RBSP essay, Thea Lee agrees with Bergsten that some businesses and well-educated people are big winners from international trade and investment, that non-college educated workers are big losers, and that trade has contributed 10 to 30 percent of the wage inequality in the United States in the last fifteen years. However, Lee disagrees that the positive effects of trade liberalization outweigh the negative, especially for most workers. In her judgment, the negative effects of trade (about 4 to 5 percent of the wages of non-college workers) are much greater than its net social gains, which are estimated by free trade activists to be less than 1 percent of GDP.

Lee contends, in addition, that "economists do not possess the theoretical tools to declare unequivocally that free trade . . . is a better policy than protectionism." In response to the argument that the impact of trade on wage inequality is smaller than other things (i.e., technology, declining unionization, and inadequate education), Lee notes that the relevant standard should be whether or not *greater* trade liberalization produces net social benefits. She concludes with measures that could be taken to make trade more of a plus-sum, or mutually beneficial, process.

Human Resource Development

Education and School Reform

Almost every economic and social policy analyst recommends improved education, especially for low-income groups, as one of the surest ways to achieve shared prosperity. There is a question, however, of whether new jobs require higher skills or whether the availability of better-educated workers enables employers to hire them for jobs requiring less education. Confusion over the relationship between education and economic outcomes results in part from using years of schooling as a measure of educational achievement (i.e., skills and knowledge). Obviously all years of schooling are not equal. There often are very different outcomes when educational achievement is measured by objective achievement assessments and compared with economic performance or social pathologies. It also clearly makes a difference what kinds of knowledge and skills people have, not how many years they spend in school. These and other inferential problems could be mitigated by a national standards-driven qualifications system of the kind outlined by Marc Tucker in his essay.

Schooling and Economic Performance

There has, in addition, been much uncertainty about how schooling improves productivity. Some analysts argue that, because of the American system's tendency to track students by income, race, and ethnicity, schooling merely sorts people into income earning opportunities and therefore does not itself improve productivity. If this is true, the almost universal belief that investments in schooling would help restore shared prosperity would be wrong.

In his RBSP essay, Mark Rosenzweig throws some valuable light on this question. He observes that the international evidence on schooling, equality, and growth is mixed. The recent experiences in industrialized and newly industrializing countries in Asia "appear to suggest that investments in schooling are critical determinants of economic growth." However, "many countries with relatively high levels of schooling compared to their level of development in the 1960s, such as the Philippines, Sri Lanka, Argentina, Costa Rica, Cuba, and Uruguay, did not subsequently achieve high growth rates over the next twenty-five years."

Rosenzweig's main conclusions are that schooling alone does not do much to improve productivity and that schooling is most productive where there are profitable learning opportunities. Even with free markets and stable macroeconomic conditions,

> if markets and technical processes have been stable for some time, or if new technologies ... actually simplify work tasks, the true returns to schooling will be low. The corollary is that where opportunities to exploit learning arise, the absence of schooling can impede economic growth and those who have invested in schooling reap rewards while those who have not share less of the growth dividends.

Rosenzweig's analyses make it clear that, to be effective, schooling must be part of economic development strategies that increase the demand for educated workers.

School Reform: Building a National Qualifications System

Marc Tucker shows how standards-based school reform could lead to a world-class American qualifications system that progressively links various levels of schooling with each other and the workplace. Tucker discusses several factors preventing most American students from performing at world-class levels. He points out that American schools are geared to the mass production system where success for all except a small professional, managerial, and technical elite could be achieved with limited intellectual skills. In order to provide the skills required for both a democratic system and an economy that could produce shared opportunities, our schools must be transformed. Tucker notes that this core challenge for education is no different from the one "that has faced American business and public administration in recent years: to make major improvements in productivity and the quality of its products and services."

Tucker argues that standards-based reform is the best way to build a world-class education system. Standards, benchmarked to the highest in the world, would perform three valuable functions largely missing from American schools. First, standards would facilitate student learning by providing incentives for teachers, parents, and students to work together to achieve the standards. Second, standards provide more information to parents, employers, other schools, and students themselves about what students know and are able to do. A standards-based system like the America's Choice Program, which Tucker co-directs, provides reference exams, which measure progress toward standards, and technical assistance and curricular materials to help students and schools meet the standards.

Finally, standards enhance systemic efficiency by improving the linkages between learning systems (i.e., families, schools, post-school training institutions, colleges and universities, and workplaces) and therefore facilitate the elimination of the enormous waste and duplication in present arrangements. Standards also increase efficiency by providing a means to monitor and evaluate a diverse, decentralized school system like the one we have in the United States.

Tucker outlines an agenda to create a world-class, standards-driven system that would require more resources, but also would rely heavily on improving the use of resources already available.

The School-to-Career Transition

School-to-career transition processes are very important for the reform of both schools and workplaces. Incentives for students to work hard in school and acquire higher-order knowledge and skills depend heavily on whether or not hard work translates into clearly better life chances. In American schools, hard work and demanding courses are important mainly for students seeking entry into colleges and universities with demanding standards. For most other students grades, courses and relationships with teachers and administrators have had limited significance for lifetime opportunities in an economy where high wages could be earned with little formal education. In the information economy, by contrast, lifetime earnings have diminished for those with high school educations or less. However, high school students with higher-order math, technical, and learning skills who get into good on-the-job post-secondary or skill development programs probably will do at least as well as college graduates without these skills.[17]

Other advanced industrial countries give much greater attention to school-to-career processes than we do in the United States. These countries facilitate the transition from school to career with high standards all students must meet before leaving secondary schools, greater attention to skill development for non–college bound students, and much closer relationships between school and workplace learning systems. Companies in other countries seem to believe that people are their most important assets and treat schools as "preferred suppliers," giving much greater attention to teachers' recommendations and school performance. Close school-work relations cause the business sector to provide greater support for schools, strengthen the status of teachers and administrators and, most important, improve student learning.

In their RBSP essay, Ahituv, Tienda, and Hotz explore racial and ethnic differences in the transition from school to work. They cite research that shows that early work experience, especially when combined with schooling, has lasting positive effects on lifetime economic outcomes. These analysts deepen and broaden our understanding of this important phase in human development. In particular, they provide useful information on Hispanics as well as blacks and whites and explore the importance of counting as work experience jobs young people hold while they are in school or the military. Military experience is more important for blacks than any other group, raising the amount of work for them by about 6 percentage points, but only 3 points for whites and Hispanics. The usual practice of counting work only for school leavers distorts measured returns to employment as well as our understanding of the racial and ethnic differences in the transition from school to work. This is so because the first work experiences occur while in school for the vast majority of all youths, but especially for whites, 83 percent of whom have worked by age 17 compared with only 70 percent of blacks, with Hispanics in between.

Ahituv, Tienda, and Hotz reveal three distinct racial-ethnic paths from school to work: Hispanics leave school for work much earlier than blacks or whites, giving them early work experience advantages but reducing lifetime opportunities because of restricted schooling. The typical black youth prolongs schooling relative to Hispanics and has less work experience than whites. White youth, by contrast, typically gain lifelong advantages by acquiring more combined schooling and work experience than minorities. However, this multivariate analysis, holding other things constant, found that young minority men were more likely than statistically comparable whites to remain in school and were less likely to be idle. This suggests that minorities' schooling disadvantages are due mainly to family background, not to race or ethnicity. Finally, the lasting effects of early work experience probably depend upon the learning opportunities afforded by that experience and its complementarity to schooling.

Labor Market Policies and Institutions

Labor markets are very important for achieving shared prosperity. External labor markets (i.e., outside of workplaces) determine access to jobs and information about workers, jobs, and training opportunities. The ease with which labor markets match workers with jobs influences the effectiveness of anti-inflation and full-employment strategies, welfare reform, and the speed with which workers displaced by technology, international trade, or other reasons find new jobs or training opportunities. The absence of the kind of positive adjustment processes available in other advanced market-oriented countries is a major reason American workers resist trade liberalization and other changes.

The absence of effective positive adjustment processes is due in no small measure to the fact that America's labor market institutions do not function very well. They are highly fragmented, inefficient, and tend to perpetuate inequality. Federal employment and training programs serve few people, are largely stigmatized as extensions of a highly flawed welfare system and provide very few resources relative to the magnitude of the problems they are intended to address. In addition, American schools and training institutions are not world class and usually lack standards to judge performance, provide accurate information, and promote systemic efficiency. Despite the almost universal recognition of the importance of labor markets for shared prosperity, there is no strong political constituency in the United States to create a world-class labor market infrastructure system.

Internal labor markets—especially those within large workplaces—that contributed to shared prosperity as part of the New Deal paradigm are undergoing dramatic transformation. Internal labor markets are linked to external labor markets at "ports of entry," usually at entry-level jobs for each career ladder. Internal labor markets allocate employment, training, income, and power within workplaces. These markets also influence such vital outcomes as productivity, quality, profits, and compensation for workers and managers. Indeed, in a more global, competitive, and knowledge-intensive world, the most basic determinants of economic success are closely related to four factors: firms' competitiveness strategies, the organization of work, human resource development, and supportive policies and institutions.

The New Deal's main influence on internal labor markets was to achieve more balance within Tayloristic management structures by providing worker protections through regulations of wages, hours, and working conditions and by giving workers the legal right to organize and bargain collectively. Unions also provided organized means for workers to influence public policies. The basic rationale for collective bargaining within the firm was to promote efficient rule-making, stability, and equity. Efficient rule-making provides the workers and managers closest to the workplace with a means for formulating the rules governing wages, hours, and working conditions. It was equitable, according to New Deal policy-makers, to give workers a modest means to balance the enormous powers governments had granted companies by permitting them to establish corporate and other forms of business enterprise. And collective bargaining stabilized internal labor markets through rules that carefully defined roles, rewards, and responsibilities.

As noted earlier, globalization and technology combined to weaken unions and transform the mass production industrial relations system. The weakening of unions therefore has reduced support for policies that contributed significantly to America's Golden Era.

Active Labor Market Policies

During the 1960s and 1970s, various governments, especially in Scandinavia, developed the concept of active labor market policies to complement macroeconomic measures. The basic theory was that full employment and stable prices could be achieved more effectively by targeted employment, training, counseling, and other policies that reduce labor market bottlenecks by overcoming skill shortages and providing a better match between the demand for and supply of labor. Active labor market policies were thought to be a much better use of public resources than "passive" policies such as "the dole" or unemployment compensation. In theory, targeted policies were justified on *equity* grounds because they reduce unemployment by focusing on those with the worst problems, on *stability* grounds because they could reduce unemployment with less inflationary pressure than macroeconomic policies that simultaneously affect tight as well as loose labor markets, and on *efficiency* grounds because they are the least costly way to reduce unemployment.

Although these programs can be defended on equity grounds, the United States has never devoted sufficient managerial, organizational, or other resources to targeted labor market policies to test the stability or efficiency rationales. Other countries, including Canada, but especially those in Northern Europe, have much higher public expenditures for training and other labor market functions. Moreover, as Richard Nathan stresses in his essay, while targeted policies have a role in overall economic and social policy, they have had serious administrative and management challenges.

A more competitive, knowledge-intensive economy shifts the emphasis and increases the importance of labor market policies. Attention now focuses less on unemployment compensation and an almost exclusive preoccupation with the disadvantaged; and more on education and school reform; school-to-work transition processes; restructuring low-wage sectors to improve their productivity; the transformation of mass production internal labor markets into high performance company-based learning systems; and the development of a labor market infrastructure to provide good information and other services to employers and workers and to support more effective positive adjustment processes. Labor market institutions likewise have important roles to play in addressing such problems as rural and urban development and jobs and training for low-income people, especially in connection with welfare reform.

Service Labor Markets

In his RBSP essay, Lester Thurow contends that "if broadly shared prosperity across Amer-

ica is to be restored, the key to unlocking this new . . . prosperity will be found in the service sector," which accounted for 94 percent of U.S. employment growth between 1980 and 1995. While services have some high-paying jobs, productivity in this sector is very low and average hourly wages in goods producing activities are 30 percent above those of the service sector, which accounts for 74 percent of part-time and contingent workers.

Thurow adds, "Services also explain much of Europe's better productivity performance." There, service-sector wages are near those in manufacturing, and capital investment, training, and productivity are much higher than they are in the United States. Thurow notes, however, that in Europe higher productivity results in slower service-sector job growth. He points out, though, that the Europeans have higher unemployment at least in part because they have failed to offset higher productivity with macroeconomic stimulus.

The policy changes required to improve service productivity and wages include "requiring identical wage and fringe benefit packages for full-time and part-time workers and for temporary or contract workers," which would reduce the demand for these non-regular workers. And this requirement would cause firms to "provide more training or undertake more capital investment to cut the unit labor costs of the services they supply," as well as to reorganize work for high performance. Thurow points out, however, that without adequate economic growth and better incentive structures, more education and training would simply push wages down faster.

Finally, Thurow concludes:

> While social legislation could alter private incentives so that the service sector would contribute to a broadly shared prosperity, this will

not happen by itself in the marketplace. As the incentives are now structured, services can only lead the economy toward a more in-egalitarian structure of wage and employment opportunities in the future as they continue to be an increasingly larger percentage of total economic activity.

Federal Labor Market Policies and Institutions

Critique of Past Programs. Garth Mangum, a major participant in the creation of American workforce development programs, provides insights into what is required to make employment and training more effective. He contends that these programs have been worthwhile despite their highly publicized shortcomings and shows that a major problem with these measures has been their short duration. Mangum notes strong correlations between the duration of training and its returns. In fact, according to Mangum, most of the modest improvements in trainee earnings have been due to steadier employment, not higher earnings. Two constraints have forced reliance on cheap training: eligibility requirements that create a much larger demand for training than can be delivered with the means available, forcing program operators to spread resources too thinly, and the inability of the unemployed and working poor to undergo lengthy training without stipends.

Mangum concludes that federal employment and training programs produced significant gains for women, insignificant and diminishing gains for men, and negative results for most youths, except for the Job Corps, which has been a clear success, though expensive in budget terms. Mangum's main conclusion is that the limited average duration of training in the past will be an increasingly serious problem in

the current labor market, where skill requirements are rising to the point where even those with college degrees have trouble maintaining their incomes.

A Labor Market Infrastructure for the Twenty-first Century. Chris King, Robert McPherson, and Don Long demonstrate the need for a new labor market system to replace the present federal programs, which are fragmented and poorly coordinated; neglect the demand side of the labor market, especially employers; have been stigmatized as extensions of welfare and therefore are shunned by many workers and employers; yield very low returns on the public's modest investments; rarely reach more than a small fraction of those who need labor market services; and, for all of these reasons, lack broad constituencies.

These analysts propose a system that would more effectively link the demand and supply sides of labor markets and provide a broad array of supportive services. Demand-side policies should provide strong incentives for the involvement of employers, without which the system is unlikely to be very effective. The supply-side policies connect individuals with education, training, and jobs. Policies to connect demand and supply include labor market information and labor exchange services. Desirable support services include dependent care and universal health insurance; fully vested and portable pensions; measures to combat discrimination; and income supports for workers in training.

The integrated labor market system recommended by King, McPherson, and Long would be governed by a system of tripartite labor market boards at the federal, state, and local levels. This infrastructure would be funded by governments, employers, workers, and a training tax that could be combined with unemployment compensation trust funds. These funds could be supplemented by general revenues and fees from employers and workers for customized services. Most revenue for the system should flow as block grants through the labor market boards. King, McPherson, and Long also recommend strengthening private training through favorable tax treatment, certifying and reimbursing private companies that establish effective learning processes, and matching training grants to companies that transform themselves into high-performance organizations. These recommendations are very important because funding instability and uncertainty have been major problems for the federal workforce development system.

Public Service Employment. Eli Ginzberg and Richard Nathan provide cautious support for the selective use of subsidized public service employment (PSE) as a component of the federal workforce development system. William J. Wilson and Harry Holzer also believe public employment programs will be necessary to provide jobs for inner-city residents—especially young black men. Nathan concludes, on the basis of extensive field evaluations, that the PSE programs of the 1970s were largely successful in creating jobs and performing useful public service. However, these programs lost political support when Congress and the Carter administration shifted their focus from a countercyclical role to the structural one of addressing the employment problems of the disadvantaged.

Nathan makes the very important point that a major problem for PSE—and other public labor market activities—is that politicians give far too little attention to the management challenges of such programs. However, he agrees with Ginzberg that if "we do the job right, there is a sizeable potential demand" for PSE programs.

Nathan suggests that PSE management problems might be reduced by giving non-profit organizations more responsibility for them. He points out that most of the nation's social and community development services already are "performed by non-profits that are in effect *extensions* of government." The growing popularity of using non-profits to deliver public services is due to many factors, including their superior ability to reach, and be more directly responsive to, target populations, as well as their ability to save money and insulate local governments from direct program management, the fickleness of the flow of federal funds, and civil service and union rules. Another important advantage of the non-profits is their considerable political power, which has disadvantages, but which also makes it more difficult for programs to be discontinued for ideological or partisan political reasons.

Ginzberg, a major participant in the development of U.S. labor market policy, provides a valuable retrospective on the role of PSE in the development of economic policy in the United States from the Great Depression until the present. He notes that the Roosevelt administration used public employment to counteract the depression, while Europeans relied more on the dole. There was fear, following World War II, that the United States might have massive unemployment, but this fear proved false because of effective conversion planning, global economic expansion, and the education and training provisions of the GI Bill. During the 1960s, concern about rising unemployment, which reached 6 percent by the end of the Eisenhower administration (when 3 percent was considered to be full employment), led to a debate about the role of targeted employment and training programs relative to the macroeconomic policies which dominated the economic thinking of the Kennedy administration. Rising structural unemployment during the 1960s and 1970s, especially for youths, minorities, and women, focused attention on the need for PSE and other targeted labor market policies. This debate apparently was settled by the end of the 1960s, when the Kennedy-Johnson tax cut (along with the "War on Poverty" and the Vietnam War) reduced unemployment to about 3 percent.

However, concern for both cyclical and structural unemployment associated with the energy price shocks of the 1970s caused the Carter administration to mount the largest PSE buildup since the 1930s. The rationale for such a large program was the belief of the administration and the Congress that unemployment could be reduced most effectively by concentrating on the groups with the highest levels of unemployment, but a secondary consideration was PSE's effectiveness in achieving macroeconomic stimulus. Labor Department analysts estimated that each PSE job could be created for about $6,000 net, compared with $30,000 or more for tax cuts and $60,000 for public works. Careful evaluations of PSE by Richard Nathan and others concluded that the program was cost effective and achieved its objective by providing useful public services. The program was particularly successful in creating jobs for young black males, who experienced their first increase in employment in the 1970s, about three-fourths of which was in PSE programs.

However, the Carter experience with PSE encountered a number of problems. First, the concern about inflation resulting from the oil price shocks caused some to conclude, without any evidence, that creating jobs for low-wage workers contributed to the high levels of inflation during the 1970s. Second, academic economists criticized PSE for not improving long-term earnings of participants, even though that was not the program's main objective—it was to put unemployed people to work providing useful public services. Third, and most important, as Nathan observes, PSE and other public employment and training programs had serious managerial problems. Some of these problems were inherent in U.S. political and governmental structures. PSE was a federal program administered as an automatic pass through of funds to state and local governments with varying degrees of competence and integrity. There was no way that federal agencies could adequately monitor this system to prevent fraud and abuse. The political problem was caused by the fact that state and local public officials strongly supported the program when they could simply use PSE funds to supplement their budgets without much accountability. They turned against it when the Department of Labor, under strong congressional pressure, attempted to strengthen the program's management and accountability. A catch-22 problem occurred when Department of Labor administrators attempted to improve the program's management and eliminate fraud and abuse, providing information for media stories that exaggerated the extent of fraud and abuse, thus undermining support for the program. Other management problems were created because the tenuous annual congressional appropriations made it hard for program administrators to retain competent staffs and develop strong management systems.

The experiences reviewed by Ginzberg and Nathan present some valuable lessons for the role of PSE in future economic and social policy. First, the main instruments to keep unemployment low must be macroeconomic measures to achieve sustained economic growth. However, targeted programs such as PSE could play a complementary role in providing training and jobs for the hard to employ, though they require major attention to management and accountability. Ginzberg and Nathan observe that community organizations with multiple funding sources could strengthen the management of public service employment. Program stability also could be strengthened through trust funds and multiple-year funding of the kinds suggested earlier by King, McPherson, and Long. Ginzberg notes, in addition, the need to address "such problems as what types of minimum income transfers must accompany low-paying jobs, as well as such supplementary supports as who will care for young children or perform other chores for women who currently face major responsibilities in and out of the home and a shortage of time." Finally, Ginzberg believes governments must be employers of last resort, especially for single-parent family heads and jobless rural and urban youth, who are

> urgently in need of assistance to provide them the education and skills to become self-supporting and . . . [to] obtain PSE jobs until they are able to move into the private economy. Only an obtuse, insensitive society would use taxpayers' money to build more jails rather than develop effective PSE programs.

Employer Training. Relative to most other industrialized countries, American companies provide little formal training to front-line workers. There are many reasons for this. One is that American employers have greater freedom to pursue cost-cutting strategies. Second, the Tayloristic organization of work, which requires that only managerial, technical, and professional employees use sophisticated knowledge and skills, was much more deeply entrenched in the United States than in Europe or Japan. Third, the United States has no system to provide secondary school leavers with the basic technical and learning skills needed for advanced on-the-job learning and is less likely to provide formal school-to-career services. Finally, unlike most other countries, the United States has no policy to encourage or require employers to provide education and training to front-line workers. As a consequence, only high-performance companies—probably no more than 15 percent of all American companies—have seen the need to provide major skill development for front-line workers. Moreover, in the absence of external requirements for training, American companies will underinvest in training because they individually will be unable to capture all of the returns on their training investment, which empirical evidence suggests are high relative to the returns to physical capital.[18]

Private-sector training experts Anthony Carnevale and Donna Desrochers stress the importance of company policies for the "high road" to shared prosperity. The "low road" "continues along the historic path of mass production, emphasizing downsizing, outsourcing, 'deskilling,' and other methods to improve productivity by slashing labor costs. While low-road strategies result in short-term productivity gains, they reduce the nation's long-term economic competitiveness, living standards, and income equality." These authors conclude that only "a minority of elite American employers have taken the high road." Moreover,

> absent alterations in the current institutional incentives, the American economy—and most workers—will never find the high road. . . . Without changes in policy and market incentives that encourage an equal opportunity to learn, uneven access to good schools and lifelong learning will only . . . [drive] an already

deepening wedge between the learning-haves and the learning have-nots, substituting an exclusive meritocracy for more traditional forms of economic elitism.

Because of the critical importance of on-the-job learning, Carnevale and Desrochers recommend policies for encouraging employer-based training that would "focus on the complementarity between employer-provided training and schooling."

Health Care

As noted earlier, diminished access to health care has contributed to serious social pathologies as well as poor economic opportunities for many low-income workers. An effective national health care system therefore could do much to restore shared prosperity. Karen Davis proposes such a policy. She would create a national health system that would assure health security for all Americans with the "long-term goal of a single system for all." She believes this single universal health care financing system could be approached incrementally and would avoid the quality, cost, and equity problems of such proposals as raising financial contributions for Medicare beneficiaries, vouchers, or other changes. She notes that Medicare's administrative costs, 2 percent of outlays, are much lower than the 15 to 20 percent of managed care systems and 30 to 50 percent of individual health insurance plans.

Corporate Governance and Internal Labor Markets

The mass production system and its supporting policies and institutions were largely responsible for America's Golden Era, but the viability of these arrangements was greatly diminished by technology and the globalization of markets. As noted in Part I, economic success in more competitive, knowledge-intensive global markets depends primarily on value added (productivity and quality) and flexibility. These outcomes, in turn, depend on business strategies, the organization of work, and supportive policies and institutions. There is mounting evidence that high-performance workplaces are needed to optimize value added and restore shared prosperity. These high-performance organizations have a number of characteristics—they adopt lean, decentralized, highly participative management and decision processes; stress the development, adaptation, and use of leading-edge technology; have positive material and non-material compensation systems that reward value added; provide for the education and training of all workers, not primarily managerial and technical employees as in the mass production system; and provide independent sources of power for all stakeholders.[19] As Carnevale and Desrochers noted earlier, very few American companies have adopted the high-road strategy.

There are many reasons for the failure of most American companies to adopt high-value-added strategies. Some of these are discussed in the following sections, beginning with the important role of corporate governance.

According to Eileen Appelbaum and Peter Berg, financial markets have discouraged firms from adopting high-performance practices that could lead to shared prosperity. This is so because high-performance practices require large upfront long-term investments in technology, logistical design, and training for front-line workers, which collide with the short-term stockholder interests that increasingly drive financial institutions and corporate managerial decisions. As with many other institutions, financial markets have been transformed by technology, deregulation, and global competition. Immediately after World War II banks were regulated, interest rates were low, and creditworthy companies financed their long-term investments mainly through retained earnings and long-term debt or bonds.

These practices changed during the 1970s and 1980s, when deregulation and globalization caused foreign competition to threaten oligopolistic domestic prices and made it difficult for companies either to achieve their financial targets or to continue traditional industrial relations practices. The deregulation and globalization of financial markets provided stockholders and investors with alternative, higher-yielding opportunities. The managers of mutual funds, pensions, and other institutional investments became more interested in short-term returns than the long-term survival of companies. In this process, the long-term value of companies was converted to short-term capital values. The results were often quick gains for financial operators, heavy debts for companies, and the displacement of workers.

These developments also altered the way companies are governed and managers are rewarded. Instead of long-term survival of the company and a community of interest with neighborhoods and workers, stockholder value became the driving force of most corporations. The primacy of stockholder value in corporate decisions relative to other stakeholders' interests causes executive compensation to be linked with stock prices, which is one of the factors responsible for short-term decision-making and the rapidly escalating salaries of corporate executives, both of which could be detrimental to the long-term interests of workers, the country, and even to companies themselves.

These new financial arrangements also cause companies to compete through cost-cutting instead of restructuring for high performance. Some of these cost-cutting activities resemble high-performance practices, but have very different motives and outcomes. For example, decentralization and flat management structures are designed to reduce costs, not to improve productivity, quality, and flexibility. Moreover, in this system, human resources become costs to be minimized, not resources to be developed.

Because high-performance systems are more compatible with the long-term interests of nations, communities, and workers, Appelbaum and Berg agree with Tom Kochan that corporate laws should be changed to give employees greater voice. Moreover, they argue that these laws should reflect the reality that "shareholders are merely one group with a stake in the corporation."

Internal Labor Markets: Industrial Relations and Worker Participation

As noted earlier, worker organizations and collective bargaining were integral components of the New Deal institutional and policy system associated with America's long period of shared prosperity. Unions and collective bargaining were sanctioned by New Deal policies as a way both to provide a democratic voice for workers in national and workplace policies and practices and to help prevent recessions and depressions by sustaining purchasing power and aggregate demand. Employer opposition to collective bargaining was moderated by taking labor out of competition through contracts and government regulations and by corporations' low public esteem during the depression. Labor economists argued that removing labor from competition strengthened economic efficiency by forcing companies to compete by improving productivity and quality instead of by reducing wages and working conditions. Furthermore, removing labor from competition promoted the development of human resources by protecting the health and welfare of workers and their families.

Workers in America were never as highly organized as those in most West European countries, but at their peak in the 1950s and 1960s unions represented about a third of the non-agricultural workforce. And the influence of collective bargaining extended to virtually the entire workforce through union-sponsored government regulations and the tendency for non-union companies to more or less match union conditions as a way to avoid unions by keeping their employees satisfied. The legal framework for union organizing in the United States was based on the implicit assumption of large oligopolistic organizations or regulated monopolies, homogeneous workforces, and adversarial relations between unions and employers.

As noted earlier, the underpinnings of the traditional American labor relations system were weakened by technological and demographic changes and the growth and intensification of competitive markets. These developments changed the public perception of the nation's most important economic problem from stimulating aggregate demand, where unions were part of the solution, to economic competitiveness, where unions often are depicted as part of the problem. American unions have never been very strong in highly competitive markets, where it is difficult to take labor out of competition. Each employer in a competitive industry will resist union actions that would raise labor costs and put their companies at a competitive disadvantage. As Tom Kochan points out, American employers resist unions more than their European counterparts, partly

because union/non-union cost differentials are likely to be much greater in the United States than in Europe. Moreover, the globalization of markets enables employers to shift work away from heavily unionized areas. Other trends weakening unions include the growth of employment in white-collar and technical occupations and in the South, where unions are generally weaker, and the increased labor force participation of women and minorities, which not only causes the union practice of a "common rule" adopted mainly for male heads of households to be more difficult to implement, but also requires unions dominated by white males to adjust their policies and practices to accommodate the interests of women and minorities. Thus, demographic, labor and product market, and technological changes combined to weaken the traditional industrial relations system and its legal and institutional supports.

Tom Kochan and Paula Voos demonstrate that labor relations have become more important for economic success at the very time private-sector unions have become weaker. These analysts confirm much expert opinion that worker-management cooperation could improve company performance as well as the enforcement of such worker protections as safety and health laws, and could strengthen education and training processes, especially for small employers.

American workers and managers would like to expand employee participation, but could be deterred from doing so by provisions of the National Labor Relations Act (NLRA) which prohibit company-dominated unions and require unions aggressively to protect and promote workers' interests. Indeed, Kochan argues that the more effective worker participation becomes, the more questionable its legality Kochan and Voos show that the main barriers to workers being able to join unions and participate in workplace decisions are employer opposition and the weaknesses of the NLRA. Indeed, while more favorable to employers than to workers, the NLRA does not meet the needs of workers, employers, or the country very well. Workers have difficulty acquiring basic rights taken for granted in other countries and good worker participation practices are of questionable legality. Moreover, because of defective labor-management processes, the resolution of many conflicts is unfair or requires time-consuming, uncertain, expensive, and inefficient legal processes for companies and workers.

Both Kochan and Voos recommend policies to improve worker representation and participation. Employee rights could be strengthened through mandated labor-management safety and health programs, which have demonstrated their effectiveness in some states and countries, and through federal legislation guaranteeing a "just cause" standard for dismissal. Voos would, in addition, amend labor law to make it easier for workers to organize and bargain collectively.

Tom Kochan believes in the soundness of the collective bargaining premise that "the parties closest to the problems . . . are best positioned to shape the terms and conditions of employment that suit their needs and circumstances." But, he argues, the most fundamental aspect of labor law, "the rules governing interactions among employees and employers in negotiating the terms and conditions of employment and their . . . administration . . . is perhaps the most outdated and ineffective of all components of employment policy." The NLRA's basic tenet, that workers should be able to freely choose whether or not to be represented by unions "often resembles a high-pitched, high-stakes battle." The level of conflict in these representation elections has steadily increased and the resulting time and resources required have caused frustrated workers and unions to doubt the value of the process. "Approximately 25 percent of representation elections result in at least one worker being illegally discharged." And even when unions win elections, approximately one-third fail to achieve a first contract.

The consequences of this system, according to Kochan, are unsatisfactory to workers as well as employers as indicated by scientific polls, which show that: ". . . nearly 25 million workers want to be represented by a union but cannot gain access to representation." Moreover, "Approximately 70 to 80 percent of the respondents . . . indicate an interest in being part of a process that consults and has significant influence in decision-making but that has the cooperation, not the opposition, of management."

Because of the well-documented competitive advantages of worker participation, "most American employers have introduced one or more types of direct employee representation," which surveys find are as likely to be in union as non-union workplaces. Ironically, "The evidence suggests that the broader the scope of the innovations, the bigger their effects on productivity and quality. Yet, the broader their scope, the more likely they are to also violate the NLRA."

Employers and their supporters in Congress advocate amending the NLRA to permit various forms of worker participation in non-union settings. However, Kochan rejects this proposal because it would leave the other problems in the law unaddressed and "make it more difficult for workers to gain independent representation since one of the most effective union avoidance strategies an employer can mount is the promise of an employee participation program."

Kochan recommends a number of institutional reforms, including the modification of corporate governance laws to shift the legal rules from maximizing shareholder wealth, which was more appropriate to early industrialization, to accommodate the representation of human assets, "the firm's most critical resource" and a residual risk-bearer.

A Corporate Perspective

Thomas J. Usher, Chief Executive Officer of USX, provides important corporate insight into what is required to restore shared prosperity. Usher's experience is that of a CEO who has led the transformation of America's largest steel company from an oligopoly with an authoritarian management system to a highly competitive and participative company. USX's Steel Group (formerly U.S. Steel) has established a good working relationship with the United Steelworkers, which is partly responsible for transforming USX into one of the world's most efficient integrated steel companies. In this sense, Usher's views probably are typical of progressive CEOs in basic industries that have been transformed from oligopolies into globally competitive companies.

USX was forced to transform itself during the 1980s when globalization rendered obsolete both its business and industrial relations policies. As the largest company in what was a critical U.S. industry, USX's pricing and industrial relations were frequent targets of government intervention. Moreover, long strikes like the one the company sustained in 1959–60 caused a loss of customers to foreign imports. In order to avoid this problem, the company and the union entered into a no-strike agreement that contained cost of living and automatic wage increases that caused prices to become unsustainable in the more competitive economy of the 1980s. The union and the company understood the need to restructure, but disagree-

ment over the terms led to a bitter six-month strike in 1986 in which, according to Usher, "all sides were bloodied, nobody won and everybody lost—we, the union, the employees, the plant communities, and our customers." The strike also caused the parties to realize that domestic steel had become much less important to the American economy: "We had a strike and nobody cared—and nobody missed us." As frequently happens after bitter and inconclusive conflicts, USX and the United Steelworkers realized that, if the company were to survive, the parties needed to establish more participative and cooperative relationships. The parties also recognized the need for continuous training and financial incentives for workers to improve quality and productivity and reduce costs. As Usher notes, while union-management relations are more cooperative, they are adversarial as well, though the parties so far have been able to resolve their differences more amicably than before their partnership agreement.

While USX's transformation into a more competitive company has improved performance, Usher notes the importance of supportive public policies to the industry's continued success. The most important of these in Usher's view include economic growth through federal budget, tax, and environmental policies to encourage investment; trade policies to prevent the dumping of subsidized foreign steel; and improved education, which "might help the country more than anything else we have talked about."

The Development of Communities, Regions, and Rural and Urban Areas

The essays in this volume make it very clear that opportunity in America depends heavily on where people live. Bill Spelman demonstrates how many neighborhoods condition young people for a life of crime and, in the 1990s, those who live in depressed rural communities and inner-city neighborhoods are not likely to have access to role models or other amenities middle-class people take for granted. As William J. Wilson and Gary Dymski show, this was not always the case. In the 1950s, people in racially segregated communities had access to jobs, middle-class and professional neighbors, local banking and credit institutions, and better schools, to name a few things that have changed. Because of shared prosperity in the 1950s and 1960s and improvements in civil rights protections, more affluent minorities were able to move to the suburbs. During the 1970s and 1980s, the deregulation of financial markets and the emergence of more intensive competition caused stronger businesses and financial institutions to flee central cities. Opportunities for the people left behind therefore have been greatly restricted. The most accessible short-term opportunities for many inner-city residents are drugs, prostitution, or other illegal activities, all of which increase poverty and greatly reduce long-term opportunities. The economic and social development of depressed urban areas therefore is a major challenge in any strategy to achieve shared prosperity.

Moreover, as William Galston shows, opportunities for many rural as well as urban residents are limited because of location. And, just as with urban areas, rural places that were major beneficiaries of New Deal policies have been transformed by the structural changes of the last twenty-five years.

Helping Communities Help Themselves

Ernesto Cortes, director of the Southwest Industrial Areas Foundation (SIAF), an affiliate of the Industrial Areas Foundation (IAF), examines the lessons learned from an effective movement to empower low-income neighborhoods to take responsibility for their own conditions. The IAF's iron rule—"Never do for others what they can do for themselves"—has enabled the organization to win impressive victories "not by speaking for ordinary people but by teaching them to speak, act, and engage in politics for themselves." Inverting Lord Acton's dictum, IAF leaders have learned that "powerlessness also corrupts—perhaps more pervasively than power itself." Cortes emphasizes, however, that rebuilding civic and political institutions requires action and hard work, not just good ideas.

The IAF's mission is to strengthen grassroots democracy by teaching ordinary citizens to build broad-based organizations that fill the vacuum in their communities left by the deterioration of such mediating institutions as families, neighborhoods, congregations, unions, political parties, neighborhood schools, and other civic organizations. The IAF seeks to rebuild the social fabric in these communities by creating a civic society, or social capital, to offset the tendency for markets and the state to work (increasingly hand in hand) to undermine whatever stability can be found for the less fortunate in our society. Broad-based community organizations are required, according to Cortes, to prevent most of the costs of change from being shifted to low-income people and most of the benefits to the affluent.

The IAF's experiences teach a number of lessons about what is required to reduce inequality, especially that

> redistributing resources to support individuals earlier in their lives is critical to sustaining a civil society in this nation. Our organizations have found that resources invested in public

education, after-school programs, preventive health care for children, summer work experience for adolescents, college scholarships, and similar strategies greatly improve the chances of those children when they become adults.

In a relatively short time in the 1990s, the Alliance Schools have made remarkable progress in improving the educational achievement of low-income children throughout Texas. The IAF has learned, in addition, that the capacity to manage change depends more on social capital (the vitality of relationships) than upon traditional economic factors: "The capacity to innovate, to readjust, and to maintain common efforts in the face of uncertainty depends upon the trust and mutual commitment among those who do the work of our society."

The SIAF has, in addition, addressed the mismatch between workers and jobs, one of the anomalies of urban America. In every metropolitan area, there are many jobless workers and many very good jobs that these workers either do not know about or have not been trained for. Some very effective programs have been initiated to address this problem. For example, two SIAF affiliates in San Antonio worked with employers to develop a successful program, Project Quest, to recruit, train, and place workers from low-income neighborhoods into high-wage jobs. The Project Quest model has spread to other Texas cities.

Urban Development

Gary Dymski analyzes three necessary elements for a healthy urban community: robust income flows, an asset base whose value increases over time, and an adequate social and physical infrastructure. "When all three elements are present in a community, they are mutually reinforcing; the converse is true when all three elements are absent." These three elements reinforce each other through spillovers transmitted by market transactions, as when strong labor markets generate higher incomes that increase home values. Dymski notes that community development is path dependent such that cumulative processes of prosperity or stagnation are not easily reversed.

Since traditional macroeconomic policies have much less effect on inner cities, targeted urban policies will be required to revive these areas. Moreover, Dymski rejects the assumption that market forces will automatically correct the problems of inner cities (e.g., that declining wages and asset values will automatically attract capital). Because of the importance of path trajectories and spillovers, inner-city areas with heavy concentrations of poor people have become degenerating or stagnant systems, even as parts of a metropolis with concentrations of wealthy people prosper.

Like most of the essayists in this volume, Dymski rejects the cultural interpretation of inner-city problems, which stresses residents' unwillingness either to take low-wage jobs or to demand capital. According to culturalists, the inner-city economies will improve only when the alternatives to work and entrepreneurship— "that is, welfare benefits and criminal activity— are made less available and less attractive." The contrasting structural perspective, which Dymski supports, stresses "an inadequate supply of capital and credit and an inadequate demand for inner-city labor." This interpretation "puts the primary blame for the current crisis on deindustrialization and discrimination in markets, not on the behavioral maladies of inner-city residents."

In Dymski's view, none of these remedies are likely to work unless they are done on an adequate scale. Moreover, when communities have stabilized with triple deficits in his three-factor framework (i.e., income flows, increasing asset values, and social and physical infrastructure), successful interventions must address at least two of the three factors.

Rural Areas

As Galston stresses, rural leaders also must produce new development strategies compatible with the realities of a global information world. These "strategies will have to be defended primarily as contributions to overall national well-being rather than in place-specific terms."

Galston believes, however, that "it would be premature to give up on the capacity of the public sector to improve rural America, even in the face of the adverse global trends." He believes that "a sounder understanding of broad developments will create a context in which policy analysts and local decision-makers can more realistically evaluate the odds of success for the options they face." And rural leaders might particularly be able to use information technology to overcome some of the disadvantages of distance.

Regions

In his RBSP essay, Norman Glickman shows that incomes vary by regions as well as by urban and rural locations. Indeed, he cites evidence that income inequality for individuals and regions varies with economic development, increasing at first as development proceeds at a faster pace in some regions compared to others and then declining as the lagging regions catch up. However, during the 1970s, inequality started increasing among and within regions as well as among individuals and families.

The causes of the differential patterns of re-gional inequality include varying rates of growth, resource endowments, and responses to national business cycles; demographic factors, including migration from poor to richer regions and different demographic mixes; technology, which changes the composition of rates of growth and the demand for skills; changing industry mixes and linkages; the differential impacts of international trade and investment; and diverse education levels.

With respect to the future, Glickman concludes that, despite economic theory to the contrary, convergence between regions is not assured. His calculations show that declines in inequality have come slowly and over long periods of time, but that these long-term trends have been interrupted by periods of increasing inequality, which are difficult to predict.

IV. Conclusions

America's long period of shared prosperity started in the 1940s and ended in the early 1970s with a sharp slowdown in the growth of productivity and total output. Since that time, only the top 20 to 25 percent of households have significantly improved their economic fortunes, while income and wealth have declined for the bottom half of the population. The big winners generally are people with post-graduate degrees and the owners of capital and their agents (managers) who make decisions about the distribution of gains. The big losers are unionized male workers, who were able to earn middle-class incomes in the mass production economy. Other losers are disadvantaged minorities, especially young black males; Latinos, especially recent immigrants who entered American labor markets after the Golden Era was over; workers without a college education; and the residents of depressed or disconnected rural and inner-city areas. As we have noted, however, the expanding college wage premium is due mainly to losses by those with only high school educations or less, not to rapid increases in the incomes of those with college degrees.

The essays in this volume show that inequality and stagnant incomes are accompanied by physical and mental health problems, crime and other social pathologies, and undermine the national unity required to gain support for the policies needed to improve opportunity. Widening inequalities would be less problematic if they were offset by upward mobility, but as McMurrer and Sawhill show, this is not the case. Upward mobility is a function of economic growth, family background, and education. Family background, while still a major factor in upward mobility, has become slightly less important, but this has been more than offset by slower economic growth and declining wages for those without a college education.

The negative impact of family background can be overcome by education, but this is a catch-22 problem because educational achievement is closely related to family incomes, so access to education also is becoming more unequal. Moreover, educational opportunity has been limited by stagnant real incomes; grossly unequal educational resources between rich and poor school districts; declining educational subsidies; the poor quality of K–12 education for low-income students; high dropout rates, especially for Latinos; and the escalating cost of higher education. Thus, declining opportunity is self-perpetuating. The widening education-income gap will narrow somewhat as more disadvantaged people seek higher education, thus increasing the supply of educated people, but this process will be more than offset by several factors, including: relatively higher increases in the demand for academic skills, especially in

mathematics, science, and technology; larger numbers of unskilled workers from immigration and natural population increases because disadvantaged minorities' younger-aged cohorts have higher birth rates; and the limited opportunity structures confronting the disadvantaged because of family background, residential neighborhoods, and job discrimination. As William J. Wilson notes, race is not the only factor limiting the opportunities of ghetto blacks, but it is a factor. Similarly, Hartmann and Chapa conclude that discrimination continues to impede the upward mobility of women and Latinos. And Ahituv, Tienda, and Hotz show that the school-to-work paths of Latinos and blacks put them at lifetime economic disadvantages relative to white youths. Hartmann notes, however, that momentum, family choices, and the narrowing of the education gap will cause women to continue advancing economically. Nevertheless, they still face obstacles to their upward mobility; this is especially true for mothers who have to balance job and family responsibilities in workplaces and families whose rules and benefits are geared to male heads of households. This challenge is especially daunting for single, less-educated mothers and their children.

A review of the forces that changed the institutions and policies responsible for America's long period of shared prosperity before the early 1970s provides insights into what, if anything, can be done to increase upward mobility. America's prosperity was based upon an abundance of physical resources, which were much more important in early industrialization than they are now; rapid improvements in productivity made possible by economies of scale in basic mass production industries; institutions, policies, and cultural attributes that supported shared economic progress; and creative, pragmatic policies that defined the working relationship between the public and private sectors.

The basic engines of growth were the mass production system and a culture that encouraged innovation and entrepreneurship. The factors that improved opportunities for low-income people included:

- the absence of rigid class identification;
- limited need for formal education for most mass production workers;
- a universal free public education system that provided workers the education they needed to succeed;
- the accessibility of higher education through numerous low-cost colleges and universities with lax entry standards, reinforced by the GI Bill for veterans as well as by grants, loans, and scholarships for non-veterans;
- a flexible, diverse post-secondary school system, especially community colleges, which provided Americans with greater opportunities for second chances at higher education than was the case in other countries;
- the social safety nets—especially Social Security, unemployment compensation, subsidized health care, Medicare, and Medicaid;
- the spread of collective bargaining, which enabled workers to share in the gains of their enterprises and to protect and promote their interests in society and in workplaces;
- a moderately progressive tax system that caused a larger share of taxes to be borne by those with the greatest ability to pay; and
- public infrastructures available to all regardless of income.

However, the most important factor in upward mobility was the relatively rapid growth of productivity, output, and employment in the three decades before the 1970s. This growth benefited greatly from the commercialization of technologies, many of which were developed during World War II, the dominant factor in the 1940–73 period; macroeconomic policies to keep the mass production system going; and the rebuilding of economies devastated by World War II—alone among the major powers, the American economy actually benefited from World War II.

As the essays in this volume demonstrate, the chief forces undermining the policies and institutions responsible for America's Golden Era were the closely related processes of technological change and globalization. The main economic force at work is the expansion of financial, service, and product markets increasingly driven by global competition. Because competitive markets provide important material benefits, especially to economic and political elites, they are powerful forces for change. The increased mobility of capital and its role in job creation and economic development have caused financial markets to impose major constraints on individuals, enterprises, and governments. Once the cycle of innovation, global economies of scale, competition, and increases in value added gained momentum, domestic economies moved from shallow to deeper integration into the global economy, with much larger and more pervasive implications for domestic institutions, policies, and values.

Globalization thus makes it increasingly difficult for governments to regulate their economies, pursue income maintenance or other equity-oriented policies that conflict with the logic of the market, and renders national macroeconomic policies much less effective.

Increased competition also makes it difficult for the mass production oligopolies that dominated basic U.S. industries to regulate prices. Market-driven systems stress productivity in the use of all resources (not just economies of scale), as well as quality and flexibility in adjusting to change.

The technological and market changes discussed in these essays not only undermined the mass production system, they also created the means for a more prosperous economy whose benefits can be more equitably shared. The keys to success are scientific and technological progress, human resource development, the organization of work, and supportive policies and institutions. However, all of the essayists in this volume agree that such an economy will not be produced by competitive market forces alone, but will require strategies and policies to take advantage of the opportunities and moderate the risks in this more dynamic, knowledge-intensive, and competitive environment.

In the new economy, competitiveness strategies are the core determinants of success. There are two basic ways to compete: reduce costs directly by lowering incomes or indirectly by improving value added (i.e., quality and productivity). For a high-wage country, a cost-cutting strategy implies lower and more unequal incomes, and improves income mainly by using more labor and physical resources, which clearly limits economic progress. The high-value-added strategy, by contrast, permits faster and shared growth because it requires the effective organization of production and the greater use of ideas, skills and knowledge to improve productivity, quality, and flexibility. High-value-added organizations require (1) lean, decentralized participative management processes with positive reward systems; (2) education and training for all participants, especially front-line workers; (3) the development and use of leading edge technology; (4) the empowerment of all stakeholders, not just shareholders and their agents (i.e., managers); and (5) supportive policies and institutions.

The supporting policies and institutions for a high-value-added system include:

- a coherent theory to guide domestic and international policies—the high-value-added concept seems most appropriate;
- open and competitive global and domestic markets;
- a full employment growth strategy;
- public infrastructure investments, including education, research and development, and the protection of intellectual property rights;
- an advanced digital network, the information infrastructure for the twenty-first century;
- a world-class standards-driven system to facilitate lifelong learning opportunities, especially for students from low-income families;
- progressive tax policies that moderate widening disparities in wealth and income, and encourage human and physical capital formation and stable economic growth;
- more effective international institutions based on sustainable high-value-added principles, including labor and environmental standards, transparency of international transactions, and international financial institutions to stabilize and prevent international financial crises;
- the development of a modern labor market infrastructure to provide information and other services to workers, employers, and learners;

- development strategies to provide greater opportunities to people in depressed rural and urban areas, including access to jobs, credit, and high-quality education institutions;
- corporate governance, worker participation, and labor relations policies to facilitate employee involvement in workplace decisions and encourage labor-management cooperation;
- adequate minimum wage and income support systems (e.g., earned income tax credits) to provide incentives for low-income people to work at a living wage;
- social safety nets for people unable to work, including positive adjustment processes for displaced workers; a national health insurance system; stabilizing Social Security; lengthening unemployment compensation from twenty-nine weeks to thirty-nine and raising the wage replacement rate to 50 percent; and strengthening private pension programs and providing for portability and joint control of corporate pensions.

It is particularly important to ensure that democratic institutions are more responsive to workers and communities. Worker participation, unions, and community-based organizations such as the Industrial Areas Foundation should be strengthened.

A High-Value-Added Competitiveness Strategy

Higher and more broadly shared prosperity requires a competitiveness theory to guide particular policies. An orienting theory enables the separation of the important from the unimportant and gives coherence to policies that other-wise might seem invalid out of context. For example, a minimum-wage law makes sense as part of a developmental process to encourage people to become self-sufficient and prevent low-wage competition, despite the assumption that minimum wages inevitably create unemployment, which is not always valid even theoretically. Moreover, trade-linked labor standards are viewed by many international trade theorists as "protectionism," even though as components of a high-value-added strategy they can help promote wage convergence between countries by improving the conditions of low-wage workers, not merely by lowering those of higher-paid workers. Similarly, a comprehensive positive adjustment program can facilitate the transfer of workers and capital from low- to high-value-added sectors and overcome resistance to changes deemed to be in the national interest.

Sensible policies to more equitably share the benefits and costs of economic liberalization are particularly important as economies become more deeply integrated into the global economy. Robert Lawrence, Albert Bressand, and Takatoshi Ito demonstrate that the movement from shallow to deep international integration erodes national sovereignty and values.[20] As a result, "Almost every aspect of domestic policy now has international ramifications," which create tension between internationalization and national sovereignty. Moreover, "Relying exclusively on competitive pressures to reduce international tensions could undermine efforts to establish sensible multilateral standards and rules."[21]

An appropriate theory also enables decision-makers to understand the consequences of various policies. For example, "free trade" usually is viewed by economists in terms of the principle of comparative advantage, which posits only winners from voluntary, short-term transactions, where specialization in products in which each trader has the greatest advantage or the least disadvantage will maximize the traders' joint product. The outcomes of such transactions are true by definition or they would not take place. In the real world, however, where global markets are deeply integrated, there are losers as well as winners from international transactions, which include not only commodities but technologies, factories and whole industries as well. In such a world, the theory of competitive advantage (i.e., competing either by value added or by direct cost cutting) is more appropriate for analyzing a particular trade liberalization proposal. It would be ludicrous to argue, as many do, that *all* trade liberalization provides net social benefits. As Thea Lee points out, economists do not have the analytical tools to support that claim. It is possible, however, to conclude that more open and expanding markets within the framework of good rules, policies, and institutions can be mutually beneficial to the great majority of people in all countries.

A Growth Strategy

As noted throughout these essays, a growth strategy could do much to provide upward mobility and increased revenues for public investments. Faster growth is particularly important for the restoration of upward economic mobility. Unfortunately, growth policies have been constrained by the NAIRU concept, which, as argued by Bob Solow and Bob Eisner in their essays, clearly is not an effective guide to policy. There obviously are limits to economic growth, but they are not easily predicted. Moreover, inflation does not appear to be a threat in a more open, competitive, and knowledge-intensive global economy. However, though he believes it is exaggerated, Solow warns us not to treat the threat of inflation lightly.

A growth strategy that includes public infrastructure investment could stimulate private investment and job creation. As Jeff Faux noted, the decline in public investment is an important factor in the slowdown in productivity growth since the early 1970s.

Faux, Eisner, Wolff, and others show where revenues could be found to finance public investment. Like Eisner, Faux calls for a more realistic accounting of public assets and liabilities. Since national output per capita will continue to grow, making future generations, on average, much better off, Faux, Eisner, and Baker also question the idea that the public debt will bankrupt future generations. Furthermore, public infrastructure investments will improve the quality of life for future generations through cleaner air and water; better transportation, communications, and education systems; and stronger knowledge and technology bases—all of which are important sources of economic growth. Of course, governments, like businesses and schools, will achieve their objectives more efficiently if they are high-performance organizations.

Learning Systems

One of the American economy's most serious problems is the inadequacy of its public schools and the huge education gaps between high- and low-income students. It is almost universally recognized that education not only yields high personal and social returns, but also is vital to upward mobility. The good news is the growing international evidence that poor people in general, and disadvantaged minorities in particular, value education very highly. We also have mounting evidence that the schools in poor communities can be transformed into high-performance institutions. Marc Tucker, for example, outlines a standards-driven system to reform schools and other learning systems. Tucker's ideas are not just theoretical because the organization he directs, the National Center on Education and the Economy (NCEE), is deeply involved in implementing extensive standards-driven reforms throughout the United States. The NCEE also is helping the National Skills Standards Board develop and implement a world-class skills development system. Moreover, Ernie Cortes and his IAF colleagues have demonstrated that low-income parents and communities can be mobilized to dramatically improve student achievement. More is required, especially reducing school finance inequities by relying less on local property taxes. And major attention should be given to removing the financial barriers to higher education. There is impressive evidence that realistic opportunities for higher education can greatly improve the performance and graduation rates of low-income students in elementary and secondary schools. The social returns to higher education are sufficient to justify making it a free good, as is done in Germany and Scandinavia. Abundant evidence for high social returns to post-secondary education was provided by the World War II GI Bill, which returned to the federal government at least five times its cost over ten years.

We also need to dramatically improve school-to-career opportunities for the non-college bound and on-the-job training for front-line workers, where the United States lags far behind other countries. As Ahituv, Tienda, and Hotz show, the disadvantages minorities suffer in the school-to-work process have negative lifetime consequences. Moreover, Carnevale and Desrochers and the Commission on the Skills of the American Workforce show that American companies invest much less in the education and training of front-line workers than their counterparts in other countries. This is a serious problem given the importance of learning, thinking, and problem-solving skills for high-performance production processes. Because they have difficulty capturing the returns to education and training, most American companies are reluctant to make these investments. Governments at every level therefore should provide technical assistance and incentives through taxes or other means for company- or industry-based training, especially for medium and small companies. These training processes should be administered jointly by employer and worker representatives to ensure that training meets the needs of employees as well as management.

Internal Labor Markets and Industrial Relations

Another serious defect in the American system is the lack of effective mechanisms to facilitate worker participation in workplace and societal decisions. Indeed, American workers have less voice at work than their counterparts in any other major industrial country. The absence of participatory mechanisms makes it difficult to ensure that enterprise and societal decisions reflect workers' interests. Without such representation, we are less likely to develop policies to promote upward mobility and high-value-added strategies. There is abundant evidence, moreover, that worker participation not only improves productivity and quality, but also enhances the effectiveness of such workplace regulations as occupational safety and health and the administration of pension funds. Participatory processes can, in addition, reduce worker compensation costs and probably help avoid expensive, time-consuming, and uncertain employment-related litigation. And a participatory system clearly is more compatible with a democratic society than the traditional authoritarian organization of work.

As Kochan and Voos show, American labor relations laws are rooted in the conditions of the 1930s and do not serve the contemporary interests of workers, employers, or the public very well. However, because the present system gives them considerable power relative to unions and workers, business organizations have been unwilling to support the modernization of labor laws to provide more effective worker participation.

For their part, unions are reluctant to support amending the NLRA to clarify the legality of labor-management cooperation processes that improve performance. As Kochan points out, the more effective these processes are, the more likely they are to violate the law. He also presents evidence that workers overwhelmingly desire to participate in workplace decisions but are unable to do so. Kochan estimates that 25 million non-union U.S. workers would like union representation but are unwilling to endure the risky contests with their employers required to unionize. Not only do American companies resist unions more than their European counterparts, but probably also are unique in considering unionization—a fundamental right in most countries—a sign of management failure.

Corporate Governance

As Appelbaum and Berg show, deregulation and globalization have combined with shareholder dominance of American corporate law to create barriers to the investments and structural changes required to be high-performance organizations. The consequence of these developments has been to focus companies' attention on the short-term interests of stockholders and less on workers, communities, and even the long-term viability of companies. Competition protects customers' interests, but there is no process to protect workers, communities, or the country's long-term interest by ensuring that companies pursue high-value-added competitiveness strategies. The recommendations advanced in this volume would do much to force companies to consider the long-term interests of workers, communities, and the country. However, the recommendations of Kochan, Appelbaum, and Berg to amend corporate law to reflect the interests of other stakeholders as is done in other industrial countries also merit careful consideration.

Safety Nets

Stronger social safety nets could simultaneously limit companies' ability to pursue low-wage options and to moderate the growing inequality of wealth and income. A combination of minimum wages, earned income taxes, and income transfers could support families, thus making them better learning systems for parents and children.[22] A national system to close the gaps in health insurance coverage could improve the health of low-income families. The present company-based system not only makes health care costs a negative factor in the employment practices of companies, but puts downward pressure on wages because workers often accept low-paying jobs in order to obtain health care coverage. Similarly, many welfare recipients are reluctant to seek employment outside their homes because they would lose health care for their children. As Karen Davis argues, the incremental development of a comprehensive national health care financing system could simultaneously contain costs and maintain the quality and accessibility of health care.

Pensions and Soci

Dean Baker and B
cial Security syste
ever problems it h
modest changes. T
resa Ghilarducci,
against privatizing
that the Social Sec
investment for ma
system's insurance
provide larger bene
for low-income fam
ent. Privatization w
low-wage workers
wealth gaps. Bake
would also increas
would not increase
Social Security taxe
ize employment, the
for lowering these ta
investment of Socia
vate securities marke
sulated from poli
investors. However,
ment income could b
tages to encourage
individual retirement

Strengthening priv
could help moderate
give workers a non-v
income. This is par
market forces and str
downward pressure o
tom 40 percent of the
strong worker partici
formance issues invol
of pension funds, whi
source of equity capi
The evidence suggest
participation in their g

the greater use of pension funds for job creation
purposes, with no increase in risk. Ghilarducci
raises the issue of whether corporate pension
funds should belong to beneficiaries and therefore be controlled by trustees elected at least in
part by employees. The superior performance of
jointly trusteed union pension funds suggests
that worker participation need not sacrifice returns or safety. And, as Kochan emphasizes, the
reduced attachment of workers to individual
companies suggests the need to make pension
and other benefits more portable.

Despite its problems, America is still the
world's strongest economy, with many advantages and considerable individual opportunity.
We therefore should use this strength to make
American prosperity more sustainable by addressing our most serious social and economic
problems. The growing inequality of wealth and
income, obsolete public schools, and limited
voice for workers on the job and in the larger
society create social pathologies as well as
long-term political, economic, and social risks.
The evidence suggests that our economy's basic
strengths, along with advances in science and
technology, provide the means to achieve an
even greater period of shared prosperity than
we had in the decades before the early 1970s.
As then, the main requirements for a new
Golden Era are human resources, the organization of production and supportive policies and
institutions. The main objective of the essays in
this volume is to contribute to this debate.

es

Some analysts dispute the extent to which real
s have declined, arguing that the official consumer
index used to deflate money incomes overstates in-
and therefore understates the growth of real in-
. There is, however, no way to know whether or by
much the official index overstates the true rate of

inflation, which is impossible to measure with precision. The official CPI is regularly adjusted and is probably as accurate a measure of changes in consumer prices as we have. Moreover, the CPI measurement issue has no effect on measures of growing inequality. (See Dean Baker, "The Measurement of Inflation," in Mishel, Bernstein, and Schmitt, *State of Working America,* Appendix E.)

2. Edith Rasell, Barry Bluestone, and Lawrence Mishel, *The Prosperity Gap: A Chartbook of American Living Standards* (Washington, DC: Economic Policy Institute, 1997).

3. Lawrence Mishel, Jared Bernstein, and Jay Schmitt, *State of Working America, 1997,* ch. 3.

4. In the tightening labor markets of the 1990s, wages increased faster for low-wage workers than for high-wage workers, but seven years into the recovery wages were still below their 1970 and 1989 levels. The median wage of male workers rose 2.6 percent between 1996 and June 1998; the median increased by 3.6 percent for low-wage workers in the twentieth percentile and 2.3 percent for high-wage workers in the ninetieth percentile. (David Wessel, "Inflation-Adjusted Wages Are on the Rise for Typical U.S. Worker, Shifting Trend," *Wall Street Journal,* July 17, 1998, p. A-2; Larry Mishel, Jared Bernstein, and Jay Schmitt, "Finally, Real Wage Gains," paper prepared for the Economic Policy Institute, July 17, 1998).

5. Considering real hourly wages alone, in 1982 the top tenth averaged $24.80, 3.95 times the $6.28 for the bottom tenth, while total hourly compensation for the top tenth averaged $35.16, 4.56 times the $7.72 for the bottom tenth. In 1996, this ratio had increased to 5.43 to 1; the highest tenth increased to $36.90, while the lowest tenth fell to $6.79. In addition, workers at the bottom of the occupational scale are more likely to have hazardous jobs and less likely to have health care or other benefits. In 1996, over 80 percent of all workers had paid holidays, but only 10 percent of those in the bottom tenth received paid leave of any kind. About 70 percent of all workers were covered by health insurance and pension plans, while less than 10 percent of the bottom tenth had such benefits. A study by Daniel Hamermesh found that in 1979 lost time from on-the-job injuries for the top quarter of wage earners was 38 percent *greater* than for workers in the bottom quarter, but in 1995 injury rates for the top quarter were 32 percent *lower* than for the bottom quarter. The reasons why low-wage workers had relatively more lost time from injuries in 1995 than in 1979 are not clear. Hamermesh does not believe safety conditions changed much in that time, but believes many high-wage unionized workers became low-wage non-union workers. This pat-

tern is particularly true of hazardous construction work like asbestos removal, which became much less unionized between 1979 and 1995 (Peter Passel, "Benefits Dwindle Along with Wages for the Unskilled," *New York Times,* June 14, 1998, p. 1).

6. The data discussed in this section are from Lawrence Mishel, Jared Bernstein, and Jay Schmitt, *The State of Working America, 1997–99* (WDC: Economic Policy Institute, 1999).

7. George Will, "Healthy Inequality," *Newsweek,* October 28, 1996, p. 92.

8. William Baumol and Edward Wolff, "Side Effects of Progress," *Public Policy Briefs,* Jerome Levy Institute, July 1998, p. 3.

9. Ibid., p. 2.

10. Baumol and Wolff cited Brent Mallinckrodt and Bruce R. Fretz, "Social Support and the Impact of Job Loss on Older Professionals," *Journal of Counseling Psychology* 35, no. 3 (1988): 281–86.

11. Baumol and Wolff, p. 4.

12. Ibid., p. 5.

13. Paul Krugman, "Competitiveness: A Dangerous Obsession," *Foreign Affairs* 73, no. 2 (1994): 28–44.

14. Robert Solow, "Europe's Unnecessary Unemployment," *International Economic Insights* (March–April 1994): 11.

15. Robert Eisner, "Social Security Is Worth Saving: Here's How to Do It," *Wall Street Journal,* March 26, 1998, p. A-22.

16. Fred Bergsten, *Competitive Liberalization and Global Free Trade: A Vision for the Early 21st Century* (Washington, DC: Institute for International Economics, 1997).

17. Frank Levy and Richard Murnane, "U.S. Earnings Levels and Earnings Inequality: A Review of Recent Trends and Proposed Explanations," *Journal of Economic Literature* 30 (September 1992): 1333–81.

18. Lisa M. Lynch, ed., *Training and the Private Sector: International Comparisons* (Chicago: University of Chicago Press, 1994).

19. There is substantial evidence that high-performance workplaces improve productivity and that performance is higher under union than non-union conditions (Richard Freeman and James Medoff, *What Do Unions Do?* [New York: Basic Books, 1984]). Sandra Black and Lisa Lynch, using data from a unique nationally representative sample of businesses, found "that those unionized establishments that have adopted what have been called new or 'transformed' industrial relation practices and promote joint decision making coupled with incentive based

compensation have higher productivity than other similar non-union plants, while those businesses that are unionized but have more traditional management relations have lower productivity" ("How to Compete: The Impact of Workplace Practices and Information Technology on Productivity," National Bureau for Economic Research Working Paper 6120, August 1997).

20. Robert Lawrence, Albert Bressand, and Takatoshi Ito, *A Vision for the World Economy* (Washington, DC: Brookings Institution, 1996).

21. Michael H. Armacost in Lawrence, Bressand, and Ito, *A Vision for the World Economy,* p. vii.

22. For a discussion of such a system, see Barbara Bergman, *Reducing Poverty Among Americans Through Help for Working Parents Program* (Washington, DC: Foundation for Child Development, November 1997).

Part I

Introduction:
Opportunity in America

1

Recent Trends in the Distribution of Household Wealth

Edward N. Wolff

Though super-salaries of sports stars and entertainers frequently grab the headlines, these figures are dwarfed by the accumulated wealth of America's billionaires. Salaries of $5 million, or even $10 million, per year (or even Michael Jordan's $30 million per year) pale in comparison to wealth figures such as $40 billion for Microsoft's Bill Gates, $21 billion for the investor Warren Buffet, $14 billion for the Dupont family, and $7 billion for the Rockefeller family. In 1997, *Forbes* magazine counted 170 billionaires in 1997, a record number.

For the very rich, large fortunes can be a source of tremendous economic and social power. A large accumulation of financial and business assets can confer special privileges to their holders and enable them to influence the political process through large donations to candidates running for public office. In some cases, it gives them a special advantage in seeking public office, as the Kennedys, Rockefellers, and, more recently, Ross Perot and Steve Forbes have demonstrated. Large fortunes are often transmitted to succeeding generations, creating family "dynasties."

These colossal sums are hard for the average American to comprehend. In 1995, the average American family was worth $45,600, a trifle compared to the Forbes 400. For the average family, wealth is our security blanket or safety net. It is what we put away for the "rainy days" in our lives and allows us to escape from living from hand to mouth. It serves as our fallback source of consumption. With the possible exception of consumer durables (cars, furniture, and the like), assets can be converted directly into cash and thus provide for immediate consumption needs. This is also true for the equity in owner-occupied housing, because second mortgages and home equity loans are also a source of credit. The availability of financial assets can thus provide for our consumption expenditures in times of economic stress, such as the loss of a job, a family break-up or tragedy, sickness or disability. Accumulated wealth is the ultimate source of economic security.

This report begins with a brief discussion of the definition of wealth (Section 1). The next section presents evidence of the dramatic rise in wealth concentration that has occurred since the early 1980s. Only a small proportion of American families reaped the benefits of the remarkable economic growth of the 1980s.

Section 3 places recent trends in wealth inequality in the context of longer-term time trends. The evidence shows a dramatic U-turn in inequality, from a generally falling trend from 1929 to the late 1970s followed by a sharp upward course.

Section 4 will analyze some of the factors

responsible for the sharp increase in inequality during the 1980s and early 1990s, particularly the reasons for the substantial gains made by the very wealthy. The last section considers the broader political and social implications of the rising concentration of wealth and possible policy remedies.

What Is Wealth?

Wealth (or net worth) is the difference between assets and debt. There are four major types of assets: (1) one's home (technically referred to as "owner-occupied housing"); (2) liquid assets, including cash, bank deposits, money market funds, and savings in insurance and pension plans; (3) investment real estate and unincorporated businesses; and (4) corporate stock, financial securities, and personal trusts. Debt consists primarily of mortgage debt (usually on one's home) and credit card debt and consumer loans.

Where do Americans put their savings? According to the 1995 Survey of Consumer Finances, real estate (other than owner-occupied housing) and unincorporated business equity is the most important asset, comprising 31 percent of total assets. The gross value of owner-occupied housing is second, accounting for 30 percent. Third in importance are demand deposits, time deposits (including money market funds), and other deposits (including retirement plans such as IRAs), amounting to 19 percent. Corporate stock, bonds, and other financial securities and trust equity amount to 18 percent. Indebtedness is also high, with debt as a proportion of total assets equal to 16 percent.

This survey provides a picture of the average holdings of all families, but there are marked class differences in how middle-income families and the super-rich save. A little less than two-thirds of the wealth of the middle class is invested in their home—a result that often leads to the misimpression that housing is the major form of family wealth in America. Another 20 percent goes into various monetary savings. Together housing and liquid assets account for 85 percent of middle-class wealth. Of the remaining 15 percent, a little over half is invested in non-home real estate and unincorporated businesses and the remainder in various financial assets and corporate stock. The ratio of middle-class debt to assets is very high, 60 percent. Even if we exclude home mortgages, the debt-to-asset ratio is still 31 percent.

In contrast, the super-rich invest over 80 percent of their savings in investment real estate, unincorporated businesses, corporate stock, and financial securities. Housing accounts for only 8 percent of their wealth, and monetary savings another 11 percent. Their ratio of debt to assets is only 6 percent.

Recent Trends in Wealth Inequality

Though the increase in income inequality has received most of the attention, the period between 1983 and 1992 has also witnessed a disturbing increase in the concentration of wealth. In many ways, this trend is even more dramatic than changes in income disparities.

My calculations from the 1995 Survey of Consumer Trends indicate an extreme concentration of wealth. The top 1 percent of families (as ranked by wealth) own 39 percent of total wealth, and the top 20 percent of families hold 84 percent. In contrast, the top 1 percent of families (ranked by income) earned 16 percent of total income and the top 20 percent accounted for 55 percent—large figures but still considerably lower than the corresponding wealth shares.

These calculations also confirm a rising level

of wealth inequality between 1983 and 1995. The share of wealth held by the top 1 percent increased by 4.7 percentage points, from 33.7 to 38.5 percent between 1983 and 1995, and the share of the top 20 percent rose by two and a half percentage points. The share of wealth held by the bottom 80 percent fell from 19 to 16 percent. The increase in wealth inequality recorded over the 1983–95 period is unprecedented except for the 1920s, when rising concentration was largely attributable to the stock market boom.

Another indicator of rising wealth concentration is the relative share of the total gain in wealth, which accrues to different parts of the wealth distribution. However, it should be noted that in these calculations the households found in each group (say the top 1 percent) *may be different* in the two years.

The results indicate that the top 20 percent of wealthholders received *99 percent* of the total gain in wealth over the period from 1983 to 1989, while the bottom 80 percent accounted for *only 1 percent*. The top 1 percent alone enjoyed 58 percent of wealth growth. Moreover, while the average net worth of the top three quintiles increased in real terms, the wealth of the bottom two quintiles suffered an absolute decline.

These results indicate rather dramatically that the growth in the economy since the early 1980s has been concentrated in a surprisingly small part of the population. This is particularly so for wealth, with the top quintile accounting for almost all of the wealth gain, and the rest of the population receiving almost nothing. The starkness of this contrast suggests a growing bifurcation within our society.

Long-Term Trends in Wealth Inequality

It is helpful to place the recent rise in wealth concentration in historical context. My estimates show a substantial increase in the share of total household wealth owned by the top percentile between 1922 and 1929, from 40 to 48 percent. This was followed by a somewhat jagged downward path, with the share of the top 1 percent declining to 22 percent in the late 1970s. A substantial increase in wealth concentration occurred between 1979 and 1989, with the share of the top 1 percent rising from 22 to 39 percent. However, in the early 1990s there was a slight remission in wealth inequality, with the share of the top percentile falling to 37 percent in 1992 but then rising back to 39 percent by 1995.

The trend line is also shown for "augmented wealth," which includes an imputation for Social Security and pension wealth. The addition of pension and Social Security wealth has a significant effect on measured wealth inequality. Because pension and Social Security wealth, particularly the latter, is distributed more equally than marketable wealth, the addition of retirement wealth to marketable wealth causes measured wealth concentration to decline. In 1995, for example, while the top 1 percent of households, as ranked by marketable wealth, owned 39 percent of total marketable wealth, the top 1 percent, ranked by augmented wealth, held only 23 percent of total augmented wealth.

The gap in the share of the top 1 percent between the marketable wealth and the augmented wealth series widened over time, from 2 percentage points in 1922 to 16 percentage points in 1995. However, the trends in the two series are very similar. Both show a gradual decline between 1929 and the late 1970s, followed by a substantial rise. The increase in the share of the top percentile between 1979 and 1995 is more muted on the basis of augmented wealth, 9 percentage points, in comparison to 17 percentage points for marketable wealth.

All in all, the evidence points to a dramatic U-turn in wealth concentration as the leveling effects of the Great Depression, World War II, and the early post-war boom wore off. We now explore some of the reasons for this turnaround in inequality.

Causes of Rising Wealth Inequality

Why has wealth concentration increased so much? One way of understanding some of the factors is to compare the 1960s and the 1980s. Both were periods of high economic growth, in terms of both GDP and GDP per capita. Yet, wealth inequality remained virtually unchanged during the 1960s but increased sharply during the 1980s, so that economic growth by itself does not appear to be a causative factor. What else might have explained rising wealth inequality? There appear to be five main factors at work:

Rising Income Inequality

Increases in family income inequality is one major factor that has led to increases in wealth concentration. Income inequality remained relatively unchanged during the 1960s but rose markedly during the 1980s.

Different Propensities to Save

Differences in income among families become magnified into differences in savings; the savings rate (the ratio of savings to income) among richer families is higher than among poorer ones. Indeed, the savings rate generally increases in step with the income level of the family. As a result, if the share of total income going to the top income class increases, the share of total savings attributable the top income class increases even more.

Compounding this effect is increased disparities in the savings propensities of different income classes. Two major changes occurred between the 1960s and 1980s. First, the percentage of income saved by the upper third of families more than doubled between 1962–69 and 1983–89, from 9.3 to 22.5 percent. Part of this change reflects the very favorable tax cuts for the rich that occurred in 1981 and 1986 during the Reagan administration. This increased the after-tax income of the rich and shows up in terms of an increased savings rate.

Second, the middle third of the population, which saved almost 5 percent of its income during the 1960s, saved virtually zero by the 1980s. This reflects the growing "squeeze" on the middle class from stagnating incomes and rising expenses as the family ages. The bottom third has traditionally saved none of its income.

Changing Importance of Savings and Capital Gains

There are two sources of wealth growth in the aggregate: conventional savings (the difference between income and consumption expenditures) and the appreciation in value of existing assets, also called capital gains. Contrary to popular perception, the predominant source of wealth accumulation is capital gains, not savings. Between 1962 and 1989, for instance, 66 percent of the growth of household wealth was from the appreciation of existing wealth and the remaining 34 percent was from savings.

One major difference between the 1960s and 1980s is that savings were more important in the earlier period. Between 1962 and 1969, savings accounted for 38 percent of the growth of wealth and capital gains for 62 percent, while from 1983 to 1989 the respective shares were 30 percent and 70 percent. The primary reason for this change is that the household savings rate has eroded over time, from 6.9 percent of family income to 4.7 percent.

Relative Movements in Asset Prices

The major household assets have historically been owner-occupied housing and business assets. Corporate stock and unincorporated business equity are owned almost exclusively by the rich (over 90 percent of its total value are held by the top 10 percent of wealthholders), while housing is the principal asset of the middle class. As a result, the share of wealth held by the top percentiles of the wealth distribution is closely correlated with the stock market, while the share of the middle class tends to move in tandem with the price of housing.

Between 1962 and 1989, annual real housing prices increased by 2.2 percent per year and stock prices by 3.6 percent. During 1983 to 1989, annual housing prices rose faster, 4.8 percent, but stock prices shot up even faster, by 8 percent. The ratio of annual stock to housing prices, the key variable, rose twice as fast during 1983–89 (3.3 percent) than during 1962–69 (1.5 percent). This factor also led to increasing wealth concentration during the 1980s.

The Homeownership Rate

A related factor is that the homeownership rate (the percentage of families owning their home) fell during the 1980s, by 0.6 percentage points. In contrast, it rose by 1.6 percentage points during the 1960s. A rising proportion of families who own their home indicates a widening diffusion of assets to the middle class. The homeownership rate, which had risen from the beginning of this century, actually peaked at 64.6 percent in 1975 and since then has gradually fallen.

Summary

Using regression techniques, I have decomposed the increase in wealth inequality into various effects. This analysis shows that the rapid increase in stock prices relative to house prices during the 1980s appears to be the most important factor, accounting for about 40 percent of the increased wealth concentration of the decade, followed by increased income inequality, which explains another 35 percent. The growing importance of capital gains relative to savings explains another 10 percent, as did the increased savings propensity of the rich relative to the middle class, and the declining homeownership rate picked up the remaining 5 percent or so.

Consequences and Remedies

The average family is better off today than a generation ago both in terms of income (27 percent greater in 1995 compared to 1962) and wealth (54 percent greater). What has changed since 1980 is that the gains in income and wealth that used to be more equally distributed over the population have now been concentrated in fewer and fewer pockets. Perhaps the most telling statistic is that almost all of the increased wealth of the 1980s went to the top 20 percent of wealthholders and three-quarters of the income growth went to the top 20 percent of income recipients.

The 1980s was also a time that saw great increases in capital gains—even more so than the 1960s. Those who had wealth at the beginning of the 1980s enjoyed considerable gains over the decade. Moreover, relative price changes favored the rich, so that capital gains were twice as great for them in comparison to the middle class.

For those without wealth, savings alone was not sufficient to amass significant amounts of wealth holdings. The overall savings rate was historically very low during the 1980s. Moreover, while the savings rate of the rich mushroomed in the 1980s, that of the middle class dwindled to almost zero.

Indeed, the growing "anxiety" of the middle class may be largely attributable to its falling financial reserves. According to my calculations, the average family in 1989 had only enough financial wealth to sustain its normal consumption for a period of 3.6 months in case of income loss and to sustain consumption at 125 percent of the poverty standard for only 9 months. Indeed, the bottom 40 percent of households had only enough savings to keep going for a month. The fraying of both the private and public safety nets has led to increasing middle-class insecurity.

Both the extreme nature of wealth concentration in the United States and its rise in recent years pose serious policy challenges. On equity grounds, can a society in which economic gains are concentrated in fewer families long endure without increasing political divisiveness? Will increasing wealth concentration further tilt political power toward the rich? Is the increasing concentration of economic resources compatible with renewed economic growth of the American economy? These questions point to the policy challenges the United States faces.

How can we reverse the rising inequality? Insofar as rising inequality in our country is a result of structural labor market shifts—shifts in relative demand toward skilled labor and away from semi-skilled and unskilled workers—there may be little the government can do to reverse the underlying causes. However, the experience of European countries, as well as our neighbor, Canada, who have been affected by the same market forces, suggests that one effective mechanism is to place more of the tax burden on the rich and less on the middle class. In the United States, the 1980s witnessed falling marginal tax rates, particularly on the rich and very rich. Though the federal government raised the marginal rates on the very rich in 1993, they still are considerably lower than at the beginning of the 1980s (and much lower than in the 1960s) and much lower than in West European countries.

Should we think about direct taxation of the wealth holdings of households? Almost a dozen European countries have such a system in place, including Denmark, Germany, the Netherlands, Sweden, and Switzerland. On the grounds of equity, a combination of annual income and the current stock of wealth provides a better gauge of the ability to pay taxes than income alone. Moreover, there is no evidence from other advanced economies that the imposition of a modest direct tax on household wealth has had any deleterious effect on personal savings or economic growth. Indeed, there are arguments to the contrary that such a tax may induce a more efficient allocation of household wealth, away from unproductive toward more productive uses. Finally, the possibility that such a levy might promote capital flight is not borne out by the facts—consider Switzerland, a net importer of capital.

I propose a very modest tax on wealth (a $100,000 exemption with marginal tax rates running from 0.05 to 0.3 percent). My calculations show that such a tax structure would yield an average tax rate on household wealth of 0.2 percent, which is less than the loading fee on most mutual funds, and would reduce the average yield on household wealth holdings by only 6 percent. Even the top marginal tax rate of 0.3 percent would reduce the average yield on personal wealth by only 9 percent. These figures suggest that disincentive effects on personal savings would be very modest indeed. More-over, as suggested above, personal savings might actually rise as a result of a wealth tax.

I estimate that such a tax could raise $50 billion in additional revenue and have a minimal impact on the tax bills of 90 percent of American families. This is not a large amount, representing about 3 percent of total federal tax receipts. However, on the margin such additional revenue could be critical. In particular, it could help provide the fiscal latitude to enact more generous social transfers, including a family allowance plan, which, if coupled with a rising minimum wage (indeed, even a constant minimum wage in real terms) and extension of the Earned Income Tax Credits, would do much to improve the financial well-being of the poor and lower middle class.

2

The Effects of Economic Growth and Inequality on Opportunity

Daniel P. McMurrer and Isabel V. Sawhill

America has always been known as "the land of opportunity." Reality has never quite matched the rhetoric, but a number of factors historically have brought us progressively closer to that ideal. The continued expansion of opportunities to previously excluded groups, the extension of education to an ever-increasing share of the population, and the impressive economic growth that prevailed for many years all made it easier for opportunity to spread broadly throughout the population.

In recent years, however, this record has not been sustained. The period since the early 1970s has been marked by a decline in opportunity for many, especially young men without college degrees. Today, it is becoming increasingly difficult for young workers to surpass their parents' standard of living, thereby achieving the proverbial American dream.

The decrease in opportunity can be illustrated by the average earnings of young men aged 25 to 34. In 1974, men in this age group had average incomes of almost $30,000 that year (in 1994 dollars). In 1994, by contrast, men in this age group averaged under $23,000 in that year—a precipitous drop. There were similar trends for family and household incomes, although an increase in the number of two-earner families and growth in fringe bene-fits partially offset the effects of the decline in individual wages. This reduction in relative well-being early in the earnings cycle is likely to persist or even worsen as this generation born after 1960 ages.[1]

Causes of the Decline in Intergenerational Opportunity

What has gone wrong? Two broad economic trends lurk behind the recent decline in opportunity. First, economic growth has slowed significantly since 1973, causing average earnings to stagnate. Almost simultaneously, earnings inequality has increased, bringing about a dramatic reversal of the trend toward greater equality that had prevailed since World War II. Either trend, occurring alone, would have had troubling consequences. The two trends together have wrought an important change in prospects for many members of the younger generation.[2]

Slower Economic Growth

Upward economic mobility and strong economic growth have frequently gone hand in hand. Indeed, in comparing the United States to other countries, some scholars have suggested that the faster rate of economic growth that prevailed in the United States until recently is the primary reason that this country enjoyed greater social mobility.

The rate of growth in living standards, as measured by per capita GDP, is driven by changes in productivity and the size of the labor force. Productivity—the only vehicle for improving living standards without increasing the proportion of the population in the labor force—has increased at an average annual rate of about 2 percent since 1870. The 1960–73 period saw especially strong growth, with productivity increasing by 3 percent per year.[3]

The good news did not last. Productivity slowed to a crawl after 1973—an average of 1 percent per year between 1973 and 1995, lower than the rates that prevailed in many other industrialized countries. Because the compensation of workers tends to track their productivity, real wage growth also slowed commensurately.

What is the impact on an average worker of this slowdown in productivity from 3 percent annually to 1 percent? In 1973, the typical male high school graduate could expect an average full-time entry-level wage, in 1995 dollars, of almost $22,000. If productivity had continued to grow at the *higher* rate of the earlier post-war period, and if that growth had benefited everyone equally, entry-level wages for a male high school graduate by 1995 would have been over $20,000 higher ($42,000). Distributed equally, the *actual* (slower) growth in productivity would have increased entry-level wages for male high school graduates by only about $6,000 from 1973 to 1995 (to $28,000).

Thus, the slowdown in productivity growth *by itself* has sharply curtailed the opportunity for the average male high school graduate to improve on standards of living enjoyed by previous generations. Because of the productivity slowdown, his entry-level wages are only slightly higher on average than those of the cohort that was born twenty years earlier.[4]

Increasing Earnings Inequality

But this is not the end of the story. An increase in earnings inequality exacerbated the effects of the decline in productivity growth. When rising inequality is also taken into consideration, the entry-level wages for a male high school graduate working full time were under $16,000 in 1995, more than $6,000 *lower* than entry-level wages in 1973. This is over $26,000 less than would have been expected if there had been a faster rate of growth from which everyone had benefited equally. Thus, the combined costs to this group of slower growth and rising inequality have been enormous. Each accounts for about half of the overall $26,000 gap, with the slower rate of growth having a slightly larger effect.[5]

The increase in inequality has been carefully documented and analyzed by numerous researchers, who have concluded that wage inequality today is higher than at any time since World War II. It began to increase during the 1970s, surged during the early 1980s, and has only recently shown signs of leveling off or declining.

Males, younger workers, and those who are not college educated have been particularly affected by the above trends. Although trends in *inequality* have been the same for men and women, male median earnings have decreased even as female median earnings have increased (in part because of their increased work hours). At the same time, work experience is more highly rewarded by employers than in the past, so younger workers lacking experience also have seen a disproportionate decrease in wages.

Most important, less-skilled, less-educated

men have experienced particularly sharp drops in real earnings. In part, this is a result of a significant increase in the pay differential between college-educated workers and others, with college graduates (male and female) earning 58 percent more than high school graduates in 1993, compared with 38 percent more in 1979. The disparity is even greater for *entry-level* wages, where the "wage premium" for college graduates was 77 percent in 1993 compared to 37 percent in 1979.

Most analysts attribute the increased wage differential for education primarily to a substantial increase in the demand for more-educated workers, a shift uhat appears to have been driven by factors related to technological change. Workers who use computers on the job enjoyed faster wage growth than other workers during the 1980s, which supports this view. Indeed, the forces related to technological change are considered so powerful that they generally are assigned a significant percentage of the responsibility for the overall increase in wage inequality in the United States.

Opportunity and Changes in Mobility

Although there is little question that economic rewards are more widely dispersed than they were a few decades ago, it is still possible for individuals to move up and down the economic ladder during their careers and for children to do better than their parents. In fact, what evidence we have suggests that there is considerable mobility—both intragenerational and intergenerational—within the United States. A brief review of this evidence can help to provide a more complete picture of the opportunities available to individuals—not just groups—in today's economy. From the perspective of the individual, what matters is not just what is happening to the sum total of good- or well-paying jobs, for example, but also how hard or easy it is to obtain those jobs.

Intragenerational Mobility

In recent years, we have accumulated a new body of information about the extent to which individuals move up and down the economic ladder during the course of their adult years. These data suggest that there is quite a lot of mobility, usually measured as the proportion of individuals in any particular income quintile who move to a different income quintile over some well-defined period of time.[6] For example, studies have found that between 25 and 40 percent of individuals move into a new income quintile in any single year. So there is a great deal of fluidity within the distribution. Those who are poor today may be middle class some years later, others may fall from the top to the bottom. But we have also learned that, despite this churning, income mobility has not changed significantly over the last twenty-five years. Indeed, among the least well educated, it seems to have declined. This is a major change from the 1970s, when the income trajectory that an individual could expect over the course of his or her adult years was much more similar across educational levels.

The bottom line is that we cannot assume that the much greater disparity in rewards provided by today's economy has been mitigated by any increase in access to those rewards, especially for those with the fewest skills. There is significant fluidity, but its extent has not changed over time and it is increasingly linked to education.

Intergenerational Mobility

A related question concerns the extent to which children are able to do better than their parents. In an economy with no growth, intergenerational mobility would be a zero-sum game: for every child that did better than his or her parents, there would be someone else who did worse. However, it would still matter to the individual, and to our sense of fairness, whether it was easy or hard to escape one's origins.

Origins matter. America has never been a classless society. However, some progress toward that ideal has·occurred. The increase in individual opportunity can be seen in the decreased importance of social background in determining individual success or failure. The link between an individual's own economic status (as measured by either occupation or income) and his or her parent's status, while still significant, has eroded in recent decades. This is true especially for individuals with a college education, for whom success or failure in the labor market is largely unrelated to their parents' status. And although children from more-privileged backgrounds tend to obtain more education, education is still a more important predictor of where one ends up in the economic system than family background per se.

The declining importance of class or family background, and the increased importance of education, provides both good and bad news. The good news is that education is, more than ever, the way to get ahead—the route to upward mobility. The bad news is that without it, even those with favorable origins or those who work hard, are unlikely to get ahead. Indeed, in an economy with little or no growth, they may very well end up moving down the economic ladder.

What Can Be Done?

Stagnating incomes and increasing earnings inequality have reconfigured the economic landscape for tens of millions of Americans—particularly younger Americans. Government did not create these problems and they are too large and deeply rooted for the public sector to solve alone. But it can help.

Government should focus its energy on areas in which it can be most effective—such as paying down the national debt, which is a drag on economic growth, and using its leverage, leadership, and limited resources to encourage early childhood education, local school reform linked to national academic standards, and more private-sector job training. It should also extend various kinds of help—such as an opportunity to go to college or secure technical training—to those for whom this would not otherwise be possible. Although a new middle-class entitlement to a college education could absorb resources better spent in other areas, there is merit in insuring that people have both the incentive and the opportunity to achieve as much education as their talents will allow.

At the same time, other social institutions (e.g., families, local communities, and churches) must all play a role in preparing the next generation for a world in which education will increasingly determine the success of both individual citizens and the nation as a whole. In this context, nothing could be more important than giving every child a good start in life by insuring that they are born to parents ready and able to care for them. Schools and other social institutions are currently overwhelmed by an influx of children from poor or inadequate homes. More than 45 percent of first births in the United States are to mothers who are teenagers, unwed, or lacking a high school degree.

There is no sense in pretending that the solutions—public or private—will be cheap or easy to finance. Indeed, in the present environment, making the necessary investments will require shifting more of society's resources from the support of an aging population to education, training, mentoring, and other types of assistance aimed at preparing young people to take advantage of today's opportunities.

Government should at a minimum avoid actions that make matters worse. Proposals to reduce assistance to lower-income families or to reduce the taxes paid by those who are doing well seem especially misguided in the face of two decades of rising inequality.

Instead, we need to forge a public philosophy that recognizes the benefits of living in a dynamic, technologically advanced economy but also is responsive to the collateral damage it inflicts on those not yet prepared to take advantage of the new opportunities.

Notes

1. This chapter draws in part on material from Daniel P. McMurrer and Isabel V. Sawhill, *Getting Ahead: Economic and Social Mobility in America* (Washington, DC: Urban Institute Press, 1998).

2. It should be noted that real wage growth has slowed and inequality has increased in other industrialized nations as well, although the trends have been most pronounced in the United States.

3. All productivity statistics reported in this paper reflect the January 1996 comprehensive revisions of the national income and product accounts and were computed using chain-type output indices. At this time, revised data are not available prior to 1959. Earlier (unrevised) data suggest that the rate of productivity growth that prevailed between the end of World War II and 1959 was slightly lower than the rate between 1960 and 1973.

4. Because this example assumes that the impact of the change in productivity is distributed *evenly* across the labor force, the preceding two sentences apply to all workers—not only male high school graduates.

5. These calculations will tend to overstate the importance of rising inequality to the extent that today's high school graduates are a more disadvantaged group than those who completed the same amount of schooling in 1973. This is undoubtedly the case, given the decreasing fraction of the population with only a high school degree and the likelihood that it is the more able or ambitious that have made the greatest educational gains. For example, individuals with a high school education or less accounted for 70.2 percent of total employment in 1973, and only 54.2 percent in 1989 (there are no reliable data for 1995 using the same definitions).

6. Most studies have looked at changes in the amount of total family income available to an individual rather than at only their earnings, but changes in earnings are a very important component of these changes in income. Existing evidence suggests the conclusions of this section would be similar if the focus were on earnings alone.

3

Economic Outcomes and Mental Health

Mary Merva and Richard Fowles

Introduction

This essay discusses the relationship between economic factors and societal well-being for the United States over the post–World War II period. We examine how changes in the distribution of wage income and poverty generate conditions that may contribute to negative mental health outcomes, thereby affecting societal well-being. At the outset, we point out that there are basic questions regarding the origins of mental health problems, now considered to be among the leading causes of disability. There is disagreement regarding the degree of psychological, cultural, biological, social, and economic factors that underlie mental health problems such as anxiety, depression, obsessive-compulsive behavior, stress, suicide, and criminal behavior. In many cases, these behavioral outcomes are the result of complex interactions of individual and environmental factors, making the determination of causality by any one factor difficult. For example, does job loss trigger depression or is a worker more likely to be fired after the onset of depression? In this essay, we examine the contribution of economic factors to a wide variety of mental health disorders. Empirical evidence supporting this relationship is abundant. In Hadley Cantril's 1965 study surveying factors mentioned most frequently by Americans in discussing their hopes, approxi-

mately 65 percent of the respondents related personal hopes to economic factors.[1] Current research clearly ties behavior that is antithetical to success with social toxicity, bred by poverty, violence, substance abuse, and crime. These problems are especially severe for urban youth and are manifested in an epidemic of violent crime. This essay examines the theoretical and empirical aspects of the relationship between wage inequality, poverty, and mental health.

Mental Health and the Distribution of Income: Absolute and Relative Income Effects

Economists generally have assumed that economic growth results in greater economic welfare or happiness. However, while cross-sectional evidence is overwhelming for a positive relationship between income and subjective well-being—defined as a positive evaluation of one's life—real increases in national income over time may not make people happier. Extensive evaluations of surveys of happiness for the United States over the period 1946 to 1970 indicate:

In all societies, more money for the individual typically means more individual happiness. However, raising the incomes of all does not increase the happiness of all. The happiness-

69

income relation provides a classic example of the logical fallacy of composition—*what is true for the individual is not true for society as a whole.*[2]

The key to this finding is the importance of both the relative and absolute economic position of an individual in his/her assessment of welfare or happiness. Complicating the evaluation of the roles of relative and absolute economic position for mental health is that what constitutes an acceptable standard of living is subjective. Needs and wants are not fixed but are generated within a society, which is constantly creating new expectations of wants and needs. In fact, it has been shown that when individuals assess what income they need, the absolute amount changes over time and this amount tends to be indexed to the average family consumption of the day, which can informally be summarized as "keeping up with the Joneses." Changes in income distribution may therefore affect societal well-being by altering both the absolute and relative socioeconomic status (SES) affecting individuals' assessment of their well-being and mental health.

The relationship between an absolute level of SES and mental health is well documented. David Williams and Chiquita Collins report that, in the largest study of psychiatric disorders ever conducted in the United States, SES predicts elevated rates over a broad range of psychiatric disturbances.[3] Bruce Dohrenwend points out there is a consistency in research, dating from 1855, that documents important correlations between SES and mental health.[4] The direction of causation, however, remains a controversial issue. Higher rates of substance abuse, schizophrenia, personality disorders, and anti-social behaviors may be the result of environmental adversity. Lack of access to educa-

tion, housing, and household possessions, each of which are related to wealth, puts people at risk. These types of mental disorders can cause a downward drift to a lower SES; people with psychiatric disabilities and high rates of substance abuse simply are unable to gain or maintain employment. Dooley, Fielding, and Levi argue that while poor mental health can lead to poor work performance and job loss, most aggregate-level studies cannot adequately control for this type of selection effect.[5] They find, though, that at a personal level, laid-off workers exhibit increased psychiatric problems such as depression and substance abuse, implying the causation runs from economic hardship to stress.

The relationship between relative economic status and mental health is based upon the theory of relative deprivation or what also has been termed the "envy effect." The theory of relative deprivation contends that individuals compare themselves to a reference group (the Joneses) when determining their subjective well-being. The reference group toward which individuals orient themselves is critical for the determination of the extent of relative deprivation. These reference groups could be contemporaneous (How am I doing now with respect to my peers?) or historical (How am I doing now with respect to myself or someone else in my position a decade ago?). Psychologists have found that assessment of relative position is an important predictor of satisfaction and mental health outcomes.

A heightened sense of relative deprivation can increase psychological stress, which may result in two general outcomes. The first is a proactive response to alter one's relative position so that current feelings of relative deprivation dissipate. In this respect, relative deprivation motivates competition among individuals to improve their economic standing by furthering their education or searching for better jobs. In fact, this is one of the adjustment processes that occurs in a dynamic, capitalistic economy as individuals adapt to changing economic opportunities. The second is that individuals interpret their declining relative position as evidence of their own inadequacies. Internalizing these feelings of failure may lead to higher levels of depression and, in the extreme, suicide. Externalizing these feelings may lead some individuals to blame others for their poor relative position, becoming angry and aggressive. Exaggerated anger and aggression toward others is more likely to occur under the disinhibiting effects of alcohol or drugs.

We now consider the trends in the distribution of wage income over the post–World War II period and examine their link to mental health. This is not a particularly straightforward task as anytime there are changes in a distribution of income, some people become relatively better off and others relatively worse off, rendering measurement of the net changes in relative deprivation for society as a whole problematic. It may be possible, however, to make general statements about societal well-being if an income distribution characterized by rising expectations is followed by one that does not allow for the realization of those expectations—a situation that we argue has occurred over the post–World War II period in the United States. This allows us the possibility to consider what may be happening over time to the level of well-being in the United States.

The post–World War II period, which continued until the early 1970s, generally is characterized as a period of capital-labor accord and a "golden age of growth" with falling inequality and rising real wages. Growth accompanied by rising real wages across all groups implies significant opportunities for individuals to make

adjustments in their contemporaneous relative economic positions and also see improvements in their relative economic position over time. Given these favorable economic trends, there is a temptation to conclude that society's level of mental health or well-being must have been improving during this period. However, incomes and educational levels also raise expectations and this may have heightened a sense of relative deprivation. As has been noted by Angus Campbell, the average level of happiness reported by both blacks and whites declined between 1957 and 1972.[6] Evidence such as this makes it difficult to reach broad conclusions about income distribution and well-being over this period. However, what this evidence clearly points out is that rising expectations without ample opportunity to realize those expectations can generate stress. In fact, the heightened expectations generated by the "golden age" may be an important factor toward understanding why the widening of the income distribution after 1970 may have contributed to a decrease in societal well-being—particularly with respect to the income and relative economic position of high school–educated workers. In sum, this historic juxtaposition of a period of rising expectations followed by a period where these expectations are not realized for a broad segment of society is the classic background for increased societal stress. The widening of the wage distribution after 1970 may have more serious repercussions for societal well-being for two additional reasons.

The changes in the post-1970 wage distribution are thought to be primarily the consequence of technological change and globalization—factors that yield economic benefits for society as a whole but have economic costs that have not been equally shared. As noted in the overview to these essays, significant groups are becoming both absolutely and relatively worse off compared to past cohorts with similar education and skills. High school–educated males and dropouts, particularly the young, have suffered significant declines in both their absolute and relative economic status. By contrast, the wages of college-educated workers have been rising. Indeed, the college/high school wage differential increased to a historic high over the 1978–88 period. While there always have been changes in the structure of employment in the context of a dynamic economy, the current trends are the result of economic changes that benefit society as a whole but with costs that are increasingly borne by workers with a high school education or less. The real issue is not only income inequality per se, but rather the unequal distribution of economic costs paid to acquire societal benefits that could be viewed as increasingly unfair.

Given these adverse developments, what has been the response of workers and what can we say about changes in the level of well-being? We answer this question by considering both individual choice and the constraints on these choices. First, in the face of falling real wages for high school-educated labor and rising college/high school wage differentials, many workers can protect their absolute and relative economic positions by augmenting their human capital. Despite negative real wage growth for college-educated workers over 1973–79, the returns for a college education and the demand for college-educated labor increased in all industries from 1968 to 1989. In addition, over 1979 to 1988, real wages for college-educated workers began to grow modestly. In response to this we see an increase in the proportion of college-educated labor from 26.7 percent in 1968 to 43.6 percent in 1988 as estimated by Kevin Murphy and Finis Welch.[7] These choices represent a proactive response to changing eco-

nomic opportunities. For workers who accumulate human capital to obtain the better jobs, their level of well-being may increase. Not only have they obtained higher-paying jobs than they would have had with a high school education, but those jobs may be more interesting. However, why have a substantial number of workers not obtained a college degree? If we put this individual choice in a historical context, we see that during the 1970s, the college/high school wage differential decreased to a historic low. This, coupled with the fact that real wages of high school-educated workers had not yet begun their serious decline, would indicate that a high school degree was adequate to achieve a desired standard of living. Based upon these expectations, the decision to forego college was rational. As a result, some workers in the 1970s who might have gone to college did not. Unfortunately, as we moved past the 1981–82 recession, it became increasingly clear that, unbeknownst to these workers, the rules of the game were changing. Optimal decisions of the 1970s turned out to be sub-optimal as both high-wage employment for high school-educated workers and their real wages began to decline. In sum, economic signals were followed and rational choices were made based upon expectations; however, these expectations turned out to be wrong for many workers.

While the decision to obtain a college degree is one aspect, not everyone has the ability or is in a situation to complete a college degree. Their standard of living is constrained by employment and wage structures. For these workers, an alternative response to adverse changes in the structure of employment and wages is to increase hours of work and, for married couples, to pursue joint incomes. In fact, average hours of market work for employed parents increased over 1969 to 1989 by approximately 72 hours more per year, or 3.75 percent overall. Mothers in these families had the most significant increase in hours, about 27 percent. What is noteworthy about these trends is that the greatest increases in hours of work occur in families in the lowest fifth of the income distribution (4.6 percent compared to 2 percent for families in the top fifth). Wives also contributed an increasing share of family income, rising from 14 percent in 1968 to 22 percent in 1988. Indeed, 64 percent of the growth in family income from 1978 to 1988 was due to increasing earnings of wives. While the higher income obtained from working more is a plus, there may be significant offsets. For some families, the higher income may be sufficient to purchase goods and services previously supplied in the home such as child care, housekeeping, meal preparation, and job expenses. For others, however, income may not be sufficient to purchase the goods, resulting in increased time pressures.

What do these wage and employment trends and accompanying adaptations imply about societal well-being and mental health? Although many workers have improved their economic position, we should be concerned about those who lack the education to benefit from today's economy. While we cannot make general statements about the overall level of societal well-being, we can say that the welfare of high school-educated workers definitely has worsened. First, current changes in the distribution of wages may be viewed as increasingly unfair by high school-educated workers who are bearing proportionally more of the costs of economic changes that produce benefits for society as a whole. Second, the absolute and relative socioeconomic position of high school-educated workers, particularly young males, has worsened dramatically relative to their historical earnings. Third, the high school-

educated male's position as a family breadwinner is eroding. Finally, people working for lower wages are working more and likely lack sufficient income to purchase products to alleviate time pressures for household activities. In fact, low-income workers, especially women with children, are at higher risk of developing stress-related health problems. These four factors may create conditions that, at the very least, do not alleviate pressures for poor mental health outcomes among groups most at risk. The fact that these wage and poverty trends have continued in an economy that is characterized by low inflation, full employment, and economic growth may exacerbate people's worries regarding their future as these trends become a more permanent feature of economic life.

Empirical Findings

In this section, we report the resulting linear regressions to empirically describe a general relationship between economic variables and stress outcomes for Standard Metropolitan Statistical Areas (SMSAs) over 1975 to 1990. Primary SMSAs include New York, Los Angeles, Chicago, Detroit, and Philadelphia. Economic stress variables include the Gini coefficient, the poverty rate, and changes in the unemployment rate. The Gini coefficient is a widely used measure of income inequality and is calculated from hourly wages reported by samples of workers drawn from the Current Population Surveys from 1975 to 1990. A higher Gini coefficient indicates greater inequality. The sample of workers are those who usually work 30 hours per week or more. This set of workers is representative of those who have a significant commitment to the workforce. The links between broad categories of economic and social stress variables were described in terms of linear

Table 3.1

Estimated Proportionate Effects of Unemployment, Poverty, and Wage Inequality on Social Stressors: Data Period 1975–90

	Unemployment[a]	Poverty[a]	Wage Inequality[b]
Stress			
Major Cardiovascular Mortality[c]	2.21	−0.39	0.11
Cerebrovascular Mortality[c]	1.85	−0.19	0.10
Suicide	1.01	2.08*	0.04
Accident Mortality	0.82	0.93*	0.18*
Homicide	5.62*	5.64*	0.59*
Aggravated Assault	1.77	5.67*	0.57*
Forcible Rape	1.90	2.92*	0.01

Source: Authors' computations.

An * indicates the ordinary least squares t-statistic was significant at the 5 percent level.

[a]Effects of a 1-percentage-point change in unemployment and/or poverty evaluated at the mean of the stressor variable.

[b]Elasticity coefficient evaluated at the means. Wage inequality measure was a Gini coefficient computed over hourly wages.

[c]Computations were based on coefficients with tight bounds from extreme bounds analysis results.

regression models, which control for other plausible explanatory effects that include demographic characteristics of the SMSAs, time trend, and functional form. With these estimates, we can hypothesize what would happen to stress outcomes given a change in an economic variable. These estimates are presented in Table 3.1, which shows the effects of a 1-percentage-point increase in the unemployment and poverty rates and a 1-percent change in wage inequality.

With the exception of the effect of poverty on cardiovascular and cerebrovascular mortality, all estimated coefficients are positive. Effects from poverty on the other stressors are

statistically significant. For accidents, homicide, and aggravated assaults, the effect from wage inequality also is significant; unemployment is significant only for homicides. These data demonstrate the effects of abstract economic changes in human terms—loss of life, disability, trauma, and pain.

Conclusion

In this essay, we have looked at the relationship between economic conditions and mental health from a wide perspective. Theory suggests that associations between economic factors and physical and mental health are important. This essay argues that economic effects should be considered in both absolute and relative terms—needs and wants are not fixed, but are referenced against societal norms that change over time. Using pooled time series and cross-sectional data from 1975 to 1990—a period of diverse economic growth accompanied by changing income inequality and poverty—we show there are unambiguous associations between key economic variables and significant measures of health outcomes. These relationships are in accord with theoretical expectations—that increasing poverty, inequality, and unemployment correlate with increasing rates of mortality, suicides, homicides, aggravated assaults, and rape. Although these results may not be surprising, they are disturbing and, as such, should be considered seriously by policy-makers when assessing the economic costs and benefits of reform programs that may affect poverty, unemployment, and the distribution of wages.

Notes

1. Hadley Cantril, *Patterns of Human Concern* (New Brunswick, NJ: Rutgers University Press, 1965),

p. 35. Cited in Richard Easterlin, "Does Economic Growth Improve the Human Lot? Some Empirical Evidence," in *Nations and Households in Economic Growth,* ed. Paul A. David and Melvin Reder (Palo Alto, CA: Stanford University Press, 1974), p. 94.

2. Richard A. Easterlin, "Does Money Buy Happiness?" *The Public Interest* 30 (Winter 1973): 3–10.

3. David Williams and Chiquita Collins, "U.S. Socioeconomic and Racial Differences in Health: Patterns and Explanations," *Annual Review of Sociology* 21 (1995): 349–86.

4. Bruce P. Dohrenwend, "Socioeconomic Status and Psychiatric Disorders," *Social Psychiatry and Psychiatric Epidemiology* 25 (1995): 41–47.

5. David Dooley, Jonathon Fielding and Lennart Levi, "Health and Unemployment," *Annual Review of Public Health* 17 (1996): 449–65.

6. Angus Campbell, "Subjective Measures of Well-Being," *American Psychologist* 31, no. 2 (Feb. 1976): 117–24.

7. Kevin Murphy and Finis Welch, "Industrial Change and the Rising Importance of Skill," in Sheldon Danziger and Peter Gottschalk, *Uneven Tides: Rising Inequality in America* (New York: Russell Sage Foundation, 1994).

4

One More Chance:
Cities in the
Twenty-first Century Economy

Elliott Sclar

Americans only dimly perceive the steep economic price they pay for the sprawled and segregated shape of metropolitan America. The idea that workforce productivity is linked to the distances between work and home is acknowledged only in the abstract. A severe fault line runs through our thinking about the relationship between space and productivity. We are an urban people who love to hate central cities.

Two stylized facts: 75 percent of us reside in urbanized places; over half of us jam ourselves into just thirty-four major metropolitan areas. Despite this reality, as a matter of official public policy we look with disdain upon the social and physical investment needs of core cities and, increasingly, the older close-in suburbs.

For most Americans, the idealized domestic landscape is a rambling house surrounded by a green lawn and shade trees, connected to the world by the two cars sitting in the attached garage and the phone lines and coaxial cable that connect the home computers, fax machines, phones, and television sets to the global infrastructure. Retail wants and outside entertainment are the province of area malls. For growing numbers of us work is located at the off ramps of the interstates, which head yet further into the rural hinterlands. Although still substantial, fewer metropolitan residents than ever commute to jobs in the central cities.

To the extent that central cities have a positive place in this spreading spatial panorama it is largely in their appeal as nostalgia. They are viewed as clusters of old buildings once important for their industrial functions, but now for the reminiscence of the bygone times, which their aging architecture suggests. To attract the suburbanized crowds, contemporary urban economic development strategy seeks to capitalize on this fad. City leaders encourage real estate developers to recycle these buildings in Disney-esque fashion as historic facades to house modern retail gallerias. The goal of many urban economic development planners is to fill these spaces with Red Lobster restaurants and Banana Republic clothing stores so popular in the suburban malls. Cities also still retain some locational importance for infrequently used institutions such as museums, concert halls, and medical centers.

On the flip-side of the coin, cities often have a negative image. They are the places where America's festering social problems threaten the idealized landscape. The response to this view of cities as social pathology is to cordon them off as much as possible so that the urban "diseases" do not seep into suburbia. This negative view is a confound of concerns over race, poverty, and central city life. The national policy response to these views is built around an amalgam of tax deductions and public spending programs that favor automobile travel and single-family homeownership. The local policy response is to rely on the mechanisms of exclusionary zoning and local property taxes to keep poverty and its public costs at arms length.

On balance, comparatively few influential policy-makers think of central cities as having much relevance to the unfolding American economy of the twenty-first century. The reasoning runs something like this: Cities are no longer economically essential because the end-of-the-century service-based economy, sustained by an abundance of relatively inexpensive and widely dispersed transportation and telecommunications infrastructure, does not need centralized locational concentration. Central location is viewed by them as a concept tied to the old nineteenth-century manufacturing-based city. Location may have mattered once, but no more. Geographic distinctions between cities, suburbs, and rural areas are viewed purely as matters of lifestyle and personal choice, not of cost.

The experience and politics that shape this reasoning are straightforward. The suburban populace is about one-half of the entire population. Many suburban residents proudly proclaim that they have not set foot in "downtown" or "the city" in years. Their daily experience convinces them that both the older cities, and, increasingly, even the inner ring of older suburbs, are places inhabited largely by poor people and racial minorities with little to contribute to the new global economy. Their everyday experience tells them that metropolitan and American futures are found in the shopping malls, office parks, and wired-up home offices at suburbia's outer reaches. The heart and soul of America resides in suburbia. This group holds the critical balance in electoral politics. They are one-half of the American population. Suburban voters are, on average, more affluent and hence have a higher rate of voter turnout than does the 25 percent of the electorate living in the central core. The suburban-based state and national political leaders who have emerged from this demographic calculus, and who shape public policy, reflect the anti-urban ideals of their constituents.

The Increasing Importance of Centrality

This view of central cities, suburbs, and the economy, although widespread, is wrong. It does not properly account for the way in which the contemporary global economy actually functions spatially, nor for the way in which American urban policy has uniquely drained cities of resources. Along the way, it has hidden the true cost of what is, in effect, an artificially constructed playing field. The most obvious immediate losers are residents of our central cities and the inner ring of older suburbs. But the long-term disadvantage burdens everyone. In both the service sector, which has risen to prominence, and the reconstituted manufacturing sector, efficient centralized density is increasingly critical to global economic success. As international competition becomes keener, the economic dysfunctionality of the policy will become increasingly apparent. Can we develop the political ability to reverse this situation before it is too late? I don't know. But the case for the economic importance of central cities is unassailable.

The New Spatial Economic Reality

The economy of the twenty-first century will be intensely information based. It will center on producer service industries. These include high-end activities such as legal services, advertising, finance, insurance, real estate, data processing, and telecommunications services as well as less-prestigious activities such as security, custodial services, and messenger and package delivery services. The tie that binds them to one another is their heavy reliance on information-processing technology. Despite the theoretical notion that one result of such technology is to permit producer services, especially the high-end ones, and information industries to locate anywhere that phone lines, satellites, and package delivery services can reach, in reality they are far less footloose. They generally prefer central locations because the quality of information processing depends critically upon the quality of the underlying information. The best information and hence the best analysis is obtained in an environment in which diverse experts have easy face-to-face contact with one another. Investment bankers want to meet the principals to whom they entrust large sums of capital. Innovative new products derive from cutting-edge research and development. Increasingly that activity is carried out by networks of closely located and closely affiliated small independent firms. Less and less of new product development derives from work undertaken in the large isolated corporate research and development campuses so popular in the post-war decades. It is no accident that the biotechnology firms that bring new products to market cluster in locations such as San Francisco even as important basic biological and medical research takes place almost everywhere. This need for face-to-face contact, com-

bined with the intensive use of telecommunications infrastructure, favors urban density. Only densely settled places can sustain enough intensity of telecommunications use to justify the high fixed costs of state-of-the-art technology.

Despite high rents, high taxes, and a host of urban problems, firms in the expansive producer services sector still prefer to cluster in cities. Job growth in these industries has sustained a rate of expansion that is more than double the overall national average. Surely such phenomena are indicative of the enduring economic importance of central location. What constrains further growth in cities is the lack of public investments in urban infrastructure and public services to make them competitive with the subsidized alternatives at the metropolitan fringe.

While manufacturing in general and urban manufacturing in particular has fallen dramatically as a share of total employment and GDP since the end of World War II, it would be a fatal mistake to dismiss it. The symbiotic linkage between producer service jobs and manufacturing is powerful. We cannot long remain a world economic power if actual manufacturing activities leave our shores. Over time, producer services follow the production base. By the same token, strong producer services can be a powerful spatial anchor for modern manufacturing. In other words, national competitiveness in services is critical to competitiveness in manufacturing, and vice versa. The question is, can we exploit our comparative advantage in producer services to spread urban prosperity via a resurgence in urban-based manufacturing? The answer is perhaps.

When it comes to manufacturing, it is important to note that past trends are not future destiny. Until recently, it was fashionable, especially in academic circles, to argue that manufacturing belonged as far away from the city as possible. The new information technology has changed everything. Mass production is continually being bested by small batch production methods. One result is that central locations are once again critical for manufacturing success. The granddad of mass production, Henry Ford, once remarked that his customers could have their Model Ts in any color as long as it was black. But with inexpensive information processing it is now possible to tailor products to individual needs without incurring meaningfully higher production costs. While mass-produced goods were most efficiently churned out ad infinitum on large sites located on cheap land far from the urban core, the customized small batch products that increasingly characterize manufactured output are better produced in small plants embedded in rich networks of transportation and communications infrastructure. These smaller, more flexible firms have proven to be a competitive match for the older industrial giants because they can quickly and continually adjust output as product demand changes. The small batch production methods that these firms employ enable them to maintain a much smaller inventory of inputs, minimizing the amount of costly capital tied up in unnecessary parts and storage space.

This production system is one element of what is now popularly called "just-in-time" production. Developed in Japan, where space always commands a premium, its successful implementation requires an extremely reliable freight distribution system and a well-developed telecommunications infrastructure linking retail outlets to factories, warehouses, and suppliers. In the most advanced systems, a product can be designed specifically to fit an individual customer's unique needs. The data is fed directly to the computers at the factory, which in turn customizes the manufacturing process and notifies a host of component suppliers of their need for additional parts. As just-in-time manufacturing becomes the standard and mass production fades, the increasing importance of transportation and telecommunications linkages between producers and retailers, and the reduced need for production space, are making urban industrial areas, once abandoned as inappropriate for mass production, increasingly valuable as efficient sites for the specialized flexible industrial activity required in the new information age.

According to the 1992 Census of Manufacturers, New York City is still home to over 12,000 manufacturing firms with 330,000 jobs that produce over $41 billion worth of goods. The Borough of Queens in New York City experienced a 30 percent decrease in the amount of its available manufacturing space between 1993 and 1995 as many small manufacturers, eager for close-in locations, scooped up available sites. Small manufacturers in New York tell anyone willing to listen that it is the lack of well-located and serviced manufacturing sites that are the limit on their urban expansion.

Yet the older view of manufacturing still holds great sway over urban economic development officials. They continue to press for the high-rise commercial and residential mega-projects favored by politically well-connected real estate developers. The virtue of these projects is that they can produce the highest short-term profits. The downside is that they effectively throttle the longer-term and more socially diffuse returns inherent in a resurgent manufacturing base. The wonder is that despite the hostility and neglect of this key sector by public officials it persists. One can only speculate on what might occur if laissez-faire policy was replaced by a more activist industrial planning.

Further, because cities are the repository of

an enormous historic national investment in physical infrastructure, it will be significantly less costly to rehabilitate that capital stock than to add new higher-cost and inherently less efficient capacity at the metropolitan fringe.

The more competitive are international markets, the more crucial will be efficient urban locations to a broad-based American prosperity. Therefore, the more valuable will be the old abandoned industrial sites on the edges of major cities. While much is made of the fact that all the new auto assembly plants being built by foreign manufacturers in the United States, called transplants, have been located in rural areas of the southeast, that trend is more a reflection of the huge locational subsidy to sprawl, which has been given to them as matters of both national and state tax policy, than it is a reflection of any inherent efficiency in these out-of-the-way locations. By way of contrast, it is noteworthy that the popular American built car, the Ford Taurus, is assembled without artificial subsidy by unionized workers in plants in South Chicago and Atlanta. These plants are certainly competitive with the highly subsidized transplants. In this modern age of inter-jurisdictional economic competition, too much of location decision-making has been reduced to a contest of competitive tax cuts.

The Need for Urban Infrastructure

Infrastructure is the invisible but tangible physical underpinning that holds up society. Cities, because of their ability to co-locate large numbers of people in small spaces economize greatly on these costly elements. If low transport and telecommunications costs, agglomeration economies (the benefits from close proximity to others in the same industry), and superior access to principal markets were no

longer important as a general economic proposition, we would be witnessing as rapid a dispersal of urban centers across the globe. But this is not the case. Indeed, as the noted urban historian Kenneth Jackson observed, "The United States is not only the world's first suburban nation, but it will also be its last."

Supporting the same level of economic activity in low-density suburban locations requires that physical infrastructure be extended and maintained over longer distances. A 1974 HUD-sponsored study, "The Costs of Sprawl," indicated that the cost of providing housing in low-density unplanned suburban areas was 60 percent higher than providing the same number of units in planned, high-density urban areas. More than half of these costs are subsidized. Sprawled development requires that ever-increasing numbers of workers commute in increasingly diverse patterns over ever-increasing distances. This in turn undermines the viability of alternative, less expensive, less polluting, and more efficient mass transit modes.

The traffic congestion associated with this development pattern is imposing severe costs on the economy. Every time a firm relocates from an urban to a suburban location the number of automobile trips made by the firm's employees during the day increases twelve times. Thus, a large part of the growth in vehicle miles traveled by U.S. citizens and traffic congestion is being driven by the relocation of firms from urban to suburban areas.

Our heavy dependence on automobile transportation and the infrastructure costs required to support it are reflected clearly in the amount of money we spend on transportation relative to other countries. The United States spends between 15–18 percent of GNP on transportation; Japan spends 9 percent. American families spend from between 15.2 percent to 22.5 percent of their annual income on transportation-related expenses, whereas a Japanese family only spends 9.4 percent of their income on transportation. These differences in costs are reflected both in the costs that firms pay directly for transportation, and also indirectly for the costs that firms pay out in wages.

The cost of building more highways to overcome increasing traffic congestion is far beyond our means. According to the Federal Highway Administration our current annual expenditures on highways of $14.6 billion annually would have to be increased by 35 percent just to bring the existing physical infrastructure back up to its 1983 physical condition. In order to maintain average user costs (which includes the costs of congestion) at current levels ($400 billion per year), current expenditures would have to be increased by 113 percent. Encouraging the use of mass transit and higher-density living and working patterns provides a more cost effective solution.

Zoning and Local Fiscal Policy

The current apparent efficiency of living and working in the outer reaches of metropolitan America is a fiscal illusion. It is created through large, but mainly invisible, public subsidies to both automobile-based travel and low-density housing. Absent these large subsidies, it would be difficult to explain, from an economic point of view, why the fastest growing portions of metropolitan regions continue to be the spatially distant periphery while decay and stagnation cover all too much of the more centrally located core. The simple, popular rationale is that the market did it. Residents and businesses made free choices to move and the efficient market merely accommodated them. True, up to a point, but trivial. Individual choices are only

made from available options. If, as a matter of public policy, relatively more heavily subsidized suburban options compete with relatively less favored urban ones, it is difficult to see how the outcome could be otherwise. A more powerful economic policy analysis must delve into the dynamics that cast up the options.

The mainstays of this policy are federal housing and transportation subsidies as well as the exemption of homeowner capital gains from taxation. The costs of mortgage interest and local property taxes are both deductible from the federal income tax, a clear advantage to suburban homeownership over urban renting, as well as an incentive to continued sprawled, gated, and segregated metropolitan development patterns.

The federal government, through its highway aid, underwrites both the capital and operating costs of highways. Cars operate most efficiently where density is lowest. Ironically, meager urban transit subsidies are under sustained attack by both the Clinton administration and Congress; subsidies to automobiles outstrip mass transit subsidies by a ratio of seven to one. The net impact of these spatially skewed transport subsidies ensures that the only individual travel costs associated with sprawl continue to be the relatively small out-of-pocket ones for gas and, occasionally, parking.

Finally, homeowners enjoy a tax-free imputed rent when their property goes up in value. The owners also receive an exemption from capital gains taxation when the property is sold to buy another house and a large tax-free gain on most of the value if they give up homeownership as senior citizens. As a result of this tri-partite federal subsidy package it is far easier for the real estate industry to focus private capital investment on the development and sale of housing built on farmland at the metropolitan periphery than to generate similar capital to revitalize the more expensive and strategically valuable space at the center. By the same token, because of the ubiquitous presence of autos, the strip mall continues to pave over America.

At the same time, the standard method of local service provision through local property taxes and zoning serves to make life in the newest and most peripheral communities seem better than it really will be in the fullness of time. When a rural community first begins to become a suburb, it has neither the historic costs of past infrastructure investment nor service costs of congestion embedded in its municipal tax rate. Its entire fiscal effort, financed off of the rising property values that accompany a new population influx, is devoted to new infrastructure for the use of the new residents. More importantly, thanks to subsidized highways, it inherits its initial access as a more or less free public good. But, as the evidence of the past half-century shows, these advantages only last until the next wave of even more peripheral development begins.

If these federal subsidies, nurtured by local fiscal zoning disappeared, refurbishing the quality of life in older urban and inner-ring suburban residential neighborhoods would prove to be an obvious highly cost-effective alternative investment. These slowly decaying places are an important undervalued asset for providing efficient high-quality housing to the diverse urban-based workforce that the next century's economy will demand. Cities and older suburbs contain a broad range of housing types for people in all walks of life in close proximity to one another and to the efficient locations of twenty-first century work. They are already connected by urban mass transit systems. If urban areas were able to receive a significantly higher per-

centage of new housing investment, the need for massive increases in highway expenditures could be avoided, as traffic could be shifted from single-occupancy vehicles to more efficient modes such as public transportation, and to walking and bicycling.

The Political Economy of Spatial Public Policy

A rational economic case is not the same thing as a viable political one. Higher-income city dwellers, not wishing to bear the nation's entire burden for the poor, as embodied in public hospitals and housing, simply avoid the problem by moving to suburban municipalities beyond the central city's taxing authority. Sometimes they remain in the cities and become a political constituency for privatizing everything. They may support the private management of their parks to exempt them from the cuts in the city's public parks budget. Sometimes they become advocates for business improvement districts—those little neighborhood tax havens that service only their immediate environment. In either case, they can feel good about the civic virtue of overcoming "bureaucracy" in the name of tight-fisted small government.

These urban conservatives may become supporters of those politicians seeking to privatize the infrastructure needed by the poor, be it public hospitals or public schools. Once more, they can claim to do so in the name of efficiency. The results of such an expansive political movement for private provisioning set in the context of a larger set of policies that spatially skew society in an anti-urban direction is two-fold. First, it inevitably lessens the public obligation to provide equal service for all citizens, a distinct political danger if we want our society to be a progressive democracy. Second, it undermines our ability to even provide for the broad base of middle-class people who live one to two paychecks from the bottom.

While the picture may seem bleak, it is far from hopeless. Since the root of the problem is more political than economic, the solution must be political. That means building coalitions among those being squeezed by these trends. There is a substantial difference between the interests of those living in the peripheral suburbs and those inhabiting the older more racially integrated ones near the center city. Residents in these older communities, regardless of income, tend to have a much larger stake in urban well-being. By the same token, the residents of the center city have a great deal at stake in the welfare of their close-by neighbors who work "downtown," rely on the city's transportation systems, fill its offices, eat in its restaurants, and shop in its stores.

A second place to build alliances is between public employees, lower-income urban residents, and political progressives. Privatization, which is now the mantra of those seeking to cut urban support for the poor, serves each of these groups badly. If we are to have a prosperous economy and social justice, we need a well-functioning and democratically accountable public sector. As part of that coalition, public employee unions must become the advocates for the efficiency and effectiveness of the public services they provide as well as defenders of their members.

Finally, environmentalists and urban activists should recognize their mutual dependence. The only cure for the environmental damage of populations expanding across the countryside is bringing new vitality to the environmental efficiency inherent in urban density.

We can no longer afford to maintain the illusion that we can move ever outward into unsullied soil. To preserve our prosperity, we must begin conserving the massive and substantial investments of our center cities and older suburbs. Our need for spatial efficiency and our desire for comfortable lives are not antithetical. They are economical, practical, and, most importantly, urban.

Three Policy Goals

If this coalition for more rational and equitable metropolitan life is to succeed, it must have a programmatic agenda. What follows are my three choices for that agenda.

1. *The playing field between city and suburb must be leveled.* The implicit subsidies to continual deconcentration must either be equalized with subsidies to urban areas or eliminated. Unless the true costs of sprawl are borne by those who engage in the deconcentration process, it will not stop.

2. *The physical infrastructure (i.e., water, sewerage, power, transportation, communications, and housing) and the service levels in education, public safety, and transit in central cities and surrounding older suburbs must be restored.* It is not enough to level the playing field. It is also necessary to make up for past disinvestment. Unless the urban public realm works well it will be difficult to effectively create the level playing field of the first objective or entice an expanded middle class back into the city. Without an expanded middle class, the social and spatial urban polarization will not stop. At present both the administration and Congress seem intent upon perpetuating the present subsidies to sprawl. Coalitions to change that must begin working now.

3. *The industrial land and abandoned neighborhoods of center cities and older suburbs must be primary targets for revitalization.* The vast expanses of under- or unutilized land, which lies within ten miles of center cities, must be given high priority as efficient locations for production in the new era of transportation- and telecommunications-intensive just-in-time manufacturing. Similarly the residential neighborhoods with their excellent stock of older buildings must be thought of once more as locations for housing all classes of citizens. These locations, near already well-developed public transportation and other infrastructure, are cost-effective places for a sustained revitalization of America's economic base.

5

Jobless Ghettos: The Social Implications of the Disappearance of Work in Segregated Neighborhoods

William J. Wilson

In 1950, a substantial portion of the urban black population was poor but working. Urban poverty was quite extensive, but people held jobs. However, in many inner-city ghetto neighborhoods in 1990, most adults were not working in a typical week. For example, in 1950, 69 percent of all males 14 and over held jobs in a typical week in the three neighborhoods that represent the historic core of the Black Belt in Chicago—Douglas, Grand Boulevard, and Washington Park. But by 1990, only four in ten in Douglas worked in a typical week, one in three in Washington Park, and one in four in Grand Boulevard. In all, only 37 percent of all males 16 and over held jobs in a typical week in these neighborhoods.

The disappearance of work has had devastating effects not only on individuals and families but also on the social life of neighborhoods as well. Inner-city joblessness is a severe problem that is often overlooked or obscured when the focus is mainly on poverty and its consequences. Despite increases in the concentration of poverty since 1970, inner cities have always featured high levels of poverty, but the levels of inner-city joblessness reached in 1990 were unprecedented.[1]

It should be noted that when I refer to "joblessness" I am not solely referring to official unemployment. The unemployment rate represents only the *official* labor force—that is, those who are actively looking for work. It does not include those who are outside of or have dropped out of the labor market, including the nearly 6 million males age 25–60 who appear in the census statistics but do not show up in the labor statistics.[2]

These uncounted males in the labor market are disproportionately represented in the inner-city ghettos. A more appropriate measure of joblessness that takes into account both official unemployment and non–labor force participation is the employment-to-population ratio, which corresponds to the percentage of adults 16 and older who are working. In 1990, for example, only one in three adults ages 16 and older held a job in the ghetto poverty areas of Chicago, representing roughly 425,000 men, women, and children. And in the ghetto tracts of the nation's 100 largest cities, for every ten adults who did not hold a job in a typical week in 1990, there were only six employed persons.

The consequences of high neighborhood joblessness are more devastating than those of high neighborhood poverty. A neighborhood in which people are poor, but employed, is much different from a neighborhood in which people are poor and jobless. Many of today's problems in the inner-city ghetto neighborhoods—crime, family dissolution, welfare, low levels of social organization, and so on—are fundamentally a consequence of the disappearance of work.

It should be clear that when I speak of the disappearance of work, I am referring to the declining involvement in or lack of attachment to the formal labor market. It could be argued that the general sense of the term "joblessness" does not necessarily mean "non-work." Many people who are officially jobless are nonetheless involved in informal activities, ranging from unpaid housework to income from work in the informal or illegal economies.

Housework is work; baby-sitting is work; even drug dealing is work. However, what contrasts work in the formal econo ay with work activity in the informal and illegal economies is that work in the formal economy has greater regularity and consistency in schedules and hours. The demands for discipline are greater. It is true that some work activities outside the formal economy also call for discipline and regular schedules. Several studies reveal that the social organization of the drug industry is driven by discipline and a work ethic, however perverse. However, as a general rule, work in the informal and illegal economies is far less governed by norms or expectations that place a premium on discipline and regularity. For all these reasons, when I speak of the disappearance of work, I mean work in the formal economy, work that provides a framework for daily behavior because of the discipline and regularity that it imposes.

Thus, a youngster who grows up in a family with a steady breadwinner and in a neighborhood in which most of the adults are employed will tend to develop some of the disciplined habits associated with stable or steady employment—habits that are reflected in the behavior of his or her parents and of other neighborhood adults. These might include attachment to a routine, a recognition of the hierarchy found in most work situations, a sense of personal efficacy attained through the routine management of financial affairs, endorsement of a system of personal and material rewards associated with dependability and responsibility, and so on. Accordingly, when this youngster enters the labor market, he or she has a distinct advantage over the youngsters who grow up in households without a steady breadwinner and in neighborhoods that are not organized around work—in other words, a milieu in which one is more exposed to the less-disciplined habits associated with casual or infrequent work.

In the absence of regular employment, a person lacks not only a place in which to work and the receipt of regular income but also a coherent organization of the present—that is, a system of concrete expectations and goals. Regular employment provides the anchor for the spatial and temporal aspects of daily life. It determines where you are going to be and when you are going to be there. In the absence of regular employment, life, including family life, becomes less coherent. Persistent unemployment and irregular employment hinder rational planning in daily life, a necessary condition of adaptation to an industrial economy.[3]

Explanations of the Growth of Jobless Ghettos

What accounts for the growing proportion of jobless adults in inner-city communities? An easy explanation would be racial segregation.

However, a race-specific argument is not sufficient to explain recent changes in such neighborhoods. After all, these historical Black Belt neighborhoods were just as segregated by skin color in 1950 as they are today, yet the level of employment was much higher then. One has to account for the ways in which racial segregation interacts with other changes in society to produce the recent escalating rates of joblessness.

The disappearance of work in many inner-city neighborhoods is in part related to the nationwide decline in the fortunes of low-skilled workers. Over the past two decades, wage inequality has increased sharply and gaps in labor market outcomes between the less- and more-skilled workers have risen substantially. Research suggests that these changes are the result of "a substantial decline in the relative demand for the less-educated and those doing more routinized tasks compared to the relative supply of such workers."[4] Two factors appear to have reduced the relative demand for less-skilled workers—the computer revolution (i.e., skill-based technological change) and the internationalization of economic activity. Inner-city workers face an additional problem—the growing suburbanization of jobs. Most ghetto residents cannot afford cars and therefore rely on public transit systems that make the connection between inner-city neighborhoods and suburban job locations difficult and time consuming.

Although the relative importance of the different underlying causes of the growing jobs problems of the less-skilled, including those in the inner city, continues to be debated, there is little disagreement about the underlying trends. They are unlikely to reverse themselves.[5]

Changes in the class, racial, and demographic composition of inner-city neighborhoods have also contributed to the high percentage of jobless adults in these neighborhoods. Because of the steady outmigration of more advantaged families, the proportion of non-poor families and prime-age working adults has decreased sharply in the typical inner-city ghetto since 1970. These changes have made it increasingly difficult to sustain basic neighborhood institutions or to achieve adequate levels of social organization. The declining presence of working- and middle-class blacks has also deprived ghetto neighborhoods of key resources, including structural resources, such as residents with income to sustain neighborhood services, and cultural resources, such as conventional role models for neighborhood children.

It is not surprising therefore that our research in Chicago revealed that inner-city ghetto residents share a feeling of little informal social control of their children. A primary reason is the absence of a strong organizational capacity or an institutional resource base that would provide an extra layer of social organization in their neighborhoods. It is easier for parents to control the behavior of the children in their neighborhoods when a strong institutional resource base exists and when the links between community institutions such a churches, schools, political organizations, businesses, and civic clubs are strong or secure. The higher the density and stability of formal organizations, the less illicit activities such as drug trafficking, crime, prostitution, and the formation of gangs can take root in the neighborhood.

It is within this context that the public policy discussion on welfare reform and family values should be couched. Our Chicago research suggests that, as employment prospects recede, the foundation for stable relationships becomes weaker over time. More permanent relationships such as marriage give way to temporary liaisons that result in broken unions, out-of-wedlock pregnancies and births, and, to a lesser extent, separation and divorce. The changing norms concerning marriage in the larger society reinforce the movement toward temporary liaisons in the inner city, and therefore economic considerations in marital decisions take on even greater weight. The evolving cultural patterns are seen in the sharing of negative outlooks toward marriage and toward the relationships between males and females in the inner city, outlooks that are developed in and influenced by an environment featuring persistent joblessness. This combination of factors has increased out-of-wedlock births, weakened the family structure, expanded the welfare rolls, and, as a result, caused poor inner-city blacks to be even more disconnected from the job market and discouraged about their role in the labor force. The economic marginality of the ghetto poor is cruelly reinforced, therefore, by conditions in the neighborhoods in which they live.

In the eyes of employers in metropolitan Chicago, the social conditions in the ghetto render inner-city blacks less desirable as workers, and therefore many employers are reluctant to hire them. One of the three studies that provided the empirical foundation for *When Work Disappears* included a representative sample of employers in the greater Chicago area who provided entry-level jobs. An overwhelming majority of these employers, both white and black, expressed negative views about inner-city ghetto workers, and many stated that they were reluctant to hire them. For example, a president of an inner-city manufacturing firm expressed a concern about employing residents from certain inner-city neighborhoods:

> If somebody gave me their address, uh, Cabrini Green, I might unavoidably have some concerns. [*Interviewer:* What would your concerns be?] That the poor guy probably would

be frequently unable to get to work and . . . I probably would watch him more carefully, even if it wasn't fair, than I would with somebody else. I know what I should do though is recognize that here's a guy that is trying to get out of his situation and probably will work harder than somebody else who's already out of there and he might be the best one around here. But I, I think I would have to struggle accepting that premise at the beginning.

In addition to qualms about the neighborhood milieu, employers frequently mentioned concerns about applicants' language skills and educational training. An employer from a computer software firm expressed the view "that in many businesses the ability to meet the public is paramount and you do not talk street talk to the buying public. Almost all your black welfare people talk street talk. And who's going to sit them down and change their speech patterns?" A Chicago real estate broker made a similar point:

> A lot of times I will interview applicants who are black, who are sort of lower class. . . . They'll come to me and I cannot hire them because their language skills are so poor. Their speaking voice for one thing is poor. . . . They have no verbal facility with the language . . . and these . . . you know, they just don't know how to speak and they'll say "salesmens" instead of "salesmen" and that's a problem. . . . They don't know punctuation, they don't know how to use correct grammar, and they cannot spell. And I can't hire them. And I feel bad about that and I think they're being very disadvantaged by the Chicago public school system.

Another respondent defended his method of screening out most job applicants on the telephone on the basis of their use of "grammar and English."

I have every right to say that that's a requirement for this job. I don't care if you're pink, black, green, yellow, or orange, I demand someone who speaks well. You want to tell me that I'm a bigot, fine, call me a bigot.

Finally, an inner-city banker claimed that many blacks in the ghetto "simply cannot read. When you're talking our type of business, that disqualifies them immediately. We don't have a job here that doesn't require that somebody have minimum reading and writing skills."

How should we interpret the negative attitudes and actions of employers? To what extent do they represent an aversion to blacks per se and to what degree do they reflect judgments based on the job-related skills and training of inner-city blacks in a changing labor market? I should point out that the statements made by the African-American employers concerning the qualifications of inner-city black workers do not differ significantly from those of the white employers. Whereas 74 percent of all the white employers who responded to the open-ended questions expressed negative views of the job-related traits of inner-city blacks, 80 percent of the black employers did so as well.

This raises a question about the meaning and significance of race in certain situations—in other words, how race intersects with other factors. A key hypothesis in this connection is that, given the recent shifts in the economy, employers are looking for workers with a broad range of abilities: "hard" skills (literacy, numeracy, basic mechanical ability, and other testable attributes) and "soft" skills (personalities suitable to the work environment, good grooming, group-oriented work behaviors, etc.). While hard skills are the product of education and training—benefits that are apparently in short supply in inner-city schools—soft skills are strongly tied to culture and are therefore shaped by the harsh environment of the inner-city ghetto. If employers are indeed reacting to the difference in skills between white and black applicants, it becomes increasingly difficult to discuss the motives of employers: are they rejecting inner-city black applicants out of overt racial discrimination or on the basis of qualifications?

Nonetheless, many of the selective recruitment practices do represent what economists call statistical discrimination: employers make assumptions about the inner-city black workers *in general* and reach decisions based on those assumptions before they have had a chance to review systematically the qualifications of an individual applicant. The net effect is that many black inner-city applicants are never given the chance to prove their qualifications on an individual level because they are systematically screened out by the selective recruitment process. Statistical discrimination, although representing elements of class bias against poor workers in the inner city, is clearly a matter of race. The selective recruitment patterns effectively screen out far more black workers from the inner city than Hispanic or white workers from the same types of backgrounds. But race is also a factor, even in those decisions to deny employment to inner-city black workers on the basis of objective and thorough evaluations of their qualifications. The hard and soft skills among inner-city blacks that do not match the current needs of the labor market are products of racially segregated communities, communities that have historically featured widespread social constraints and restricted opportunities.

Thus, the job prospects of inner-city workers have diminished not only because of the decreasing relative demand for low-skilled labor, the suburbanization of jobs, and the social deterioration of ghetto neighborhoods, but also because of negative employer attitudes. This combination of factors presents a real challenge to policy-makers. Indeed, considering the narrow range of social policy options in the "balance-the-budget" political climate, how can we immediately alleviate the inner-city jobs problem—a problem that will undoubtedly grow when the new welfare reform bill takes full effect.

Public Policy Dilemmas

To what extent will the inner-city jobs problem respond to macroeconomic levers that can act to enhance growth and reduce unemployment? I include here fiscal policies that regulate government spending and taxation and monetary policies that influence interest rates and control the money supply. If jobs are plentiful even for less-skilled workers during periods of economic expansion, then labor shortages reduce the likelihood that hiring decisions will be determined by subjective negative judgments concerning a group's job-related traits.

But given the fundamental structural decline in the demand for low-skilled workers, fiscal and monetary policies designed to enhance economic growth will have their greatest impact in the higher-wage sectors of the economy. Many low-wage workers, especially those in high-jobless inner-city neighborhoods who are not in or have dropped out of the labor force and who also face the problem of negative employer attitudes, will not experience any improvement in their job prospects because of such policies.

If firms in the private sector cannot use or refuse to hire low-skilled adults who are willing to take minimum-wage jobs, then the jobs problem for inner-city workers cannot be adequately addressed without considering a policy of public-sector employment of last resort. Indeed, until current changes in the labor market are reversed or until the skills of the next generation can be upgraded before it enters the labor market, many workers, especially those who are not in the official labor force, will not be able to find jobs unless the government becomes an employer of last resort. This argument applies especially to low-skilled inner-city black workers. It is bad enough that they face the problem of shifts in labor-market demand shared by all low-skilled workers; it is even worse that they confront negative employer perceptions about their work-related skills and attitudes.

Prior to the late 1970s, there was less need for the creation of public-sector jobs. Not only was economic growth fairly rapid during periods of expansion, but "the gains from growth were widely shared." Before the late 1970s, public jobs of last resort were thought of in terms of "a counter-cyclical policy to be put in place during recessions and retired during recoveries. It is only since the late 1970s that the disadvantaged have been left behind during recoveries. The labor market changes . . . seem to have permanently reduced private-sector demand for less-skilled workers."[6]

For all these reasons, the passage of the recent welfare reform bill, which did not include a program of job creation, could have negative social consequences in the inner city. Unless something is done to enhance the employment opportunities of inner-city welfare recipients who reach the time limit for the receipt of welfare, they may flood a pool already filled with low-skilled jobless workers.

New research into urban labor markets by Harry Holzer reveals the magnitude of the problem. Surveying 3,000 employers in Atlanta,

Boston, and Los Angeles, Holzer found that only 5 to 10 percent of the jobs in central-city areas for non-college graduates require very few work credentials or cognitive skills. This means that most inner-city workers today not only need to have basic reading, writing, and math skills but also need to know how to operate a computer as well. Also, most employers require a high school degree, particular kinds of previous work experience, and job references. Because of the large oversupply of low-skilled workers relative to the number of low-skilled jobs, many low-educated and poorly trained individuals have difficulty finding jobs even when the local labor market is strong.[7]

The problem is that in recent years tight labor markets have been of relatively short duration, frequently followed by a recession which either wiped out previous gains for many workers or did not allow others to fully recover from a previous period of economic stagnation. It would take sustained tight labor markets over many years to draw back those discouraged inner-city workers who have dropped out of the labor market altogether, some for very long periods of time. We are currently in one of the longest economic recoveries in the last half century, a recovery that has lasted eight years and generated more than 14 million net new jobs and the lowest official unemployment rate in twenty-four years. This sustained recovery is beginning to have some positive effect on the hard-core unemployed. The ranks of those out of work for more than six months declined by almost 150,000 over a two-month period in early 1997. And, as reported in early 1998, the unemployment rate for high school dropouts declined by five points since 1992, from 12 to 7 percent. Two-fifths of this decline has come in the last year.[8]

How long this current period of economic recovery will last is anybody's guess. Some economists feel that this period of tight labor markets will last for at least several more years. If it does it will be the best antidote for low-skilled workers whose employment and earning prospects have been diminished in the late twentieth century. For example, in the inner cities the extension of the economic recovery for several more years will significantly lower the overall jobless rate not only for the low-skilled workers who are still in the labor force but for those who have been outside the labor market for many years as well. It will also enhance the job prospects of many of the welfare recipients who reach the time limit for the receipt of welfare. But, given the decreased relative demand for low-skilled labor, what will happen to all of these groups if the economy slows down? Considering the changing nature of the economy, there is little reason to assume that their prospects will be anything but bleak. Why? Simply because the economic trend that has twisted against low-skilled workers is unlikely to reverse itself, thereby diminishing over the long term their job prospects and earnings.

Concerned about these issues, I sent President Clinton a memorandum in August 1996. I pointed out that, although he has long realized the crucial relationship between welfare reform and job creation and that his initial welfare plan emphasized job creation, the bill he signed had no such provision. I pointed out that to remedy the most glaring defects of the bill, a mechanism for state and local governments to respond to widespread joblessness in the inner cities was essential. I was aware that the president was giving some thought to tax credits and wage subsidies to encourage businesses to hire welfare recipients. I pointed out that although giving subsidies and tax credits to private employers may help, research suggests that subsidies and credits are hardly sufficient by themselves to accomplish this goal.

The track record of private employers is not especially encouraging. Past efforts to subsidize employers to hire welfare recipients and other disadvantaged individuals have generally failed to work on a large scale. For example, during the late 1960s and early 1970s, the federal government funded a program by the National Alliance of Business (NAB) in which employers received a $3,200 subsidy for each disadvantaged worker, including welfare recipients, they hired (an amount that would be much higher in inflation-adjusted terms today). That effort resulted in a very low take-up rate among employers. Why? Simply because not enough employers have been willing to hire people whom they view as troublesome or "damaged goods." Indeed, a study by the economist Gary Burtless revealed that the low-income individuals who were supposed to be aided were *less* likely to be hired as a result of a targeted wage subsidy. Employers evidently thought that if the government was willing to subsidize the hiring of these individuals so heavily, they must have serious work-related problems.[9]

Studies also show that when employers do receive a subsidy for hiring such individuals—whether a tax credit or a direct subsidy—the subsidy often rewards employers for hires they would have made anyway. When that occurs, it costs the government money but the number of jobs for this population does not increase.

Although a new study by Lawrence Katz reveals that one tax credit program, the Targeted Jobs Tax Credit, "may have modestly improved the employment rates of economically disadvantaged youth,"[10] an impressive array of other studies over the past two decades suggests that a single approach involving tax credits or wage subsidies will fail to move a significant number of welfare recipients into employment.

In my memorandum to the president, I therefore urged caution in placing too many of his "eggs" in the private-sector job-placement basket. We will need a mix of both private- and public-sector initiatives to enhance employment. In inner cities, where the number of very low-skilled individuals vastly exceeds the number of low-skilled jobs even before welfare reform adds tens of thousands more people to the low-skilled labor pool, a healthy dose of public-sector job creation will be needed. Public jobs can help people shunned by private employers initially to learn acceptable work habits and build an employment record, from which they may be able to graduate to private-sector positions. In order to really make my point clear, I pointed out to President Clinton that I am not suggesting a new federal public works program because I understand the difficulties in getting such a program approved in today's political climate. I am only recommending that he enable governors and mayors to use a mix of private- and public-sector approaches as they see fit, based on local conditions. I pointed out that he could not be criticized for a "big government" approach if he allows state and local officials, so many of whom are now Republicans, to make this choice. Indeed, Governor Tommy Thompson's welfare plan in Wisconsin includes provisions for significant public- as well as private-sector employment.

The president responded that several of my recommendations were already under consideration by his administration. And during the presidential campaign, he outlined a proposal that included both tax credits to companies that hire welfare recipients and $3 billion to create public and private work slots in localities that have high unemployment and welfare dependency.

However, in the tax bill submitted to Congress on February 6, 1997, the president's proposal to strengthen the welfare-to-work initiative did not include language that would allow governors and mayors to create private or public work slots in areas plagued by high rates of unemployment and welfare receipt. Indeed the focus, although stated in vague language, was entirely on initiatives to place recipients in private-sector jobs, including a larger tax credit for businesses that hire long-term welfare recipients. The new tax credit would allow employers to deduct 50 percent of the first $10,000 in wages paid to recipients who had been on welfare for at least eighteen months.

The conclusions I draw from the current evidence is that as the president and the Congress take future steps to address the jobs problem for welfare recipients and other disadvantaged workers, they ought not rely on a stand-alone strategy of employer subsidies—either tax credits or wage subsidies. Instead, they ought to consider a mixed strategy that combines employer subsidies with job creation in the public and non-profit private sectors.

It is especially important that this mixed strategy include a plan to make adequate monies available to localities or communities with high jobless and welfare dependency rates. At the same time that the new welfare law has generated a greater need for work opportunities, high-jobless urban and rural areas will have more difficulty placing individuals in private-sector jobs. To create work opportunities for welfare recipients, these areas will therefore have to "rely more heavily upon job creation strategies in the public and private non-profit sectors."[11] West Virginia, plagued with a severe shortage of work opportunities, has provided community service jobs to welfare recipients for several years. In Wisconsin, Governor Thompson's welfare reform plan envisions community-service jobs for many parents in the more depressed areas of the state, and the New Hope program in Milwaukee provides community-service jobs for those unable to find employment in the private sector.

Thus, we could face a real catastrophe in many urban areas if steps are not taken soon to enhance the job prospects of hundreds of thousands of inner-city youths and adults.

Notes

1. Parts of this essay are based on my latest book, *When Work Disappears: The World of the New Urban Poor* (New York: Alfred A. Knopf, 1996), which included three research studies conducted in Chicago between 1986 and 1993. The first of these included a random survey of nearly 2,500 poor and non-poor African-American, Latino, and white residents in Chicago's poor neighborhoods; a subsample of 175 participants from this survey who were reinterviewed and answered open-ended questions; a survey of 179 employers selected to reflect the distribution of employment and firm sizes in the metropolitan area; and comprehensive ethnographic research, including participant-observation research and life-history interviews in a representative sample of inner-city neighborhoods.

The second study included a survey of a representative sample of 546 black mothers and up to two of their adolescent children (ages 11 to 16—or 887 adolescents), in working- and middle-class neighborhoods and high-poverty neighborhoods. Finally, the third study featured a survey of a representative sample of 500 respondents from two high-joblessness neighborhoods on the South Side of Chicago and six focus-group discussions involving the residents and former residents of these neighborhoods.

2. Lester Thurow, "The Crusade That's Killing Prosperity," *American Prospect,* March–April 1995, pp. 54–59.

3. Pierre Bourdieu, *Travail et Travailleurs en Algerio* (Paris: Editions Mouton, 1965).

4. Lawrence Katz, "Wage Subsidies for the Disadvan-

taged," Working Paper 5679, National Bureau of Economic Research, Cambridge, MA, 1996, p. 2.

5. Ibid.

6. Sheldon Danziger and Peter Gottschalk, *America Unequal* (Cambridge: Harvard University Press, 1995), p. 174.

7. Harry Holzer, *What Employers Want: Job Prospects for Less-Educated Workers* (New York: Russell Sage Foundation, 1995).

8. Sylvia Nasar, "Jobs Juggernaut Continues Surge: 30,000 Find Work," *New York Times,* March 7, 1998, pp. 1A and 1B.

9. Gary Burtless, "Are Targeted Wage Subsidies Harmful? Evidence from a Wage Voucher Experiment," *Industrial and Labor Relations Review* 39, October 1985.

10. Katz, op. cit.

11. Center on Budget and Policy Priorities, "The Administration's $3 Billion Jobs Proposal," Washington, DC, 1996.

6

The Labor Market for Young African-American Men: Recent Trends, Causes, and Implications

Harry J. Holzer

The labor market experiences of young African-American men in the United States have greatly deteriorated in the past few decades. Their employment rates have declined dramatically, while the improvements in their relative earnings during the civil rights era have been at least partly eroded.

Recent Trends and Their Causes

Declining employment among young black men is not necessarily a new development; indeed, these rates have been falling at least since the 1950s. Declines that occurred at that time have been attributed to forces such as the mechanization of southern agriculture, which eliminated many jobs among rural blacks and contributed to their "Great Migration" to the industrial centers of the urban North. Some part of the decline also reflected rising school enrollment rates of young blacks.

Both of these developments were, of course, part of the general improvement in the labor market status of blacks over most decades of the twentieth century, as the quantity and quality of education received by blacks improved. In addition, there were two periods of rapid im-provement in the relative earnings of blacks that have been widely attributed to rapid declines in labor market discrimination: during the 1940s and the civil rights era of the mid-1960s through mid-1970s. Improvements in the earlier period were likely related to the tight labor markets of the World War II era, while those of the later period seem to reflect implementation of the equal employment opportunity (EEO) legislation and affirmative action. Improving education attainment and declining labor market discrimination seemed to reinforce each other, as young blacks improved their relative occupational status and earnings at a rapid rate.

But, in the 1970s and 1980s, many social scientists and policy-makers became alarmed at the continuing decline in employment rates and rise in unemployment rates among young black men. By the end of the 1980s, roughly one-third of young black males who were out of school also were without work at any point in time. Among high school dropouts, about 60 percent were not employed.

The deteriorating employment rates of young blacks in the latter period have also been accompanied by some reversals of earlier improvements in relative earnings among young blacks. By the mid-1970s, the gap in wages between young black and white men (after controlling for differences in educational levels) had fallen to 10 percent or less; by the end of the 1980s, this gap had risen to 20 percent or more.

But, without "controlling" for differences in educational levels, the numbers look far worse. Both black and white men with high school or less education have experienced earnings declines of over 25 percent since the early 1970s, and young blacks remain more heavily concentrated among these groups than whites. Even the earlier improvements in relative educational attainment among blacks began to dissipate, as college enrollment rates among black high school graduates declined in the 1980s relative to those of whites.

What has caused this deterioration in the employment and earnings status of young black men over the past 20 to 25 years? The research literature has identified the following important causes of these trends:

Declining Demand for Less-Skilled Labor

As noted above, the earnings of less-educated men in general have declined in the United States over this period, and black men have been particularly hurt by these developments. Most economists identify technological change (especially as it relates to the development and spread of personal computers) as the primary cause of this shift, while growing international trade and immigration have also contributed somewhat.

Even aside from educational attainment, employer skill needs appear to be rising. The vast majority of new jobs for less-educated workers now also involve direct customer contact, reading/writing, arithmetic, and/or use of computers on a daily basis. Most employers require previous experience in the relevant line of work, previous training, and/or references as well.

Many of these rising skill requirements clearly cause disadvantages for black male applicants when they are seeking work. Though their levels of educational attainment and even their test scores have improved in recent years, these measures of cognitive ability among blacks continue to lag behind those of whites, and the improvements have apparently occurred more slowly than employer demand for them has risen. Indeed, gaps between whites and blacks in education and written test scores can account for much of the differences in their wages.

Declining Industrial Employment and Unionization

One of the channels through which declining demand for less-educated labor has reduced the earnings of black men has been through the disappearance of production jobs in manufacturing. By the early 1970s, less-educated black men in some parts of the country (particularly the Midwest) had become quite heavily concentrated in this sector and benefited from the relatively high wages paid there. Consequently, declining manufacturing employment over the past few decades generated particularly large losses in relative employment and earnings for black males.

Blacks also have been hurt by the growing disappearance of private-sector unionism in the United States and a relative decline in the wage premium associated with unionized jobs. As blacks had been relatively more concentrated in these jobs and had enjoyed relatively greater gains for such membership, the decline in this institution over time has been particularly harmful to them.

Growing Spatial Imbalances Between Residences and Employment

Over the past several decades, both U.S. residential populations and employment have been growing more "suburbanized." But while suburbanization has grown among blacks as well as whites, a relatively large part of the black residential population remains in central-city areas, often in neighborhoods that remain highly segregated by race and by economic status. Even within the suburbs, employment growth is often strongest in those parts of the metropolitan area furthest away from where blacks live.

These developments contribute to a "spatial mismatch" between locations of employment and residences among lower-income blacks that reduce the employment and earnings of the latter to some extent. If these individuals had easy access or transportation to, full information about, and social contacts in all parts of the metropolitan areas in which they live, their residential locations would not necessarily impede their labor market opportunities. But many inner-city blacks rely on public transit, which does not easily provide access to many outlying areas; many lack knowledge of and contacts in these areas; and many perceive (accurately or not) racial hostility there. Thus, their ability or willingness to seek employment in these areas is limited, and they "crowd" into areas closer to home where job opportunities or wages for the least-skilled may be lower.

Continuing Racial Discrimination

While employment discrimination against blacks clearly declined in the 1960s and 1970s, there also is clear evidence that it persists to some extent. Recent "audit" studies, in which matched pairs of black and white jobseekers with identical credentials are sent to apply for listed job openings, demonstrate quite clearly that blacks are less likely than comparably qualified whites to receive job offers. Employers also frequently espouse strong negative stereotypes about the attitudes and performance of young blacks, especially men, in the workplace.

Employers generally seem to prefer Hispanics (particularly immigrants) to blacks for jobs requiring few skills, and they prefer black females to black males. They are also especially reluctant to hire black applicants in small establishments (i.e., those less closely scrutinized by EEO officials), in the suburbs, and in jobs where they deal primarily with white customers.

Have any of these problems actually grown worse over the past few decades? Though we have no direct evidence, it is certainly plausible that employer reluctance to hire young and less-educated black men has risen as the violence, crime rates, and so on associated with them have increased. A growing fraction of jobs also involve the kind of direct customer contact (with predominantly white customers) and social/verbal skills at which employers seem to think blacks are relatively weak.

Furthermore, affirmative action enforcement at the federal level weakened in the 1980s, and EEO litigation involving blacks focused more on promotion/discharge cases rather than on hiring. Indeed, employer fears of legal problems and conflict with prospective black employees may make them more reluctant to hire blacks in the first place.

Growing Social Isolation of the Poor

While residential segregation by *race* has declined somewhat in recent decades, segregation by *income* or *class* actually grew in the 1980s, and, in at least some large metropolitan areas, the concentration of poor black residents in predominantly poor neighborhoods increased in both of the previous two decades.

What are the consequences of this growing "social isolation" of the black poor? In terms of their ability to gain employment, fewer will have contacts with working people, and they will have greater difficulty obtaining information about and referrals into jobs that employers frequently fill through informal means. More broadly, young people growing up in predominantly low-income neighborhoods will obtain less (or lower-quality) education and may be more likely to engage in behaviors such as crime, drug use, or teen pregnancy that will almost certainly reduce their labor market opportunities later in life.

Wage Expectations and Alternative Income Sources

Wage expectations that exceed those available in the labor market might have contributed to lower employment levels among young blacks in various ways. For one thing, the rising expectations associated with the civil rights era likely made young blacks less willing to accept "menial" or low-wage jobs that earlier they might have found acceptable. Indeed, wage demands among young blacks are somewhat higher than among young whites *relative to what each faces in the labor market.*

But, in recent years, the declining wages available to less-educated men apparently have led many (both white and black) to withdraw from the labor force. Young black males' willingness to pursue income through means such as crime, especially drug "trafficking," clearly has grown in the past decade. Indeed, roughly one-third of all young black men are now involved with the criminal justice system, and

among young black high school dropouts the proportion appears to be well over half. Criminal activity among young blacks has risen the most in those metropolitan areas where income inequality has widened by the greatest amount.

Thus, the combination of declining rewards for legal work and growing rewards (at least financially, and in the short term) for illegal work apparently has convinced young black men to avoid the former and pursue the latter in very large numbers.

Social Implications and Future Trends

What are the implications for the black community and the country overall of declining earnings and employment of young black men? What are the likely future trends in this area?

The answers to these questions are not very encouraging. Clearly, the reduced earnings of the young men themselves represent a social cost. These will likely hamper them throughout their future working lives, as the loss of current work time prevents them from accumulating skills, labor market experience, and seniority that are generally rewarded in the labor market.

But there are other costs. The tendency of so many young black men to engage in illegal activity clearly entails the obvious risks of incarceration and personal harm to the individuals themselves. Also, employers are extremely wary of hiring young men who have criminal records. This likely results not only in the reduced future employment and earnings of those actually engaging in crime, but also those of other men whom employers may incorrectly *suspect* of having been involved. Of course, there are high personal costs for individuals who live in or near high-crime neighborhoods, and the social cost to the United States of policing and incarcerating so many individuals, as well as the loss of economic output, has become extremely high as well (as much as $300 billion a year by one estimate).

Another likely consequence of the low earnings and high rates of non-employment among young black men is the declining rate of marriage within the black community and the consequent growth of out-of-wedlock births to never-married women, often teens. William J. Wilson has hypothesized that these employment problems (along with the high percent of young black men who are either incarcerated or in the armed forces) reduce the pool of "marriageable men" (i.e., those capable of supporting a family over time). While the causes of declining marriage rates in the black community clearly go beyond the economic problems of black men (and are occurring among all U.S. racial and socioeconomic groups), these problems certainly appear to be among the causes of this trend.

The costs of declining marriage rates and resulting unwed motherhood to the mothers themselves, especially among teens, likely include reduced educational attainment, employment, and future earnings. And the children are more likely to grow up in lower-income families, live in lower-income neighborhoods, and be at risk for a variety of behaviors (e.g., dropping out of school, engaging in crime or drug use, etc.), which clearly will hamper their own future earnings capacity. While social scientists continue to debate the exact magnitudes of these costs, their existence seems in little doubt.

Given that the costs of low employment and earnings of young black men, to themselves and society more broadly, appear to be quite high, what can we expect the future to hold? There is at least some basis for hope in the rising educational levels and test scores among young blacks alluded to above. High school dropout

rates in the black community have fallen quite significantly, and the gap in cognitive performance between young whites and blacks has certainly narrowed. More black children today are born to parents with high school and even college diplomas than was true a generation ago, which suggests some chance for them to achieve higher educational status themselves.

More generally, as the gap widens between the earnings of more- and less-educated U.S. workers, the incentives grow for individuals (and their employers) to invest more heavily in education and job training. Indeed, college enrollment rates among both young whites and blacks have already begun to increase in response to these incentives, and there is every reason to expect these trends to continue. As the relative supply of workers with education and training grows over time, more individuals will earn the higher returns associated with those skills, and even those without the skills may earn more, as the skills themselves become relatively less scarce in the market. Thus, the labor market itself should help to generate some "self-correcting" forces to narrow these widening earnings gaps, and that should be relatively more beneficial to blacks than whites.

On the other hand, there are several potential problems with this optimistic scenario. For one thing, the demand for skills in the labor market will likely continue to increase and may even accelerate. The high-paying industrial jobs that have already disappeared will not return, and many more will likely be eliminated as new technologies and international trade continue to expand. Thus, our hope that the supply of skills (especially among young blacks) will "catch up" with and eventually overtake the growing demand for skills on its own may be unrealistic. Indeed, the improvements to date in educational attainment have not been sufficient to begin reversing the widening gaps between education groups that have developed over the past twenty years. Furthermore, there apparently have been many other sources of growing inequality in the labor market besides just education, and these show few signs of being fully understood by the academic community (much less addressed by policy-makers).

There are also specific barriers that young blacks will face. One such problem is the rising cost of obtaining a college education relative to the diminishing sources of state aid and family resources that are available to many young blacks. In the current political environment of public budget cutbacks in education and programs serving the disadvantaged, these relative costs may well grow worse in the coming years. Other dimensions of government policy, such as rollbacks in enforcement of (or even wholesale elimination of) affirmative action programs, also may cause the labor market opportunities of many young blacks (even those with college or more education) to worsen rather than improve over the next several years. If large numbers of women who are currently on welfare are pushed into the labor market in these areas, young males may face even greater competition for the limited number of low-skill jobs that are available there.

Finally, we note that the future prospects of young blacks growing up in poor families and neighborhoods look particularly grim. For those young black children who grow up in single-parent families with relatively low incomes, attend low-quality schools, and live in dangerous neighborhoods of concentrated poverty, it is hard to see how their chances of escaping these outcomes will improve in the foreseeable future without quite dramatic changes in their economic and social environments and in public policy.

Policy Implications

Given the enormous labor market problems that young black males currently face, and the low likelihood that these conditions will dramatically change in the foreseeable future, what can public policy do to help generate improvements?

1) *Improved Education and Job Training.* Improving the relative skills of young black males should remain the most important long-term goal of policy in this area. A number of dimensions of skills are relevant here: high school dropout prevention, basic cognitive skills improvement, increasing college enrollment rates, smoothing the "school-to-work" transition for the non-college bound, enhancing occupational skills of adults, including those employed, and so on.

Programs are already in place that address some of these problems (e.g., Pell grants for college attendance among low-income students), and others have recently been developed in response to new legislation (such as the School-to-Work Act). While some programs targeting disadvantaged young people have not been very effective, at least a few that provide intensive treatments for a year or more (such as Head Start and the Job Corps) have been more successful. Some new approaches, such as the "Quantum Opportunities" Program for high school students, also look promising and need to be seriously evaluated.

Two other points are worth mentioning here. First, whatever basic skills young blacks develop in secondary school or beyond must be clearly demonstrated to employers. It is obvious that employers *perceive* a lack of skills among young blacks; whether the actual gap is as great as they believe is another story. Thus, having a clear set of credentials or signals of what they actually can do might encourage employers to hire more young black job applicants and invest more training in them. Second, it is important that young blacks perceive large market returns to skill development; otherwise, they will have little incentive to perform well academically in high school and pursue skill training after graduation. Creating better linkages between employers and schools might help to change both sets of perceptions.

2) *Job Placement, Transportation, and Residential Mobility.* The imbalances that exist between the residential locations of inner-city blacks and the locations of employers suggest that there might be strong returns to low-cost interventions, such as transportation and job placement assistance, that help to improve the mobility and access to suburban jobs of inner-city young people. Indeed, a variety of such programs already exist in many localities. They are also far less costly than are approaches such as "enterprise zones" (where the cost of each new job for the disadvantaged can be over $30,000 per year).

Of course, these approaches will work only for young people who are readily "employable," with good basic skills and attitudes toward work. Job placement officials must be prepared to screen out those applicants who will likely be less successful, so as to maintain the trust of employers with whom they are working. These approaches may also be most successful for young people, for whom the returns to early work experience can be quite substantial (and for whom the lack of such experience can be quite damaging).

A much more ambitious, long-term goal is to remove the various obstacles (such as housing market discrimination and the lack of financial resources and information) to residential mobility for lower- and middle-income black families.

These approaches would likely generate larger benefits over the long run than those mentioned above, as they would help overcome not only the spatial imbalances that impede current workers but also the negative consequences of having young people grow up in neighborhoods of concentrated poverty. Unfortunately, political and social resistance to such efforts among middle-class whites is often quite high.

3) *Anti-discrimination Efforts.* Given the clear persistence of discrimination against young black males, EEO monitoring and enforcement must be maintained or even expanded. Indeed, improving the access of inner-city blacks to suburban employers and equal employment efforts that increase their chances of being hired there should probably go hand-in-hand. Furthermore, recent research has found little evidence of substantially weaker job performance among minorities in firms that use affirmative action in hiring; at least in terms of productivity, there appears to be little basis for the current attack on affirmative action in many political circles.

4) *Public Job Creation.* While the U.S. economy has been enormously successful in creating jobs over the past few decades, many of these jobs do not appear to be obtainable for less-educated, inner-city young males. Job creation efforts therefore must be part of any strategy to improve the employment outcomes of the least-skilled black males. A number of approaches are available, from those that subsidize private-sector employment (targeted to varying degrees on the least skilled) to public-service employment. The former generally are lower in cost and higher in productivity, but the latter may be necessary as well if we expect to see employment for a large portion of the currently non-working population.

5) *Raising the Rewards to Low-Wage Work.*

Given the declining wages of legal relative to illegal work, it is little wonder that so many young black males opt out of the former to pursue the latter. In order to change the relative returns to these activities, skill enhancements and other approaches identified above must be pursued. But in the short term, this can be accomplished through approaches such as the Earned Income Tax Credit (EITC) and higher minimum wages. While these may not be fully sufficient to dramatically change the perceived relative rewards of work versus other activities, at least they constitute the beginning of such an effort.

6) *Support for Local Efforts and Community Institutions.* In an era of federal government cutbacks, the role of state and local public efforts will grow far more important. Furthermore, governments at *any* level will not be able to provide all of the resources and efforts needed to generate major improvements in these problems.

Therefore, we must support the activities of private agencies and community institutions wherever possible. Local institutions such as churches seem to have major positive effects on labor market outcomes for some young people; these and other community groups might be important sources of mentoring, information, and contacts for those who are involved. More research is needed into the nature and effectiveness of community group activities, and more government support should be provided to local groups that demonstrate such effectiveness.

7

Including Latinos
in Broadly Shared Prosperity

Jorge Chapa

Introduction

The majority of Latinos have not shared in the United States' past prosperity. In fact, the recent era of rapid Latino population growth began in the early 1970s, just as prosperity was becoming more unequal. Indeed, the interaction of restricted opportunities with the growth of the relatively less educated Latino population is the reason that the U.S.-born children, grandchildren, and other descendants of Latino immigrants have not followed other immigrants up the educational and economic ladder. This problem is compounded by the fact that the proximity of the United States to Mexico and other originating countries impedes the assimilation of Latinos into the U.S. population. Now there are 30 million Latinos in the United States, and according to the latest Census Bureau population projections:

> Every year from now to 2050, the race/ethnic group adding the largest number of people to the population would be the Hispanic-origin population. In fact, after 2020 the Hispanic population is projected to add more people to the United States every year than would all other race/ethnic groups combined. By 2010, the Hispanic-origin population may become the second-largest race/ethnic group.[1]

There are five major trends or tendencies shaping the role Latinos will play in America's future. First, as seen above, Latinos are and will continue to be a growing part of the population and workforce. Second, our future will be conditioned by decreasing demand for unskilled workers. Third, the persistent education gap between Anglos and Latinos will restrict upward mobility for Latinos. Fourth, because much of the projected Latino growth is from relatively high fertility categories, Latinos have and will continue to have a much higher proportion in the younger ages. For example, in 1996, Latinos constituted a little more than 10 percent of the U.S. population, but had more than 14 percent of the nation's children. Fifth and finally, because of their relative youth, future economic growth may slow if Latino levels of education and work skills do not improve.

There are several policy-relevant areas where these age-ethnic differences are likely to be most noticeable. The increase in Latino youth will surely also result in an increase in the number of school districts that are composed largely of Latinos and other minorities. Second, a larger proportion of the working-age population will be made up of Latinos and other minorities, particularly in the ages of entry into the labor force. This change could be large enough to have a noticeably negative impact on the U.S. economy.

The third policy-relevant area where the age distribution of the population could cause trouble is the rapidly growing number and proportion of mainly white seniors as the mass retirement of the baby-boom generation in the first decade of the twenty-first century puts large demands on public retirement and health care resources. This will occur at the same time that Latinos and minorities become a larger part of the workforce. The increased demand by the elderly for public services may compete for resources needed to increase the education, skill levels, and productivity of growing numbers of Latinos and other minorities. These developments could add generational stress to the other conflicts that could greatly damage the quality of life for twenty-first century Americans.

Latino Social and Economic Characteristics

This paper discusses the characteristics of Latinos that must be considered in policies and plans to help this growing population group become part of a future with broadly shared prosperity. Perhaps the most important of these considerations is the recognition that the low educational, employment, and economic status is true of all categories of Latinos, not just immigrants. It is true, of course, that many newly arrived Latino-Americans do have low levels of education and earnings, but so do many U.S.-born Latinos, who constitute a majority of the Latino population.

For reasons noted elsewhere in this volume, since the early 1970s, the real wages of Americans with low levels of education have fallen dramatically. This must be considered in the historical context of rising expectations that have shaped the assumptions of most adults in the United States. The failure of the economy to meet the traditional assumptions of continual growth undoubtedly is a source of the public discontent that now seems ubiquitous. Now, most workers do not enjoy the high rates of economic growth they or their parents experienced during the economic boom years from World War II to 1973.

Latino discontent is compounded by the fact that Latinos, for a number of reasons, did not fully enjoy the fruits of the post-war boom and, like all workers with low levels of education, have been increasingly marginalized since 1970, absolutely and relative to Anglos and blacks (see Tables 7.1A and 1B).

Table 7.2 shows that immigrant Latinos have very low levels of high school completion and that U.S.-born Latinos have substantially higher dropout rates than non-Latinos.

Thus, compared to the non-Latino population, both immigrant and U.S.-born Latinos have less schooling, lower earnings, and higher levels of unemployment and poverty.

The post-North American Free Trade Agreement prospect is for more, or much more, of the same. While Latinos have had substantially lower unemployment rates than African-Americans since 1973 (when such statistics were first collected for Latinos), in the last few years, Latino unemployment rates have risen relative to Anglos and African-Americans. In January 1995, for the first time ever, the unemployment rates of Latinos equaled that of African-Americans.

It is, of course, difficult to distinguish a long-term trend from the expected, but random, variation in recurrent measures. Nonetheless, it would be foolish to ignore the potential significance of the convergence of Latino and African-American unemployment rates. Traditionally, monthly unemployment rates for African-Americans have

Table 7.1A

Male Median Income by Race: 1970, 1980, and 1990 (in U.S. dollars)

Median income, all males, 15 and over (1989 constant $)	1970	1980	1990
Anglo	21,160	21,830	22,070
Black	12,800	13,130	12,970
Latino	18,440	15,120	13,500

Table 7.1B

Male Median Income by Race: 1970,1980, and 1990 (in U.S. dollars)

Median income, male year-round, full-time workers (1989 constant $)	1970	1980	1990
Anglo	28,510	30,430	30,760
Black	19,060	21,240	21,690
Latino	22,110	21,730	20,320

Source: Tables 7.1A and 7.1B: Harrison and Bennett, 1995, pp. 204–5. Roderick J. Harrison and Claudette E. Bennett, "Racial and Ethnic Diversity," in Reynolds Farley, ed., *State of the Union: America in the 1990s. Volume Two: Social Trends* (New York: Russell Sage Foundation, 1995), pp. 204–205.

Table 7.2

Percent of Status Dropouts Among 16- to 24-Year-Olds, by Recency of Migration and Ethnicity: November 1989

Recency of immigration	Total	Latino	Non-Latino
Total*	12.5	31.0	10.3
Born outside U.S.	28.9	43.0	7.9
First generation U.S.-born	10.4	17.3	6.2
Second or more generation born in U.S.	11.2	23.7	10.7

Source: U.S. Dept. of Education, "Are Hispanic Dropout Rates Related to Migration?" (WDC: U.S. Government Printing Office, 1993).

*Total includes a small number for whom recency of migration is unknown.

almost always been twice those of Anglos, while Latino unemployment rates typically were in the middle. However, over the last few years, Latino unemployment rates have been increasing compared to Anglos and African-Americans. In January 1995, the Anglo rate was 4.9 percent, compared with 10.2 percent for both African-Americans and Latinos. Until now, it could accurately be said that many Latinos were poor because they work in low-wage jobs. If this pattern and level of unemployment is sustained in the future, many more Latinos and African-Americans may not be able to find jobs at all.

Once all the data are available, it is certain that the recently measured high rate of Latino unemployment will be tied to both long-term and short-term factors. The relevant long-term economic and demographic factors shaping unemployment must include the fact that since the early 1970s, all workers with low skills and educational levels have had decreasing wages *and* diminishing opportunities for employment. The future employment prospects for workers with low levels of education are even more bleak than those of the recent past.

Additionally, as noted earlier, the continued rapid increase in young Latinos, especially those of working age, might add an age component to higher Latino unemployment—that is, for two interrelated reasons, Latino youth could have an unusually high rate of unemployment: being Latino and young. These factors are exacerbated by the massive educational failure for Latino children across the nation. Finally, the fact that many jobs do not pay a living wage may increase joblessness by acting as a work disincentive.

Table 7.3 shows the drastic recent decrease in earnings and employment for high school dropouts. In addition, similar analysis by Johanne Boisjoly and Greg Duncan found that Latino workers had substantially higher job displacement rates between 1987 and 1992 than blacks or whites:

> The reasons for the higher Hispanic rate include a more youthful demographic composition, a much lower level of education, and a much higher rate of employment in occupations vulnerable to layoffs.[2]

As shown previously in Table 7.2, Latinos have, by far, the largest proportion of adults with less than a high school education.

Latino Employment, Education and Skill Levels

The following example from San Antonio, Texas, illustrates the negative impact on Latinos of low education and skill levels. Approximately 80 percent of the non-Latino adults in the San Antonio metropolitan statistical area, but only about 55 percent of Latinos, had completed high school. In addition, the proportion of college graduates in 1990 was far lower among Latinos (7 percent), than in the city as a whole (about 20 percent).

In contrast to many other major cities with high concentrations of Latinos, manufacturing was never significant in San Antonio. In 1990, less than 10 percent of the city's civilian workforce held jobs in this industry. And census publications show that the number of jobs related to manufacturing was low as far back as 1940. After World War II, employment opportunities in San Antonio grew rapidly in producer services (e.g., financial services, insurance, real

Table 7.3

Changes in Wages and Employment by Education Level, 1989–92

Education level	Percent change in real hourly earnings	Employment share	1989
High school dropout	−15.9	18.2	14.3
High school graduate	−6.4	31.1	34.2
BA or higher degree	−6.9	20.9	23.4

Source: David A. Brauer and Susan Hickock, "Explaining the Growing Inequality Across Skill Levels," *Federal Reserve Bank of New York Economic Policy Review*, January 1995, p. 65.

estate), social services (especially health services), and entertainment/tourism. Each of these sectors offer bifurcated employment opportunities characterized by either high-wage/high-skill or low-wage/low-skill jobs. As a result, many San Antonio residents, especially those with little education and skills, are faced with the prospect of part-time, seasonal, or low-wage employment. The final result is a large portion of the total population, and an even larger portion of the Latino population, mired in poverty.

One example clearly demonstrates the connection between the low economic status of most of San Antonio's Latinos and the globalized economy. Between 1985 and 1990, Levi Strauss & Co. closed ten manufacturing plants in San Antonio. The last and largest closing, in February 1990, displaced more than 1,000 garment workers, almost all of whom were Latinos. The *San Antonio Light* summarized the situation as follows:

> Levi Strauss & Co. said it had no choice but to close its San Antonio plant and move the jobs to Costa Rica and the Dominican Republic. The lure of Third World workers performing the same tasks at half the cost is proving irre-

sistible to the garment industry. Levi simply joined an inexorable trend.[3]

One cruelly ironic aspect of this closing is that by moving the plant to Costa Rica, Levi Strauss not only found cheaper wages, but, since it paid relatively high wages by Costa Rican standards, better-educated workers. The newspaper further reported that "Reading is fundamental: 25 percent of San Antonians are at least marginally illiterate; in Costa Rica, only 7 percent can't read and write."[4]

The basic elements of this story are repeated in countless decisions by employers. Many Latino workers in San Antonio and across the United States have very little, if anything, to distinguish themselves from their cousins south of the border. In the future, they may not be able to find jobs at all.

The Future for Low-Skilled Workers

The Hudson Institute's report, *Workforce 2000,* created a stir by asking if our future workforce would have the skills necessary to be economically competitive. The authors argued that the following trends would have a great impact on America's economic future: (1) the continuing growth of service employment and continuing decline in manufacturing; (2) an increasing demand for more highly educated workers; (3) as the population ages, the majority of a decreasing pool of future labor force entrants will consist of women and minorities; (4) inadequate child care and other support systems will continue to limit the potential productivity of women; and (5) ineffective educational institutions will continue to limit the potential productivity of minorities. One major potential consequence of the interaction of these trends is a future shortage of well-educated workers rela-

tive to the requirements of newly created jobs *(Workforce 2000).*

How do these considerations apply to the future for a broadly shared prosperity? If our economy is requiring an increasing supply of highly trained and skilled workers, does this mean that the skill requirements of all jobs will likewise increase? Also, what do these matters portend for Latinos, the group with the lowest levels of skills and education? Will the predicted mismatch between the educational requirements of new jobs in the future and our inadequate educational system create a relative surplus of workers with low or medium skill levels?

Some of the apparent differences between the projected supply and demand for highly educated workers comes from comparing the needs of jobs with the fastest growth rates to current levels of educational attainment. Even though many new jobs do require highly educated workers, the foreseeable future also includes a need for the services of relatively unskilled workers.

The report of the National Center on Education and the Economy (NCEE), *America's Choice: High Skills or Low Wages,* provides a very helpful complement to *Workforce 2000.* The fact that the new jobs created by economic growth and change generally do require higher educational levels, as *Workforce 2000* indicates, does not mean that the skill requirements for existing jobs are increasing.

The authors of *America's Choice* argue that unless skills improve dramatically, most new jobs will be like the large majority of existing jobs with low formal educational requirements and therefore give no indication of a demand for change. In this analysis, America's jobs are composed of three groups of roughly equal size. The first requires no more than eighth grade competency in math and language, the requisite physical ability to do the work, and an agreeable personality. Service workers, operatives, and laborers are examples of this group. The second group of jobs requires specialized training beyond basic literacy and numeracy, but not a four-year college degree. Many of the clerical and craft occupations are examples of these jobs. The third category encompasses occupations that require college degrees. The skill shortage identified in *America's Choice* consisted of interpersonal and higher-order thinking skills, reliability, communications ability, and the other work-related attitudes and manners.

Making Work Pay and Making Schools Work for Latinos

This essay earlier presented evidence that employment opportunities for Latinos with low skill and educational levels are diminishing. While the evidence is far from conclusive, this may indeed be true. However, even if it is, the weight of the arguments presented in *America's Choice* is that there are still many low-skilled jobs available. Common sense and casual observation indicate that this is true. The increases in unemployment discussed earlier may be temporary, but the decreases in real earnings have been unambiguously shown for much of the U.S. population, including Latinos. The first step in restoring broadly shared prosperity, particularly to Latinos, is to increase the wages paid to workers with low-skilled jobs. Setting the minimum wage at a level where it is also a living wage and keeping it there by indexing is a good place to start. While we can hope that Latinos will someday have the educational attainment and the proportion of very highly trained workers equal to that of any other group, these goals will never be achieved if the economic situation of Latinos now working at

low-paying jobs is made worse. The labor market floor must be stopped from sinking further. In addition to low pay, more than a third of Latinos and almost 40 percent of Latinos living below the poverty level do not have health insurance coverage.

A large proportion of jobs in the future will require workers with basic cognitive and work skills. One of the great problems with our educational system is its failure to provide high school graduates with an institutionalized connection to employers. One approach that is more consistent with the thinking presented in *America's Choice* is to make high school coursework more "relevant" to employers. Another key point of *America's Choice* is that education should be available over the life course. Instead of telling teenagers that they have to finish high school or never hold a job, the authors of *America's Choice* call for a flexible education structure that imparts basic workforce skills to all students at a very early age and would then permit every individual to tailor the combination of education and work experience that would meet their needs and abilities.

Conclusion

If every American were fully committed to restoring widespread prosperity and sharing that prosperity with Latinos, it would still be a very difficult goal to attain. However, we know that many people do not share that commitment. In fact, some large and effective factions active in American politics seem to be working to exclude Latinos from obtaining prosperity.

Recent initiatives, court cases and laws are likely to further restrict Latino rights with an evident vengeance. The first of these is California's Proposition 187, passed in 1994, which intends to deny government services to undocumented immigrants. While Proposition 187 was targeted at undocumented immigrants, there can be little doubt that its blunderbuss impact has hit Latino citizens and documented residents as well. It probably is no coincidence that Latino unemployment rose to equal that of African-Americans a few months after the ratification of Proposition 187.

California also has led the way in obstructing access to higher education for Latinos and other minorities. This occurred first in the decision of the University of California Regents to end their affirmative action programs, followed by the passage of Proposition 209, which ended affirmative action measures in all state institutions. The number of minority students in many higher education programs already has dropped drastically.

Again, California is home to almost a third of all Latinos in the United States; another quarter live in Texas, where the U.S. Fifth Circuit Court's Hopwood decision banning the consideration of race in higher education admissions and financial aid also has decimated minority enrollments. There are efforts under way to bring similar suits in all regions of the United States.

The end of affirmative action and continued discrimination would be bad news in any case. However, it is tragic in face of the fact that, even with the enhanced opportunities offered by affirmative action, even Latinos who have been in this country for many generations are not attaining educational, economic, or occupational parity with Anglos. Any movement to share prosperity with Latinos has to begin by countering these efforts that would relegate Latinos to the bottom of the economy and society.

Notes

1. Jennifer C. Day, *Population Projections of the United States by Age, Sex, Race and Hispanic Origin*, U.S. Bureau of the Census, Current Population Reports, Series P25–1130 (WDC: U.S. Government Printing Office, 1996), p. 1.

2. Johanne Boisjoly and Greg J. Duncan, "Job Losses Among Hispanics in the Recent Recesssion," *Monthly Labor Review,* June 1994, p. 16.

3. *San Antonio Light,* "A Thousand Lives" (Special Report), November 13, 1990, p. A1.

4. *San Antonio Light,* "A Thousand Lives" (Special Report), November 14, 1990, p. A3.

8

Crime and Prosperity: Neighborhood Explanations for Change in Crime Rates

William Spelman

Are there people really walking around saying there is no relationship between crime and unemployment? Are we beating a dead horse here? Is there a unanimous consensus on the subject or do we have something more to prove?

—Representative John Conyers

The absence of an impact of the unemployment rate on the rate of crime appears at this time to be unequivocal.

—James A. Fox, Professor of Criminology

It is just common sense that unemployment leads to crime. People unable or unwilling to make money in the legitimate economy turn to the illegitimate economy. If the legitimate economy falters—due to a downturn in the business cycle or to changing economic conditions—we should expect more people to turn to crime to make up the lost income. The notion is simple, plausible, and in keeping with most people's experience. But if one is to take the bulk of expert economic opinion at face value, it is also wrong.

Since the late 1960s, several dozen statistical studies have measured the effects of unemployment on crime. Most find no significant effect,

and most of those that do find it to be relatively small. As Richard Freeman put it,

> In studies that include measures of criminal sanctions and labor market factors, sanctions tend to have a greater impact on criminal behavior than do market factors. . . . [T]he "stick" looks relatively more important than the "carrot."[1]

Freeman is cautious, asserting that the jury is still out. Nevertheless, results like these have led many economists to argue that the mammoth rise in crime between 1960 and 1980 was due almost entirely to non-economic factors and that economic policy was not a useful tool for crime reduction. By default, the best way to stop crime was still to catch crooks.

A closer look at the research suggests that the consensus is premature, based on oversimplified criminological theories and inappropriate research designs. When a theory more in keeping with mainstream criminology is tested using a more appropriate design, the results are quite the opposite: Economic factors, particularly unemployment and poverty, emerge as the most important indicators of crime rates. Any attempt to reduce crime must thus come to terms with the economic conditions that create it.

Before turning to new analysis, let us first take a closer look at previous research and the theory that underlies it. In this case, small changes in theory and design may have a large effect on the findings and conclusions.

Previous Research

Most studies of the relationship between economic conditions and crime owe a debt to the pioneering work of Gary Becker, who first developed a coherent microeconomic theory in the late 1960s. Stripped of its mathematical details, the theory behind most such studies is simple. The decision to commit a crime is rational, in that it responds to two kinds of incentives.

- *Positive incentives* are measures of the opportunities available in the legitimate economy. These are usually measured by unemployment rates (the unlikelihood of successful participation in the economy) and prevailing wage rates (the benefits of success). Lower unemployment and higher wages should lead to less crime.
- *Negative incentives* are the costs of participating in the illegitimate economy. The usual measures are arrest and conviction rates (the likelihood that one will be punished for each crime committed) and average prison sentences (the severity of that punishment). Higher arrest rates and longer sentences should reduce crime.

Prospective criminals compare the positive and negative incentives and choose accordingly. The relative importance of carrot and stick is measured by the *elasticity,* the percentage change in crime rate associated with a one-percent change in positive and negative incentives. The conclusion that negative incentives dominate offenders' decisions is based on the finding that the elasticities of negative incentives (particularly arrest rates) are usually statistically significant and often large, while those of positive incentives are usually insignificant and small.

Like all microeconomic theories, the weakness of this one is its assumptions. The critical assumption here is that prospective offenders are free to make decisions to get a job, commit crimes, or both, depending on current conditions in the economic and criminal justice systems. Thus, changes in arrest or unemployment rates are reflected in more or less immediate changes in crime rates. The problem is that there appears to be substantial "stickiness" in offenders' decisions. Most crimes are committed by a relatively small percentage of especially frequent and dangerous offenders. They start committing crimes early in life, continue at a fairly constant rate for twenty years or more, and make most of their money in the illegitimate economy. Although virtually all are eventually caught, many are clever or experienced enough to avoid being arrested and punished as often as less-frequent but less-sophisticated criminals. Frequent offenders are more likely to deal drugs, consume a variety of different kinds of drugs, and commit violent acts than other criminals. They also appear to resist rehabilitation more than others. Although it may be a stretch to call such a record a "career," it seems unrealistic to expect that the activities of these offenders will be much swayed by short-term changes in incentives, positive or negative.

Even those less committed to a criminal lifestyle may find it difficult to respond to immediate incentives. Offenders justify their acts in ways that make further offenses easier to commit; ex-cons find it more difficult to get a legitimate job, even when more jobs are available; and fellow gang members and other criminal associates provide a constant source of temptation. Once started, criminal activity takes on a momentum of its own.

This is not to say that offenders do not respond to positive and negative incentives at all. It is very likely that they do. But the extent of the response is liable to be limited. On the other hand, it is certainly possible that, before becoming committed to an illegitimate lifestyle, youths considering criminal activity may respond considerably to positive and negative incentives. Here, the theory is somewhat different.

The neighborhood in which a young person grows up sets expectations and defines opportunity structures. If unemployment and poverty are high, a straight job may look to be a loser's game. Participation in the illegitimate economy can appear to be a reasonable alternative, and youths begin to explore crime. William J. Wilson quotes a 25-year-old Chicago man who says this about his neighbors:

> They try to find easier routes and had been conditioned over a period of time to just be lazy, so to speak. . . . They don't see nobody getting up early in the morning, going to work or going to school all the time. The guys they be with don't do that . . . because that's the crowd you choose—well, that's been presented to you by your neighborhood.[2]

Conversely, if neighborhood unemployment is low and prevailing wages are high, a youth may never seriously consider crime. In a sense, crime causes crime, as failure in the legitimate economy is passed down from generation to generation in an urban community.

When rational choice theories are recast in this way, they begin to resemble more traditional sociological theories such as differential opportunity, drift, and strain. They relocate the engine of crime and jobs from the macro-level of nation and state to the micro-level of social group and neighborhood. The reality of young people is what they see around them, and opportunities beyond their immediate experience may as well not exist. We would thus expect the primary effects of economic conditions to be found at the neighborhood level, not the city or metro area, and certainly not at the state or national level.

There is another, more prosaic reason for thinking the neighborhood to be more important than the state or nation. With very few exceptions, states and nations do not present unitary labor markets. A few people drive from one end of Los Angeles to another to get to work every day, but no one drives from LA to Sacramento. Although relatively few people live and work in the same urban neighborhood, the poor in particular find it difficult to take advantage of job opportunities far across town. Thus, even the city may be too big a unit to analyze.

These sociological and economic explanations all hold that crime results when people cannot get what they want through the legitimate economy. Another class of sociological explanations also is neighborhood-based, although at first blush not at all economic in orientation. These *control theories* hold that crime results form a failure of society to control the activities of would-be criminals. Especially important are informal social controls—that is:

> informal mechanisms by which residents themselves achieve public order. Examples of informal social control include the monitoring of spontaneous play groups among children, a willingness to intervene to prevent acts such as

truancy and street-corner "hanging" by teen-age peer groups, and the confrontation of persons who are exploiting or disturbing public space.[3]

When neighborhood controls are lacking, kids run rampant and grow up to become criminals—making it all the more difficult to maintain order in the future. Because some neighborhoods are more effective at applying informal controls than others, this should be an important cause of variations in neighborhood crime rates.

Clearly, a neighborhood's capacity to apply informal social control will be affected by social and economic factors. As Robert Sampson, Stephen Raudenbush, and Felton Earls stated in a recent influential study of Chicago:

> A high rate of residential mobility, especially in areas of decreasing population, fosters institutional disruption and weakened social controls over collective life. Perhaps more salient is the influence of racial and economic exclusion on perceived powerlessness. The alienation, exploitation, and dependency wrought by resource deprivation act as a centrifugal force that stymies collective efficacy. Even if personal ties are strong in areas of concentrated disadvantage, they may be weakly tethered to collective actions.[4]

Their hypothesis is borne out by empirical tests. Fully 70 percent of the variation in use of social control among 343 Chicago neighborhoods could be explained by social and economic factors, principally unemployment and poverty. And social control itself was an important factor in explaining neighborhood crime rates—somewhat more important than residential stability and immigration, somewhat less important than the direct effect of unemploy-

ment and poverty. Simply put, residents of low-unemployment and low-poverty neighborhoods enjoyed lower crime rates in part because they made it harder for their neighbors to commit crimes. Thus, there are at least two routes by which neighborhood-level unemployment and poverty increase crime rates—by motivating people and by making it more difficult to stop them.

Viewed in this context, the basis for economists' "consensus of doubt" looks shaky, indeed. Theodore Chiricos reviewed sixty-three studies of the relationship between positive incentives (usually unemployment rates) and crime. More than half (54 percent) were at the state, provincial, or national level. Only eight studies (13 percent) were at a level of aggregation less than the city. Thus, the vast majority of the statistical evidence on this relationship is taken from an inappropriate level of aggregation.

There is evidence from Chiricos that the level of aggregation matters. When studies of the relationship between unemployment and crime at all different levels of aggregation are examined, the probability is quite high for the eight neighborhood-level studies ($p = .68$), but drops quickly as the level of aggregation increases. For national-level studies, the probability was only .20. We may reasonably conclude that cross-sections between nations, or national time-series, are simply too far removed from the psychological and economic engines of crime causation to be of much use.

The eight neighborhood-level studies were all cross-sectional designs and thus suffer from the problems of all cross-sectional analyses: they provide only a snapshot of current conditions, so it is difficult to generalize the results over time; although they measure association, it is dangerous to infer causation; they are subject to considerable specification errors due to unmeasured (and perhaps unmeasurable) variables;

and finally, because they measure crime and social conditions at a low level of aggregation, there is much potential for errors in measurement due to random fluctuations.

One way to solve many of these problems is through use of cross-sectional/time-series, or *panel* designs of the kind used in the study reported in this essay. By measuring crime and its correlates in a particular place over several decades, we can reasonably expect a panel study to produce better resolution on the connection between unemployment and crime, a more robust specification that deals adequately with variables that have been left out of the analysis, and better generalizability over time. In the study described below, a panel of crime data is assembled for census tracts in Austin, Texas. In addition to creating results of theoretical interest, these data may help answer the question: Why did the crime rate double in Austin, Texas?

Data

Until the late 1960s, Austin, Texas, was a typical state capital. Home of the flagship campus of the University of Texas and America's largest state capitol building, Austin's economy was dominated by government and education. Then, in 1967, Tracor established a small factory. IBM and Texas Instruments quickly followed, and the high-tech boom was on. A bust came in the mid-1980s; manufacturing employment leveled off and construction employment fell 57 percent. Still, by 1990, Austin had recovered the lost employment and growth continued. Altogether between 1970 and 1990, Austin's population doubled. Manufacturing jobs went up 300 percent, and real income per capita (expressed in 1990 dollars) grew from $9,812 to $14,285, an increase of nearly 50 percent.

In the midst of such prosperity, Austin's crime rate doubled. Most crimes remained petty thefts and burglaries, and the violent crime rate was still among the lowest in the country. But the fact that the increase was primarily in property crimes appears to question any link between prosperity and crime reduction. For anyone interested in showing the link between economic conditions and crime, Austin appears to represent a worst-case scenario. If the neighborhood-based model works here, it is reasonable to suspect it would work anywhere.

To test this model, index crime and arrest data were collected, by census tract, for the census years 1970, 1980, and 1990. The study was restricted to census years for the practical reason that neighborhood-level data were simply not available for unemployment, income, labor force participation, and other variables for the intervening years.

Nevertheless, the lack of annual data limits our ability to test the theory. If in fact the major effect of social and economic factors is on the future behavior of children, not the current behavior of criminal offenders, then the immediate effects of changes in these factors may be relatively small. Thus, changing the minds of (say) twelve-year-olds will not affect crime much today (few pre-teens commit many crimes), but it may reduce crime considerably when these kids grow up. According to national figures, the peak ages for crime commission are between sixteen and eighteen years. Thus we might expect a lag of five years or so between changes in social and economic factors and resulting changes in crime rates. Because census data are only collected every ten years, we will not be able to use these data to test any delayed effects.

There are a variety of other flaws. For small areas such as census tracts, reported crime rates can change dramatically from year to year due

Table 8.1

Predictors of Neighborhood Crime Rates (in percent)

Variable	Minimum	Best guess	Maximum
Central Business District (CBD)	587.3	816.8	985.5
Unemployment/poverty index	29.3	35.3	44.1
Young adult (percent of population 20–24)	15.9	27.4	33.1
Over 65 (percent of population over 65)	17.3	23.2	29.3
Socioeconomic status index	−8.4	−22.4	−24.2
Arrest rate	−12.1	−20.5	−22.3
Labor force participation index	7.4	14.9	27.4
Youth dropout index	7.2	14.3	19.0

Note: Figures shown are *standardized regression coefficients.* That is, they represent the approximate effect of a one-standard-deviation change in each variable on the neighborhood crime rate, measured in percent. Exception: The figures for CBD show the extent to which crime rates are higher in the central business district than elsewhere in the city.

to random factors. The Census Bureau split some tracts in 1980 and split others in 1990; this makes it difficult to compare across neighborhoods directly. The practical effect of all these flaws turns out to be the same, however: The effects measured here are likely to be underestimates of the true effects of social and economic factors. Better data would produce effects that were larger and more statistically significant.

This analysis includes most variables that were collected in a consistent manner between the 1970 and 1990 censuses and were conceivably related to crime. They also include index crime and arrest rates, as reported to the Federal Bureau of Investigation by the Austin Police Department, and a variable representing the central business district, which includes both the downtown commercial area and the Sixth Street entertainment district.

A series of tests were applied to arrive at refined measures or diagnostics. Each of these diagnostics produced a range of effects for each of eight, basic predictor variables. Table 8.1 shows the minimum and maximum effect estimated for each variable, taken over all diagnostics, together with a "best guess" that represents

the median of all effects estimated. Each figure in the table is a *standardized regression coefficient;* that is, it represents the effect of a one-standard-deviation change in the predictor variable on the crime rate. Thus, our best guess is that a one-standard-deviation increase in the unemployment index for some neighborhood would cause the crime rate in that neighborhood to increase by 35.3 percent; the effect may be as low as 29.3 percent, or as high as 44.1 percent, however. For most variables, the minimum and maximum effects cover a fairly narrow band— evidence that the initial prediction was fairly robust. In addition, no other variables emerged as being consistently effective predictors.

In summary, the eight-variable working model works about equally well over a wide range of statistical assumptions. Further, it applies about equally well throughout the period studied and for all neighborhoods sampled. Let us now use this model to interpret changes in Austin crime rates over the 1970s and 1980s.

Interpretation. We can get a clue as to what happened over this period by simply looking at the relative size of the coefficients in Table 8.1. The central business district is obviously an anomaly: Very few people live downtown, but crime rates are high due to the large number of daytime and evening users. Thus, the high figures associated with the CBD are largely due to failure to effectively measure the denominator (that is, the number of people at risk of becoming victims downtown).

Aside from this, the biggest coefficients are on demographic variables (the number of young adults and older people) and economic variables (unemployment and socioeconomic status, or SES). As one would expect, the more young adults, the higher the crime rate (they are especially likely to be both victims and offenders); the more old people, the higher the crime rate (though less likely to be victimized, they are at greater risk per unit of exposure and are also less able to exercise control over local hoodlums). And, as the economic model developed above suggests, crime rates are highest in places and times where unemployment is high and SES low. The apparent effects of arrest rates, labor force participation, and teenage dropout are smaller, but in the expected direction.

Although all of these coefficients are interpretable and of reasonable magnitude, the variables that do not appear to be important may be even more interesting. One set of variables left on the cutting room floor measures the racial composition of the neighborhood. Previous studies have found that high concentrations of black residents, and to a lesser extent Hispanic residents and recent immigrants, are associated with higher crime rates. The usual explanation is that members of these groups have less access to education and good jobs than whites, and thus have fewer incentives to participate in the legitimate economy. Some have gone beyond these economic theories to posit subcultural theories: Poor neighborhoods that are also racially homogeneous develop subcultures that

support crime. My findings support the economic theories, not the subculture theories. Poor blacks and Hispanics appear to be no more and no less criminal than poor whites; middle-class blacks and Hispanics and middle-class whites commit crimes at the same (low) rates. Once economics has been controlled for, race appears to be irrelevant.

The effects shown in Table 8.1 apply about equally well for 1970, 1980, and 1990. The practical significance of this is that citywide (or larger) changes over time not captured by the other variables have little effect on crime rates. Some changes offered as explanations for crime rate increases include: the development of crack cocaine and increasing gang activity in the 1980s; the slow erosion in the length of the average prison sentence between 1970 and 1990 (since reversed with a vengeance); and the increasing portability of consumer electronics (making valuable items easier to steal). I had no need for any of these hypotheses. My results suggest that, had social and economic conditions and arrest rates been in 1970 what they were in 1990, the crime rate would have been just as high 20 years before.

Finally, my results provide no evidence as to why unemployment and poverty affect crime so much. Informal social control is more often exerted in middle-class, stable neighborhoods with low unemployment and poverty rates—exactly the same neighborhoods that provide the weakest economic motivations for potential criminality. Thus, it is impossible to tell whether unemployment and poverty cause crime primarily through the "carrot" of many criminal opportunities or the "stick" of few legitimate economic opportunities. The similarity of these results to those of the Chicago study suggest that carrot and stick may be about equally important, but a full test would require a sample survey (at least) to obtain information about mediating variables.

The results described above only measure the marginal effects of a change or difference, if it occurs. To estimate the relative importance of changing conditions—that is, to solve the original problem—we need to couple these results with evidence of what actually *did* change between 1970 and 1990.

The changes were dramatic: Austin became richer on average, poorer in places, more heavily industrialized, and so on. We can use the results described above to measure the marginal effect of each of these changes on the crime rate, while holding all other characteristics constant. That is, we can estimate the amount by which crime would have changed in each neighborhood, had the *only* differences between 1970 and 1990 been on each of the eight basic variables. We may then estimate citywide changes by averaging the effects over all neighborhoods, weighted by population.

The most obvious conclusion from my analysis is the overwhelming importance of general unemployment and poverty. Even if nothing else had changed, increases in these components alone would have driven crime rates up by 67 percent. This is reinforced by the relative importance of a closely related factor, young male unemployment and dropout rate. Taken together, these components—measuring opportunities in the legitimate economy, especially for high-risk individuals—account for the vast majority of the increase over the 1970s and 1980s. In fact, these two factors are more important than all the rest of the variables combined.

The 1970s and 1980s saw dramatic increases in Austin's industrial base and its general prosperity. Average real income per capita, housing values, and other indicators of prosperity also increased. Why, then, did unemployment and poverty increase as well? The explanation lies in the nature of the changing economy. In 1970, Austin's economy was dominated by state government and the University of Texas. Over the next two decades, high-tech manufacturing, software development, and back-office operations (telemarketing and customer support) moved in and became dominant. Although these are highly productive industries, they also require a workforce with high levels of education and training. New immigrants sought jobs, but many did not have the experience and education needed to compete. Neither did many long-term residents: Increases in unemployment and poverty were especially pronounced in traditionally poorer sections of town—the black and Hispanic neighborhoods of the East Side. Schools, colleges, and state and local governments reacted slowly to the shift and did little to prepare low-status residents for these changes. Thus, poverty and joblessness increased despite growing general prosperity.

The slow decline in arrest rates may well have been related. One (albeit rough) measure of police workload is average annual number of crimes per sworn officer; the higher the figure, the less time each officer has, on average, to spend per crime reported. In 1970, forty-seven crimes were reported per sworn officer; by 1990, this figure had climbed to seventy-one crimes per officer. This suggests that police spent less time on follow-up investigations in 1990 than in 1970. Perhaps more important, they also had less time to spend on drug enforcement, order maintenance, and "soft crimes" such as panhandling, minor fights, and traffic violations. In fact, the number of arrests made for these offenses actually *declined* from 1970 to 1990. These activities may be even more important deterrents to crime than arrests for index crimes. Simply put, the police department could not keep up with growth, particularly given concomitant increases in unemployment, poverty, and associated criminal activity.

Other social changes were relatively unimportant. The age distribution and labor force participation may be important indicators of crime in a neighborhood, but they did not change much on a citywide basis over the twenty-year period. What changes there were tended to increase the crime rate: There were a few more young adults, more older people, more working mothers. But these effects were not large.

Finally, these effects were offset somewhat by citywide increases in the wealth and status of the average resident. Increases in educational opportunity, occupational status, real income, and wealth tended, all else equal, to reduce crime rates. Had the city been able to achieve these gains without also increasing unemployment and poverty, crime rates might in fact have gone down. Unfortunately, the increase in unemployment and poverty was far greater than the increase in average status, with a higher crime rate the apparent result.

Conclusions

At least in Austin, Texas, during the 1970s and 1980s, changes in local economic conditions appeared to have a far greater impact on crime rates than changes in the criminal justice system or other social conditions. Where crime is concerned, it *is* the economy.

This has clear implications for local economic development policy. Growth in primary industries may bring jobs and wealth, but if it also leaves some citizens behind—and particularly if these citizens are concentrated in underclass neighborhoods—increased crime will be an unfortunate side effect. As my results show, wealth reduces crime, but not so much as poverty and joblessness increase it. From the viewpoint of crime reduction, our aim should be to provide full employment, especially for young men, not merely to attract and grow the most lucrative businesses.

Job training programs were relatively undeveloped throughout this period, so it is impossible to tell whether improvements in the extent and availability of these programs would have reversed these trends. And it may be that, even today, a city can maintain a low crime rate by attracting and growing relatively low-tech industries that require little education and specialized training of its workforce.

Nevertheless, Austin, like most cities, has little choice in the long run. The fastest-growing and most productive industries are those that put the greatest intellectual demands on their workers. Improving workers' ability to meet these demands is not just a sound development strategy; it may prevent leaving behind an underclass and a crime problem that could inhibit growth for years to come.

Notes

1. Richard Freeman, "Crime and Unemployment," in *Crime and Public Policy,* ed. James Q. Wilson (San Francisco: ICS Press, 1983), p. 106.

2. William J. Wilson, "When Work Disappears," *New York Times Magazine* (August 18, 1996): 30.

3. Robert J. Sampson, Stephen Raudenbush, and Felton Earls, "Neighborhoods and Violent Crime: A Multilevel Study of Collective Efficacy," *Science* 277 (1997): 918.

4. Ibid., p. 919.

9

Closing the Gap: Women's Economic Progress and Future Prospects

Heidi Hartmann

Introduction

This essay reviews several areas of economic life in which women have made substantial progress in recent decades, assesses their prospects for future success, and recommends policies to help further close the economic gap between women and men. Closing that gap would ensure the more equitable sharing of economic prosperity. The areas of progress include the increase in women's labor force participation, the growth in women's earnings relative to men's, the gain in women's education, the broader range of occupations and jobs open to women, and the increasingly shared financial responsibility for families.

One of the most interesting aspects of women's economic progress is that it generally continued beyond 1973, the year men's earnings peaked. Since 1990, median earnings have fallen slightly in real terms for all women working full-time, year-round, but whether this reflects the recession or a new trend toward stagnation in women's earnings is not clear. The narrowing of the wage gap between women and men resulted both from the fall in men's real earnings and the steady rise in women's real earnings.

Several other negative labor markets trends either did not affect women or affected them less severely. For example, between 1975 and 1985 when the proportion of male workers in unions declined sharply, the decline in union density for women workers was less sharp. The number of women union members has been increasing steadily since at least 1955, while among men the number has fallen since 1975, so that now women's share of all union members at 37 percent is the largest ever. And while contingent work is difficult to measure, a recent Institute for Women's Policy Research (IWPR) study shows that between 1987 and 1990 the share of women working in contingent jobs fell slightly while the share of men working in such jobs grew slightly. While the "degradation of work" may be growing and spreading, women's share of degraded work seems to be falling.

What accounts for this difference of experience between women and men in the labor market? One very important factor is human capital accumulation. Since women are newcomers to the labor market (with women's labor force participation increasing most rapidly in the decade of the 1970s), as women began to stay in the labor market longer, their average experience increased more than did men's. Also, during the 1970s and 1980s, women's rate of college graduation began to catch up with men's (finally overcoming the advantages in that regard that the GI Bill gave men). By 1984, more women than men were obtaining bachelor's degrees, and by 1986, more were obtaining master's degrees. Women committed more of their time to the labor market and prepared themselves for their participation by investing in training and education.

Another important factor has been the differential impact of economic growth on women and men. Growth in services, health care, education, and white-collar work of all kinds tended to favor those areas of the economy in which women were disproportionately located (while the decline in manufacturing affected more men than women). The skills that women workers have developed in these economic sectors are likely to stand them in good stead in terms of future economic growth as well. Through their domination of "office work" and work that involves personal contact, many women workers have access to and experience with the new information and communications technologies, and they understand the customer and work relations required in a more customized and less mass produced work process. To the extent that new job growth may be in "high-tech, high-touch" jobs, women may well have an advantage relative to men.

Third, there is no question that a cultural revolution of profound proportions has occurred for America's women. The virtuous circle of prosperity and economic growth of the 1950s and 1960s assigned many women to full-time work in the home and to family care and community service. While poor and working-class women, immigrant women, and women of color have always worked to support themselves and their families, even sometimes after marriage and child bearing, most wives and mothers did not work for pay outside the home. By 1977, the revolution in women's labor force

behavior had occurred: more mothers participated in the labor force than stayed at home caring for their children. The change in women's economic behavior, their commitment to a life-pattern of work not unlike men's, now seems irreversible. Women's drive to full participation and citizenship requires them to participate equally in the economy, to end their dependence on men for their economic survival, and to shoulder an equal share of the financial burden of self and family support. As women take on more roles outside the home, men must take on more inside the home, sharing more of the responsibility for the personal care of family members. Moreover, many long-standing institutions and policies, both public and private, must adjust to take into account the new fact of life in the United States—that virtually all adults today both work and nurture and their needs to do both must be accommodated.

Let us not forget, though, that the revolution in women's status is not complete. Women have not yet reached economic parity with men. With median earnings for full-time, year-round work by women at about 70 percent of men's median earnings, women still have a long way to go. Moreover, politically women are, if anything, even further behind, holding only about 10 percent of the seats in the U.S. Congress and only two governorships of the fifty states. Sharing prosperity more broadly clearly requires the completion of the revolution and the granting to women of full citizenship, both economically and politically. And it requires a revolution in our institutions which is only just beginning.

Women Are Closing the Labor Force Participation Gap

Women are entering the labor market in greater numbers, and in a sense, as economic actors, women are becoming more like men. The historic growth in women's labor force participation has occurred in three ways. First, each new cohort (age group) has worked more than the one before. Second, each cohort has generally worked more as they have aged (until reaching retirement age). And, third, each cohort has worked more steadily during the child-rearing years, spending less time out of the labor force when they have children. There is now no dip at all in average labor force participation rates for women in their twenties and thirties. Simultaneously, men's labor force participation has been falling, at almost every age. Today, women constitute 46 percent of the labor force and are expected to reach 50 percent, or even more, over the next decade or two.

Because so much of the change is driven by family preferences, it is likely to continue. Although much is written about the time pressures on everyone, especially on working parents, many of these parents could work less in exchange for a lower standard of living, one more comparable to that achieved in the 1950s and 1960s, but they do not make that choice. The size of the average home continues to grow, despite falling family size, and it contains many more consumer goods than it did decades ago. And more money is spent on leisure-time activities; in a sense even our leisure time is becoming more productive as it is combined with more and more purchased goods and services.

In particular, the notion that women have mainly been forced to work by men's falling real wages is wrong. Women's rising real wages are likely to have been much more important in pulling them into the labor market. Moreover, their rising education levels are also likely to continue to lead them into the labor market. And finally, the cultural transformation in women's life expectations leads them to want

to increase their control over their own economic destinies. Women will not easily give this up, even when men's economic prospects improve, as surely we all hope they will do.

Women Are Narrowing the Earnings Gap

When women are asked, in survey after survey, what they want, most women respond: "pay equity," "better wages," or "more money." In a 1994 survey by the Women's Bureau, women at every occupational level report that they believe they are not getting paid what they are worth. And this is so despite the fact that the pay gap between women and men has narrowed significantly in recent decades.

In the late 1960s and early 1970s, women earned 59 percent of what men earned (comparing the median earnings of men and women who worked full-time all year). Women now earn about 71 percent of what men earn. That is a significant change, though many would argue it is too little, too late—or at least too little, too slow. As mentioned above, part of the reason for the narrowing of the gap is that things have been getting worse for men. Men's real earnings (in 1994 dollars) have been gradually falling since the early 1970s, while women's earnings have continued to rise fairly steadily. According to IWPR calculations, nearly three-quarters of the narrowing of the gap since 1979 is due to the fall in men's real earnings.

Yet, despite the negative wage trend for men, they still out-earn women (on average) at every age. In fact, the wage gap grows as women and men age. The gap is relatively small for young women and men, but thereafter men's wages increase sharply while women's do not. The average woman in her working prime, that is, in her early forties, makes only about the same as a man in his late twenties.

Although the gap remains large and worsens for women as they age, the wage gap is likely to continue to close over time. Just how much, and how fast is the important question. In the past several years, there appears to have been less progress in narrowing the gap than during the 1980s. While it is too soon to confirm a trend, this tendency toward stagnation is troubling.

The factors that will affect the rate of closure include:

• *Resumed Real Wage Growth for Men.* Men's real wages are likely to begin to grow again, because U.S. productivity is growing at an improved rate. Obviously, it will be beneficial if they do increase, but if so, women's real wages will have to increase even faster than they have been in order for the wage gap to continue to narrow. Women's real wage growth should, like men's, get a boost from increased productivity growth, but women work disproportionately in low-productivity service sectors.

• *Growing Inequality.* In general, less-well-educated workers at the bottom have been doing less well than those higher up. Earnings of women of color still lag behind those of white women, and in recent years, the gap has stopped closing and has even widened a bit, perhaps also because of reduced returns to those at, and near, the bottom. Since more women than men are clustered at the bottom of the wage scale, the continuing growth of inequality between the bottom and the top may affect women more than men, contributing to a tendency to widen the female/male wage gap, rather than narrow it. The failure of the federal minimum wage to keep up with inflation contributes to this growing inequality, as does the falling share of unionized workers in the labor force as a whole.

• *Uneven Economic Growth.* The wage gap is affected by the job sectors in which growth occurs. In the past few decades, women have benefited from high growth in areas in which they were already working—health, education, and clerical work, for example; many of these areas employed women at relatively high wage levels. High rates of growth are no longer expected to continue uniformly in all these areas. And government cutbacks are likely to affect women's employment disproportionately, especially in the professions and management, since a high proportion of women professionals and managers work in the public sector.

• *The Changing Nature of Jobs.* Contingent work, work that does not entail a stable relationship with an employer, has been growing, reducing opportunities for job security and advancement. Women hold a disproportionate share of temporary jobs, part-time jobs, and, most likely, other harder-to-measure forms of contingent work, such as contract work or direct-hire temporary jobs (temporary jobs not filled by temporary help services firms). While at least some measures suggest that women's share of these jobs may be falling, their share remains higher than men's. To the extent women work in these kinds of jobs, women's wages overall will be held down, since these jobs tend to pay less than regular full-time work. And women, more frequently than men, currently hold two or more part-time jobs in an effort to obtain full-time employment. Approximately 9 percent of women workers simultaneously held more than one wage or salary job compared to only 7 percent of male workers. Since 1970, women's employment as a whole has doubled, but women's multiple job-holding has increased sixfold.

• *Government Enforcement.* The size of the gap will also depend on government action in enforcing equal employment opportunity and affirmative action. Research done by the National Research Council/National Academy of Sciences, as well as by the Institute for Women's Policy Research has shown that these programs do work when enforced; they benefit both white women and women of color (as well as men of color). Cutbacks in budgets for the government enforcement agencies that occurred in the 1980s have not yet been fully restored.

Women Are Closing the Education Gap

Despite the mixed future suggested by these factors, however, one trend that is likely to continue to benefit women's wages is women's increasing educational attainment. Young women today are earning more than half the bachelor's and master's degrees, and about 40 percent of the Ph.D. degrees each year (as of 1992). Women are increasingly pursuing fields more like those of men, earning degrees in business, law, medicine, and computer science. In 1992, women earned 36 percent of medical degrees and 43 percent of law degrees. Despite greater similarity in women's and men's courses of study, however, there is still room for improvement in several areas. Fewer than 10 percent of engineering Ph.D. recipients in 1992 were women, and psychology is the only broad science field in which women receive the majority of doctorates. Also, minority women still comprised only 5 percent of Ph.D. degrees earned by U.S. citizens in 1992.

As we have seen, women's earnings have been growing much faster than men's since 1975, and a large part of that growth is due to their rapid accumulation of human capital, both in the form of formal education and in labor market experience. However, despite women's recent catch-up in college graduation rates, statistics on the stock (rather than the annual flow) of college graduates in the adult population reveals that women still lag behind men in college education; the catch-up in the stock occurs more gradually. Substantially more adult men than women have college degrees. Women still have some distance to go before their educational attainment equals that of men. As the catch-up, both in education and in life-time labor force participation, continues, women's wages should continue to gain on men's.

Like government enforcement of and government assistance with equal opportunity in employment, government assistance with equal opportunity in education is necessary to women's continued educational achievement. Any reductions in grants and loans could seriously handicap women as they attempt to continue to close the education gap.

Whatever the difficulty, women are likely to continue to improve their educational status. Women are the ideal workers for the new economy, those who are constantly retraining and upgrading their skills. A U.S. Department of Education study based on a longitudinal survey of the high school class of 1979 found that more women than men took post-secondary courses while working. Women's actions seem to suggest that they understand the new economy will be increasingly based on skills. What you know and how you learn may become more important in advancing economically than who you know.

Women Are Closing the Jobs Gap

The types of jobs that women hold are now more similar to those men hold. Women have been entering the professions and management jobs especially rapidly and have reached the point at which their representation in these occupational groups approximately matches their representation in the labor force as a whole. In 1993, women held 47.8 percent of all professional and managerial jobs. Some examples: from 1983 to 1993 they increased their proportion of personnel and labor relations managers from 44 percent to 61 percent and their proportion of financial managers from 39 to 46 percent. The health and medicine managerial occupations increased from 57 percent female to 71 percent female in this period.

However, women's and men's job patterns are still not substantially equal. Considerable sex segregation remains. In 1993, women made up only 23 percent of the law occupation and only 8.6 percent (a 0.5 percentage point increase from 1983) of the precision, craft, and repair occupations. And they experienced a decline in their representation as machine operators, assemblers, and inspectors (from 42 percent in 1983 down to 39 percent in 1993). Women are still overrepresented in women's jobs, despite the general improvement that has occurred. One measure of overall change is the index of sex segregation, which represents the proportion of women (or men) who would have to change occupations in order for women and men to be distributed equally across all occupations. According to Barbara Reskin, the index has fallen from 67.6 in 1970 to 57 in 1990—reflecting both considerable improvement and substantial room for further improvement. Since the higher the proportion of women, the lower the pay, other things equal, reducing segregation is an important strategy for closing the pay gap between women and men.

Women are also beginning to close the "entrepreneurship" gap; women's self-employment has nearly tripled since 1970 and women start about twice as many new businesses as men. Nevertheless, women are still underrepresented in self-employment and business ownership and their businesses are much smaller than men's. IWPR research also shows that among the self-employed, women earn about 63 percent less per hour than do men. Thus, the earnings gap is even larger here than in wage and salary work.

What about the future of the jobs gap? Both high-tech and high-touch jobs are expected to grow more rapidly than total employment. The fastest-growing jobs include the following high-touch jobs traditionally dominated by women:

- personal and home care aides;
- home health aides;
- physical therapy assistants and aides;
- occupational therapy assistants and aides;
- human service workers;
- teacher aides and educational assistants.

Rapid job growth is also predicted in the following high-tech jobs, most of which are not typically held by women:

- systems analysts;
- computer engineers;
- medical records technicians;
- operations research analysts
- data processing and equipment repairers;
- sales workers in securities and financial services.

Combining some of the characteristics of both high-tech and high-touch types of jobs are several additional occupations that are expected to have high job growth: paralegals, medical assistants, surgical technologists, and dental hygienists. All of these occupations—high-tech, high-touch, or some of both—are expected to grow by 40 percent or more by the year 2005, compared with only 14 percent for the overall labor force.

The occupations that are expected to add the

largest number of jobs, include several disproportionately held by women: cashiers, janitors and cleaners including maids, retail sales workers, waitpersons, registered nurses, and nursing aides, orderlies, and attendants. Each of these occupations is expected to grow by 400,000 to 600,000 jobs by 2005.

Thus, many of the new jobs that will be available to women are those in which women already predominate and many also are among the lower-paying jobs (e.g., home health aide, personal and home care aide, cashier, and maid). It will be difficult to reduce the concentration of women at the bottom of the labor market if the bottom experiences most of the job growth. And if 2 million more women with lower skills enter the job market from the welfare rolls, there likely will be further downward wage pressure on already low-wage jobs. If the public sector continues to be cut back and employment growth in education, health, and management slows, many of the labor market sectors that provided excellent job growth at good wages to women in the past will shrink in relative importance.

Barring a recession, there will be plenty of new opportunities for women, but many will not be especially well paying. And, since integrating jobs, with or without government help, is far easier when employment is growing, it is clear that women in particular are dependent on the success of a "high-road" approach to United States economic growth, an approach that seeks to ensure that well-paid jobs will be created as the United States successfully competes with other nations in the production, design, or marketing of goods and services with high value added.

Closing the Family Gap?

One of the areas more resistant to change than labor markets is family work, and women's continued disproportionate share of responsibility for family care affects their ability to participate in the labor market on equal terms with men. Clearly, women do not have the same relationship to families as men, but in several ways their relationship *is* becoming more similar, although important differences remain. Women in particular, have been taking on greater financial responsibility for families. Dual-earner couples, in which both parents work for wages, have grown from about one-third of families with children in 1975 to nearly half in 1994. The proportion of families with only working mothers (no working fathers) in the family has nearly doubled from about one-tenth to nearly one-fifth. Women are more likely to be breadwinners than ever before—they are now just about as likely as men (about seven out of ten) to be working to support children at home. Women are not, however, equally likely to have a "wife" at home to take care of daily family life. Twenty percent of families with children have a father working outside the home and a mother at home, whereas only a very few of the 19 percent of families with working mothers (in single-earner families) include a husband at home. Most of the latter families are headed by mothers alone; only about 3 percent of all families with children are headed by an unmarried working father, so that men are much, much less likely than women to experience the difficulties of single parenthood.

Women have closed the gap of family provider; what needs to be done is for men to close the gap of family nurturer. Men are able to have a family and a career, and in this realm, some progress has been made; not only have men been increasing, slightly, their time spent on housework, women have been spending less time on housework—for several reasons. First, when women work outside the home they simply spend less time working inside the home (teenage children are apparently doing more and more and families are using child care providers). Second, women have reduced family care time by having fewer children and having them closer together. Third, men are spending more time on a few of the domestic chores, especially child care, cooking, and shopping.

What does the future hold for the family gap? Clearly the underlying demographic and economic trends toward women's greater financial responsibility for families will continue. The birth rate is likely to continue its historic decline (although short-term increases will also likely occur from time to time), and the proportion of families headed by single parents is likely to continue to rise. Since women's labor force participation is likely to continue to approach parity with men, more and more families will have two earning parents: The proportion of so-called traditional families, distinctly in the minority now, will become even more of a minority, and men probably will continue to close the family nurturing gap.

The most important issue for the families of the future is how much help they will get from social institutions—schools, churches, governments at all levels, and corporations—in supporting the decisions adults make about how to spend their time. While some of the "overwork" by adults results from the failure of our institutions to adjust and support the new family forms, given the present institutional arrangements, families are no doubt making the choices that make the most sense to them. They clearly choose "overwork" rather than "underwork."

Since women appear to be happy with the economic control they have gained over their lives, if men's real wages started rising rapidly, we would not see a rapid return of women to the home. Provided women's real wages also continue to rise, women are likely to continue to their commitment to the labor market, and the pressure to change our institutions to accommodate families' choices will continue to grow.

Women and Poverty

The other side of the coin of increasing economic autonomy for women is the disproportionate share of poverty borne by female single parents. During the 1960s and early 1970s, poverty among families with children decreased. This was also true of single-mother families, whose poverty rate fell from 60 percent in 1959 to 40 percent in 1979 (the year with the lowest rate). In the 1980s and 1990s, poverty increased for most groups, with poverty rates worsening in recession years and never fully recovering to their earlier lows. Generally, poverty rates have continued to decline only in the elderly. In 1994, 44 percent of all single-mother families and 22 percent of all children (1993 data) had incomes below the poverty line. Even though these poverty rates do not take into account the value of non-cash benefits such as food stamps, which help many families rise above the official poverty threshold, such large and growing numbers are very troubling.

Several reasons for the poverty of single-mother families provide some insight as to how poverty can be reduced. First, women earn less than men, so even with the same family composition, women would be poor more often than men. Second, women generally do not abandon their children; thus, a single mother has not only herself to support but her children. Third, the fathers of the children do not contribute much to them financially: child support awards are spotty at best and collections are even more dismal. In addition, these mothers' single status and their low pay make it difficult for them to work full-time or to earn enough to cover the costs of working. While one approach to reducing poverty lies in reducing the numbers of such families, other approaches could focus on increasing women's wages, improving the structure of low-wage labor markets, providing greater cash and non-cash supports to working parents (such as publicly subsidized child care), and increasing child support awards and collections. Most of these policies, while they would be especially useful to single mothers, would also benefit most working parents.

Reducing the numbers of single-mother families involves either preventing the birth of a child to an unmarried woman or encouraging the marriage of the mother. Birth rates among teenage women has fallen substantially since 1960. There has been a small increase in infertility among young women since 1985. While birth rates are generally down, more of these births are to young unwed women. Among women 15 to 19 years old, non-marital births outnumbered marital births 2 to 1. However, the demise of the "shotgun" marriage is not necessarily a bad thing either for the young mothers or their children; rather it represents the greater range of choice available to young women. Indeed, not entering into a marriage actually makes it more likely that these young women will complete high school. Given that surviving in today's labor market requires more education than heretofore, early marriage, with its attendant responsibilities, should be avoided by both women and men. Early childbearing is undoubtedly harmful to the prospects of many young women, and their children, and so should also be discouraged. Making better access to birth control, including abortion, a priority is probably the single most effective policy for reducing early childbearing.

Non-marriage itself, and childbearing outside marriage, is a growing social trend affecting all adult women, not just young women, at all income levels, and in many countries around the world. It is a trend that is associated with the greater choices women have to support themselves outside marriage. And, a contributing reason for the greater share of all births to non-married women is the reduced birth rate among married women. In 1970, about half of non-marital births were to teenagers, but now teenagers account for fewer than one-third of all non-marital births. Increasing birth rates among married women, one "solution" to the problem of the rising number of births outside marriage, may be difficult unless men adjust their behavior and take on more family nurturing responsibilities.

A key solution to these problems is to adjust public policies to new realities, and key among these is tax policy. The tax burden on low-income working couples is very high—double taxation in the Social Security system for working couples (with virtually no extra benefits compared to the couple with only one working adult) is an especially severe problem for low earners. The lack of refundable tax credits for child care expenses, and their small size, also makes working less rewarding. High taxes for working married couples, coupled with high rates of benefit loss as incomes rise, make marriage an unattractive option for the working poor.

Are We Closing the Policy Gap?

In view of the progress women have made and our knowledge of likely future sources of economic and other change, what public policies are needed most to ensure that the new lifestyle choices are supported, not distorted by outdated public policies? Our most difficult problem is that we continue to base public policies on the "traditional" model of a male worker with a wife at home.

The federal income tax system, for example, does more for the family with a male breadwinner and an at-home wife, despite public opinion to the contrary. When a working wife earns about the same as a working husband, the tax penalty on marriage itself is fairly high (it can be several thousand dollars per year), so that the couple would be, tax-wise, better off unmarried. Under Social Security, married women who have worked all their lives and contributed taxes to the system often receive no more in retirement benefits than wives who never worked outside the home. Unemployment insurance benefits are more generous for those workers who are "fully committed" to the labor force, generally defined as working full-time. Recent IWPR research shows that many part-time workers and those with inconsistent labor force attachment or low earnings tend to be excluded by earnings tests, which measure not only the level of earnings, but also the accumulated annual amount of earnings. In addition, family-related reasons for leaving work are generally not considered valid and eligibility is often denied in such cases. Thus, women workers are more likely to be excluded from receiving unemployment insurance benefits.

Many public policies need to be reformed in order to spread the benefits of public programs more equitably across genders and family types. But the way the market operates must be changed as well if women are to share equally in the benefits of work. Despite many advances, women are still largely confined to the lower-paying occupations; such negative incentives likely reduce investments in human capital and in work. Women's lower wages translate into a life-time loss of several hundred thousands of dollars, a significant loss of income to families. Because of biases in wage setting and women's occupations, comparable worth could remedy this form of wage discrimination and pay equity policy is essential but not sufficient to raise women's wages. An IWPR study of pay equity adjustments in state civil services shows that pay can be raised in women's jobs without major disemployment effects and that the male-female pay gap is narrowed by such measures.

Other ways to improve women's wages include raising the national minimum wage and increasing union representation among women workers. Our research at IWPR shows, for example, that unions tend to raise women's wages more than men's, other things being equal. And two-thirds of minimum-wage workers are women; raising the minimum wage, and thereafter keeping it in line with inflation, will help women disproportionately.

If women's needs are placed more at the center of analysis, rather than ignored or subsumed as they frequently are, public policies based more on the model of a typical woman's life cycle would be developed. The United States should have dependent care policies that accord with women's growing participation in the workforce. Universally available, publicly funded child care, like that in other advanced industrial countries, should be a priority in the United States. Much as we try to encourage businesses to participate in providing child care, giving children a good start in life through organized child care is a public function and should be publicly subsidized if not publicly provided. Investing in our children is simply good public policy. Paid family-care leaves would also be of great benefit to workers, women and men who are raising children or have elderly parents to care for. IWPR research shows that a new temporary disability insurance system, much like those in five states, could also provide partial wage replacement for family care as well as sickness and disability (as they do now) for about the same cost as the current unemployment insurance system. These policies, while universal, would help low-income families disproportionately.

Shorter working days is a policy initiative that is less discussed but is just as central to enabling workers to cope with their personal lives and family needs. For example, a six-hour working day for employees would contribute enormously to the quality of life as it would relieve the family time squeeze and contribute to gender equality in the home and workplace. The standard workday has not been reduced since the 1938 Fair Labor Standards Act set the work week at forty hours and the standard day at eight hours. One way for workers to share in future productivity growth, in addition to or in lieu of future wage increases, is to reduce working hours (but not total pay). This option is now being seriously considered in other countries and deserves greater consideration here. The leisure time to enjoy the standard of living that a high-value-added economic growth strategy can produce should be a priority.

The policies discussed here—tax reform, pay equity, public provision of child care, paid family care leave, and a shorter working day— are integral to the task of restoring a more broadly shared prosperity. We have a tremendous opportunity now to lead, to point to the real problems and offer real solutions that take into account the needs of all adults as workers and nurturers and of dependent family members as well.

Part II

Forces for Change: Technology, Globalization, and Demographics

10

The Workplace Implications of Global Technological Advance

Robert M. White and Richard H. White

The technological changes shaping U.S. institutions and their workforce portray a workplace situation that is either calamitously poor or rosily encouraging. The conflicting evidence is inherent in the dynamics of an evolving transnational technological and economic system that is increasingly borderless. This system underlies and motivates the allocation and reallocation of productive resources worldwide through a tightly woven fabric of global interdependencies among national and multinational enterprises. We review the causes and consequences and suggest some actions that might ameliorate adverse effects.

The Confluence of Technological Advance and Economic Globalization

The power of technological advance and global economic integration to change social conditions is hardly a new topic. However, for the first time in our 220-year history these events appear threatening to growing segments of the U.S. population. Present concerns about the plight of U.S. institutions and the workforce in the 1990s are reminiscent of those that received attention in Europe and America around the turn of the twentieth century. During that period technological changes already had allowed private enterprises and government to extend their collective reaches within and across borders. Alfred Chandler pointed out that, "Well before 1914 a number of American firms were operating fully integrated foreign subsidiaries. . . . By 1914 American direct foreign investment was impressive [and] amounted to a sum equal to 7 percent of the United States' gross national product."[1]

In nations with democratic traditions, the political system empowered people to seek remedies for social and economic imbalances. Child labor laws, antitrust statutes, and other socially conscious legislation were enacted to restrain the more pernicious attributes of economic systems driven by rapid cycles of innovation. In retrospect, the period from 1914 to 1989, with its hot and cold world wars, might be considered as one of painful global adjustment to accelerating technological advance.

Technology as Driving Force

The economic and social changes fostered by global technological developments in information and telecommunications combined with parallel developments in fields such as space, energy, materials, and biotechnology have been profound. Almost every technological advance opens new horizons. The Global Positioning System of earth orbiting satellites, first developed for military purposes, combined with new wireless communication systems, now permits wholly new kinds of applications for a wide range of purposes. Automated, precision farming becomes possible. Transportation systems change as automated navigation of automobiles and other vehicles opens up the possibility of "smart" highways. Health care is radically transformed as it becomes possible to diagnose illnesses and provide advice remotely and as the application of molecular biology to genetic engineering transforms the understanding and treatment of disease. Precise monitoring of environmental conditions is a reality as changes in sensor technology are wedded to new information-processing systems.

Humanity's adjustments to technological advances over long periods of time result in social and economic transformations on a grand scale. And, as now, when fundamental new technologies are unfolding across the entire frontier of scientific and engineering research, major social and economic upheavals are occurring. For a half-century, economists and technologists have sought to understand the relationships between technological innovation and the economy. Much has been learned, but there is still no comprehensive, workable economic theory for forecasting the impacts of technological change on the economy or focusing private or public investments.

In spite of such ambiguity, the notion that technological advance has broad societal and economic implications is universally accepted. There is general agreement that the impacts are positive over the long term, but leave in their wake winners and losers. In particular, today more than in the past, there are growing disparities between the local and global effects of tech-

nological change. Locally, technological change affects individuals personally in the products they buy, the services they use, the games they play, the work they do, and the careers they pursue. Globally, the ultimate winners and losers from technological advances are scattered worldwide.

Effects on Employment

Technological changes are perceived by most people through such daily events as new models of autos, televisions, telephones, and computers as well as improved medical treatments. For the most part, these advances are embraced as enhancing the quality of life. The unanticipated side effects of technological change, such as environmental pollution, have until recently been grudgingly accepted as part of the price of the benefits. But the most palpable of all effects of technological advance is on jobs.

Workforce trends are characterized in many ways, but wage and productivity disparities, discussed elsewhere in this volume, deserve heightened attention, as do widespread displacements of workers from technological and economic changes.

It is easy to gain the impression from highly publicized downsizing and economic disruption that technological advance and employment are antithetical. The race between job creation and displacement from technological advance has always been close, but from a historical perspective, technology has been a net job creator. A classical example has been the technological transformation of U.S. agricultural practices. The technologically driven productivity of U.S. agriculture enabled the 30 percent of the workforce on farms at the turn of the century to be reduced to 3 percent of the workforce on farms today. That displaced workforce, with considerable disruption and pain, became employed in manufacturing and service industries as new technology created new enterprises and services. The process continues today, but the circumstances are fundamentally altered because of economic globalization and the fact that technological advance in one country frequently results in job creation in another as advances are quickly exploited.

The continued creation of jobs depends on the formation and expansion of new industries or new markets, usually both. Technological changes have created them. The software industry hardly existed twenty-five years ago. In 1993, it provided employment for 435,000 workers. By 1993, it was a $32 billion industry. This story is repeated endlessly. Since 1985, new and growing corporations have increased their workforces. MCI has grown from 12,445 employees, to 47,500 today. Sprint has increased its workforce from 27,415 workers to 51,500. According to the FCC, cable operators and television companies increased their workforces from 23,538 in 1978 to 112,239 in 1997. The cellular telephone industry, since its inception in the 1980s, employs 300,000 workers, directly and indirectly, according to the Cellular Telecommunications Industry Association. The biotechnology industry, capitalizing on the scientific discoveries in molecular biology, can expect a world market for its products to grow from $5.7 billion in 1992 to almost $94 billion in the year 2000.

What this mixed employment message shows is that social dislocation is a natural result of technological advance. The post–World War II U.S. experience confirms that such change need not lead to net employment loss, and the growth of new firms demonstrates the constructive effects of technological innovation in the marketplace. In all, according to the Bureau of Labor Statistics, from 1991 to 1996, net U.S. job growth has been 11.2 million, largely in services, with a large percentage of these of the high-skill, high-wage variety.

The Effects on Enterprise Structures

Make or buy decisions have always been a way of life for companies. There is nothing new in contracting out for parts, and retaining the key design, systems engineering, product assembly, and technological and marketing functions in the corporation. But many of these functions now migrate from country to country. A proliferation of cross-border business and supplier relationships now forms the backbone for international technological and industrial exchanges of information, financial support, and know-how, and provides the basis on which a truly integrated world economy is emerging. Advances in transportation and communications technologies have brought about cost-effective, transnational integration of the research, development, engineering, production, and marketing activities of enterprises worldwide.

While air transport often is cited when describing the facilitating role of transportation in globalization, just as apt an example comes from marine transportation. Within the past five decades, advances in the design and operation of large bulk commodity carrying vessels have revolutionized the transportation of raw materials so that it is now possible to cost-effectively source them from any corner of the globe. According to Martin Stopford, "By 1986, the rail freight for a ton of coal from Virginia to Jacksonville, Florida, was almost three times the sea freight from Hampton Roads to Japan, a distance of 10,000 miles."[2] The introduction of unitization has led to the integration of systems consisting of containerships, unit trains, and trucks. In this case, perhaps just as important as the cost reductions have been increases in the speed and certainty (i.e., the efficiency with which such freight now moves).

Advances in telecommunications technologies continue to permit even greater integration of international markets. Capacity for international communications continues its explosive growth. From 1988 to 1995, the capacity of submarine cables increased twentyfold. Constellations of satellites in low-earth orbit that will provide worldwide cellular communications capabilities are planned. The novel uses of the Internet, growing at a rate some estimate as high as 1.5 million subscribers per month, overlay the power of telecommunications with a new dimension of integration. The number of World Wide Web servers has grown from 50 in 1993 to over 120,000 today. These and other capabilities now enable the management of industrial enterprises located anywhere in the world to oversee globally dispersed production and service activities. A harbinger of the future is in the fact that Nike, Mattel, and to a large extent Apple Computer, do no manufacturing in the United States.

What emerges is a new kind of international corporation. The aerospace industry provides a good example. Technology now makes it possible for a U.S. company like Boeing to have the fuselages of its new 777 aircraft manufactured in Japan, the rudders in Australia, main and nose landing gear in Canada and France, portions of the flaps in Korea, and primary flight computers in the United Kingdom. For Boeing, such moves are essential to its survival as a global supplier of passenger aircraft, and indeed as an employer of highly skilled workers. Boeing's announcement that it is increasing its workforce in Seattle to enable it to cope with a rush of orders from abroad for its new aircraft illustrates the point.

As continued transnational integration of enterprise continues, it becomes less and less appropriate to view production activities simply as geographically static pyramids of companies engaged in assembling components and parts and delivering services. Within global production, research, development, and design activities are continuously redistributed among firms in many different countries to take advantage of diverse technical specialties. Industrial activities become grand endeavors cutting across national boundaries. Profit-making enterprises seek competitive advantages by relying on the lowest-cost and highest-quality technological sources worldwide, regardless of geographic location. Firms that do not engage in such efficient forms of collaborative behavior do not survive in the global marketplace.

Conflicting National and Corporate Interests

So long as international technological connectivity intensifies, trading regimes remain permissive, and managements flexibly adapt to changing circumstances, the current trend toward independence from national territories for commercial endeavors will continue. The result is unavoidable tension between the objectives of national political leaders and private-sector managers seeking to maximize return on investment. Politicians seek to advance the standard of living of citizens within national boundaries; corporate managers seek the maximization of the welfare of their firms irrespective of such boundaries.

The most prominent examples of multinational enterprises (MNEs) are large globally based corporations, most of which, unlike thirty years ago, are no longer U.S.-based. According to the Office of Technology Assessment (OTA), "Of the 500 largest MNEs in the world today, 157 are based in the United States, 168 in Europe, and 119 in Japan. In the late 1960s 304 were U.S. companies, 139 were European, and 37 were Japanese." Their political importance may be measured in terms of the economic power they are capable of wielding. According to the OTA, "The foreign affiliates of MNEs control a substantial portion of the world economy, perhaps as much as one-quarter of all economic activity in their host countries. Intrafirm trade (IFT) may account for as much as 40 percent of all U.S. merchandise trade."

We are seeing the birth of multinational collectives of corporations. These new virtual multilateral "enterprises" function almost as single corporate entities and in fact are very tightly coordinated webs of supplier relationships, which weave within and across corporate and national boundaries. Whereas in the past, firms were thought of as vertically or horizontally integrated, or both, today the extent of integration within the firm is less important than the ability to rapidly reconfigure the enterprise to take advantage of internal or external core competencies. New terms have sprung up such as agile, virtual, lean, and flexible to describe the characteristics of emerging organizational paradigms. In a rapidly growing number of cases, the implementation of these new business practices is leading firms to abandon domestic suppliers in favor of foreign competitors when such changes make economic sense. In some cases, the largest of such enterprises are single-handedly capable of changing the terms of trade between nations, mobilizing or displacing thousands of workers with little or no notice, and determining the growth and overall health of the national economy.

Employment dislocation, temporary or not, is socially disruptive and very difficult to cope with for the vast majority of U.S. workers who dream of steadily growing incomes, job security, and recognition of their self-worth. An important consequence for the world of work is the attenuation of firm loyalty by workers who will no longer be able to count on a lifetime of work for a single corporation. They will need to be comfortable with change, with a life's work for many entities, with loyalty only to themselves and their careers. This prospect was recently outlined by James Meadows, one of AT&T's vice presidents for human resources in connection with a planned layoff of 40,000 AT&T employees. "People," he said, "need to look at themselves as self-employed, as vendors who come to this company to sell their skills." He then went on to say, "We have to promote the whole concept of the workforce being contingent."[3] We are giving rise to a society that is increasingly "jobless, but not workless." The sociological ramifications of this kind of job insecurity are only poorly understood.

Technology, Education, and Social and Economic Inequalities

While economic globalization is the overriding consequence of technological advance, the attendant effects of restructuring enterprises become pervasive. Today, corporate downsizing in production, service, and management in large part results from increases in productivity brought about by the introduction of new technology and the nature of the global economy. New technologies permit the realization of economies of scale and scope, as well as in a greater variety of what is produced to serve global markets. Technology also is replacing mass production with mass customization in enterprises of all sizes.

The implications of global integration for social and economic equity are profound. On a global basis, a single world marketplace leads to the emergence of co-extensive two-tier compensation systems: One tier provides high-paying career tracks for technologically adept workers, the other relatively low-paying ones. Market access is one reason for job and technological migration, but wage advantages, not only for production workers but also for highly skilled technical workers, are among the most important driving forces.

The Council on Competitiveness reports that skilled U.S. workers are facing increased competition from abroad. The jobs at stake are white-collar, high-tech positions in computer programming, design, and financial services, many of which are going to China, India, Singapore, and Taiwan as well as to low-wage countries in Eastern Europe at a fraction of U.S. wages. The cost of hiring an English-speaking computer programmer in India is only $15,000–18,000 per year compared with $120,000–150,000 for an American programmer. Salaries for programmers in Bulgaria range from $10,000–$20,000 per year, one-fifth of the compensation for U.S. programmers.

Set against the migration of jobs overseas, there has been a counter-flow of jobs as foreign-based corporations employ U.S. workers at all levels. Foreign automobile transplants now employ tens of thousands of U.S. workers. Ten percent of all industrial research and development in the United States today takes place in U.S. subsidiaries of foreign corporations.

If education is essential to high wages, indicators of educational levels and achievement among African-Americans and Hispanics suggest the nation has a formidable problem. Quite apart from their availability, high-paying jobs and rewarding careers will require high levels of educational achievement. Managerial and technical, professional, and highly skilled support jobs will be open only to those who have had the requisite education. Today, Caucasians and Asians are heavily represented among the students seeking higher education. African-Americans and Hispanics are heavily represented among the students who do not pursue higher education. In one group, many members are trained to exploit the opportunities of the new economy; in the other, fewer are trained and able to prosper. This unfortunate ethnic correlation with economic opportunity could become a flashpoint in U.S. society. The remedy is nowhere in sight.

The American Dilemma

Intellectual knowledge diffuses and leaks. Laws may slow the diffusion, but cannot stop it. Technological know-how migrates from countries with high know-how to countries with low know-how. Japan and the other Asian countries demonstrate that technological comparability can be achieved in less than half a century. The competition among nations, however, will not only be in the efficient production and marketing of goods and services, it will be a new kind of competition for intellectual advantage.

In the face of the mobility of factors of production such as capital, technology, productive enterprises, and material inputs, labor is geographically relatively immobile. The well-educated and trained U.S. worker will still be in competition with knowledge workers from around the world with vastly differing standards of living. As such, their wages will be determined within a labor market where similar talents may be procured much more cheaply abroad. The ability to attract and retain investment is limited by the extent to which firms can re-orient and relocate their activities to take advantage of marginal economic opportunities worldwide. Other considerations being equal, if quality labor is cheaper in India or Bulgaria than in the United States, then U.S. companies will choose to move overseas.

Constancy of Principles

We do not presume to suggest how the dilemmas and perversities created by economic and technological change should be addressed, but there are some principles, adherence to which should tip the probabilities of prospering in the global economy.

1. Appreciate the formidable power of science and technology. The country must remain at the international forefront in scientific and technological research from which technological innovation stems. To do this it must take whatever steps are necessary to see that the education of our young can produce the world-class scientists and engineers that industry and government need. Science and technology literacy for the population as a whole will be necessary if the United States is to remain globally competitive.

2. Create incentives to invest in science and technology—both in the public and private sectors. The federal government has an important role in the support of basic and applied research. Whether such incentives are incorporated in the tax code or provided through direct government investment, some combination of such incentives is essential. Throughout its his-

tory, the United States has oscillated between strong and weak roles for the federal government. There have been many successes and failures. The preeminence of our agricultural, aerospace, and biotechnology industries are largely attributable to strong government roles. On the other hand, there have been prominent failures such as in supersonic transport, nuclear breeder reactors, and the synthetic fuels corporation.

3. Formulate trade and domestic economic policies that will require that, in the net, the migration of jobs among nations must be a two-way phenomenon, with traffic in both directions being roughly equal. On the one hand, U.S. multinational corporations should not be restricted from taking advantage of the global labor, economic, or capital markets if that is what is required for their viability. On the other hand, policies need to assure that the United States retains a fair share of the attractive jobs in the world.

4. Make the United States an attractive country in which to do business of all kinds—from routine production and services to the most esoteric research and development. The public policies that will encourage this at both the federal and state levels consist of a complex mix of actions to ensure an attractive and well-trained workforce and associated educational institutions.

5. Continue to build a modern infrastructure of roads, airports, and communication systems. A significant comparative advantage in attracting foreign and retaining domestic investments stems from efficiencies in production and distribution of goods and services.

6. Educational opportunities for economically disadvantaged citizens must be increased. But this will not suffice by itself. There is a problem in the distribution of the benefits of the

technological productivity explosion. The tax code has traditionally been used to bring about a more equitable distribution of the wealth generated by productivity gains. However politically charged that issue, it must be addressed because the alternative of a socially explosive income inequity situation is even less attractive.

We sum up by recognizing that the problems generated by the global technological system fall into a class that do not have unique solutions. They fall into the class of problems that need to be continuously monitored and managed for prosperous outcomes.

Notes

1. Alfred D. Chandler, Jr., *The Visible Hand: The Managerial Revolution in American Business* (Cambridge, MA: The Belknap Press of Harvard University Press, 1977), p. 369.

2. Martin Stopford, *Maritime Economics* (Boston, MA: Unwin Hyman, 1988), p. 4.

3. "Don't Go Away Mad, Just Go Away," *New York Times,* February 13, 1996, pp. C1, C4.

11

The Networked Economy

Daniel F. Burton, Jr.

The United States is in the midst of an extraordinary economic transition. The oil shocks of the 1970s were the first warning that the U.S. economy was facing fundamental new challenges. At stake is not only the internationalization of economic activity, or the much-publicized shift from an industrial to an information economy; it is the emergence of a *networked* economy.[1]

In this new environment, computing and telecommunications are converging to create an electronic marketplace in which huge amounts of economic activity are transformed by and are utterly dependent upon powerful information networks. As the pioneer of this economy, the United States is poised to play a defining role in how it evolves and how governments react to it. Our ability to do so will depend on how quickly we grasp the new ground rules and how willing we are to restructure existing institutions and policies to accommodate them. If U.S. policy-makers fail to recognize the scale of its impact and do not respond swiftly to its relentless march, they are likely to be left manning irrelevant institutions and insisting on counterproductive policies. By restructuring existing institutions and policies to accommodate them, however, the United States will be able to drive the creation of the networked economy and extend its power in international affairs.

As the networked economy matures, it will change our notions of both government and markets. To master this new environment, policy-makers must take their cue from the private sector. Like business, government must re-examine the demands of its customers, the nature of its alliances, the face of its competition, and the management of its operations. To fathom the forces driving this new world, we must understand the evolution of the network. To take advantage of it, we must grasp the network's governing principles. And to determine where America stands, we must look at a new set of indicators that profiles our performance relative to other countries. Only then will we be able to determine how to shape U.S. policy in this new environment.

The Evolution of the Network

The network consists of a backbone of computing power, software, and telecommunications. Its evolution has been so rapid that it caught even keen observers of the computing scene, such as Bill Gates, off-guard. The network we know today is the child of tremendous advances in software, hardware, and communications technology.

The Internet is often viewed as synonymous with the network, but in fact is only one component. The Internet consists of thousands of independent computer networks. It is best understood, however, not as a specific kind of network but as a set of standards or protocols that enables different types of networks to communicate. A protocol called TCP/IP enables Internet users to communicate with each other easily even though they may use different kinds of computers that are attached to different kinds of networks and that communicate over different mediums. It is this ability to link together diverse platforms and systems that makes it such a powerful tool.

The Internet is an outgrowth of a 1960s Department of Defense project known as ARPANET, which was established to allow defense scientists doing research on supercomputers around the country to share their results and communicate with one another. During the 1980s, the National Science Foundation took over ARPANET and changed its name to NSFNET, but it still had much the same function, allowing scientists around the country to communicate. In 1989, the U.S. government decided to lay plans for a commercial successor. Even when it became a commercial service, however, its first customers remained mostly scientists at universities and computer companies who used it to exchange research results and e-mail.

The real explosion of the Internet has come during the past few years as massive communications capabilities were coupled with powerful computers and sophisticated software. The net effect of two decades of steady increases in the capacity of microprocessors has been to drive down prices and put tremendous computing power in the hands of the average citizen. Today's desktop computers, for example, are over 1,000 times more powerful than the first mainframe and have several million times as much memory. And we are still in the early stages of this technological evolution.

Despite these hardware advances, the network did not achieve star status until the World Wide Web was created. The Web makes it easy for someone using a computer connected to the Internet to grab information across the network merely by clicking on little symbols displayed on the computer screen. The basic Web software was created by Tim Berners-Lee, who developed the standards for addressing, linking language, and transferring the multimedia documents on the Web. With the advent of the World Wide Web, the Internet was suddenly accessible to anyone with a computer, a modem, a browser, and some time on their hands. It was no longer restricted to scientists and researchers, but open to everyone from teenagers to business professionals and retirees. As a result, usage soared. Today, over 100 million people use the Internet.

To grasp the full implications of the network, it is instructive to review the evolution of the computer. First came the mainframe. The Electronic Numerical Integrator and Calculator (ENIAC), built fifty years ago, is commonly thought of as the first modern computer. It was designed to calculate firing trajectories for artillery shells and could execute the then-astonishing number of 5,000 arithmetic operations per second. It weighed 30 tons, filled entire rooms at the University of Pennsylvania, consumed 140,000 watts of power and employed 18,000 vacuum tubes. The mainframe's value proposition, which launched the computer industry, was its ability to increase business productivity. With the mainframe, businesses could automate their accounting systems, inventory controls, travel needs, and so on and thereby dramatically increase their efficiency. During the 1950s, IBM and BUNCH (Burroughs, Univac, NCR, Control Data, and Honeywell) drove this market. In the 1960s, however, IBM's 360 series, which allowed for scalable architecture, helped IBM dominate this market.

The second phase of the computing revolution was the stand-alone personal computer (PC), which offered a totally new value proposition—personal productivity. With a PC, individuals could enhance their own productivity with word processors, spreadsheets, and personal databases. This shift from the mainframe to the PC was made possible by awesome technology advances. For example, Intel's Pentium microprocessor is built on a piece of silicon about the size of a dime and can execute more than 200 million instructions per second—a long way from the days of ENIAC. As a result of this increased computing power, terminals emerged as power centers in their own right, and for millions of PC users the computing center shifted from the mainframe to the desktop. Apple pioneered this market, and Microsoft and Intel took advantage of the shift in computing platforms to wrest control of standards from IBM.

Today, we stand at the edge of a third major shift in computing—the rise of the network. Driving this shift is the ability to make connections with the outside world. Businesses are striving to connect with their partners, their vendors, and their customers. And individuals are striving to connect with each other and the information they need. The network is not just the Internet, as the press would have us believe. It started off with LANs (local area networks) that linked different groups of computers together, such as those in a company or small office. Novell pioneered this market and still stands out as the premier network software company. LANs soon grew to WANs (wide area networks), and ultimately to the Internet and the World Wide Web. Companies like Sun and Oracle are now predicting a new phase of the network, in which inexpensive network computers will replace expensive PCs and plug into the Internet. We will no longer purchase big software programs with multiple features, but instead rent specific applications, or "applets," from the Internet as we need them.

One of the most important lessons in the evolution of computing is that each transition has been compounding, not serial. The PC did not really "replace" the mainframe. Today, IBM still sells huge numbers of them. Similarly, it is doubtful that the network will really replace the PC. Instead, network computers will probably exist alongside millions of PCs, just as private networks will continue to exist alongside the Internet. The same lesson holds true for the nation-state. The networked world will not replace it, but will coexist with and transform it.

Rules of the Road

To see how profound an impact the networked economy will have, one need only look at trends in the private sector. The ability to communicate, transfer, store, and access information instantly has already revolutionized traditional manufacturing industries and routine services. And it is laying the groundwork for whole new markets. While it is impossible to anticipate all of the changes, we can identify some of the key trends.

1. *The networked economy will be connected.* By providing a portal to the outside world, it will connect people with each other and the information they need, enabling them to act on it anytime, anyplace. In doing so, it will fundamentally change the idea of what computing and communication is about. The network is not about productivity or typing, but the value that comes from connecting to a wide world of people and interesting information. These connections will allow for heightened access and

foster the creation of new electronic communities built around shared interests. Initially, these communities will be based on messaging and bulletin boards, but eventually they will expand to include audio-visual communications, shared data bases, and transactions. Since they will not be limited by geography, they will redefine our sense of community.

2. *The networked economy will be heterogeneous.* It will consist of many different types of computing devices and operating systems that are linked together via diverse modes of transmission. When we think of a computer today, we usually think of a keyboard, a screen, and a processing unit, much like a PC. In fact, computers are found in telephones, cars, microwave ovens, refrigerators, washing machines, and even wall switches. The value of these non-traditional computing devices increases dramatically as they are connected to resources on the network, since they can be monitored, controlled, and even serviced remotely. The multiplicity of computers will be matched by the diversity of operating systems and modes of transmission, which will span different industries and countries. Just as technology will be heterogeneous, so will the national assets necessary to take advantage of it. No one party, government, or country will have a monopoly on all the answers or resources. Instead, the constant intermingling of people, ideas, and markets will be the key to dynamism and growth.

3. *The networked economy will be decentralized.* It will consist of a broad base of people, organizations, markets, hardware, and software. There will be no Fort Knox of computing that holds the keys to the network in one reserve location. Instead, assets and information will be dispersed, giving rise to more individualized and, hopefully, more informed decision-making. If the mainframe is analogous with

centralized political power in Washington, D.C., and the PC is analogous with the shift of power to the states, then the network can be seen as the dynamic union of the two. Some have gone so far as to say that the networked computer will do away with the mainframe world altogether. But just as IBM still sells a lot of mainframes, it is much more likely that the power of Washington will not vanish, but coexist alongside more dynamic state governments and more empowered individuals.

4. *The networked economy will be open.* Although privacy and security will remain paramount concerns, it will thrive on openness. The initial appeal of the network was easy access to information and immediate communication. As these benefits became widely available, usage soared. Today, entrepreneurs are exploring ways to make electronic commerce a reality. None of these activities would be possible were it not for the network's intrinsic openness. Countries that try to manage this new medium too closely or that restrict access severely will find not only that their efforts are frustrated, but also that they harm their constituents. The openness of the network will give economies such as the United States big advantages over more closed ones like Japan.

5. *The networked economy will place a high value on content.* The promise of the digital revolution is a powerful pipeline that allows instant delivery of electronic information and entertainment in all its forms. But if the pipeline leaks—if there are not adequate intellectual property safeguards to protect the content—the creative environment will wither. America's copyright industries (which include movies, television, home video, books, music, sound recordings, and computer software) account for nearly 4 percent of U.S. GDP and employ more than 3 million workers. During the past five

years, these industries have grown much more rapidly and created jobs much more quickly than the overall U.S. economy. If the recent past is prologue, this trend will accelerate in the future. As digital information proliferates around the world, there will be tremendous battles over intellectual property. Consumers will want cheap and easy access, but unless content providers can be assured that their intellectual property is adequately protected, they will be loath to release it. Countries that establish strong intellectual property regimes will attract new investments and see their involvement in the networked economy grow; those that do not will find that investment, especially foreign investment, slows and that entry into the electronic marketplace is more difficult.

6. *The networked economy will be very sensitive to markets, which for the foreseeable future will be in flux.* Economic forces are driving this new environment. We are still in the early stages of the digital revolution, and markets are sure to go in startling, unexpected directions. In light of this uncertainty, it is essential to give them room to develop. This is more easily said than done. During times of transition, economic and political anxiety are rife, making it hard for governments to be patient. Concern about the exodus of American jobs and the widening gulf between information haves and have-nots are sure to lead to calls for the government to do *something,* even if it is unclear just what. Unfortunately, quick solutions will be hard to come by, and we should be cautious about implementing elaborate government programs. Government-imposed standards and regulations that clamp down on markets that are still in their infancy may only exacerbate the problems they are intended to solve.

7. *The networked economy will offer an abundance, not a scarcity, of choice.* This is the real lesson of the 1996 telecommunications bill. The future will witness an abundance of technologies, providers, services, information, and consumer choices. During much of the twentieth century, there was only one major telephone company (AT&T), which provided a standard telephone (for many years, a black rotary dial) and offered a homogeneous service (local or long distance) over one path (twisted-pair copper wires). Today, there are hundreds of telephone companies (from MCI to Teleport Communications Group), which provide numerous kinds of communications devices (including cellular phones and pagers) and offer a wide range of services (such as voice mail, call-waiting, and conference calling) that can be delivered over numerous channels (such as fiber optics, ISDN, and satellite). This proliferation of choice will be reflected in a host of products available to consumers in the marketplace. And, as countries such as China are discovering, greater economic choice creates tremendous pressure for political systems to be more open.

8. *The networked economy will place a premium on soft assets, not just hard ones.* During the cold war era, the world was obsessed with hardware. We kept careful count of nuclear warheads, armored divisions, and military personnel. In the economy, the manufacturing sector reigned supreme. The Dow Jones Industrials dominated the stock market, and analysts looked at such statistics as durable goods purchases and machine tool orders to gauge economic trends. The networked economy will marry the traditional reliance on hard assets with a new premium on soft ones. The skills of our people, the management of our R&D enterprises, the ability to manage information, and the vitality of our intellectual property will drive economic performance.

9. *The networked economy will be lean.* The information revolution has already resulted in massive realignments in corporate America. Its real promise, however, is not the heightened productivity that it affords individual companies, but its ability to restructure entire markets. Eventually, the networked economy will create a market environment in which consumers can communicate their needs directly to suppliers, thereby allowing products to be customized to their specifications and reducing the need for intermediaries. Prices will be driven down as consumers compare competing offers and switch vendors easily. Vertical suppliers will disappear in favor of network specialists. As these markets emerge, many new jobs will be created, but many traditional ones will vanish. The resulting dislocation will lead to increasing calls for protectionism and will severely test governments. While there is no easy solution to this problem, the best defense is a good offense. We should focus on creating new industries and the jobs that come with them, instead of just trying to hang onto old ones. This is the course that the United States has taken, with the result that it remains an impressive engine of job creation. Europe, by contrast, has been more prone to a defensive strategy that focuses on preserving existing jobs and has watched its unemployment rate rise to double digits.

Many of the characteristics listed above—decentralized, heterogeneous, open, market-driven—are textbook descriptions of the United States. As the creator of the network, this similarity should not be a surprise. These elements were necessary to give birth to the network, and they will be essential to its evolution. Indeed, the United States currently finds itself in a strong position to lead this new economy.

Where Do We Stand?

Almost any assessment of the U.S. economy begins with a look at macroeconomic indicators. In recent years, these have reflected a sustained U.S. recovery. American GNP growth, productivity, employment, inflation, and even investment rates have all turned in strong performances, especially compared to the other G-7 countries. These rosy numbers, however, mask some fundamental problems. Our national savings rates are abysmal, and our education system is facing a crisis. Chronic trade imbalances and a widening disparity between the rich and the poor compound the gloom.

Usually the debate stops here, with analysts picking their indicators, going into minute detail and arguing at length whether the glass is half-full or half-empty. Underneath these macroeconomic statistics, however, lies another set of indicators that reveals a very different picture. These indicators are technology-related and show just how far the United States is along the path to a networked economy—and how much more rapidly it is moving than its competitors.

The data are not yet available for a systematic comparison of the United States to many other countries. It is possible, however, to make some direct comparisons with Japan. Viewed through the lens of the 1980s, Japan was an awesome competitor. Five years ago, conventional wisdom held that Japan's version of developmental capitalism was far superior to the American laissez-faire model. Japan's combination of flexible wages, lifetime security, mega banks, incremental innovation, and industrial policy were said to produce a workforce, a financial system, and an industrial base that were unbeatable.

Technological indicators, however, paint a very different picture. Let us look at a few:

- In 1995, the United States had 365 personal computers for every 1,000 people compared to 145 in Japan.
- In 1996, 66 percent of U.S. homes subscribed to cable television, compared to only 29 percent in Japan.
- In 1994, the United States had over 5,500 domestic commercial databases, compared to only 1,050 in Japan.
- In 1995, 23 percent of U.S. workers used network-connected PCs, compared to only 1.3 percent in Japan.

Other indicators also highlight America's dominant position in the networked economy. The U.S. software industry accounts for three-fourths of the world market, and eight of the world's ten largest software companies are located here, as are most of the major computer-related companies. Business-use of PCs in the United States is already saturated at about 90 percent, and one-third of American families have them in their homes.

Moreover, America's Internet use is soaring. The majority of Internet users are in the United States. And the United States dominates Internet hosts by region, accounting for about two-thirds of the total, while Europe accounts for about one-fifth and Asia/Pacific for only about one-tenth.

In short, no other country has moved as far toward the networked economy as fast as the United States. We have a robust computer hardware industry, the world's leading software industry, a telecommunications sector that is being deregulated and strong consumer demand. Japan, by contrast, has a strong computer hardware industry, but is weak in software and has not yet begun to seriously deregulate its telecommunications sector. Europe also has its problems, lagging in hardware and software, as well as moving slowly toward telecommunications deregulation.

Policy Implications

During the 1980s, many Asian and European nations looked at Japan's runaway economic success and concluded that the corporate state was the wave of the future. Japan's combination of centralized decision-making, industrial policy, and emphasis on producer interests seemed like the key to winning in world markets. No more. Although the corporate state may work well when the trajectory of the economy and the scope of industrial competition are fairly predictable, it does not work well in times of transition. In such times, qualities that are anathema to the corporate state—such as decentralized decision-making, entrepreneurial risk-taking, and open markets—are most prized. These characteristics are at the core of the networked economy and endow it with a flexibility and a dynamism that are lacking in more closed, centralized states.

In order to create the markets, industries, and jobs that will power economic growth in the twenty-first century, the U.S. government must focus on three core public policy goals: create a world-class environment for innovation and investment, spur the development of digital markets, and harness investments in the training and education of people. By themselves, these measures are not exceptional; taken together and fully implemented, they constitute an extraordinarily powerful combination.

Creating a world-class environment for investment and innovation is the mantra of the high-tech community. In many ways, the R&D tax credit has come to symbolize this priority—

high on rhetoric, but low on implementation. For almost a decade, both Congress and successive administrations have announced their support for a permanent R&D tax credit, only to extend it temporarily or let it lapse altogether when it came time to make hard choices. Fortunately, they have shown more courage in reforming securities litigation to prevent frivolous lawsuits that prey on the inherent volatility of high-tech stocks. And they have seriously taken up the effort to extend U.S. copyright laws into digital environments to protect intellectual property and creative works in cyberspace. They need to back up these initiatives with incentives to bolster national savings and keep our university research base healthy.

Spurring the development of digital markets may seem like a more abstract pursuit, but here too the government can take several concrete steps. It can assure that the regulatory legacy of the telecommunications industry does not bleed into cyberspace. The U.S. computing and software industries grew up in a market that was largely free from stringent government regulations. As these industries converge with telecommunications, government must strive to keep regulations to an absolute minimum. Two immediate actions the government can take to accelerate digital markets are to allow U.S. companies to provide strong security to their customers in the form of robust encryption and to provide incentives for the private sector to expand significantly the bandwidth that is available for digital transmissions around the country.

The last core policy goal is not new. No political speech today is complete without reference to the need to harness investments in the training and education of the American people. There is a serious debate under way about educational standards, and the government is working with industry and the education community to make our schools Internet-ready. The education debate shows that the rise of the networked economy will not be led solely, or even primarily, by government, but by a combination of forces that include private-sector, civic and non-profit organizations. One of the most important lessons for public policy-makers is to be receptive to these outside agents of change. A good example is "Net Day." On March 9, 1996, thousands of volunteers wired many of California's 13,000 public and private schools to the Internet. This action was conceived by the high-tech community, which rallied the education community behind it and subsequently received broad political backing. The goal is to provide every school in California with its own home page and the ability to connect to the Internet at virtually no cost to taxpayers. Today, there is a similar program in almost all fifty states.

At bottom, the essential challenge facing the U.S. economy is one of adjustment and adaptation. In itself, this is not a new problem. What sets it apart is the sheer scope and pace of the transformation. Fortunately, the United States is already well on its way down the path to the networked economy. To capitalize on America's inherent strengths, the U.S. government must maintain a vigilant competition policy, while refraining from implementing elaborate policies that are predicated on a fixed view of the future. Instead, it must establish a climate that encourages private initiative, fosters innovation, and rewards flexibility.

Note

1. A modified version of this paper was published in *Foreign Policy* 106 (Spring 1997).

12

Globalization of Financial Markets

Jane W. D'Arista

Introduction

In the years 1946 to 1969, the U.S. Federal Reserve System (the Fed) perfected ways to implement monetary policy that were critical in creating financial and economic stability. The Fed's success created the conditions that supported other public- and private-sector initiatives aimed at ensuring broadly shared prosperity in the United States.

The method of policy implementation that the Fed refined involved the use of open market operations to change the reserve base of the banking system and thus directly influence both the demand for credit and the amount of credit that could be supplied by banks. The Fed did this by buying or selling U.S. government securities in the open market and by developing the Fed funds market in which banks with surplus reserves sold their excess to other banks. This made it possible to transmit the effects of changes in reserves throughout the system. Moreover, changes in reserves affected the Fed funds rate and, given the preeminent role of the banking system in financial markets at that time, directly influenced other market rates of interest and thus the demand for credit.

The critical component of the post–World War II U.S. monetary system was reserve requirements. Banks were required to hold a certain percentage of their deposits in the form of reserves with the Fed or as vault cash rather than use all their deposit liabilities to make loans or investments. Thus, the Fed's actions in creating or extinguishing reserves directly determined the total amount of credit that could be extended by the banking system. This gave the Fed the unique ability to undertake countercyclical policies. It could increase total reserves and encourage an expansion of bank credit when the economy was slowing. The ability to moderate changes in the business cycle and minimize the disruption and damage of the wide swings characteristic of earlier periods resulted in stable growth in credit, stable interest rates, and virtually no bank failures.

The golden age of central bank effectiveness began to erode in the 1960s as banks discovered ways to move funds offshore and evade the restrictions of interest rate ceilings and the cost of reserve requirements. Lending dollars in London was more profitable than lending in the United States because all of a bank's deposits could be loaned or invested in the unregulated offshore market. The implications of the central bank's loss of control over the supply of funds was reflected in its response: as credit continued to expand, the Fed continued to press on the brakes, driving the Federal funds rate up to the then-historic level of 9.7 percent in October 1969.

The events of 1969 are most often discussed in the context of decisions to end the convertibility of the dollar into gold (1971) and adopt floating exchange rates (1973). Their domestic effects were equally important. They were the beginning of a seemingly inexorable expansion of offshore dollar credit markets that increasingly undermined the Fed's ability to control the supply of domestic credit. In the process, the distribution of credit narrowed as greater reliance on changes in interest rates to influence the demand for credit resulted in higher and more volatile interest rates that favored more affluent investors and borrowers and the larger institutions that served them.

The Fed's inability to maintain a stable financial environment conducive to economic growth and broad-based prosperity became glaringly apparent in the inflationary environment of the 1970s. Nevertheless, the central bank made no effort either to discuss or to confront the issues related to the loss of effective monetary control. It continues to ignore the fact that its policy actions have global implications and that the credit supply is now global, not national.

The following discussion examines some of the more recent developments and changes associated with the continued globalization of financial markets. It presents evidence of the intensified pace of financial market integration, describes changes in market structure, and examines their effects on monetary policy implementation and credit allocation programs. It also describes how globalized credit markets facilitated the U.S. slide into debtor-nation status in the 1980s and how the enormous increase in debt made possible by foreign capital inflows acts as a continuing restraint on spending by governments and households. A major focus of the discussion is on the shift to foreign portfolio investment as the primary channel for international capital flows in the 1980s and 1990s and how the procyclical bias that characterizes this channel undermines stability and impedes sustainable growth. It concludes that, unless steps are taken to restore the Fed's ability to implement countercyclical policies, the future prosperity of the U.S. and global economies may be at risk.

Globalization of Financial Markets

A number of changes over the last decade have resulted in wider, more globalized linkages between national and international financial markets. The most important new development is "greatly" increased capital mobility, one measure of which is the daily volume of foreign exchange transactions, which rose to $1.5 trillion in 1998, up from $820 billion in 1992 (when their volume was sixty times the volume of world trade) and $590 billion in 1989. The various factors contributing to increased capital mobility—financial innovation, deregulation, and structural change—were augmented by several additional developments that intensified the pace of global market integration: the removal or relaxation of capital controls by many developed and developing countries, a wave of privatizations of state enterprises initiated by the Thatcher government in the United Kingdom in the early 1980s and culminating in the restructuring of third-world economies and formerly centrally planned economies in the 1990s, and the dramatic increase in foreign portfolio investment flows that these developments facilitated.

The increased dominance of foreign portfolio investment that became apparent in the mid-1980s reflected significant changes in saving and investment patterns in major industrialized countries. These changes were due largely to the growth of private pension plans. Because pooled funds held by such plans are invested primarily in securities, the role of institutional investors (e.g., pension funds, life insurance companies, mutual funds, and investment trusts) became more important than that of banks and other depository institutions. In the United States, for example, the Fed reported that the share of total financial-sector assets held by institutional investors rose from 32 percent in 1978 to 52 percent in 1993, while the share of depository institutions fell from 57 to 34 percent over the same period. Although the rising dominance of pooled funds as channels for saving is particularly pronounced in the U.S. and U.K. financial markets, the growth in the assets of institutional investors in Canadian, German, and Japanese markets is no less significant. Measured as a percentage of GDP, the assets of these investors doubled over the period from 1980 to 1994 in four of these countries and almost doubled in Canada. In 1993, the assets of U.K. institutional investors rose to 165 percent of GDP and those of U.S. investors to 125 percent of GDP. As their assets expanded, institutional investors' diversification strategies increasingly included cross-border investments. According to the Bank for International Settlements, cross-border securities transactions among the G-7 countries (excluding the United Kingdom) rose from 35 percent of their aggregate GDP in 1985 to 140 percent of aggregate GDP in 1995.

It is now widely believed that, with strong capital market integration, most of the impact of monetary policy in an open economy is transmitted through exchange rates rather than interest rates—a shift that, some economists believe, imposes serious constraints on policy, sacrifices other objectives such as credit allocation to ex-

change rate stability, and allows lenders and investors to ignore local credit needs in favor of global opportunities.

Highly accessible external markets also increased pressures for financial liberalization as the expansion of the unregulated Eurocurrency markets—markets for transactions denominated in currencies other than that of the country in which the transactions take place—contribute to the volume of international short-term credit flows by opening up an additional, very convenient channel for such flows. The ease with which national regulations could be evaded prompted national regulators to relax domestic restrictions in efforts to repatriate outflows that reduced the amount of savings available for productive investment at home. But the removal of interest rate ceilings, lending limits, and portfolio investment restrictions have significantly weakened central banks' interest rate transmission mechanisms while further weakening their ability to allocate credit.

The most serious blow to national monetary control, however, began in 1990 with the removal and/or relaxation of reserve requirements. These actions reduced the direct impact of monetary policy initiatives on the supply of credit. The erosion of control over the supply of bank credit and the declining role of bank lending in total credit flows forced central banks to rely more on their ability to change interest rates through open market operations to influence the demand for credit. Efforts to control aggregate demand consequently require higher and more variable interest rates, which in turn become a powerful inducement to procyclic surges of foreign portfolio investment that undermine the restrictive policy objectives sought by the change in interest rates.

It is now widely acknowledged that implementing monetary policy has become more difficult as a result of increased capital mobility, the liberalization of domestic financial markets and shifts in credit flows to channels outside the direct influence of monetary policy. Moreover, the globalization of financial markets has altered the relevance of assumptions about the impetus for capital flows and the effects of policy initiatives. The following section examines some of the ways in which these assumptions have been challenged. It describes how the effects of globalization precipitated the U.S. slide into debtor-nation status in the 1980s—one of the critical developments that continues to undermine efforts to restore the broadly shared prosperity that the United States experienced between the end of World War II and the early 1970s.

Capital Flows in the 1980s: The U.S. Experience

Surges of capital inflows into the United States in the 1980s created problems similar to—but less severe than—those experienced by emerging market countries in the early 1990s: an overvalued currency, rising current account deficits, and a boom in consumption.

It is now widely agreed that the combination of the Reagan administration's easy fiscal policy, resulting in widening budget deficits, and the Federal Reserve's tight money policy raised real interest rates to historically high levels in the first half of the 1980s, attracted foreign savings into dollar assets, and caused an unrealistic appreciation in the purchasing power parity of the dollar. These effects were exacerbated by opposite policy positions—tight fiscal policies and monetary ease—taken by German and Japanese authorities. As a result of the overvalued

dollar, U.S. companies lost market shares abroad as dollar appreciation raised the relative prices of U.S. goods and services and lost market shares at home for the same reason. The capital inflows that sustained the overvalued dollar thus drove the U.S. current account further into deficit, helped along by the immense U.S. consumer credit structure that easily accommodated borrowing by U.S. residents to buy cheaper foreign products. By the middle of the decade, the United States had become the world's largest debtor nation in nominal terms.

The U.S. credit expansion in the 1980s was unprecedented in both nominal and real terms. The aggregate debt of U.S. borrowers doubled in the seven-year period from 1983 through 1990—from $5.4 to $10.9 trillion. The debt of the three major borrowing sectors—the U.S. government, households, and corporations—more than doubled in this period. The debt of state and local governments and non-corporate and small businesses almost doubled. Only the farm sector experienced a contraction in outstanding debt. It was, obviously, an unprecedented development in U.S. financial history since two centuries of saving and lending had been required to reach the level of inflation-adjusted debt outstanding in 1983.

The explosion of U.S. debt in the 1980s was possible only because of the infusion of foreign savings, since expanding U.S. budget deficits absorbed the majority of domestic savings. But if the debt explosion itself was unprecedented, so was the monetary context in which it occurred. The tight money, high real interest rate environment that prevailed until 1985 was expected to curb the rise in total credit. Instead, given the openness of the U.S. economy and financial markets, the monetary environment fueled credit expansion.

Unlike the 1960s and 1970s, flows of foreign private capital into and out of the United States were not primarily intermediated by the U.S. banking system in the 1980s, which undermined the Federal Reserve's ability to sterilize or offset their effects. One important channel for inflows—loans to U.S. businesses by foreign banks from their offshore offices—was not even captured in the data on inflows and escaped notice until the end of the decade. Because U.S. banks were subject to reserve requirements on domestic lending from offshore offices from 1978 to 1990 while foreign banks were not, foreign banks could lower rates on credits to U.S. corporate customers, forcing U.S. banks to expand lending to other, more risky sectors such as commercial real estate and for highly leveraged buyouts. Moreover, the Federal Reserve's failure to extend reserve requirements to expanding non-bank financial institutions further exacerbated the banks' competitive disadvantage.

Another important channel for inflows in this period was foreign portfolio investment, a channel over which the Federal Reserve's influence is limited, resulting in redistributions in the portfolios of domestic financial institutions. There were sizable contractions in net issues of corporate equities from 1984 to 1990, when the market value of outstanding equities doubled as mergers and acquisitions and leveraged buyouts and stock buybacks reduced the supply of equities, raised their price, and increased their attraction for foreign investors. Foreign portfolio investment differs from inflows through loans, deposits, or direct investment in plant and equipment because securities markets permit larger amounts of foreign capital to be absorbed in less time. However, outflows of foreign portfolio investment will also have a larger impact on national financial markets than outflows through other channels for the same reason (i.e., the price effects will be larger and will occur more rapidly).

Some Policy Implications of Foreign Portfolio Investment

As noted above, net foreign capital inflows influence how and to whom domestic lenders and investors allocate credit. Foreign investors did not make loans for housing or buy large amounts of mortgage-backed securities (MBS), but they indirectly stimulated an expansion of MBS by reducing the supply and raising the price of other financial assets, thus inducing domestic lenders and investors to increase their holdings of assets not held by the foreign sector. As a result of the price/substitution effects of foreign inflows, the value of outstanding residential mortgages more than doubled from 1983 to 1990 and loan concentrations involving real estate proliferated in the portfolios of U.S. banks and non-bank lenders. However, the increased amount of investment in mortgages in these years was not matched by an increase in the supply of affordable housing, thus tending to raise the median price of housing. Moreover, a larger share of the benefits of the tax deduction for interest on home mortgages shifted to upscale homeowners as more families failed to qualify for mortgages at the higher price levels.

The most important and damaging effect on macroeconomic policy of foreign portfolio investment is that it is procyclical. The rising importance of institutional investors channeling funds through securities markets at home and abroad has seriously undermined the ability of central banks to control credit expansion. But it was equally difficult to revive borrowing, lending, and economic activity in industrialized countries in the early 1990s. As U.S. growth slowed at the end of the 1980s, interest rate reductions intended to re-ignite the economy precipitated outflows of U.S. portfolio investment.

The Destabilizing Effects of Foreign Official Investment

Because of the dollar's role as an international reserve and transactions currency, the United States is uniquely at the heart of an increasingly globalized financial market system. At year-end 1995, total outstanding dollar reserves held by foreign official institutions were $882 billion— 65 percent of total official foreign exchange reserves—of which about $600 billion were held in the United States. Most official reserves are invested in interest-bearing credit instruments and the majority of dollar reserves are invested in U.S. Treasury securities.

Indeed, foreign central banks' holdings of U.S. Treasury securities have, in some periods, been larger than the Fed's own holdings, and changes in foreign holdings also are often larger than the Fed's open market purchases and sales of U.S. Treasuries—the primary tool for implementing U.S. monetary policy. Thus, changes in international dollar reserves result in de facto open market operations by foreign central banks in U.S. credit markets. And since most changes in international reserves result from interventions by central banks in foreign exchange markets, U.S. credit markets are necessarily heavily influenced by fluctuations in exchange rates.

But, as had been the case in the 1970s, the investments of foreign central banks in U.S. Treasury securities in the 1980s produced effects counter to those intended by their interventions in foreign exchange markets. While net inflows of foreign official investment were positive in the early years of the decade, major industrialized countries were net sellers of U.S. financial assets, liquidating their holdings to obtain dollars to sell in support of their own currencies. However, by selling U.S. financial assets, they contributed to the increase in real interest rates that resulted in dollar appreciation. Then, in the period 1986 through 1989, as real interest rates declined and the dollar depreciated, foreign central banks' investments of dollar reserves acquired to prevent appreciations of their own currencies also backfired. Large foreign official purchases of U.S. Treasury securities in those years helped finance U.S. budget deficits, lower U.S. interest rates, and thus support a lower dollar exchange rate.

In the 1990–1992 period, foreign central banks again intervened in foreign exchange markets to halt the fall of the dollar. Again, their actions were counterproductive in terms of their exchange rate objectives. Treasury securities purchased by foreign official institutions during these three years would have raised the dollar exchange rate if the Federal Reserve had cooperated by sterilizing the inflow. This would have meant shrinking its own holdings of government securities (or its own new holdings of foreign exchange reserves acquired during the Bush administration) and accepting an increase in interest rates—an unthinkable policy choice in a recession. In fact, foreign official inflows in this period undoubtedly helped cushion the effects of foreign private disinvestment in 1990 as well as domestic outflows, providing a softer landing for some overextended U.S. debtors than might otherwise have been the case.

Foreign Private Portfolio Investment in the 1990s

The onset of recession and lower interest rates in all the major industrialized countries at the beginning of the 1990s precipitated a major shift in foreign private portfolio investment from developed to emerging markets, especially Mexico. According to the International Monetary Fund (IMF), the Mexican stock market rose 436 percent in dollar terms from 1990 through 1993.

Domestic political shocks and delay in devaluing the peso are usually cited as the primary causes of the Mexican peso crisis in December 1994. The massive capital outflows that followed resulted in soaring interest rates and deep devaluation that plunged the Mexican economy into depression virtually overnight. In the aftermath of that experience, there has been much official discussion of ways to control or manage capital inflows into emerging markets, but no official discussion of ways to control or manage flows at the source (i.e., the institutional investors in industrialized countries) or ways in which cross-border securities transactions among the G-7 countries themselves may undermine the degree of monetary control necessary for stable, sustainable growth and prosperity.

Confronting the Legacy of the 1980s

Capital flows into the United States in the 1980s resulted in debt levels for the government and household sectors that continue to slow economic growth and impede efforts to restore the broadly shared prosperity enjoyed in the years between World War II and the early 1970s. While the corporate sector was able to repay substantial amounts of debt with increases in equity issues, the shares of tax revenues and household income that are allocated for debt service remain historically high, constraining aggregate demand and the growth potential of the U.S. economy.

The U.S. external position also remains a constraint on growth and prosperity. Like any other country with a high level of external debt, the United States must export both goods and capital to avoid sliding further into debt. Increasingly, it is not only the trade deficit that is a source of concern, but the shrinking services account as well since interest payments to foreign holders of U.S. government and private financial assets have grown so large. So far, the international role of the dollar as a reserve and transactions currency has permitted the United States to continue to run current account deficits on a scale not possible for other countries. But whether or not these deficits (which result in a continuing expansion of foreign ownership of U.S. financial assets) are sustainable or desirable are questions that must be addressed.

The U.S. and Mexican experiences with capital flows in recent years suggest that there is an urgent need to begin to reform the international monetary system by creating a new international reserve and transactions instrument not based on the monetary or debt obligations of one or a few countries. These experiences also suggest that, in the near-term, the most pressing need is to restore monetary control. This will require new paradigms and tools for policy implementation. Central banks must begin to identify and influence monetary and credit aggregates within the context of global—not national—credit markets. New policy tools must be developed that take into account the shift in investment and borrowing from banks to securities markets and ensure that central banks have better control over total credit by expanding their direct influence over the supply of credit provided by all major sectors of the financial system. Finally, a new macroprudential regulatory framework is needed to moderate the volume of transactions in securities, foreign exchange, and financial derivatives markets; increase the transparency of over-the-counter markets; and cushion the bandwagon effects of international capital flows.

In summary, it is clear that the increasingly integrated and deregulated global financial system that now dominates national markets and policy initiatives responds only to market performance. Its procyclical bias has a destructive potential that undermines stability and impedes sustainable growth. Efforts to restore broadly based prosperity can only succeed in an environment in which monetary policy regains its effectiveness as a countercyclical influence on financial markets.

13

Why the Baby-Bust Cohorts Haven't Boomed Yet: A Re-Examination of Cohort Effects on Wage Inequality in the United States

Diane J. Macunovich

Between 1968 and 1994, inequality in the United States increased 22.4 percent—more than wiping out the 7.4 percent improvement that had occurred in the 1950s and 1960s. Analysts tend to trace a large proportion of this change in family and household income inequality to increasing inequality in male earnings. It is true that the rich have been getting richer and the poor, poorer. As a result, the United States enjoys the unenviable distinction of having the largest inequality of earnings in any developed country.[1]

What has been the cause of this dramatic deterioration in the relative (and absolute) position of lower-paid workers over the past twenty-five years? There has been no shortage of research addressing this question over the past decade—the literature is extensive—but as yet there is little consensus regarding the cause(s). Early researchers identified the labor market entry of the post–World War II baby boom as an important factor: a dramatic increase in the supply of younger, less-experienced workers that depressed their wages and generally reduced their employment prospects. In recent years, re-

searchers have focused on other factors such as sectoral shifts ("deindustrialization"), technological change such as computerization, and globalization of the economy reflected in immigration and the trade deficit.

It is agreed, however, that inequality has increased along many dimensions: both "between group"—between younger, less-experienced and older, more-experienced workers, and between those with and without a college education—and "within group." The purpose of this paper is to demonstrate that the age structure of the population has had a significant effect on the structure of wages throughout this entire period, and that this factor in combination with international trade and the composition of the military explains a large share of the growth in "between group" wage inequality.

Defining Cohorts and Cohort Sizes

Researchers often hypothesize that there are three specific types of effect on labor market outcomes of individuals: age-specific (are they young and inexperienced or older and more experienced?), period-specific (is the economy growing rapidly or in a recession?) and cohort-specific (is this a large or small birth cohort?). A birth cohort is a group of people born in the same year or span of years. They thus share, throughout their lives, the same age-specific and period-specific characteristics.

The annual pattern of births in the United States during this century shows very dramatically the effects of the post–World War II baby boom, when the annual number of births shot up from less than 2.5 million in the 1930s to nearly 4.5 million in the 1950s. But cohort-size effects generally refer to some *relative* measure of cohort size, not to the *absolute* numbers presented here. The relative measure used in this study is the ratio of the population aged 20 to 22 (representing new labor market entrants), to those aged 40 to 49 (representing prime-age workers). A closely related measure—the General Fertility Rate (GFR) lagged about twenty-one years—is also used, since it is a similar type of ratio, and its use permits us to forecast twenty years in advance.

Relative Cohort Size and Inequality

But why should relative cohort size affect the distribution of incomes? Economists have found—perhaps not surprisingly—that younger workers are not good substitutes for more-experienced older workers, so that when their ranks swell relative to those of older workers, their wages will tend to be depressed in relative terms—a simple supply/demand story, with younger and older workers as complements in the labor market. Labor economists began to examine this effect of changing relative cohort size in the late 1970s. Finis Welch estimated that the entry-level wage relative to that of peak earners was depressed as much as 13 percent by the increase in relative cohort size between 1967 and 1975. Both he and Richard Freeman identified a further aspect of such cohort-size effects: large relative cohort size tends to depress the relative wages of young college graduates more than those of workers with less than a college education, since substitutability between older and younger workers declines with increasing levels of education: that is, it is even more difficult to replace an experienced worker with an inexperienced college graduate.

However, Welch's results suggested that wage growth for large cohorts would improve rapidly with experience, allowing them to "catch up" to more normal cohorts as they aged, and that in any event, the advent of smaller cohorts in the 1980s promised a recovery even in entry level wages. His projections suggested career earnings for 1990 entrants equal to those of the "most favored" cohorts of the mid-1950s and early 1960s.

This was a common refrain among labor economists during the period: The prospects for the 1980s and 1990s looked rosy—not only for the smaller cohorts entering the labor market in that decade, but even for the baby boomers as they aged. But the 1980s have come and gone and, while they did witness a marked increase in both inequality and the "return to education" (i.e., the wages of college graduates relative to high school graduates) there was little help for younger relative to older workers. The assumption had been that since the relative size of new cohorts entering the labor market began to fall sharply in the 1980s, the wage effects of cohort size should begin to be positive in that decade—but wages continued to stagnate, and inequality to grow. So, what happened to cohort-size effects?

Re-examining the Theory of Relative Cohort-Size Effects

A majority of the studies over the past twenty years that attempted to measure cohort-size effects had two features in common. First, they assumed cohort-size effects to be symmetrical about the peak of the baby boom. That is, members of the baby boom born prior to the peak in 1957–59 are assumed to have experienced the same effects of cohort size as individuals born after the peak, other things equal, as long as their relative cohort sizes were the same. It was this assumption of symmetry that led researchers to expect that labor market conditions for the large baby boom cohort size would begin to improve immediately after 1980, when relative cohort size would begin to decline for labor market entrants.

Second, they examine these (assumed symmetrical) cohort-size effects on the return to experience only *within* education groups, and using labor force counts as measures of relative cohort size. For instance, among college graduates, they analyze the number of labor force participants with one year of experience relative to the total number of college graduates in the entire labor force.

But this approach tends to underestimate the full effects of relative cohort size. Why? Because the amount of education an individual receives, and his or her chances of finding a job—or being able to work full time if he or she chooses—are affected by relative cohort size, in the same way that relative wages are affected. Completed education is affected by cohort size because cohort size adversely impacts the return to education (since the relative wages of young college graduates are depressed more than those of young high school graduates). Young men in

a relatively large cohort see that they will not gain much by going to college, and so fewer choose to do so. Thus, if we look only at the effect of relative cohort size on the wages of inexperienced relative to experienced *college graduates,* we miss the fact that many who in a smaller cohort *would* have been earning college wages, are instead earning only high school graduate wages—or are perhaps even unemployed, or involuntarily working less than 40 hours per week. That comparison (of inexperienced to experienced college graduates) does not show us the full effect that relative cohort size has had on individuals.

The approach taken in this essay is a simple one, aimed at avoiding the problems of underestimation and measuring the effects of relative cohort size on

- the average expected earnings of *all* unenrolled inexperienced male workers (those with only 1–5 years of work experience) relative to those of *all* peak male earners (those with 25–34 years of work experience);
- the college to high school wage ratio, separately for men and women;
- the general unemployment rate.

Relative Cohort Size and Position Measures

The basic premise underlying the results presented here is that we must estimate the *full* effects of relative cohort size—including those on wages, on educational attainment, and on hours and weeks worked—and that relative cohort *size* alone will not be sufficient to predict these effects. It is hypothesized that a cohort's *position* relative to peaks and troughs also is important—that the effects of cohort size are not symmetric about the peak of the baby boom.

It is hypothesized that those who tend to fare worst as a result of large cohort size are those born on the "trailing edge" of the boom: these young people enter a labor market already congested with previous baby-boom entrants, and so take longer to establish themselves in a career trajectory. In addition, economists have begun to identify strong macroeconomic effects of the age structure of the population on such factors as real interest rates, inflation, incomes, unemployment, housing investment, consumption, and money demand. Age has strong effects on all of these factors, with higher levels of consumption relative to income when the population contains a larger proportion of young adults.

This suggests another reason for asymmetry in the effect of cohort size: those on the "leading edge" of the baby boom will benefit from the effects of an expanding economy, while those on the trailing edge will enter the market in a period of reduced and declining economic activity. Since it has been observed that younger workers tend to be the hardest hit by cyclic effects ("last hired, first fired"), this differential aggregate demand effect could be significant on relative income. This will depress the relative wages of cohorts on the trailing edge even more than those of same-sized cohorts on the leading edge.

As a result of these considerations, this study makes use of an additional measure to control for relative cohort *position*: the *rate of change* in that variable, which is calculated for any year *t* as the difference between relative cohort size in year *t* + 2 and relative cohort size in year *t* − 2, and will be positive on the leading edge and negative on the trailing edge of the baby boom.

Additional Factors Affecting Between-Group Wage Inequality

In addition to cohort-size effects, we must take into consideration the effects of the military on young men's labor market outcomes. David Ellwood, for example, estimated that "over half the rise in the civilian labor force for young men during the 1970s can be traced not to the baby boom, but to the military 'bust.'" His figures show that while nearly 30 percent of youth aged 18 to 24 were in the military in the 1950s, that figured dropped to 15 percent before the Vietnam War and then increased to 20 percent before declining to below 8 percent.

In the results presented here, it is assumed that the number of active military aged 20 to 24 relative to the remaining active military will have two effects on the relative income of young males. On the one hand, there will be an aggregate supply effect resulting from the removal of young males from the civilian labor market—which is expected to have a positive effect on the relative wages of young civilian males. On the other hand, there will be an aggregate demand effect created whenever the level of military expenditures changes. The effect of this second factor on young males' relative wages depends on the extent to which there are distributional effects of such changes in aggregate demand (i.e., the extent to which older males may benefit to a greater or lesser degree than younger males from military expenditures). Because changes in the size of the active military normally are accomplished by hiring more young men, we can use changes in the proportion of the military aged 20 to 24 as a proxy for changes in the level of military expenditures.

Effect of International Trade

Finally, the per capita levels of real durable exports and imports are included in the models tested in this study under the assumption that there may be distributional effects of imports and exports in the economy. The assumption in this study is that imports may disproportionately affect the labor market outcomes of unskilled young males, since they may be closer substitutes for foreign workers than are older and more skilled males. Exports also may have distributional effects, particularly to the extent that they are composed of "high-tech" goods and services provided by college-educated workers, where young workers are disproportionately represented.

We will see that over the last three decades trade, along with cohort size, has had strong effects on the college wage premium, but that trade effects appear to have been much less—although still measurably significant—on male relative earnings.

Thus, the aim of this paper has been to determine how well a model based on the following three elements—

- cohort relative size and position
- level and rate of change in the proportion of young men in the military
- level of durable goods imports and exports

—performs in explaining the historic patterns of the following crucial factors in growing income inequality:

- average expected wages of young inexperienced men relative to those of older, more experienced men (male relative earnings, or the "return to experience")

- average expected wages of young college graduates—males and females separately—relative to those of young high school graduates (variously referred to as the "college wage premium," the "return to education," or the "return to skill")
- the general unemployment rate of males aged 16 and over

The attempt has been to explain the longer-term trends in each of these four variables—thus each model uses a moving average of the observed data.

How Well Do These Models Perform?

Very well. These simple models are able to explain 99 percent of the longer-term variation in male relative earnings over the past twenty-five years, 90 to 91 percent of the longer-term variation in the general male unemployment rate over the past forty-two years, and 95 to 98 percent of the longer-term variation in men's and women's return to a college education over the past thirty-one years. (The different estimation periods for the models are due to problems of data availability.)

Results for Male Relative Earnings

The estimated model indicates that male relative earnings will be lower when relative cohort size is large, but that this effect will be somewhat less on the leading edge of the baby boom than on the trailing edge. A 10 percent increase in relative cohort size would cause a 1 percent decrease in male relative earnings and a 10 percent increase in the rate of change in cohort size would produce a 1 to 1.85 percent increase in male relative earnings.

Military buildups have a beneficial effect on male relative earnings (a 10 percent increase in the proportion of the military aged 20 to 24 would produce a 1.7 percent increase in male relative earnings)—an intuitively pleasing result—but this effect is somewhat less when the military is on the increase than when it is declining, suggesting that older males benefit disproportionately from increases in the military establishment. This favoring of older, more skilled workers would cause young men's wages relative to those of older men to be depressed *more* in periods of increasing military expenditures than during cutbacks.

International trade deficits have a negative effect on male relative earnings, as indicated by a significantly negative effect of per capita durable goods imports (a 10 percent increase in the trade deficit reduces male relative earnings by 0.5 to 0.7 percent), and the significantly positive effect of per capita durable goods exports (a 10 percent increase in durable goods exports increases male relative earnings by 1.3 percent). The larger effect of exports suggests that overall, international trade has the beneficial long-term effect of increasing male relative earnings, as the volume of international trade increases (assuming that imports and exports move somewhat in tandem!).

The General Unemployment Rate

The variables in these models explain over 90 percent of the long-term variation in the male unemployment rate over the last forty-five years. A 10 percent increase in relative cohort size raises male unemployment by 6 percent, but this effect is less for leading-edge cohorts than for those on the trailing edge (a 10 percent decrease in the rate of change of cohort size would decrease the long-term unemployment

rate by 7 to 10 percent); an increase in the size of the military reduces male unemployment by reducing the supply of civilian workers (a 10 percent increase in the military reduces the unemployment rate by 8 percent); and a 10 percent increase in durable exports tends to reduce male unemployment by about 4.5 percent. Durable imports appear to increase unemployment, but this effect is less certain.

Male and Female College Wage Premiums

Here again the models fit the data very well, explaining over 97 percent of the variation in male and female college wage premiums over the last three decades. Both cohort size and cohort position exert a negative effect (large cohorts receive a lower wage premium, and this effect is stronger for leading-edge cohorts); the military exerts a positive effect (strong military recruitment while a cohort is in college raises the opportunity cost of education and thus improves cohort quality at the margin), net per capita durable imports exert a positive effect (since foreign workers tend to substitute more for high school than college graduates); and the male unemployment rate exerts a positive effect (the wage premium is countercyclical, since less-educated workers suffer more during economic downturns than do more-educated workers).

Simulations: What Might Have Been— and What Might Come to Be

In order to see the strength of the effect of relative cohort size and position, simulations have been prepared for each of the four dependent variables—male relative earnings, the unemployment rate, and male and female college wage premiums—in which both the military and real trade variables are held constant at their 1980 levels. These simulations have been prepared with the alternative cohort measure—the GFR lagged 20–22 years, which produces very similar results to the current population ratio because the GFR allows us to make projections for the next twenty years. These simulations are presented in Figures 13.1–6. Figure 13.1 shows that male relative earnings began declining in the early 1960s, and then stopped their decline—as an effect of cohort size—but not until the mid-1980s, because of cohort position effects, and then began to increase. Then, after yet another decline in the early 1990s, also caused by cohort-size effects, male relative earnings should begin once again to experience strong increases in the late 1990s. That increase, in the absence of other effects, would take relative earnings back up to levels not seen since the 1960s (raising young men's earnings to over 60 percent of older men's earnings from their current level of just over 40 percent). The simulation shows clearly the pronounced characteristic effects of cohort position: the "hump" in male relative income in the late 1980s and early 1990s.

Figure 13.2 presents the simulation for the unemployment rate: the pattern that would have occurred if both the military and trade had remained at their 1980 levels throughout the study period. Here we can see very clearly, in the simulated curve, the unemployment pattern that has been the result of changing relative cohort size—rising steeply through the 1970s and then beginning to decline in the late 1980s. If trade and military were held at their 1980 levels throughout the 1990s, we would see steeply declining unemployment rates during the rest of this decade, on the basis of declining relative cohort size.

Figures 13.3 and 13.4 show the patterns that the male and female college premiums would

have followed over the last three decades, if all factors other than cohort size had remained constant at their 1980 levels—thus all movements in the simulated wage premiums are due to cohort effects in this figure. The figures on the vertical axis in Figures 13.3–13.6 should be read as an index, with the high school wage equal to 100. Thus "1.8", for example, indicates that the college wage is 180 percent of the high school wage. We can see the dramatic effects that cohort measures have had on the college wage premiums during this period. They exerted forces sufficient to make the male premium decline by 17 percent (and the female premium by 11 percent) during the 1960s and 1970s. But this negative effect of cohort size was reversed in the 1980s, so that cohort effects have exerted sufficient force to make the male premium rise from its 1980s' low of 145 percent to about 180 percent in 1991 (and the female premium rise from its low of 150 percent to 175 percent). And based on cohort effects alone, the female premium will rise another 8 percent by the turn of the century, to 190 percent, and the male premium will rise another 14 percent, to 210 percent.

In this figure, it is clear that the strong positive force acting on the college wage premium in the latter half of the 1980s has been cohort size. In another way of looking at this issue, Figures 13.5 and 13.6 show the patterns that the premiums would have followed if only cohort size had remained constant at its 1980 level throughout the study period: in these figures we can see what the pattern of the premium would have been in the absence of any cohort effects. We can see that without the cohort size improvement that has occurred since 1980, the male premium would be 18 percent lower than its current level (and the female premium would be 11 percent lower).

Summary

We have found that by using just three variables—relative cohort size, relative military size, and international trade—we can explain almost all of the variations over the last thirty or more years in the earnings of young men relative to older men, the unemployment rate of males aged 16 and over, and the male and female college wage premiums.

Even more important, we have established that relative cohort size and position—as measured by a simple variable such as the ratio of the population aged 20–22 to that aged 45–49, or the GFR lagged 20–22 years—are the dominant factors in determining the variations in these economic variables. This is a finding that would have generated little controversy ten or fifteen years ago; labor economists at that time were deeply involved in measuring and explaining these effects. But in the intervening years, as more data became available for the early 1980s, it became common to dismiss or downplay cohort-size effects—they were assumed important only through the 1970s.

But the results presented here constitute strong evidence that cohort-size effects since 1985 have become, once again, the most important factor in determining the labor market outcomes of young men and women, and are showing signs of becoming even stronger. The pattern of cohort-size effects on male relative earnings and on the college wage premiums for men and women exhibits a pronounced "U" shape as had been expected by researchers fifteen years ago, but the upswing of that "U" begins not in 1980, when it was expected, but in 1985. The work presented here suggests that this difference in turning points was due to the fact that cohort-size effects are not symmetric about the peak of the boom, and that when this asymmetry is taken into account, we can fully explain the strange pattern of ups and downs we have seen in these economic variables over the past decade.

And the value of a model whose dominant factor is the lagged GFR is that it allows us to look forward and prognosticate about future paths of these economic variables. The indication from these models is that the future holds good news: higher relative earnings for young men, lower overall unemployment, and further increases in the college wage premium before it finally stabilizes at a level of about 200 percent. The bad news in all of this is that inequality is likely to continue increasing because of the continuing rise in the college wage premium—although indications are that high school graduates will benefit in an absolute sense from these cohort-size induced trends. These results suggest that much of the stagnation and growing inequality observed in the labor market over the past twenty years did not represent a secular trend that can be expected to continue in the future, but rather one more manifestation of the post–World War II baby boom.

Note

1. For a more complete discussion of the results described here, using wage data for all individuals during the period 1963–1996, please see my article, "The Fortunes of One's Birth: Relative Cohort Size and the Youth Labor Market in the U.S.," *Journal of Population Economics* 12, Spring 1999.

165

Figure 13.1 Actual and Simulated Male Relative Earnings Using Lagged GFR, Holding all but Cohort Variables Constant at 1980 Levels

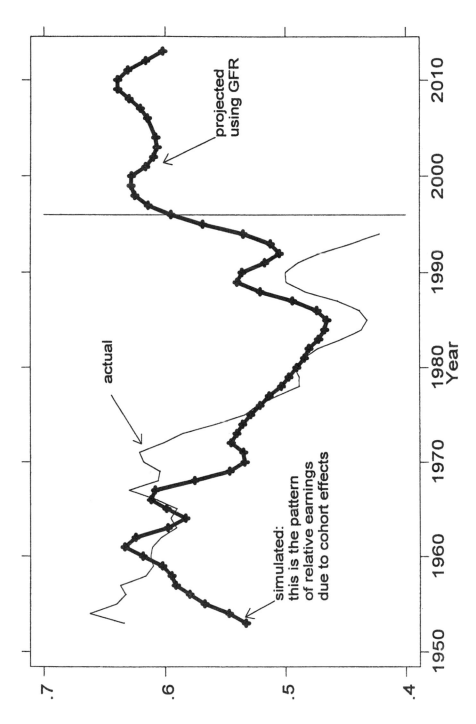

Figure 13.2 Actual and Simulated Unemployment Rate, Male Aged 16 and Over Using Lagged GFR, Holding all but Cohort Variables at 1980 Levels

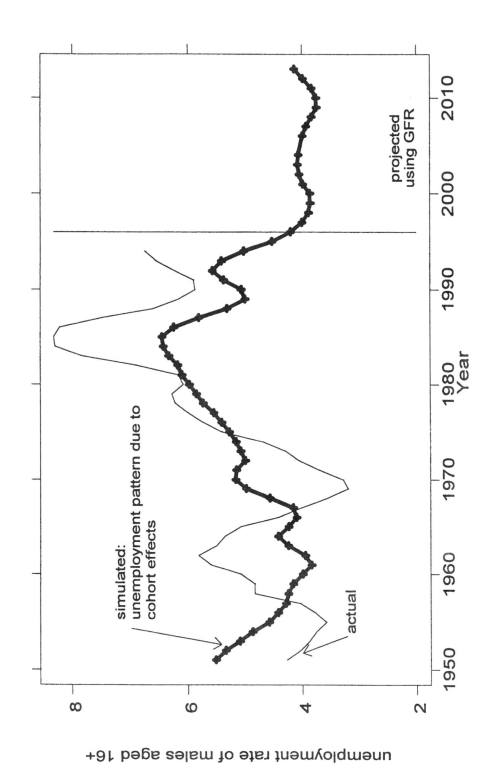

Figure 13.3 Actual and Simulated Male College Wage Premium Using Lagged GFR, Holding all but Cohort Variables at 1980 Levels

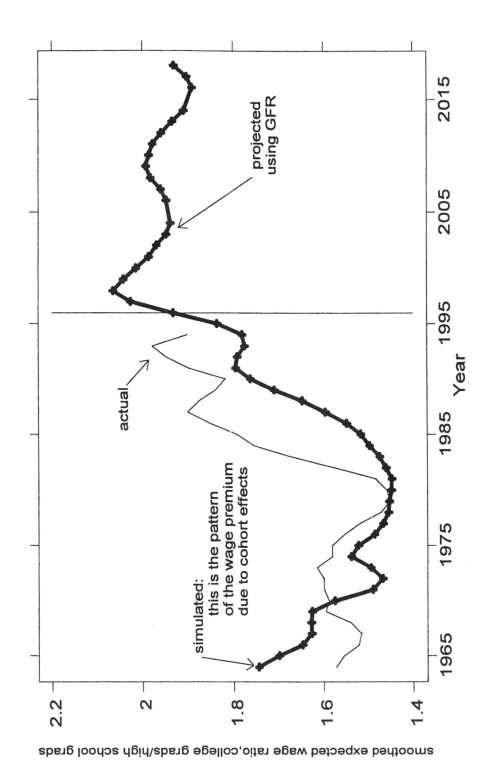

168

Figure 13.4 Actual and Simulated Female College Wage Premium Using Lagged GFR, Holding all but Cohort Variables at 1980 Levels

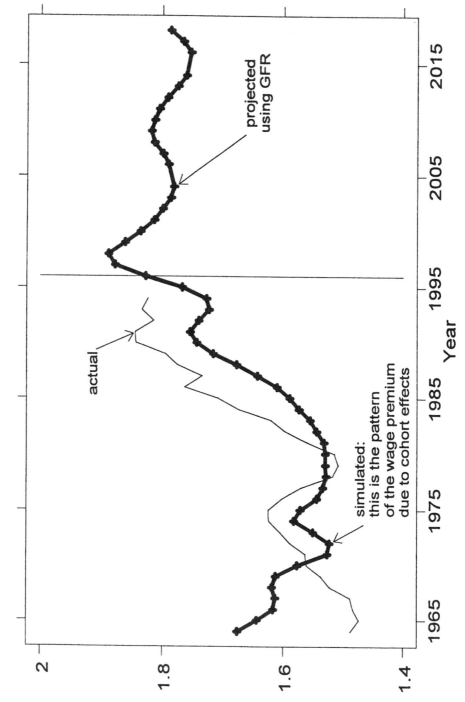

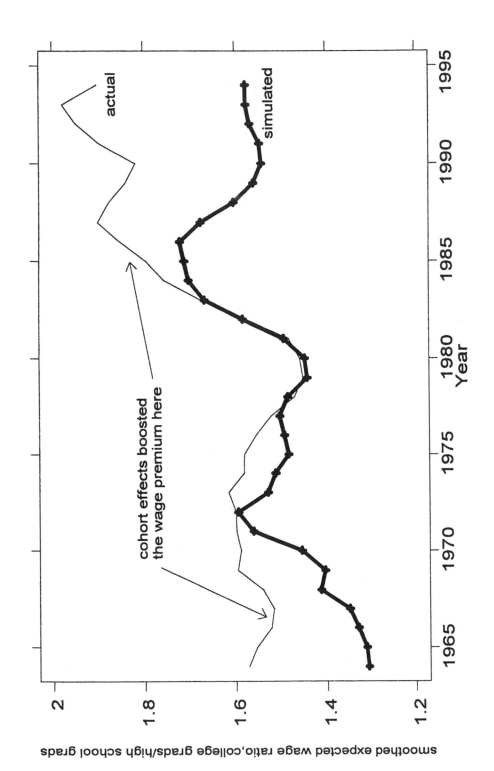

Figure 13.5 Actual and Simulated Male College Wage Premium Using Lagged GFR, Holding Only Cohort Variables at 1980 Levels

Figure 13.6 Actual and Simulated Female College Wage Premium Using Lagged GFR, Holding Only Cohort Variables at 1980 Levels

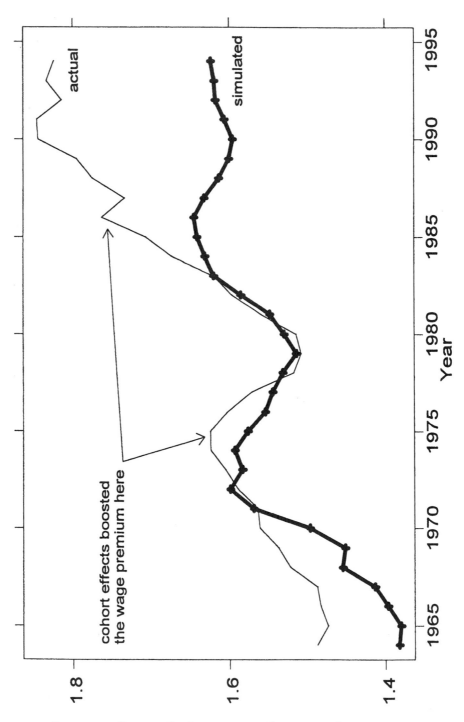

14

Social and Political Impacts of Recent Trends in U.S. Immigration

Michael S. Teitelbaum

The primary hypothesis to be tested in this volume is that fundamental economic trends underlie many of the nation's most serious social problems. What conclusions might be drawn from a balanced consideration of international migration trends under this overarching hypothesis?

The answer is hardly obvious. Nor are the debates surrounding the issues—those in the domains of politics, in the courts, and in the academy alike—notably balanced or objective. To the contrary, discussions of both the impacts and the driving forces underlying recent immigration are deeply affected by powerful currents of ideology, self-interest, ethnic/racial identities, absence of reliable data, passionate advocacy, and frank misunderstanding.

Yet for immigration, loud dissension has long prevailed. At the extremes, immigration is portrayed as either the lifeblood of America's future or the death knell of its promise. Even among responsible mainstream commentators, dissonance prevails: Some portray immigration as a positive force for economic growth and sociocultural energy, others as a source of economic burden and sociocultural turbulence.

Objective assessment is further confounded by the paucity of reliable data. The statistical functions of the Immigration and Naturalization Service (INS) have long been criticized, and

justifiably so. Only since 1994, after continued urgings from the INS statistical office, has any information on national origin been collected as part of the monthly Current Population Survey of the Bureau of Labor Statistics. Even now, very little information is sought about hundreds of thousands of workers, students, and businesspeople who are admitted annually, often for stays of many years, but are not counted as "immigrants" in the official data.

In addition to these data limitations, a substantial fraction of "research" on immigration has a tendentious quality that belies its nominally objective basis. The findings of immigration research also appear to be acutely sensitive to certain critical assumptions. In one recent and disturbing case, two groups of analysts assessed the difficult and contentious question of whether immigrants pay more or less taxes than they receive in social benefits. The research teams used similar datasets and cost-benefit analytic frameworks, yet embraced sharply differing accounting assumptions about revenues and services to include. The result: one study concluded that there was an annual net *cost* of $40 billion, while the other that there was an annual net *benefit* of $27 billion.

Finally, two common confusions have vexed recent debates about immigration. First, with twenty-twenty hindsight, we can say that earlier immigration has, on balance, had positive economic and social impacts on the United States. The large numbers of immigrants admitted during the first three decades of the twentieth century have succeeded well in the United States, and they and their offspring have contributed in important and constructive ways to American society, culture, and economic growth. So, too, did the much smaller numbers admitted during the 1930s, 1940s, and 1950s as refugees from fascism, World War II, and communism.

The problem, however, is that—Shakespeare notwithstanding—what is past is not necessarily prologue. The most recent wave of immigration—of very large and growing magnitude—began only within the last two to three decades. The last large wave of immigration essentially was terminated by public policy decisions during and following World War I and by the economic crisis of the Great Depression, whereas the current immigration wave continues to rise and shows no sign of inflection or reversal. All who comment upon the implications of current immigration patterns must acknowledge that no one can predict whether the experiences of these more recent immigrants will track those of earlier groups. Hence arguments based on experiences before the 1950s offer little insight.

The second source of confusion concerns the level of analysis. All too often, both positive and negative commentaries about *immigration policy* are confused with contentions about individual *immigrants*. Reports proliferate about immigrant valedictorians and immigrant drug-lords, about military heroes and serial murderers, even though these special cases have little to do with the size and composition of immigrant admissions.

This confusion is both incorrect and invidious. Immigrants (at least those admitted lawfully) are in the United States on the basis of federal policies. Assertions about benefits or costs should address the relevant governmental policies, rather than immigrants *per se*. To do otherwise is to romanticize or demonize selected immigrants rather than assess alternative immigration policy frameworks.

In this spirit, this essay will first synthesize evidence on the implications of immigration trends for wage distribution, economic opportunity, and social and political relations; and second, offer suggestions on how immigration policy might contribute more positively toward broadly shared economic growth.

Overall Economic Impacts

As noted above, immigration often is characterized as a powerful force for aggregate U.S. economic advance or decline. In a recent well-informed and balanced appraisal, the National Research Council (NRC) reported that the aggregate economic impacts of U.S. immigration were positive, but small, ranging from $1 billion to $10 billion per year in additional GDP, or between .01 and .1 percent of GDP and between 0.5 and 5 percent of annual GDP growth. The NRC panel concluded:

> Overall, immigration is unlikely to have a huge effect on . . . gross domestic product per capita. Many other factors are far more critical to the U.S. economy than is immigration, including savings and investment and the human capital of U.S. workers.[1]

As to the fiscal effects, the NRC panel reported that immigrants receive more in publicly financed services annually than they pay in taxes, especially at state and local levels. Their case studies of California and New Jersey show that immigration imposes a net fiscal burden of $1,178 per native-headed household (1996 dollars); in New Jersey, with a less recent and older immigrant population than California, the net fiscal cost per native-headed household is $232. The principal reasons for such outcomes are three: immigrant-headed households have more school-age children and hence require more educational expenditures, are poorer and hence receive more income transfers, and pay less in income and property taxes. The NRC case studies suggest that there is a small federal surplus from immigration—amounting to only $2–4 per year per native household. Finally, the NRC estimates the longer-term fiscal impacts of an immigrant over his/her lifetime and finds that these range from modestly negative to strongly positive, but vary greatly with education level and age of arrival. Though these latter findings will surely be misinterpreted as "forecasts" or "predictions," the reality is that some of the assumptions embodied in those simulations are truly Olympian, and it is these assumptions that drive the numerical outcomes.

Income Distribution

There has been much discussion, and not a little agonizing, about the fact that over the past two to three decades U.S. average wages have stagnated and the wage gap between the highest- and lowest-paid workers has increased by perhaps 40 percent. Over the same time period, there has been a very substantial increase in international migration—legal, illegal, permanent, temporary—to the United States. However, as discussed elsewhere in this volume, it would neither be correct nor responsible to conclude that immigration is the dominant cause of growing inequality. Nonetheless, the particularities of immigration are such that it also is wrong to

dismiss immigration as irrelevant for income distribution and related trends. These particularities include the numerical increase, the age composition, and the skills distribution of recent immigration.

There is a broad consensus that the maturing of the massive baby boom has been an important element in the relative wages paid to older and younger workers. This purely domestic factor was, however, probably exacerbated by the fact that it was precisely during these same decades that immigration to the United States accelerated rapidly. These increases were due in large part to dramatic and long-term changes produced by the 1965 Immigration Act, changes that were neither intended by the Act's supporters nor expected by its opponents. These increasing flows of immigrants were concentrated heavily in the same 20–to–35–year-old age group as the baby boomers. In effect, and unintentionally, the already-large demographic bulge of the baby boomers entering the labor force during the 1970s and 1980s was expanded and magnified by the increased flows of immigrants of the same ages.

The distribution of skills among the large and increasing flows of immigrants to the United States has been peculiarly bimodal. The largest peak represents those with very little education and low skill levels: 26 percent of adults with eight or fewer years of education versus 9 percent of native-born. But a second peak of immigrants has higher education levels: 9 percent with masters' degrees or higher, compared with 8 percent of native-born.

This bimodal character of the immigrant skills distribution has facilitated the remarkably energetic advocacy that has surrounded the issue. One advocate will report that a higher percentage of recent immigrants hold advanced degrees than does the general U.S. population, which is both true and incomplete. Others will counter that a higher percentage of recent immigrants have little or no education than the U.S. population, which is also true but partial. A more accurate and fair statement is by the NRC panel:

> A higher proportion of immigrants than of the native-born work in many jobs that call for high levels of education—they are college teachers, medical scientists, economists. But they are even more disproportionately represented in many of the lowest-paying jobs: waiters and waitresses, agricultural graders and sorters, private household workers.[2]

Hence, a useful orienting hypothesis would be that recent and prospective immigration patterns magnify and intensify the polarization of U.S. incomes resulting primarily from other, more basic factors.

Economic Opportunity

The convergence of global economic and domestic demographic trends with immigration significantly impacts the economic opportunities experienced by some important sectors. These impacts were unintended, unanticipated, and largely unnoticed.

The large peak of recent immigrants with very low skill levels introduced a strong surge of new workers into an already large indigenous low-skill labor force. This occurred just as trends in world trade and technology were reducing the relative demand for such workers in the U.S. economy. A recent paper by three Harvard labor economists, George Borjas, Richard Freeman, and Lawrence Katz, estimated the relative contribution of these two factors to the substantial decline in the wages between 1980

and 1995 of U.S. workers who had not completed high school relative to those with higher education. They attributed 27 to 55 percent of this decline to immigration and less than 10 percent to trade.[3]

At the other end of the skill/education scale, the secondary peak of high-skilled immigrants provided economically valuable and well-remunerated services in such industries as computers and telecommunications during the 1980s, when these were experiencing dynamic growth and strong labor markets. There were many complaints from highly skilled workers as these labor markets weakened during the early 1990s, just as the numbers of such high-skill immigrants increased and U.S. workers were being displaced because of layoffs and downsizing. More recently, such complaints have been more muted as these high-skill labor markets have again become stronger.

In less dynamic employment sectors such as academe, however, there has been sharp deterioration in labor market conditions even for recent Ph.D.s in science and engineering. After investing six to ten years of their lives in postgraduate education, these scientists have emerged in growing numbers from U.S. graduate schools to an extraordinarily chilly job market. As *Science* Magazine reported in 1995, "The U.S. science Ph.D. seems to have hit a wall—hard."[4]

At the same time, others almost certainly benefited substantially from these weak labor markets. Owners and operators of California agricultural land realized significant economic gains from the availability and increasing cheapness of migrant farm labor, primarily from Mexico. The U.S. Commission on Agricultural Workers reported that following passage of the 1986 Immigration Reform and Control Act (IRCA), which legalized the status of over 1 million putative farm workers,[5] "agricultural wages have stagnated [and] . . . most farmworkers' real . . . hourly, weekly, and annual earnings have fallen."[6] Similarly, foremen and other managers of low- and semi-skilled workers in construction and service sectors are thought to have benefited from weaker labor markets.

Meanwhile, as engineering salaries stagnated, owners and managers of firms employing these workers benefited, as did universities and non-academic research labs, which benefited from an employers' market for highly skilled recent Ph.D.s in the sciences. Over this period, the salaries available to recent Ph.D.s in science and engineering diverged dramatically from the robust remuneration offered to those who had undertaken fewer years of post-baccalaureate education in professions such as medicine, law, and business.

Interpretation of such trends vary. Some believe that U.S. citizens and permanent residents are deterred from considering scientific and engineering careers by relatively deteriorating career prospects. Others reject arguments that recent immigration has had negative impacts even upon weak high-skill labor markets. Still others forthrightly acknowledge such negative effects, but welcome the resulting cheapening of costs for research and development with, they believe, positive impacts upon U.S. economic performance. There is no obvious way to resolve such profoundly different perspectives.

Social/Political Relations

Such overarching labor force trends were complicated by perceptions of unfair competition that emerged from the longstanding dilemmas of racial and ethnic inequality. American elites chose affirmative action programs as their preferred solution to such disadvantages. When this approach was officially embraced by the Nixon administration in 1969, its principal intended beneficiaries were African-Americans, and its preferred action mechanisms were incentives and mandates to encourage employers to affirmatively seek out qualified minorities. Whether inevitably or not, the political dynamics of such categorical preference systems led, over time, to the expansion of "disadvantaged" groups to include Hispanics (a demographic category originally created by the U.S. government in the 1970s), Native Americans, and other groups defined by race and ethnicity. When affirmative action preferences came to be applied to women, a substantial majority of the U.S. population fell under the official designation "disadvantaged groups."

African-Americans have long been ambivalent about the extension of affirmative action to these other categories. The fact that recent international migrants—both permanent immigrants and those admitted on temporary visas—have originated heavily from regions populated by persons of Hispanic and African origins has complicated and intensified such concerns. Should immigrants of African origin (whether from Africa itself, or from Caribbean island nations such as Haiti, Jamaica, and the Dominican Republic) be "counted" against the numerical goals and targets adopted to facilitate the integration of African-Americans? Does the large fraction of the Hispanic category who are recent immigrants have the same moral and historical claim for affirmative action as those whose ancestors were held in slavery and then under the strictures of segregation? Should foreign students and faculty be "counted" in universities' affirmative action data? Advocates for immigrants, and many who administer affirmative action programs, reply that affirmative action programs should be applied without regard to whether beneficiaries are native-born or foreign-born.

Overall, have social and political relations among diverse racial, ethnic, regional, and political groups been affected by recent immigration patterns? On this one can find little consensus. Some argue that intercommunal tensions are on the rise, pointing to recent political initiatives and counterinitiatives in California and to a series of violent intercommunal episodes that engulfed the metropolitan areas (Los Angeles, New York, Miami) experiencing substantial immigration.

Others detect no such rising tensions, arguing instead that the grassroots initiatives against current immigration policies are driven by longstanding xenophobia and racism and that immigrants are being "scapegoated" for the short-term traumas produced by economic restructuring and recession.

There is no obvious way an objective observer might resolve such fundamental differences. What can be said without reservation is that immigration issues have become fundamental elements of state and local politics in California and Florida, that there is a looming gap between elite and public opinion, and that immigration debates are as divisive within political parties as between them.

The contentious Proposition 187 in California is a case in point. This ballot initiative was framed to deny illegal aliens access to California income transfers and services, including public education. Its co-authors sought endorsements from both the Democratic and Republican gubernatorial candidates, Kathleen Brown and Pete Wilson, respectively. Both declined. Later, when Wilson found himself lagging some 20 percentage points behind Brown about six months before the November 1994 election,

he shifted positions to become an outspoken advocate of Proposition 187.

At that time, California public opinion polls were showing landslide levels of 2-to-1 support for the proposition, despite opposition from nearly every elite organ of California society— business, labor, professional, editorial, religious, and academic. Ultimately, Proposition 187 passed 59 to 41 percent and Wilson came from well behind to win re-election by a substantial margin.

While Proposition 187 seems to have provided dramatic political advantage to the 1994 Republican gubernatorial candidate, its implementation has been blocked by federal courts in response to lawsuits filed by opponents, and similar efforts in other states have not yet been adopted.

What Will Conditions in the United States Be Like if Population and Income Trends Do Not Change Between Now and 2030?

Credible predictions about what the United States will be like more than three decades from now are very difficult to make, and even harder to believe. What can be said is that current tendencies toward polarizing income distributions and a hollowing out of the great middle class are not favorable for the maintenance of stable social/political relations.

The importance of immigration for such tendencies is not entirely clear. The expert consensus is that the overall impacts of immigration on the economy are positive but quite small, and that the really important impacts are upon the distribution of income and wealth. The major winners are those who employ immigrants, owners of capital, and the immigrants themselves. The main losers are those workers whose occupations cause them to compete with immigrants, and taxpayers (mostly at state and local levels) who are required to finance the income transfers and public programs used by immigrants.

Economists are not noted for a high level of consensus on such matters. Yet on the basis of what we now know about the characteristics and behaviors of recent immigrants, at least one declarative conclusion seems to be unassailable: A continued influx of large numbers of immigrants with very low levels of education and skills can be expected (other things being equal) to exacerbate the poor economic prospects of similarly situated U.S. residents.

At the upper education/skill levels, where there is a secondary peak of immigrants, the situation is more varied, depending heavily upon the particular area of expertise in question and the unpredictable future demand for such services. Continued substantial inflows of foreign-born scientists and engineers might be expected to have negative impacts in academe if current weak labor markets persist, and positive or benign effects in the computer and telecommunications industries if tight labor markets persist.

What Immigration Policies Would Help Restore Broadly Shared Economic Growth?

Policies that might contribute to a restoration of broadly shared economic growth must distinguish between illegal and legal immigration. For the former, the most important would be to make effective the to-date largely rhetorical "employer sanctions" against those who knowingly hire undocumented workers. The measures adopted in 1986 were in a sense ineffectual by design—deliberately hobbled by provisions demanded by their opponents that made it in essence impossible for honorable employers to detect document fraud and impossible for federal officials to act against employers who knowingly winked at fraudulent documents. The most promising remedy for this situation would be a secure, non-discriminatory verification system based on a computerized registry, as recommended by the U.S. Commission on Immigration Reform.

As to legal immigration, perhaps the most destructive single barrier to broadly shared economic growth would be to acquiesce to demands by California agribusiness for a new "temporary worker" program to import low-wage workers from Mexico or elsewhere. One of the few universals in international migration is that low-wage "temporary workers" imported into high-wage economies hardly ever prove to be temporary (the only partial exceptions seem to be in authoritarian countries such as those of the Persian Gulf). Both the temporary and the permanent residents attracted by such a program would contribute even further to the growing income gap between America's rich and poor.

One affirmative measure affecting legal immigration that might promote broadly shared economic growth would be the enforcement of labor laws that currently are unenforced. The number of wage-and-hour inspectors fielded by the Department of Labor has been in decline for two decades and now is remarkably small for an economy the size of the United States'. These two decades saw the re-emergence of the sweatshop in New York, New Jersey, and California, and in some notorious cases the recrudescence of outright slavery or peonage— illegal immigrant workers detained by force. In its assessment of how credibility could best be restored to U.S. immigration policy, the U.S.

Commission on Immigration Reform concluded that:

> Labor standards and employer sanctions should be seen as mutually reinforcing. . . . Employer sanctions alone will not effectively deter unlawful employment practices. The Commission also firmly believes that enhanced enforcement of labor standards must be seen as a complement to employer sanctions enforcement and an integral part of the strategy to reduce illegal immigration.[7]

As to policies intended to deal with the adverse labor market impacts of legal immigration, the Inspector General of the U.S. Department of Labor has reported as "ineffectual" its programs of "Permanent Labor Certification" (PLC) and its "Labor Condition Application" (LCA) program for temporary foreign workers in "speciality occupations." In unusually outspoken words, the Inspector General's report stated that:

> In our opinion, while DOL-ETA [Department of Labor-Employment and Training Administration] is doing all it can within its authority, the PLC and LCA programs do not protect U.S. workers' jobs or wages because neither program meets its legislative intent. DOL's role amounts to little more than a paper shuffle for the PLC program and a "rubber stamping" for LCA program applications. . . . We believe changes must be made to ensure U.S. workers' jobs and wage levels are protected.

> The PLC program . . . does not currently protect U.S. workers' jobs; instead, it allows aliens to immigrate based on their attachment to a specific job and then to shop their services in competition with equally or more qualified workers without regard to prevailing wage.

> The LCA program . . . does not always meet urgent, short-term demand for high skilled,

unique individuals who are not available in the domestic workforce. Instead, it serves as a probationary try-out employment program for illegal aliens, foreign students, and foreign visitors to determine if they will be sponsored for permanent status.[8]

Despite such criticism, a lobbying effort led by immigration lawyers and industry associations and supported by employers such as Microsoft and Intel produced 1998 legislation to dramatically expand the visa program for such temporary workers in "specialty occupations" (known as H-1B visas).

A second area deserving scrutiny is whether foreign-born persons (and especially those who did not grow up in the United States) should continue to be treated the same as U.S.-born-and-raised minorities for affirmative action purposes.

A third area deserving attention concerns that large fraction of legal immigrants who are low-skilled and poorly educated. Most of these are admitted solely on the basis of family ties to U.S. residents, with literally no attention to their impacts upon similarly low-skilled U.S. citizens and earlier immigrants. Those concerned about deteriorating economic conditions for low-skill, low-wage workers in the United States certainly need to acknowledge that inflows of immigrants depress wages and working conditions in these labor markets.

Employers understandably welcome such workers and lobby fervently for their continued importation, which helps sustain employers in marginal, low-wage industries. But this is special-interest lobbying *par excellence*. From a U.S. national perspective, it would be far better if employment in such sectors were to be upgraded to higher-value-added and better-paid activities, so that all U.S. workers could receive decent wages and benefits. Where such upgrading is impossible (because of trade competition from countries where wages are miserable by U.S. standards), the best approach would be that long followed by Japan with its "co-production zones" on the Pacific Rim: conscious efforts to move these low-value-added jobs to labor-surplus, low-wage developing countries (Mexico, Caribbean Basin, etc.) in a manner designed to integrate them with higher-value-added activities remaining behind.

Finally, at high-skill levels, thoughtful scrutiny is warranted for the U.S. practice of financing postgraduate education in science and engineering research assistantships through federally funded research grants. Over the past decade, an enormous expansion in the number of postgraduate "slots" was justified by National Science Foundation forecasts of a looming "shortfall" of hundreds of thousands of scientists and engineers. The number of U.S. students entering such graduate programs increased, but not as rapidly as the number of funded "slots." The difference was made up by an exceptionally rapid growth in the number of foreign graduate students, many (if not most) of whom were financed by the U.S. government.

These augmented cadres of new science and engineering Ph.D.s have emerged into a labor market with few openings for such highly skilled workers. Though it is impossible to be sure, these experiences may limit the appeal of science and engineering careers for undergraduates now considering whether to pursue a Ph.D. or more lucrative professional degrees in law, medicine, or business.[9]

Notes

1. National Research Council, *The New Americans: Economic, Demographic, and Fiscal Effects of Immigration* (Washington, DC: National Academy Press, 1997), pp. 4–25.

2. Ibid., pp. 5–33.

3. George J. Borjas, Richard B. Freeman, and Lawrence F. Katz, "How Much Do Immigration and Trade Affect Labor Market Outcomes?" *Brookings Papers in Economic Activity* 1, 1997, pp. 46–47, 50–51. See also John Casey, "The Melting Pot Myth," *New Yorker*, July 14, 1997.

4. "Science Careers '95: The Future of the Ph.D.," *Science* 270, no. 6 (October 1995): 121.

5. Most observers believe that on the order of 50 percent of those applying for legalization as farm workers submitted claims based upon fraud.

6. U.S. Commission on Agricultural Workers, *Report of the Commission on Agricultural Workers* (Washington, DC: Government Printing Office, 1993), p. xxii.

7. U.S. Commission on Immigration Reform, *U.S. Immigration Policy: Restoring Credibility* (Washington, DC: Government Printing Office, 1994), p. 89.

8. U.S. Department of Labor, Office of Inspector General, Office of Audit, *Final Report: The Department of Labor's Foreign Labor Certification Programs: The System Is Broken and Needs to Be Fixed* (Washington, DC: Department of Labor, Report Number 06–96–002–03–321, May 22, 1996), p. 1.

9. For a discussion, see Alan Fecter and Michael S. Teitelbaum, "A Fresh Approach to Immigration," *Issues in Science and Technology* 13, no. 3, Spring 1997, pp. 28–32.

Part III

Policies to Restore Shared Prosperity

A. National and International Economic Policy

15

What Can Macro-Policy Do?

Robert M. Solow

I am going to start with an analogy that you will not like. I am not crazy about it either, but it is important to understand it, even if you would like to undermine it. I, myself, will do a little bit of that in a moment. Imagine a fairly high-cost paper mill, specializing in the production of a kind of paper that is gradually being replaced by computer networks. Naturally, the production of this paper is more profitable when the whole economy is prosperous, because the demand for paper is greater. But it does poorly in recessions. The company is gradually losing its markets, and would lose them more rapidly were it not making bigger and bigger price reductions. There may even be some import competition to contend with. Macro-policy probably should not be much concerned about this situation, and probably could not do much about it even if it were concerned. It looks like a case of shape up or ship out.

The case of the paper mill is a lot like the case of unskilled labor in the United States. Nearly everything I said about the paper mill could be said about unskilled labor. Does the same conclusion follow? Well, there are some major differences between the two cases. For one thing, the life chances of people, including unskilled workers, is the main object of public policy, including macro-policy. The same cannot be said about paper mills.

Second, unskilled workers have not chosen their status in the same way that investors in paper mills have chosen theirs. Buying stock is a business decision, known to be accompanied by risks that presumably have been evaluated by equity owners or their representatives before they bought in. Individual stockholders can get out pretty easily (even the mill itself can be allowed to depreciate, sold for scrap, etc.). Getting out of the unskilled-labor business is a lot more complicated.

Finally, unskilled labor is a much bigger part of the national economy than the paper business. So maybe the issue of macro-policy is not settled by the paper mill analogy, despite the real similarities.

It cannot be said too often that maintaining high aggregate employment is *basic*. But this is not simple, and it is probably not enough. Macroeconomic policy can go a long way toward giving us prosperity, but it does not guarantee that it will be broadly shared.

Despite the high employment associated with the long upswing of the 1990s, there has been very little of the wage compression that usually goes along with a strong economy. The past year or two has brought some income equalization, but only a little. And it is much too soon to be sure that this was not noise—a statistical fluctuation that could be reversed. Converting rising employment into wage compression is not as automatic or as easy as it used to be.

Besides, there are limits to what macro-policy can be expected to do with aggregate employment. The danger of faster inflation is not just phony. The notion that there is a non-accelerating inflation rate of unemployment (NAIRU) cannot be dismissed as nonsense. Please notice this choice of words. I do not think much of the underlying theory myself. If there is a NAIRU, it appears to be a poor guide to policy. There is even a real possibility that the experience of high unemployment leads to a high NAIRU, and vice versa, and that would change the picture drastically. Except for certain countries in certain periods, the whole apparatus does not fit the facts very well, as Ray Fair has shown. As of now, the NAIRU story gets more respect than it deserves. (It must be said, however, that the Federal Reserve has felt its way flexibly and open-mindedly; otherwise the long upswing would have ended long ago.) None of this means, however, that it would be sound policy to proceed as if the sky is the limit when it comes to employment.

No case can be made for the "European" belief that avoiding inflation is not only necessary for sustained prosperity, but also sufficient. Too rigid a belief in this doctrine, and in a solid NAIRU, has led to a decade or more of destructively high unemployment in much of Europe. (It supports a point I made earlier that this bad experience in Europe has been accompanied by only a little widening of inequality, if any.) There is every reason to want to avoid the European foolishness. But we should not kid ourselves: a burst of inflation in the United States would be unpopular and would damage both the administration that allowed it to happen and the whole idea of expansionary macro-policy.

A good case can be made, however, for cautious exploration of lower unemployment rates.

If lower unemployment can be safely achieved, that would be good in itself, and it would surely do no harm to the goal of broadly shared prosperity. The danger of irreversible overshooting has been grossly exaggerated. If the safe limit to unemployment (or, in the other direction, employment) is overshot, the fact can be recognized and policy can be reversed. There do not appear to be any fatal "slippery slopes" or other loose metaphors for runaway inflation triggered by small, brief excursions into overemployment. Preemptive strikes are unnecessary and self-confirming. But that is about all that can be soberly said.

Two cheers for macro-policy. But now come back to the issue. It is very doubtful that even the best macro-policy can do the distributive trick by itself. With luck it can achieve continuing prosperity, but that prosperity will be shared the way current conditions of supply and demand determine. If broadly shared prosperity is the goal, then macro-policy will have to be supplemented by the usual strategies: more and better education, well-aimed vocational training, improved health care, and possibly some public employment. Those are discussed elsewhere in this volume.

This does not let macro-policy off the hook. The standard devices for improving the supply side of the labor market are unlikely to do much good unless macroeconomic forces, including policy, generate some pull from the demand side of the labor market, along with or even ahead of the supply-side policies. This is what is so clearly lacking in Europe. Manpower-type policies will work only if there is clear demand for the graduates of manpower programs. Some of this can come from public or semi-public sources. In the U.S. context, however, there is no substitute for the availability of jobs in the business sector.

I have said nothing about direct redistribution because that is not macro-policy as we usually classify these things. An alternative to wage compression (or to lifting the lower tail of the wage distribution) is transfer payments to supplement low earned incomes. The Earned Income Tax Credit has a lot to be said for it, despite the inevitable problems arising from a fairly high marginal tax rate when earnings improve. I would only mention the importance of not financing social costs by raising the payroll tax on low earnings.

A one-sentence summary: good macro-policy can do definite but limited good for the goal of broadly shared prosperity, but bad macro-policy can do unlimited harm.

16

Budgets and Taxes

Robert Eisner

Economic policy has been paralyzed by a combination of outworn economic dogmas and strident political ideology. The dogmas and ideology are tied to faulty measures and uncertain theory that defy the accumulating weight of evidence.

We have not counted right and have not focused on what counts:

- total output and income,
- its equitable distribution,
- provision of productive jobs for all able to work, and
- saving and investment for the future.

We are misled by narrow, limited measures of national and personal income, unemployment, and investment.

Policies to pursue what counts have been blocked by a cultivated paranoia about mismeasured and misunderstood government budget deficits. Attempts to improve our tax system have been frustrated by a plethora of politically influential special interests. Possible reforms have been distorted by the fairly transparent efforts by many to focus on changes in the system that would be of overwhelming benefit to the richest, least deserving, and least needy strata of the population, to the detriment of almost everybody else. And generally emasculating macroeconomic policy has been accep-

tance of the dogma that fiscal and monetary policies cannot affect the level of employment; demand-side efforts to get and hold unemployment below its "natural" or "non-accelerating-inflation rate," the infamous NAIRU, can only doom us to ever-increasing inflation.

A nation earns income from output. The more we produce, the more we earn. The output we should maximize should include not only the conventional (essentially business) market production, but also all of the output of government and households, much of which is not produced for the market.

A nation's output grows from investment. But this includes all investment—public as well as private. The definition is broad enough to encompass intangible investments in research, human capital investments in education and health, as well as tangible investment in machines, brick and mortar, and other physical capital. Appropriate measures would facilitate public enlightenment and public decisions on the proper role of government, where it should be reduced and where, contrary to the assertions of many, it should be increased, in the interest of our well-being now and in the future.

We should, similarly, recognize household investment in durable goods and education. And we should recognize the value of household labor services, whether hired or, more usually, unpaid. It is desirable to offer women in the household every opportunity and incentive to become productive members of the labor force. But we must not neglect support for all they do or can do in raising children and maintaining a home. Our children are our greatest investment in the future.

The Mismeasured, Misunderstood Deficit and What to Do About It

Almost everybody talks against "the deficit" and almost nobody knows what he or she is talking about. The federal deficit in the "unified budget," which gets most attention, is defined as the excess of "outlays" over "receipts." This does have some meaning as the equivalent of the excess of what the public receives from the federal government over what it gives. Hence, the greater the federal deficit the more solvent and able to spend are state and local governments, those in the private sector, and, to some minor extent, foreigners. Generally, the more the federal government is in the red the more the rest of us are in the black. It should seem a bit puzzling that many of those so concerned about private interests should wish to eliminate the deficit and thus benefit the government income statement at the expense of the income statements of the private sector or of the state and local governments to which they generally wish to devolve responsibilities.

But the deficit in the federal budget is calculated in ways at wide variance with business and private accounting practice. A U.S. corporation would not show a loss in its income statement—a deficit—because it had invested in new plant and equipment. Such expenditures would be viewed as capital outlays, not a charge against income. Only the depreciation or consumption of existing capital would turn up as a negative item. Official federal accounting provides for no separate capital budget; all outlays are lumped together.[1]

The federal deficit, therefore, offers no indication in itself of "borrowing from our children" or passing on a burden to future generations, presumed characteristics that convey the view that it is irresponsible and, worse, immoral. The effects on future generations depend instead upon the federal budget's contributions to real investment, both public and private. A deficit that finances public investment in roads, bridges, waste disposal facilities, and our air and water hardly hurts our children. Nor does a deficit that finances investment in basic research, new technology, education, training, and health. Our failure to correctly measure the deficit invites efforts to eliminate it, in the name of increasing investment, which in fact reduces public investment and the private investment that government outlays may finance.

The problems of measurement and implications for policy go further. Deficits, it must be understood, add to debt. The federal deficit adds to the financial liabilities of the federal government and, correspondingly, to the financial assets of other sectors. Changes in asset positions affect the economy. The more our net worth is increased by our holdings of Treasury bills, notes, and bonds, the more we are able to spend, both as consumers and investors. We must clearly view ourselves as richer if we hold a U.S. government security than a receipt for payment of taxes.

Many are quick to accept the argument that raising taxes makes us poorer and in some way injures the economy. But eliminating deficits by cutting government outlays has precisely the same effect of holding down the net worth of the private sector as a tax increase would have. The spending cuts may, admittedly, have a different incidence, though, and therein may lie their appeal to some in our body politic. Taxes, particularly income taxes, tend to come more from the relatively well-off; the government outlays that more generally benefit the middle class and the poor are those which deficit hawks seem most ready to cut.

Nominal deficits, or deficits in current dollars, unadjusted for inflation, add to the debt in nominal dollars. But like all other economic variables, they must be adjusted for inflation. Increases in our holdings of Treasury securities will make us feel richer and make us spend more if the increases are sufficient to overbalance the loss in their real value due to inflation. To understand the impact of the deficit we must then calculate it in real terms; that is, we must subtract from the nominal deficit, which adds to the nominal debt, the loss in the value of the debt due to an "inflation tax." With a debt held by the public of some $3.7 trillion at the end of the 1996 fiscal year, a 2.5 percent inflation rate means an inflation tax of $92 billion.

The 1996 fiscal year deficit was $107 billion, far below the 1992 deficit of $290 billion. As a percent of GDP, a more appropriate measure, the deficit declined sharply, from 4.72 percent to 1.44 percent. When adjusted for inflation, the real deficit in 1996 dollars is only $15 billion, or 0.34 percent of GDP. Were we to "balance the budget," as so many demand, we would have a real surplus.

At the assumed 2.5 percent inflation rate, this surplus would come to about 1.25 percent of GDP (the debt-to-GDP ratio of about 0.5 multiplied by the inflation rate). We would thus be losing to the federal government, net, an amount of wealth or potential purchasing power equal to 1.25 percent of our income. This can only prove a serious drag on the economy. Whether such a drag would at any particular time pull it down to a recession and stagnation is never certain. But one should ponder carefully the justification for taking such a risk—a risk with no evident reward.

Not only is there no economic reason to balance the budget, let alone run a real surplus, but achieving balance could incur major costs. Properly measured deficits, it turns out, can be good for us. And deficits can be too small as well as too large.

If the economy is operating at full employment, using all of its productive capacity, any increase in demand or purchasing power, whether due to increased government spending or decreased taxes, it can only increase prices, that is, raise the rate of inflation. Over almost all of the past half-century, however, with the exception of the Vietnam War years, we have operated at less than full employment and less than full capacity. In such a situation, increased spending, whether by government or the private sector, stimulates production. Ultimately, to produce more, more people must work. Thus employment is higher and unemployment lower.

I have in fact repeatedly related the appropriately measured, inflation-adjusted, high-employment deficit over the years beginning in 1956 to subsequent growth in real GDP and to unemployment.[2] The results are clear. Larger budget deficits were associated with greater subsequent growth in GDP and lower unemployment.

Proponents of lower deficits claim that otherwise investment will be "crowded out." According to this argument, the Treasury will borrow funds that would otherwise finance business capital expenditures, absorbing private saving to finance the public dis-saving.

The claim of drainage of loanable funds misses the point that the public uses money to buy Treasury securities issued to finance the deficit that the public would not have in the absence of a deficit. A deficit of $117 billion means that the public is getting from the Treasury $117 billion more than it is turning in. Without that deficit, the public would have $117 billion less to lend. Further, if increased public spending as a consequence of a deficit does cause a shortage of loanable funds or a rise in the rate of interest, our Federal Reserve is fully capable of supplying additional funds and keeping the rate of interest from rising.

The argument that national saving and investment must be reduced by a deficit, because a deficit is public dis-saving and total, national saving is the sum of public and private saving, misses two fundamental points. First, since the conventional deficit does not exclude capital outlays, it is not a measure of public saving. National saving, properly measured, must include public investment. Eliminating the deficit may well mean reducing public investment and hence reducing national saving.

Second, the argument confuses an identity with predictions of behavior. It is true that national saving is the sum of private saving and federal, state, and local saving. We can then safely say that a reduction in the federal deficit, by reducing federal dis-saving, must increase national saving *if state and local saving and private saving are unchanged.* But how in the world can such an assumption be reasonable? One way of reducing federal dis-saving, for example, is to reduce federal grants in aid to state and local governments, currently totaling over $200 billion a year. How can we assume that this will leave state and local surpluses or deficits unaffected and/or not force cuts in state and local outlays or increases in state and local taxes? And how can we assume that any cut in outlays or increase in taxes, at any government

level, would leave private saving unaffected? Clearly, if we have less after-tax income we are compelled to reduce our saving.

But further, as we spend less, what happens to business investment? If we decide not to buy that new Buick, will General Motors decide to invest more—or less? That indeed suggests the way to analyze the issue. Since total saving is identically equal to total investment, we can answer the question of the effects of the deficit on national saving by determining its effect on investment. As additional evidence, I can report the results of regressions relating the inflation-adjusted, high-employment deficit to subsequent gross private domestic investment and net foreign investment, the sum of which is equal to total investment and national saving. The results are clear. Larger deficits over the past forty years have been associated with *more,* not less, domestic investment. There has been "crowding-in," not "crowding-out."

Larger deficits, it is true, have also been associated with less net foreign investment. This is readily understandable when it is recalled that larger deficits are also associated with more GDP and less unemployment. As we become more prosperous, we buy more Buicks but we also buy more Toyotas, not all of them made in Kentucky. The increase in imports, a negative item in its total, reduces net foreign investment. The sure way of cutting imports, and hence raising net foreign investment, would be a substantial recession—which sufficiently reduced budget deficits might well bring about.

Reductions in net foreign investment brought on by larger deficits have been dwarfed, however, by corresponding increases in domestic investment. Larger standardized deficits have thus been associated with more total investment and hence more national saving. A bigger federal deficit, as conventionally measured, does mean less public saving—or more dis-saving—but it also has brought even more private investment and private saving. And to the extent larger deficits have been associated with more public investment, as they have, they bring an even greater increase in national saving, properly measured.

Prudent deficits, then, can be good for us. They maintain aggregate demand and purchasing power and support both private consumption and private investment. But what is "prudent?" I offer, as a rule of thumb, a deficit that allows the debt-to-GDP ratio to remain constant. This is, after all, a measure that households, businesses, and banks look at. Banks will not lend if the resulting debt seems beyond the income out of which it must be serviced. If our debt is twice that of our parents, we do not consider ourselves more burdened than they were if our incomes are also two times theirs.

The federal government suffers no income constraint in servicing a debt denominated in dollars because it can always raise all the dollars it needs by taxation or by creating them. And since this is true, the federal government can always find new lenders. It need never be insolvent unless Congress, by a misguided act like refusing to raise a debt ceiling, makes it so. But the rule of thumb of maintaining over the long run, at least, a constant debt-to-GDP ratio is consistent with balanced growth. If followed, it would permit financial portfolios to remain with the same proportions of government securities and other assets. It would imply a constant deficit-to-GDP ratio and would offer support to purchasing power equal to a constant proportion of GDP.

In the current situation, with the debt-GDP ratio of 0.5, as indicated above, and a rate of growth of (nominal) GDP of about 5 percent per year, that would mean a deficit-GDP ratio of 0.025: the deficit would be 2.5 percent of GDP. With a GDP of some $7.5 trillion, that would imply currently a deficit of $188 billion, well above this year's actual deficit.

My rule of thumb for prudent fiscal policy would then suggest as well that the deficit be used to finance net public investment. This would imply vastly more public investment than we have now. And it would permit the considerable investment in human and other intangible capital—education, training, research, and health—which analysts increasingly agree is the key to maximum economic growth.

As a rule of thumb, it would hardly be inviolate. We might well invest more and run a bigger deficit where we discerned the possibilities of increased, productive investment. We clearly should be prepared for increased deficits in times of economic downturn when tax revenues decline and public expenditures for unemployment benefits and welfare payments rise. Inflationary booms, by contrast, might well be accompanied by increases in tax revenues such that the deficit would be below its long-run target.

The Deficit and Social Security

The argument for deficit reduction frequently is related to the alleged need to curb "entitlements," particularly Social Security.[3] Indeed, we are told, speciously, that Social Security is in "crisis" because of the impending increase in the proportions of elderly as the "baby boomers" reach retirement age. The deficit can be lowered by reducing Social Security cost-of-living adjustments, by taxing benefits more, or by further raising the retirement age at which full benefits are received. Without justification, however, such moves single out the elderly to make the heaviest sacrifices.

The facts are that there is no crisis in Social Security now, and there is none looming in the future. There is no need or justification for demanding sacrifices of the elderly of today or tomorrow. And whatever the merits—and there can be substantial demerits—of some form of privatization, it is utterly unnecessary to "save" our retirement benefits.

The issue of Social Security may only be understood by recognizing two separate problems: (1) the use and financing of the Old Age and Survivors and Disability Insurance trust funds (OASDI), and (2) the real support of those not working—the dependent population, young and old—by those working.

The problem with regard to the first of these, the OASDI trust funds, if there is one, is utterly trivial. Many act as if these "funds" contain piles of hundred-dollar bills, which we replenish with our contributions. In fact, there is no "money" in the trust funds; their assets are Treasury obligations, as good as money but essentially computer entries, printed out each month. These indicate that the Treasury has credited the funds amounts which correspond to our payroll taxes and the interest payments on these balances.

Since our Social Security checks come from the Treasury in any event, there is no real reason we have to go through the accounting procedure of building up the computer balances and then drawing them down. The funds could be abolished and the Treasury ordered to go on paying the benefits prescribed by law, borrowing to finance these expenditures, if necessary, just as it does now to finance Social Security or anything else. Payroll taxes, like other taxes, go into the general Treasury pot that finances expenditures, and dropping a separate account for them would make no difference. It is argued that retirees would be less secure without the funds, and some politicians play to these fears of insecurity. We are warned of the dangers of "raiding" Social Security to finance other government outlays. But the integrity of commitments to the elderly depends ultimately on the political will to meet them and our real economic ability to do so. Neither of these should be in doubt.

As to the alleged future problems of the solvency of the funds under current law, they stem from what is known as the "intermediate" long-run projections of the fund trustees (and their actuaries and economists). These indicate now that by the year 2029 the fund assets, which will have grown enormously in the intervening years, exceeding $1.3 trillion in 2015, will be exhausted by the year 2029. At that time, current receipts will be insufficient to fully finance expenditures. What most alarmists fail to mention is the observation, in the trustees' report, that an increase in taxes of a mere 2.19 percent of taxable payroll would, by these intermediate projections, keep the funds fully solvent through the year 2070!

I can offer an easier solution that entails no increase in taxes on anybody. Simply credit the funds with: (1) the income taxes now paid on the Social Security payroll "contributions" that are not deductible in computing taxable incomes, and (2) higher interest returns on the fund balances.

The non-deductible Social Security contributions, attacked by some as double taxation, include all of employee payroll taxes and half of the taxes paid by the self-employed. Their total is now running about $200 billion a year. With income tax rates averaging about 17 percent, crediting the trust funds with the income taxes on these payroll taxes would give them this year an additional $35 billion, about half of the 2.19 percent of taxable payroll that the intermediate projections indicate would be adequate for long-term solvency. Crediting the funds with returns on their asset balances of two percentage points more than under current law, thus about 9.8 percent instead of 7.8 percent, would easily make up the rest of the gap.

The Treasury is already contributing out of general revenues to Medicare—$39 billion in 1995. Crediting to the Social Security trust funds the income taxes on the payroll contributions is entirely reasonable and would make no difference whatsoever to government financing, the taxpayer, or the economy. The Treasury, after all, would be collecting these taxes as before and spending as before. Instead of the taxes going into a general funds account, they would be credited to the OASDI accounts. And those worried about fund solvency might breathe more easily.

Crediting the fund balances with higher returns is also amply justified. It would bring them closer to the market equity return that advocates of privatization promise. Payroll contributions to the funds have saved the Treasury from public borrowing that would have substituted for private investment. It is only appropriate that Social Security contributors have their funds credited with the higher returns to private investors that their contributions made possible. And again, this additional credit to the funds would make no difference of any real magnitude; it would not even add to the relevant figure for the federal debt, which is the gross federal debt *held by the public,* currently some $3.7 trillion, not the "debt" of one part of the government to another.

Not often noticed are the fund trustees' "low-cost" projections. They differ from the somber intermediate projections partly in assuming a long-run unemployment rate of 5 percent instead of 6 percent and a twenty-first-century annual rate of growth of GDP of about 2.2 percent, instead of a very low 1.3 percent. They also assume higher fertility and mortality rates and greater immigration. With the low-cost projections, fund balances reach a temporary low in 2040 of four times annual expenditures! And then they mount indefinitely thereafter. If even some of the more "optimistic" assumptions underlying the low-cost projections are realized, the fund will remain solvent indefinitely.

The only meaningful problem that Social Security faces is the real one of the working population producing the goods and services to be acquired by those not working. We are told that instead of the current ratio of almost five people of working age—20 to 64—for every potential dependent aged 65 and over, by the year 2030 that ratio will fall to less than three.

The relevant numbers, though, relate to all potential dependents, the young—under 20 years of age—and the old. Currently, for every 1,000 people of working age there are 709 young and old potential dependents. In the year 2030, the intermediate projection puts the number at 788. That means that 1,000 people of working age would have to support 1,788 people—themselves and their dependents—instead of 1,709, a 4.62 percent increase in their burden.

But if productivity per worker grows at a modest 1 percent per year, well within historical experience, total output per worker will grow by more than 40 percent by the year 2030. This one-third increase in output and income per capita would support improvements in the standard of living for all—the elderly, the young, and those in their working prime.

Of course, greater growth will improve that lot all the more. We can promote that greater growth by getting our policy-makers out of the game of slowing the economy in dubious efforts to fight an imagined danger of inflation.

Over the long run, we can promote greater growth by bringing about more productive investment of all kinds. And most important, as economists have been increasingly recognizing, is investment in human capital—in jobs and in the skills and health of our people.

But cutting the retirement benefits or other "entitlements" that a rich and great economy has been able to provide has no part in that picture. Our Social Security system ain't broke. There is no excuse for emasculating it in the guise of fixing it.

The Furor over Taxes

It is said that the only things inevitable are death and taxes. We might say that taxes are like living into old age, not all that pleasant, but usually viewed as better than the alternative.

Politicians make much of the desirability of lower taxes, and raising taxes can prove fatally injurious to political health. But despite the feasibility of keeping them lower by financing some government outlays by a deficit, as indicated above, clearly most outlays must be financed by taxes and the question then becomes one of efficiency and equity. How can we collect taxes equitably and thus improve the performance of the economy—or at least avoid harm?

The current federal income tax is an awful mess. Its complications, inequities and diseconomies baffle ordinary imagination. Enforcement and compliance, to the extent we comply, costs many billion hours of time and perhaps $200 billion dollars annually. It is true that more than half of Americans avoid most of the hassle because they do not earn enough to pay any income tax, or can use the simpler, shorter forms of the infamous 1040. But for many of the rest, the appeal of a tax return that

can be filled out on a post card—or junking the system entirely and substituting a national sales tax—appears great.

With all the government-bashing that is heard, one might suspect that many would do away with taxes entirely—and the government they finance. We might privatize Social Security, which takes some 36 percent of the revenues the federal government collects. We might privatize all schools and go to the further extreme of asking all students or their parents to pay for schooling themselves. I am not sure that any would opt for privatizing defense and have us hire private armies to protect our turf, although many seem willing to pay more for private protection agencies than for public police. And we could, particularly with improving technology, shift to traveling on private toll roads. But while differing both on optimum size of government and just what its role should be, most of us recognize that there are major government expenditures to be financed and that we cannot rely exclusively on borrowing or on printing money to do so. The central question is what kind of tax system to have.

What kind do we have now? At the federal level, the individual income tax, about which we hear so much complaint, actually takes in less than half of government revenues, 43.7 percent in the last fiscal year. The share from corporate income taxes, despite booming profits, was only another 11.6 percent. And most Americans pay more in "social insurance taxes and contributions," 12.4 percent of their wages and salaries, including their own contributions and those paid by employers on their behalf, than in individual income taxes.

But who actually pays these taxes? Economists largely agree that all of the payroll taxes, regardless of whether they are dubbed employee or employer contributions, come out of wages. None of the prominent proposals of flat taxes or sales taxes would change this. That burden on working Americans would remain.

The incidence of corporate and other business taxes is somewhat more elusive, but one axiom must be accepted. Businesses do not pay taxes; people do—in this case, those who buy business products. To stay in business and pay investors a return that warrants their investments, businesses generally must pass on all of their costs, including those imposed by Uncle Sam. In effect, then, corporate income taxes are akin to sales taxes, paid for in higher prices of the goods and services we all buy.

Individual income taxes have the clearest incidence. We can tell exactly who is paying them. The income tax system is moderately progressive. Those with higher incomes not only pay more taxes but pay a higher *proportion* of their income in taxes. In 1993, those with adjusted gross incomes between $20,000 and $30,000 paid taxes equal to 6.3 percent of their total income, while those earning $75,000 to $100,000 paid 11.5 percent, and those with incomes over $200,000 paid 21.1 percent.[4]

The various "flat" taxes would change that drastically. They would offer great savings for the relatively rich, not only because of the elimination of progressivity in the rate structure. Of major importance is the exclusion of all but wage and pension income from individual taxes. The rich get a tremendous boon because the proportion of their earnings coming from such income is much lower, 57 percent in 1993 for those earning $200,000 and over, as against 90 percent and over for those earning less than $100,000. Indeed for the $1,000,000-and-over group, for which I had data for 1991, only 31 percent of income came from wages and pensions, which would alone be taxable under the usual flat tax proposals; 23 percent was in the

form of capital gains and another 23 percent in interest and dividends. The elimination of direct taxation of capital income is touted as an encouragement to investment in productive physical capital but, if so, does it not tilt the playing field against labor and possibly more productive investment in human capital?

All this, though, is only part, and a misleading part, of the story. The tax savings touted by flat-tax proponents are in the individual income tax. These are balanced, if there is to be revenue neutrality, by corresponding increases in the business tax. Despite the lower "flat" rate, the loss of such major deductions as interest payments, state and local taxes, employer payroll tax contributions, and all employee fringe benefits, including health insurance, would raise business taxes by some $200 billion.

Who will pay these increased business taxes? Again, those who buy business products. *The flat tax is a combination wage and sales tax.* And since all business capital expenditures will be immediately deductible, as widely recognized and indeed boasted, it will be a tax on consumption. Consumers will pay in proportion to their consumption, and their consumption of domestic products only. Since at higher income levels lower proportions of income are spent on consumption, the flat tax is clearly regressive when all taxes paid under such a system are taken into account. It turns out that, looking at *total* taxes paid, individual and business, all income classes up to $100,000 would pay more under, for example, the Armey-Shelby flat tax than under current law while those in the $100,000 to $200,000 group would see the proportion of their income going to taxes fall by about 15 percent and those in the $200,000-and-over group would see their taxes cut in half. Lower income groups would suffer particularly from the loss of the Earned Income Tax Credit, once hailed by Ronald Reagan as the best anti-poverty program ever, while very high income groups would benefit in addition from abolition of estate and gift taxes.

A national retail sales tax, obviously also a consumption tax, unlike the combined wage-and-sales "flat" tax, could in principle, eliminate the income tax entirely. But since the proportions of income spent on domestic consumption rise as we go down the income scale, sales taxes are uniformly regressive. Despite this regressivity, perhaps because those affected adversely do not understand it—or do not vote—sales taxes seem to arouse less political opposition than income taxes.[5]

The big appeal of consumption taxes—whether the flat tax or a pure sales tax—is that they would encourage work and saving. There may be something to the first claim. The work-leisure choice would be altered as the loss of income from foregoing work would be greater without the income tax bite. But the value of income would be correspondingly reduced for that major portion going to consumption, as prices would be higher by the amount of the sales or consumption tax. And the transition to the sales tax would entail some major inflation. Efforts to curb this inflation by tight money policy and higher interest rates would depress the economy in general.

The effect on total saving and investment would be more dubious. Contrary to popular argument, most saving, which takes place through pension contributions and IRAs and gains in the value of assets, including housing, is already tax exempt. And saving, properly measured, including all these gains in equity and household and government investment in durable goods and intangible capital, particularly human capital, is not nearly as low as is frequently charged. But fundamentally, discouraging consumption by putting a tax on it does not necessarily add to national saving. Again, national saving has to be embodied in investment; no increase in investment must mean no increase in saving. If a 20 percent sales tax discourages us from buying new cars—an important form of investment which produces transportation services for a number of years—will the automobile manufacturers invest more in new facilities, or less?

Our current income tax system can be improved. We should move to broaden the base of taxation by removing many exemptions, deductions, and preferences, and generally reduce tax rates. This was the philosophy of the Tax Reform Act of 1986, which included all of realized capital gains in taxable income, eliminated some $200 billion in "tax expenditures," and provided essentially a two-rate system with a maximum of 28 percent. We might well return to that approach and add further reforms, replacing tax incentives with direct expenditures to support desirable goals of health insurance, home ownership and state and local services. We could go further still and eliminate the corporate income tax, and integrate it and payroll taxes in one comprehensive tax.

But the political caution at the drastic changes proposed in the flat taxes and sales taxes now on the table is well placed. Taxes are onerous, but despite all the complaints, we have probably the best system in the world for collecting them. Our system strives to make people pay their "fair share," which means that those who get the most from the economy pay the most and those at or below the poverty level should pay the least. With increasing evidence that, even aside from taxes, our economic system is generating increasing disparities of income and wealth, it might well be dangerous to the social compact to change the tax system in a way that drastically exacerbates those disparities.

Rather, changes in the tax system should be directed at encouraging investment in human capital and reversing the increase in income inequality. While it would generally be preferable to rely on direct government outlays, a worthwhile tax incentive to consider is a refundable tax credit for education and training. Such a credit should be equal in real magnitude to the GI Bill after World War II, which financed my studies for the Ph.D. Much of the disparity in incomes relates to differences in education, with college graduates now earning far more than those with only a high school diploma who, in turn, earn more than dropouts. More education for the less educated would lead to higher incomes.

We might consider introducing vouchers equal to the full cost of education that could be used by parents to send their children to private or public schools, the latter of which would also charge "tuition" that could be paid for with the vouchers. Faced with vastly increased competition among schools, the quality of both private and public schools might improve. It would be important, however, that the vouchers be sufficient for poor children to attend private schools. Small vouchers would merely create a subsidy to the relatively rich currently in private schools, and to the schools themselves if they then find it feasible to raise tuition.

It would also be important to avoid direct support of religious instruction, to the extent the vouchers are used for attendance at parochial schools. And the vouchers should not be a substitute for the considerable investment necessary in public school facilities, teachers, and programs to permit them to offer excellent education and thus be competitive with the best in private education. The backbone of our educational system is public and certainly will remain so for the foreseeable future. Private schools should not be encouraged at the expense of public education.

An expanded Earned Income Tax Credit, with provisions that would make available quality child care and eliminate the loss of Medicaid, food stamps, and other benefits for the working poor, would also both help generate a more equitable distribution of income. By making it more rewarding for potential workers to take jobs and more profitable for employers to hire them, the larger credit will increase employment and aggregate output.

Conclusion

I return to the focus I urged at the beginning. We can contribute significantly to economic well-being if budget and tax policy are aimed uninhibitedly at maximizing and equitably distributing total output and income, offering productive jobs to all able to work, and fostering adequate investment in our future.

Notes

1. The Bureau of Economic Analysis has recently begun separating out tangible capital outlays in its national income and product accounts and measuring the deficit, accordingly, as receipts minus *current expenditures*.

2. This corresponds to the "standardized" or cyclically adjusted deficit calculated by the Congressional Budget Office and others to separate out the component of deficit that affects the economy from the component that is affected by the economy.

3. This section is adapted from my article, "What Social Security Crisis?" which appeared in the *Wall Street Journal*, August 30, 1996.

4. Only the non-business portion of individual income taxes is used in these calculations.

5. John Kenneth Galbraith has suggested that liberals might well soften their opposition to sales taxes in the interest of securing more tax revenues for public schools and other government services they would like to expand. This might be a second-best solution to the problem of financing increased public investment—if one could be sure the sales tax revenues would go to that.

17

Social Security: A New Deal Program for the Twenty-first Century

Dean Baker

It has become fashionable to speak of Social Security as an outdated relic of another era that is in dire need of an overhaul, if the program should exist at all. In fact, Social Security is a remarkable success story. It provides retirement income to over 35 million people. As a result of Social Security, the poverty rate for the elderly fell from about twice the average for the non-elderly adult population to just about the same as for the rest of the adult population. The median income for an elderly household is now about $18,000. This is far from luxurious, but sufficient to meet basic needs.

Social Security also provides disability insurance to virtually the entire working population, as well as survivor insurance for families in the event of the death of a parent or spouse. It provides these benefits in a manner that is progressive and fair. Lower income people get a higher percentage of their earnings back as Social Security benefits, but the more someone has paid in, the more they get back. The system is also efficient; there is a minimal amount of waste and fraud. The cost of administering Social Security is less than 0.8 percent of annual benefits. Administrative costs at private insurance companies are, on average, more than thirty times as high. Social Security is a model program where the government meets a public need in a fair and efficient manner.

This essay will examine the nature of the Social Security "crisis." It is divided into four parts. The first part will examine the changes needed to preserve the solvency of the program. It will show that the necessary tax increases are relatively minor and that they will not significantly impinge on the living standards of future generations. The second part will discuss the privatization option. This section will show that privatization does not affect the problems resulting from demographic shifts at all. The third part will briefly explain why a public pension system, such as Social Security, is more efficient than a private system. The last section is a brief conclusion.

The Nature of the Problem

In spite of the constant talk of a "Social Security crisis," for the next thirty-five years the program faces no problems whatsoever. The fund currently has an annual surplus of more than $60 billion per year. According to Social Security's 1996 annual report, the surplus is projected to rise until it peaks at about $85 billion in 2003. According to the Social Security

Administration's intermediate projections, the standard basis for policy analysis, the fund will continue to run an annual surplus until 2019, after which it will begin to dip into the assets accumulated over the previous thirty years. It will be able to draw on these assets until 2029, at which point they will be depleted. In that year, annual tax revenues will still be sufficient to cover 76 percent of the benefits. This means that if absolutely nothing is done over this whole period, the fund will still be able to cover more than three-fourths of its benefit obligations at the point where its reserves will be depleted.

The tax increases that would be needed to maintain the fund's solvency are not onerous. According to the Social Security Trustees' report, if the Social Security tax was increased by 2.19 percentage points immediately, it would make the system fully solvent for the next seventy-five years. By comparison, due to the recent upward redistribution of income, hourly wages for the median male worker have been falling at the rate of nearly 1 percent a year for the last fifteen years. This means that for typical male workers, the entire burden of making Social Security solvent for seventy-five years will be less costly than what they have been losing to upward redistribution every three years.

An alternative tax approach to making the fund solvent would be to increase the Social Security tax at a rate of 0.1 percent a year (0.05 percent each on the employer and employee) for thirty-eight years, from 2010 to 2048, a total of 3.8 percentage points. This rate of tax increase would allow the average real wage, net of taxes, to rise 0.9 percent a year, so that in 2048 it would be approximately 60 percent higher than it is today. This "burden" should not give our children and grandchildren too much to complain about.

It is possible that even these tax increases will be larger than what is needed to keep Social Security solvent. The economic assumptions used for the Social Security projections are extremely pessimistic. They assume that growth will average just 1.8 percent over the next twenty years, slower than any comparable period in U.S. history. The projections assume that growth slows even further in later years, until the growth rate is less than half the 2.8 percent rate of the last twenty years.

The cause of the growth slowdown in the projections is a slowing rate of labor force growth, at times approaching zero. The projections assume that the resulting labor shortage leads to neither more rapid wage growth nor an increase in immigration. Slightly more optimistic projections will significantly reduce the size of the tax increase needed to support the system. For example, if average real wages were to grow 1.5 percent a year, instead of the 1 percent in current projections, the tax increase could be lowered by 30 percent to 2.7 percentage points over thirty-eight years. This rate of real wage growth is still far below the 2.5 percent annual rate from 1947 to 1973. If the economy were to return to this rate of wage growth, it would virtually eliminate the need for any Social Security tax increase for the next seventy-five-year planning horizon.

It is difficult to design policies that will increase wage growth; however, the amount of immigration into the country is very much under government control. For the foreseeable future, there are going to be hundreds of millions of people in less-developed countries who would be delighted to immigrate to the United States and work in less-desirable jobs. If immigration were allowed to increase enough to keep the labor force growing at the rate of 1 percent a year from 2010 to 2040, it would push back the date when any tax increase would be needed to beyond 2050. It is worth noting that if the severe labor shortage implied by the Social Security projection develops, it might be difficult to *prevent* immigration from increasing to these levels.

The Problem with Longer Lives

The real problem with Social Security is very simple: People are living longer. This is the main long-range problem facing Social Security, and contrary to the "crisis" portrayed in the media, it has nothing to do with the baby-boom generation. Current projections show that the annual deficit will be 5.71 percent of payroll in 2070, long after the baby-boom generation has passed into history. By comparison, the annual deficit is projected to be only 4.44 percent of payroll in 2035, when the worst crunch from retired baby boomers will be felt.

If the retirement age is not raised beyond what is specified in current law, and life expectancies continue to increase, then a larger portion of people's lives will be spent in retirement, requiring that they either accept reduced retirement benefits relative to their working years or that they increase the portion of their income (higher taxes) that they put aside for retirement during their working years.

Since all projections show that future wages will, on average, be considerably higher than they are at present, even if people in the future are accepting relatively lower benefits, or paying relatively higher taxes, they still can enjoy substantially higher living standards than present workers. A simple example can illustrate this point. At present, the average annual before-tax wage is approximately $25,000. If the average Social Security payment is 40 percent of this wage, then an average retiree would receive $10,000 a year in benefits. In 2050, the average

before-tax wage will be more than $40,000. If typical retirees receive just 30 percent of this wage in benefits, they will be getting $12,000 a year, or 20 percent more than current retirees. Alternatively, looking at the tax side, if the current rate of payroll taxes is 15 percent, then an average worker would have $21,250 left after paying payroll taxes. If the tax rate was 20 percent in 2050, then an average worker would have $32,000 left after payroll taxes. The fact that real wages will rise means that future workers can have both a relative reduction in benefits and an increase in payroll taxes, and still enjoy a better living standard through their working careers and retirement than present workers and retirees.

The fact that the long-range problem facing Social Security is increasing life expectancies is particularly important in evaluating the intergenerational equity of public policy. The reason that life expectancies of younger generations are increasing is the greater wealth and improved technology that is being passed onto them by the generations that preceded them. It is hard to have too much sympathy for young people that are unhappy that they will have to pay a higher tax rate during their working lives to support the longer retirement that the sacrifices of previous generations allow them to enjoy. By all accounts younger generations will, on average, have better living standards than those that preceded them *solely* because they were born later. If the higher living standard comes with a higher tax rate, it is hard to see this as an injustice.

The Privatization Solution

There have been a series of plans put forward to address the long-range problems confronting Social Security by wholly or partially replacing the existing system with government-mandated individual savings accounts. The proponents of these plans argue that the high returns from holding stock and other private assets will allow workers to enjoy comfortable retirements without imposing as large a tax burden on the workers of the future. Under these proposals, workers would be required to place a portion of their payroll taxes to the Social Security fund into a personal retirement account instead. The Schieber-Weaver plan, for example, requires that workers place 5 percent of their wages in a personal retirement account. Workers would be obligated to leave money in these accounts until they reached retirement age, although there are differences between the plans about the extent of individual control over the accounts, and what can be done with the money upon retirement. The specific problems created by this type of mandatory saving system will be discussed in greater detail in the next section. The discussion in this section will only deal with the question of whether these plans offer any solution to the demographic problems noted above.

The advocates of privatization note that the average return from holding stock in the United States has been about 7 percent above the rate of inflation over a very long period. Their calculations show that even a relatively small amount invested at this rate of return and compounded over a working lifetime will lead to a very large retirement nest egg. For example, if a low-wage worker earning $10,000 a year can place just $500 a year in such an account, every year from age 20 to 65, they will accumulate more than $150,000. This is not a bad retirement nest egg for someone who never earned more than $10,000 a year. The returns would be proportionate, so that a person earning $20,000 putting $1,000 a year aside would have $300,000 upon retirement, and a person earning $40,000 would have $600,000. These sorts of returns should allow the current generation of workers to enjoy a very comfortable retirement, and significantly reduce the tax burden that future workers would otherwise confront.

These numbers sound very appealing. Unfortunately, there is a basic logical problem with the story. Privatization by itself will not generate any additional savings. In the scenario described above, 5 percent of wages (about $160 billion a year, at present) is shifted from the government in the form of Social Security taxes into private saving accounts. This means that private capital markets will see an additional $160 billion a year from these new accounts. However, the government will also have to borrow an additional $160 billion a year to make up for lost tax revenue, exactly offsetting the gain. The result is that there would be no net addition to national savings. Every additional dollar placed in private accounts is exactly offset by an additional dollar that the government has to borrow.

If there is no increase in national savings, then the economy will be no larger in the future than is indicated by current projections. This means that the economy in 2030 will be in no better situation to support the retirement of the baby boomers under privatization plans than it is under the current projections with the Social Security system left in place. If the privatization system leads to greater retirement incomes for today's baby boomers, then the burden imposed on future generations of workers must be even larger. The most obvious way in which this could be the outcome is if the increase in the deficit led to much higher interest rates for the government, compounding the tax burden associated with the higher debt. In this case, the tax burden might be felt through higher income or excise taxes, or through some other form of taxation, rather than the payroll tax. But the actual tax burden imposed on future generations will not be reduced, just shifted from one type of tax to another.

In fairness to the advocates of privatization, most proponents also support a large tax increase to get through the transition from the current system to a largely privatized system. For example, the Schieber-Weaver plan calls for an immediate tax increase equal to 1 percent of GDP (approximately $80 billion a year) to finance the transition. Raising taxes can raise national saving. However, this is true whether or not the tax increase is associated with privatizing Social Security. In other words, if it is a desirable policy to raise taxes in order to increase the level of national saving, this policy can be carried through without dismantling the Social Security system. Therefore, the merits of maintaining a public social insurance system can and should be considered independently of the question of whether additional taxes are needed to raise national saving.

It also is worth noting the relatively small impact that raising national savings can have on future income. According to the Clinton administration, the effect of reducing the deficit by about 1.75 percent of GDP (approximately $140 billion a year, at present) is to raise average wages by approximately 3.75 percent after thirty years. This is approximately equal to the loss due to upward redistribution that a typical male worker has been experiencing every four years since 1979. For most workers, the effect of changes in the distribution of income are likely to dwarf the effect of growth on the overall level of income.

Social Insurance Versus Government Mandated Savings

Many advocates of privatization speak as though Social Security is an outdated New Deal relic that needs to be replaced by a modern market-oriented private retirement system. While this caricature may have some initial appeal, a more careful investigation reveals a far more complex story. Most advocates of "privatization" are actually advocating systems of government mandated savings, which raise many thorny questions generally ignored by the privatizers. Instead of reducing government involvement in the economy, these systems may well end up increasing the extent of government involvement.

At the most basic level, there is a question of what type of account would qualify as an acceptable savings vehicle. There are two issues that arise here. First, how does the government ensure that the worker actually is depositing money in a real retirement account, and second, how does it ensure that the account is being managed in a responsible manner?

The first issue stems from the fact that the government will be *requiring* that workers place their money in retirement accounts. There may be many people who would prefer to spend their money now and not save for retirement. If the government wants to be certain that workers will actually have money when they retire, it has to make sure that money from the workers' paychecks goes into an account and stays there. This will require some agency comparable to the Internal Revenue Service to ensure that the mandated savings are withdrawn from workers' paychecks. It also will require an agency to oversee the accounts to ensure that they actually retain the savings. Without such oversight, many banks or brokerage houses may find it a very lucrative practice to obtain accounts by promising the opportunity for quick withdrawals of mandated savings.

The second issue addresses the need for the savings accounts to provide a secure retirement, which means the government must establish oversight to ensure that the accounts are invested in a relatively risk-free manner.

A further issue to consider in establishing a government-mandated saving system is the question of government guarantees. If the government is forcing individuals to contribute to these accounts, deciding which accounts they can contribute to, and constraining the behavior of the accounts, it would seem to bear some responsibility for the security of workers' investments. This would lead to the creation of a government agency comparable to the Federal Deposit Insurance Corporation, which would insure the value of the individual accounts. This creates a further set of regulatory problems since the existence of a government guarantee will provide an incentive for individuals to pursue more risky investment strategies. This exact problem pushed the cost of the savings and loan bailout to over $150 billion. The potential for losses will be even greater under the system of mandated savings since the government would be guaranteeing the value of the stock market.

If the mandated savings accounts are intended as a way to ensure that everyone has some minimal level of retirement income, they are a very indirect and inefficient means to accomplish this result. The regulatory complexity of maintaining such a system is considerable, as indicated above. In addition, the administrative and marketing costs incurred under this system are likely to be enormous. According to the American Council of Life Insurance's *1995 Life Insurance Fact Book Update,* the operating expenses of American private life insurance companies are approximately 27 percent of the benefits paid out. The operating expenses of the privatized Chilean pension system are approxi-

mately 15 percent of annual contributions, and over 60 percent of annual benefits. By comparison, the cost of operating the current Social Security system is less than 0.8 percent of annual benefits.

The reason why a government-run program is so much cheaper is simple: A single program eliminates all the costs of competition, regulation, and oversight. It also eliminates the six- and seven-figure salaries that would be earned by executives at private financial companies. In addition, it tremendously simplifies the process of collecting savings (taxes) from workers. If the intent of forcing everyone to save is to ensure that everyone has at least some minimal retirement income, it is much more efficient for the government to force the saving and provide the income itself than to involve hundreds or thousands of separate firms.

It makes sense to have a market where people can voluntarily choose the amount to put aside in savings and the assets in which they will place their money. It does not make sense to have a market where the government already made these choices for individuals. This is the basic flaw in all the government-mandated savings plans. The proponents want to force individuals to save, and to restrict the ways in which they can save, but prefer to accomplish this through a web of government regulatory agencies policing the actions of the market. The market is prevented from performing any useful function in this situation; it simply wastes resources.

Conclusion: Government Efficiency Versus Market Ideology

The basic story of Social Security is that it is a model program. The program is very efficient and does exactly what it was designed to do in providing a basic income to retirees. With relatively small changes, the program will be able to continue to serve this function throughout the next century. There is no Social Security crisis, now or in the foreseeable future. It would be a tragedy of great proportions if the proponents of privatization seized upon a false sense of crisis and the current ideological hostility to government to destroy the system and replace it with an ill-conceived system of mandated savings. Unfortunately, by the time the public came to fully realize what it had lost, it may well be too late.

18

Pension Policies to Maintain Workers' Access to Retirement

Teresa Ghilarducci

Pensions are an economic Rorschach test. Depending on the viewer, the system supplies the largest and fastest growing source of finance capital, provides vital worker income security, has been a major component in employee reward systems, and is a key element in labor market policies. Most pension policies either focus on capital or labor market effects. Policies that encourage pension fund liquidity and short-term profits can make patient capital and long-term investments costly, leading to lower wages and unstable jobs. In turn, declining real wages weaken a pension system as workers' deferred compensation falls. An integrated economic policy focused on restoring broadly shared prosperity for working Americans must therefore address the role of pensions in both labor and capital markets. Focusing on restoring prosperity for working Americans means that it should be the prime goal, and all other policies, whether they address deficits, taxes, interest rates, trade, or the environment, must meet the broadly shared prosperity test.

America's pension system resulted from the institutions and policies associated with our long period of broadly shared prosperity before the early 1970s; the weakening of these policies and institutions therefore has changed the pension system. Lower wages, more retirement years, and job shifts from manufacturing to service are the most important economic trends affecting the pension system. Indeed, pensions and retirement themselves are an important aspect of prosperity. Workers fought for a system to provide retirement income after a long career of work. In 1940, 42 percent of men over 65 worked or were looking for work; this rate fell steadily during the golden age of American prosperity to 20 percent in 1976. Elderly men's rate of labor force participation has remained fairly steady (though the trend has increased in recent years) at between 14 to 16 percent in the late 1980s. This trend may be explained by former labor secretary Robert Reich's observation that "employers are expanding their search to groups not otherwise thought to be in the labor force, including the elderly and the poor." He observed that the chances for seniors to find work may be improving in today's tight labor market, especially if they are willing to start at the bottom.

Unfortunately, prosperity that provides leisure at the end of a work life may be eroding. Workers' "old-age leisure" comes mainly from early retirement, not increased longevity. One of the striking trends in the post–World War II period is the slight improvement in the number of years of life a 65-year-old man can expect. In

1950, his life expectancy was 78.1; by 1991, it increased only 2.9 years to 81.[1] The idea that life expectancy trends are threatening pensions is misplaced; most of the boost in life expectancy comes from decreasing infant mortality. Increased longevity and old-age and disability pensions are complementary developments that improve workers' standard of living and are a hallmark of a prospering economy. Therefore, increased longevity does not mean people should work longer and accept cuts in Social Security and pensions.

However, in the last ten years, the amount a typical middle-income retiree household receives from pensions has fallen from 19 to 16 percent. Meanwhile, throughout the 1970s and 1980s, the proportion of all workers who are covered by voluntary employer-provided pensions remained steady at 45 to 46 percent but declined to 44 percent in 1993. The real value of the private pension benefit fell from $745 to $735 from 1984 to 1991. Therefore, it is not surprising that middle-class retirees expect more from Social Security than private pensions. Indeed, 57 percent of retirement income for middle-class retirees came from Social Security, up from 47 percent in 1980.

Paradoxically, while pension benefits are falling, pension funds, fueled by soaring stock prices, are increasing their importance in capital markets. Pension funds make up the largest source of U.S. finance capital and, as a share of total financial assets, surpassed banks in 1989. The paradox—large funds and small pensions—cannot be explained by fund growth that will eventually go to workers when they retire. Nor can the paradox be explained by a growth in pension fund coverage that yields a small benefit to new people. The factors that do explain the paradox bode poorly for workers' retirement income security.

Why Growing Funds Do Not Mean Growing Benefits

There are three major reasons linked to basic economic trends that explain why pension fund growth does not mean improved retirement income security. First, the rate of pension coverage has stagnated in the last twenty years at 50 percent of the workforce. Unions and the size of firms are the most important factors determining workers' pension coverage. Eighty-nine percent of union members versus 34 percent of all workers have a pension. Three out of four large firms have pension plans compared with only one out of four firms with fewer than 100 workers. Yet even low-income, mobile unionized workers in retail, mining, construction, and unskilled manufacturing have multi-employer pensions funds. Multi-employer funds collect contributions from many employers whose workers typically belong to one union that negotiates pension benefits. A board composed of equal numbers of members from management and the union establish benefit levels and investment policy.

Second, the positive union effect on pension coverage can be partly explained by the psychological and political effects of people making savings and spending decisions in a group. A group can enforce a savings norm and negotiate automatic workplace deductions (whether implicit or explicit). By themselves, individuals are tempted to spend more of what they earn.

Third, the number of participants and the size of funds in defined contribution and individual savings plans are growing relative to defined benefit pension plans. In 1988, over 50 percent of workers reported their primary pension was a defined benefit plan; less than 30 percent said a defined contribution plan was their primary benefit. In 1993, the ratios had nearly reversed.

This shift means benefits are not distributed to workers who stay with a firm, acquire skills, and who live the longest, as is the case with defined benefit plans. Not only do workers lose the security of the insurance inherent in a defined benefit structure, they also are more likely to spend their funds before retirement. Defined benefit funds cannot be spent and are trusteed by professionals who invest in a large portfolio, in contrast to individual accounts, which lose the advantages of economies of scale and professional investment strategies.

Increasingly, middle-class workers are using their so-called retirement accounts as liquid savings to buy housing, finance periods of unemployment and fund children's education. Research by the Public Agenda Foundation and Employee Benefits Research Institute found that people generally do not participate in voluntary pension plans and withdraw funds before retirement because saving is not a priority. A full 34 percent are convinced they do not earn enough; 37 percent underestimate how much they need to save for retirement; 68 percent say they could eat out less, but 18 percent say they will not (oddly, the higher the income, the less likely people are to identify unnecessary expenditures).

Fourth, pensions grew because of the unexpected boom in financial markets. Corporate funds—90 percent of all funds—turned those earnings back to corporate treasuries. In contrast, jointly trusteed pensions used the excess earnings to better fund the pensions and improve pension generosity (i.e., normal cost divided by the number of participants). In 1981, the generosity of corporate plans was approximately $700 per person per year while union funds were about $400. After 1991, when financial markets boomed, generosity soared to over $1,000 in union plans and increased to only a little over $900 in corporate plans.

Social Security and pension reformers must acknowledge the weaknesses in voluntary and individual approaches to retirement income security. These include: the decline in union power to obtain adequate pension benefits, the loss of group norms to enforce savings, and the propensity of corporations to take "Wall Street" gains in the pension funds for corporate rather than pension purposes.

Pension Reform Ideas from the World Bank and Wall Street

Wall Street interests in the United States, as well as the World Bank, have offered up several pension reform strategies. The failed proposals of Senators Robert Kerrey and John Danforth— chair and vice chair of the 1993–94 Bipartisan Commission on Entitlement and Tax Reform— to drastically alter the system appeared again in a minority report of the 1994–95 Social Security Advisory Council, the Schieber-Weaver privatization proposal, and in various proposals advocated by the Wall Street–funded campaign of the Cato Institute.

Substituting mandatory IRAs for Social Security replaces insurance protection for a risky investment fund. Individual accounts are not insurance—they do not redistribute funds to those who pay to protect themselves from risk. The clear winners would be money managers who, in 1993–97, would have received between $70 and $160 billion in new assets if Social Security had been privatized.

The World Bank released its comprehensive report of the world's old-age programs in 1994 at the same time the business members of the biennial Social Security Advisory Council and the Entitlement Commission started to float privatization proposals. The World Bank argues that national old-age programs must have a first pillar that protects the old against poverty; a second pillar of *mandatory,* perhaps occupational-based, pensions that are privately managed; and a third pillar of voluntary savings. The pillar metaphor implies that all three sources are equally important.[2] The metaphor is sloppy and inaccurate. A better metaphor is a pyramid: Social Security is the base, employer pensions are in the middle, and savings are on the top. The most affluent elderly receive one-fourth of their retirement income from both Social Security and private pensions. The bottom one-fifth (those with incomes below $6,570) receive 80 percent of their income from Social Security.

The World Bank also argues that people should work longer to accumulate a bigger individual account to fund retirement. Yet, raising the age at which people can collect full benefits hurts those who cannot find work because of old age. They are, in effect, disabled but cannot meet the strict tests that younger people must meet for disability and unemployment insurance. Thus, raising the retirement age is not just a happy adjustment healthy people make for living longer but an erosion of disability and survivors insurance. Individual and voluntary approaches are the weakest link in any old-age program and should always be at the top, not the base, of the retirement income-support pyramid.

The World Bank's exemplar model is the 1981 Chilean pension reform. General Pinochet fully dismantled Chile's Social Security system with individual accounts. For most workers to be better off under the Pinochet system, individual funds will have to earn rates of return that far exceed the average growth in the economy (over 7 percent). This is only possible if real wages lag growth. Furthermore, the system is mandatory only for workers and firms in the formal sector. The high rate of contributions for the new system, 13 percent of payroll, could encourage a shift to the informal sector, resulting in smaller accounts and final pensions.

These problems of inadequacy, reliance on capital markets, and spotty coverage will plague any retirement system that is not based on universal social insurance. A mixed system is desirable, to be sure. However, a three-pillared system is much less reliable than a pyramid system.

The World Bank's Ponzi Scheme

One concern raised by proponents of the privatization is that the current pay-as-you-go system is like a Ponzi scheme. Under this assumption, workers can fund retirees only if the workforce is productive and large enough. As the baby boomers start retiring, the ratio of workers to retirees will decrease—reaching an all-time low by 2020—forcing increased taxes to fund the retirees. Instead, advocates for advanced-funded systems argue that workers should save for their own retirement and not put the burden on future workers.

Those that advocate advanced-funded systems contend that the bulge in the population (i.e., people born between 1945 and 1996) should save and invest while working. When they retire, they should sell off the capital and live on the income. However, just as their demand for financial assets would lift stock and bond prices, their sell-off starting in the year 2020 would lower asset values.

The boomers caused a surge of kindergarteners and college students in the 1950s and 1960s. Therefore, the estimated percentage of the U.S. population aged 65 and over will increase from 12.6 percent in 1990 to 16.3 percent in 2020 (incidentally the lowest percentage among the

twenty-nine Organization for Economic Cooperation and Development [OECD] countries).
Not only will pay-as-you-go systems such as
Social Security face increasing costs—which
we could pay for now with a 2.2 percent increase in payroll taxes—defined benefits plans
will have to adjust to the increase in the aging
population and fund more. Defined contribution
plans and personal savings will also generate a
huge growth in asset pools in the next ten to
twenty years. Wall Street firms would benefit
greatly if even 2 to 5 percent of total wages
($70 to $160 billion) were diverted to over 100
million new individual privatized accounts from
Social Security each year.

But, according to economists Sly Schieber
and John Shoven, as the bulge in the population moves through the age cohorts, the
United States will begin a de-accumulation
period around 2025. This de-accumulation
could cause a decrease in asset values. The
only hope for picking up the surplus capital in
2020 to 2035 is from the young populations
of Mexico, Brazil, and, perhaps, China and
India. Of course, this only works if these
countries have advanced-funded pension systems that invest in foreign assets. This may
explain why the World Bank's effort to privatize pension systems spans the globe. The
high return to privatizing only works in an
elaborate system in which populations with
different age distributions are buying and selling each other's investments.

In addition, pension investment policy must
learn from the failure of private pension systems to expand and provide significant retirement income to the middle class. The economic
activity generated by directing pensions to "targeted" job creation could be as important to
workers as the pensions they provide.

Pension Erosion—What to Do?

There are several approaches in Congress to expand pension coverage, and they all are designed
to enhance the defined contribution system. The
most promising idea explores the "reverse match"
concept where, instead of workers' making voluntary contributions to 401(k)s, employers would
contribute to employee accounts, thereby allowing workers to decide whether or not to *match* the
employer's contribution. The funds should be un-
available for withdrawal since workers often are
tempted to cash in pension funds for more immediate needs.

Senator Bingaman's plan, called Pro-Save,
considered a similar strategy in November
1996. Employers may be drawn to the Pro-Save
approach to escape the complex anti-discrimination rules that limit how much of the tax benefits go to high-paid workers. The "reverse
matching" concept allows employers to avoid
the anti-discrimination rules in return for contributing a "safe-harbor" amount for each employee. This amount could be, say, 3 to 5
percent of payroll (in addition, of course, to the
current Social Security tax).

Since 1994, the Clinton administration has
focused on the Savings Information Project, a
broad-based "public"-service campaign in
which the government uses private foundations
and organizations to issue basic information on
the "magic" of compound interest and retirement income needs. However, historically U.S.
group savings and consumption norms significantly influence behavior for middle- and low-
income workers. The most effective way for
workers to save is to face automatic contributions (within the context of group norms) into
funds that cannot be spent for any purpose other
than retirement.

Private Pensions in the Capital Markets: Effect on Wages and Employment

Private management of pension funds must factor in the fundamental problems in the way capital is allocated to productive investments. And as Jane D'Arista states in her essay, pension funds have been important causes of the globalization of financial markets. The promise that the growth will continue forever is a risky basis for a pension system. Pension management has been accused of distorting financial markets. Private pension investing may contribute to a short-term mentality in capital markets, and the funds' current management techniques are not amenable to targeted and relationship investing. Policy-makers and scholars are demonstrating increasingly that, if left alone, institutional investors will not necessarily make productive investments that further economic development. Studies of the role of pensions in takeovers and leveraged buyouts conclude that, without a huge pot of pension money controlled by a few managers, arbitrageurs could not quickly assemble these deals.

Moreover, the costs of administering pension plans, especially 401(k)s, have been masked somewhat by high returns. The private pension management industry has not endured the scrutiny that the health care industry underwent especially in regard to the ever-present possibility of churning and agency problems.

In addition to the costs, there is an important issue of who owns, and therefore should control, pension fund assets. The unionized multi-employer funds are jointly controlled by employee and employer trustees and are more likely to benefit workers. The corporate programs are controlled by, and therefore are more likely to benefit, corporate managers. Workers own and bear the risk of failure if pension funds collapse. The first principle of property rights is that risk-bearers are property owners and have the right to some control. Workers in U.S. corporations are denied these rights.

In 1994, the Clinton administration issued an interpretative bulletin that gave approval for funds to consider ancillary beneficial effects on employment and regional development when choosing investment vehicles. The bulletin was mild because the vehicles also had to meet traditional market tests for risk and return. More importantly, the Department of Labor contracted out for a clearinghouse that would document and explain how a fund can get good returns and promote economic development. The Republican Congress accused the Clinton administration of tampering and the initiative was frozen.

Securities Transactions Tax

Many economists, including Joseph Stiglitz, have proposed a securities transactions tax. So far, pension fund managers have opposed it. The AFL-CIO opposed Senators Nancy Kassebaum and Robert Dole's initiative for a securities transactions tax because it felt it was a start down the slippery slope of taxing pension funds. Randy Barber and this author proposed to impose a twist by penalizing short trades and credit long trades. This would do what the Fed's Operation Twist tried in the 1970s—to raise short-term cost of capital and reduce long-term cost of capital.

Joint Trusteeship

In 1990, a proposal was initiated to put worker representatives on single-employer pension fund boards of trustees; presently 90 percent of funds in the private sector are controlled solely by the employer and 10 percent by joint boards. The arguments for joint control were that management could benefit from worker participation and that workers would have a say.

Investigate the Pension Fund Management Industry Like Health Care

Active money managers may not earn their fees, but since every fund hires one, any one fund is loath to fire an active manager. Pension participants pay for this collective action problem. The industry faces only self-regulation. All funds are required to act "like prudent experts." This behavior is defined in a circular fashion: "standard practice." If the standard practices are inefficient and self-serving, they are still protected. Pension fund management needs as much scrutiny as the health care industry.

Conclusion

The pyramid supporting U.S. workers' retirement income security is under fundamental attack. Many new employers are moving toward self-directed individual accounts that put more risk on workers. Notably, union plans and large firms still provide insurance-type pensions (defined benefit). The move from collective to individual pensions also poses challenges for collective control of assets needed to promote targeted investments. Underlying the attack on the pension system is the World Bank and neoliberal policies worldwide that challenge workers' right to retirement and the very meaning of prosperity.

Notes

1. Black male longevity has actually decreased. A young black male entering the workforce at age 20 in 1985 could have expected to live 67.1 years. By 1990, the life expectancy of this group fell six months to 66.7 years. The average black male entering the workforce today cannot expect to retire at the age when he is eligible for full Social Security benefits (though he will receive disability and survivors benefits).

2. The report is silent about how the investments of the privately managed tier would be controlled and regulated. The report also acknowledges, but glosses over the fact, that means-tested programs are politically fragile. The report does not sufficiently warn readers that Chile's system is projected to work well only if annual financial returns exceed 9 percent and people keep their jobs continually for forty years.

19

Public Investment for a Twenty-first Century Economy

Jeff Faux

Investment is the act of shaping the future. Public investment in infrastructure is a major way democratic people shape their collective future and is an essential complement to private investment. Government spending on schools, roads, bridges, and basic research and development is a foundation upon which the private sector builds profit-making enterprises.

Public investment is also a generator of specific private investment opportunities. America's history is studded with grand economic sectors opened up by government and profited on by business. Early in our republic's life, we built canals and highways and provided land for towns and schools in the territories. Government financed the first assembly lines, subsidized the railroads to settle the West, and developed long-range radio technologies. It created the suburbs after World War II and explored space. Government leadership developed the jet engine, the computer, and the Internet. Each of these programs generated jobs and businesses. Just as important, they spun off technological advances that became what Robert Heilbroner calls economic "klondikes"— massive veins of investment opportunities that have been the building blocks of American prosperity.

Finally, public infrastructure is a major way

a democratic society balances the tendency of the market to concentrate wealth and economic opportunity. By providing commonly owned spheres of "enabling" activity accessible to all—schools to all students, roads to all truckers, telecommunications to all businesses—public infrastructure extends the web of upward mobility to a widening circle of the population. And by providing the public sector with leverage over resources, infrastructure spending allows government to redirect resources to citizens and regions that the market leaves behind in its pursuit of narrower, shorter-term goals.

Not all basic infrastructure is financed by direct government expenditures. Railroads were subsidized with undeveloped land; airlines with rights to airspace and a flight control system; and radio and television by privileged access to the public's airwaves. In these and other cases, public and private funds and interests were and are co-mingled.

Because of the alarming deterioration of public support for traditional infrastructure—education and training, public works, and civilian research and development—the bulk of this brief essay is addressed to those sectors. But the reader should also be aware that the deregulation of telecommunications, transportation, electric utilities, and even finance also has the potential for eroding the opportunity-widening functions of public infrastructure.

The Importance of Public Infrastructure

Until very recently, standard statistical descriptions of the economy (e.g., the basic national income accounts) treated all government spending as consumption and thereby ignored the contribution that public investment makes to productivity and overall economic growth. Economists who have studied the issue in depth have found that public investment produces substantial gains in productivity, private investment, and overall economic growth. Studies of physical infrastructure spending by David Aschauer, Alicia Munnell, and Sharon Erenburg found that every dollar of public investment raises private investment another forty-five to fifty cents. Indeed, Aschauer, Munnell, Douglas Holtz-Ekins, and Amy Schwartz concluded that, because of years of neglect, investment in public infrastructure now produces a higher return (measured by increases in productivity) than investment in the private sector. Although government reports now make some attempt to separate capital from operating expenditures, the way in which macroeconomic data are collected, analyzed, and discussed still systematically undervalues public investment.

Economists may quarrel over its exact contribution, but there is little doubt among serious observers that public investment plays a major role. In 1995, over 400 prominent economists wrote an open letter to the president and the Congress warning of the dangers of neglecting public investment. "Just as business must continually reinvest in order to prosper," they wrote, "so must a nation. Higher productivity—the key to higher living standards—is a function of public as well as private investment." They concluded that "compared with what we need in order to compete and to make all segments of our society productive, we are still not investing enough."

In this new global economy, public investment is even more important than it used to be. Where private investment has become footloose—forcing American workers to compete with workers from countries where wage growth is deliberately kept below productivity growth by public policy—public investment, in both human and physical capital, is by its very nature targeted at improving the competitiveness of those who produce in America. Indeed, those who urge us to "embrace" the global marketplace have a special obligation to assure that we raise the level of public investment.

Today, by any measure, public investment in the United States is falling further behind that necessary to maintain a productive and stable society. A decreasing share of gross domestic product is devoted to federal non-defense spending (including transfers to state and local governments) for physical infrastructure, education and training, and research and development. In 1996, it was some 40 percent less than it was twenty years earlier. The sharp downward shift in the share of GDP going to public investment occurred in 1981, after which the federal government invested considerably less in real terms than in the previous fifteen years.

Nor has the slack been made up by state and local governments. As a share of GDP, state and local government spending on capital projects and for education has fallen since the early 1970s.

Internationally, the United States now invests relatively less in its basic infrastructure than other major industrial nations. For more than two decades, it has ranked lowest in public works spending among the G-7 nations.

For the past decade, the existence of a large federal fiscal deficit has been the excuse for squeezing public sector investment. When President Clinton early in his term decided to make balancing the budget his economic priority, the concerns of supporters of public investment were assuaged by the promise that once balance was achieved, the government could return to neglected public investments.

The budget could have been balanced in a number of ways, including tax increases. But the process was concentrated on cutting discretionary spending—the source of public investment funds. Moreover, it was accompanied by rhetoric, for example, "The era of big government is over," that tended to deny the importance of public spending to the country's economic health. Not surprisingly, the political constituency for public investment became intimidated and discouraged. As a result, after the budget was balanced in 1998, the debate over how to use the surplus centered around Republican demands for tax cuts and a defensive Democratic strategy that purported to save the surplus for Social Security. Public investment needs were largely forgotten.

In his budget for the fiscal year 2000, the president proposed a small spate of programs—some of which did reflect new investments in education. But overall, the downward trend in domestic spending was continued. The president's plan called for a further reduction of domestic spending's share of GDP by fiscal year 2004, from 3.5 to 3.2 percent.

In addition, the devolution of highly visible and politically sensitive social-service programs to the states will put increasing pressure on their budgets. As Timothy Bartik has suggested, there is already a systematic bias against state and local government spending on infrastructure because local taxpayers must pay all the costs while the benefits often spill over to others.

Two decades of neglect have already taken a huge toll on our public capital. A comprehensive survey of public- and private-sector expert estimates of physical, human, and technological capital needs in 1991 concluded that, in order to keep from widening the gap between needs and actual investment, the federal government should have been spending a minimum of $60 billion and possibly as much as $125 billion. The estimates were based on a modest definition of investment; it did not include spending on health, housing, environmental cleanup, public safety, and other purposes that also add to our nation's economic strength. The 1991 investment gap was as follows:

Human Resources (billions of dollars)	
Education and Training	$23.3–45.0
Children	6.1–12.5
Physical Capital	22.7–54.8
Research and Development	10.8–13.5
Total Investment	$62.9–125.8

Since then, new studies have shown even wider gaps. For example, in 1996, the General Accounting Office reported that the nation's schools needed another $100 billion just to fix up public school buildings—repair the roofs, get the rats out of the basements, and wire the school rooms for computers. The Republican congressional leadership was completely unresponsive. The president suggested spending $5 billion over three years.

The human side of the ongoing public investment crisis was reflected in a recent interview with the retired chief engineer of New York City. Speaking of the deterioration of the city's crucial web of bridges, he noted that a bridge is in fact a series of interlocking flexible parts that, if not lubricated, will crack. In 1900, the city had 200 people painting and lubricating the Williamsburg Bridge. Now there are three. "You can take your hand and go right through the concrete—the bridge has moved so much because they didn't lubricate the bearing plates."

The Public Balance Sheet

Despite the growing gap, public investment has virtually disappeared in the national discussion over economic policy. It is now completely overwhelmed by the obsession with cutting back government spending. The problem is symbolized by "national debt clocks"—clicking away with so many dollars a second. The device is used as a prop by politicians (and often affixed to billboards) to frighten the populace with the nightmare of government spending out of control.

The debt clock is a half-truth, which is often worse than a lie. It reflects an absurd accounting notion that is concerned exclusively with the liability side of the ledger, ignoring the assets. Also missing is another dial—the value of what we are getting for government borrowing.

This is not just a problem of public accounting; it points to the misguided moral motivation behind many people's concerns with the public debt (i.e., the concern with the kind of economic future we are leaving our children and grandchildren). It is frequently claimed that "every new American baby is presented with an $18,000 debt"—representing its per capita share of the federal government's outstanding liabilities. Indeed, if that were the complete story, we would be guilty of burdening our children's future. But in fact, the newborn baby is also entitled to a share of the federal government's

assets that, as indicated below, are just a shade lower than its per capita liabilities. Moreover, the child is also entitled to its share of assets financed by that public debt and now owned by state and local governments—schools, highways, water systems, and so on. Beyond that, the child is eligible to share in the nation's productive private assets, many of which would not exist if they had not been stimulated by public investment.

Part of the problem is, of course, politics. The national debt clock is sponsored by people interested in discrediting government. And part of the problem lies in bad economics.

But part of the problem is also with the way that we keep the federal books. First, all expenditures, whether for operations or capital investment, are lumped together in one year. Thus, both a one-year subsidy to a farmer and an investment in a bridge that takes three years to build and will bring the farmer's goods to market more rapidly over the next fifty years are lumped together in the federal budget. No sensible business or householder manages its own finances this way. A business or household knows that its financial health depends not on just how much cash it takes in and spends each year, but also on the condition of its "balance sheet," a comparison of assets and liabilities. When a family borrows money to buy a house, it does not normally consider itself to be worse off because in that one year it ran a deficit (i.e., the cost of the house is more than its annual income). On the contrary, it considers itself to be better off because it has bought an asset that can rise in value. The same is true for a business buying a new plant or a piece of machinery that will last more than a year. As with households and business, the question is not the size of the government's debt, but on what one has used the proceeds. If a family borrows to buy a house, it may improve its financial condition because it now has an asset. If it borrows to take a vacation, it probably will not.

From 1980 to 1993, the federal government's debt rose more than 400 percent. During that time per capita liabilities rose from $12,130 to $18,110. Per capita federally owned and financed assets actually dropped, from $17,670 to $17,109. In 1980, the balance sheet of the U.S. government showed that assets exceeded liabilities by 27 percent. By 1993, liabilities were some 4 percent greater than assets. Had we maintained our national assets at the same level that they were in 1980—that is, had we used the increase in the national debt for investment—the federal balance sheet would still be in the black.

A balance sheet approach is not by any means a definitive measure of the government's health or, more importantly, the effect of government investment on the economy. It does not, for example, adequately capture the effects of education, health care, and similar investments that, in the new global economy, are arguably more important than traditional public works. But it serves as a proxy for the shift away from investment—and to remind us that the composition of spending is as important as its totals.

It is often argued that the problem of government investment is not that we are not spending enough, but that the government is not spending it wisely enough. There is always need for more improvement in the efficiency of the public sector. But there is no serious evidence that the public sector is less efficient than it was in the past, when the valuable investments we are currently living on were made. Indeed, a good case can be made that the public sector as a whole is more efficient than it used to be. Moreover, many of the measures used to denounce the public sector—like the calculation of liabilities

without assets—are misleading. Thus, for example, it is commonly charged that funding of the public schools has doubled with no commensurate rise in SAT scores. But the great bulk of the increase in school funding has been for special education—largely to extend school services to the physically and mentally handicapped. One can argue the merits of such policy, but spending on such disadvantaged groups cannot be expected to affect the performance on SATs. Moreover, SAT scores, after declining between 1965 and 1975, have held steady since, which is a remarkable performance considering that one-third more students (primarily those who rank lower in school achievement) take the SATs than in the 1970s. Finally, as a very labor-intensive service, education costs should be expected to rise somewhat faster than the costs of other goods and services. Adjusted for inflation, education spending has risen a modest 1 percent per year. More money is not the sole answer to the problem of education in America, but in a market economy, little improvement can be expected without it. If money were not important, we would not see the huge disparity in funding between schools in upper- and lower-income neighborhoods.

Where Will the Money Come From?

Despite the growing investment gap in each of the three major public investment categories—education and training, infrastructure, and research and development—the problem of funding remains.

Capital Budgeting

The first step toward solving the money problem is to keep in mind that there is nothing wrong with borrowing if the proceeds are dedicated to investment that generates a return greater than the cost of borrowing. And in any sensible accounting system, investments would be separated from operating expenditures and amortized over time. The revenue stream can come from the tax proceeds of a more efficient economy and, where appropriate, fees or tolls from specific projects. The treatment of less-tangible investments such as education and training is more complex than, say, the investment in fixed assets such as bridges or schools. But the U.S. government already has developed statistical techniques for doing so. In any event, it is hard to argue that in an information age, the improvement of skills for the working population is not an investment in the future. Thus, if it makes sense for an individual to borrow for his or her education, it surely makes sense for the U.S. government to borrow to educate its people.

Beyond education and training there are other human investments that one can argue are equally important—spending on children's nutrition, public health, and public safety. Indeed, many argue that the reason not to have a capital budget is that there are so many government activities that might arguably be considered as investments that a capital budget would rationalize borrowing for any purpose. This is an exaggeration, but in any event, it would be healthy to have a public debate over defining public investment. Certainly, there is little reason to hide these problems from the public.

Capital budgeting is not compatible with the demand to put the budget, as we now calculate it, into permanent balance. But it is compatible with federal fiscal responsibility. For example, the current Republican-led Congressional Budget Office has pointed out that it is not necessary to achieve balance in order to assure a sustainable budget as far into the future as we can see. A budgetary strategy aimed at stabilizing the ratio of national debt to GDP would permit us to run permanent deficits on the order to 1.5–2 percent of GDP. Without going to a full-fledged capital budget, we could raise the level of public investment by this amount (representing over $130–175 billion in 1999) and remain within the bounds of sensible fiscal discipline.

Infrastructure Bank

Even within the balanced-budget framework, there remains a number of strategies to raise public infrastructure investments. For example, as suggested by financier Felix Rohatyn and former New York City budget director Carol O'Cleireacain, the federal government could create an off-budget infrastructure fund with a fixed long-term revenue stream—say a gasoline or energy tax. The fund would permit a much-needed investment catch-up within the confines of fiscal austerity. A $10 billion revenue stream could generate $25 billion in federal investment over the first ten years, much of which would be concentrated in the nation's cities, not only to repair and replace much-neglected transportation and water systems and other capital stock, but also to provide jobs and opportunities. These investments become the backbone of a twenty-first-century program of urban revitalization, and the jobs created would not simply be pick-and-shovel jobs. Today's public work construction requires computer skills and technical knowledge that would represent career opportunities for thousands of young people in the inner city.

Human Capital

Money for more investment in education and training could come from a small dedicated tax on financial securities. Such a tax would have the added benefit of helping to discourage financial market speculation and reduce market volatility. It would also be highly and appropriately progressive, shifting resources from often empty and speculative "investment" in stocks and bonds to real productive investment in people.

A 0.25 percent tax on all stock transactions, for example, with an appropriately weighted tax applied to bonds, options, futures, currency swaps, and other financial instruments would raise over $30 billion per year with little impact on the normal functioning of financial markets. The costs of transactions on the major stock exchanges have fallen rapidly over the last twenty years. So even if the full cost of the tax is passed on to the buyers of financial instruments, average transaction costs would be raised only to their 1982 levels.

Finding the Peace Dividend

We now plan to spend as many real dollars on defense in the year 2000 as we did in 1975—in the midst of the cold war, when the Soviet Union, armed to the teeth, was threatening to bury us. The rationale is that we must be prepared to fight two simultaneous wars with "rogue states"—North Korea, Cuba, Libya, Syria, Iraq, or Iran. The *combined* military budgets of these nations in 1995 was at most $15 billion, as opposed to a $265 billion U.S. military budget. We are spending roughly $80 billion for the defense of Western Europe alone at a time when the Soviet Union has disappeared and the former communist nations of Eastern Europe are clamoring to join the Western alliance. We spend at least $35 billion to maintain a bloated and unaccountable Central Intelligence Agency at cold war levels.

Defense experts such as William Kaufmann and Lawrence Korb estimate that we could easily cut another $40 billion a year from the Clinton military budget, and more from the even greater military spending advocated by the Republican leadership. Such a cut would still leave the United States with by far the single most powerful military force in the world.

The prize here is not just the saving of money. It is the opportunity to find civilian uses for the technical resources that the nation has bought and paid for in the decades of high defense spending. Successful conversion can happen only if it is linked to a public investment strategy, because there is almost no private market for the technology we built to fight the cold war. Either we continue to waste it by producing and exporting weapons that neither we nor the rest of the world needs, dismantle it and lose our investment, or apply it to the great internal development project of rebuilding America.

Other Potential Sources of Dedicated Taxes

The United States is the least-taxed economy in the advanced world. One reason is that our tax system remains riddled with preferences and unequal treatment. The politics of tax policy make it extremely difficult to eliminate many of these tax loopholes because the benefits are general (deficit reduction) and the costs are specific to industries, individuals, and firms. But if the benefits were dedicated to specific public investments, whose case has been effectively argued, the potential for raising revenues could be enhanced.

Many billions of dollars for investment might be shifted from tax expenditures that do neither the economy nor the society any good.

Examples include loopholes through which for-eign corporations avoid paying U.S. taxes, in-terest subsidies to state and local bonds used for private purposes, and specific tax preferences for the insurance, thrift, mining, pharmaceuti-cal, and timber industries. Other possibilities in-clude the taxation of air and water pollution, which in effect would represent a collection of rent for the use of the public's domain.

Public Leadership

Implicit in the call for expanded infrastructure investment is an assumption of a civilian public sector capable of allocating resources and un-derstanding the long-term needs of the econ-omy. After at least two decades of systematic ideological attack, this assumption is problem-atic. The reason for some of the opposition to more public investment is the widespread con-viction that the government is, by its very na-ture, incompetent. In fact, the decline in public confidence in government over the last twenty years has mirrored the decline in public invest-ment. Yet the bulk of the American people re-main convinced that the government should be responsible for providing opportunities for work, training, social services, and the regula-tion of the marketplace. A 1995 Harris poll for *Business Week* showed 70 percent or more of the electorate thought the federal government had a responsibility for providing a job for those willing to work, providing continued ac-cess to job training, providing a minimum level of health care, and making sure that business sells safe products.

One clue on how to solve this puzzle is a comparison of the civilian government's lead-ership role in America's past economic devel-opment. Unlike many other nations, where civilian government *per se* is accepted as im-portant, government in America has by and large been successful when it has been "mis-sion" oriented, when its energy has been ap-plied to specific national goals—creating a barge canal network, a transcontinental rail-road track, a space program, or a more pro-ductive agriculture. For most of the past half-century, the overriding public investment task has been prevailing in the cold war. In fact, the two major civilian infrastructure ef-forts of the post–World War II period—edu-cation and highways—were promoted as part of national defense. With the end of the cold war, it may well be that in order to obtain the political support for investing in a twenty-first-century infrastructure, we need to define a new national task for the twenty-first cen-tury—the domestic redevelopment of the United States, its cities, its transportation sys-tems, its telecommunications networks, and, most of all, its people.

20

Trade and Inequality

Thea Lee

Globalization: For Better or for Worse?

There is a certain schizophrenia in public discourse about globalization. On the one hand, free trade and investment flows are touted as policies bringing remarkable benefits: efficiency, faster growth, more jobs, and good jobs. On the other hand, it is also common to read that "we" must tighten our belts and sacrifice now that the United States is part of the global economy. Many people outside of Washington policy circles are understandably confused over whether they personally can expect to reap gains from freer trade or whether they will be called on to sacrifice their jobs or income for the sake of "the global economy."

While many of the advocates for continued or accelerated globalization appear untroubled by the contradiction inherent in these two positions, ordinary people tend to fixate on the implied threat and the negative message in the belt-tightening exhortation. This may be because it resonates with their own experience, or because it is more concrete than the vague allusions to widespread benefits.

Hurting Some and Helping Others

While many economists and journalists express frustration with what they perceive as ignorance or shortsightedness on the part of the public,

this popular distrust of globalization or "free trade" is rooted in real and concrete economic facts. Trade liberalization does not benefit all members of society equally: In fact, it makes some people worse off, even in absolute terms, while making others better off. This is true even in those cases when trade liberalization can be said unequivocally to make the country (or the sum of individual incomes in the country) richer. Capital outflows, particularly direct investment in low-wage countries, can exacerbate the polarizing impact of trade, especially when companies use the credible threat of shifting production to low-wage countries as a bargaining lever.

This basic finding is not new. It is as old as trade theory itself, although it was formalized mathematically in 1941 by Wolfgang Stolper and Paul Samuelson.[1] The modern theory predicts that less-skilled labor in a country such as the United States, which is relatively abundant in skilled labor and capital, will be made worse off as trade barriers are lowered: The price of labor-intensive goods will fall, as cheap imports gain better access to the domestic market, and thus the wage of less-skilled (often described as non-college-educated) workers will fall. Since non-college-educated workers make up almost three-quarters of the U.S. workforce, this is a powerful and politically relevant prediction.

It is important to note that this prediction

holds even when the dollar value of imports is equal to the value of exports (that is, trade is balanced) and when the domestic economy is at full employment. It occurs because trade liberalization causes production to shift between sectors—out of those where the domestic advantage is weakest into those for which the domestic climate, factor endowments, and technology are best suited. Any efficiency benefits from trade are directly proportional to the inter-sectoral disruptions that are caused.

However, in the real world, trade is not always balanced; the economy is not always at full employment; and markets—both for goods and for labor—are not always perfectly competitive. Thus, there are several other channels through which trade and investment could affect the distribution of wages: large and chronic trade deficits, which reduce the demand for labor, particularly in the manufacturing sector; outsourcing of the labor-intensive portions of the production process; the erosion of monopoly profits in domestic industries, which can in turn be passed on in the form of lower wages; spillover effects of displaced manufacturing workers on service-sector wages; and weakening of the bargaining power of less-skilled labor vis-à-vis owners of capital. These effects overlap, as do the impacts of technological change and declining unionization.

Traditionally, economists have readily admitted that there are "winners and losers" from freer trade (as is the case with virtually all economic policy changes). But they finesse all distributional implications with a neat sleight of hand: *if* the net social gains from trade liberalization were to be redistributed from winners to losers, *then* it would be possible for every individual to be better off with lower trade barriers. The problem with this formulation is twofold. First, the redistribution does not occur. Second,

the focus on net societal gains has left too little attention for the issues related to distribution: Who gains and who loses? Is the impact of trade regressive or progressive? How large are the losses relative to the gains?

The Social Context

In this paper, I offer an organizing framework for examining these issues. I review the evidence and put the research into a larger social context. I conclude that trade has indeed contributed to the dramatic decline in wages and loss of jobs for non-college-educated American workers, and that the employment impact, both gross and net, has been large relative to the social benefits of trade liberalization. I argue that the size of trade's effect on wages and jobs should be judged relative to the net social gains from trade, not according to whether trade is the only or largest measurable factor.

Furthermore, current trade and investment flows are exacerbating existing inequalities—between production and non-production workers, between college- and non-college-educated workers, and between high- and low-paid workers. These conclusions hold true, based on measured changes in trade volumes, import prices, and capital flows.

Since some of the impact of changes in trade policy stems from institutional changes rather than actual trade or investment flows, the measures described here necessarily represent a lower bound estimate of trade's impact on wages. For example, when Xerox recently extracted wage concessions from its workers in New York by threatening to move production to Mexico, that threat was made more credible by investment protections and tariff provisions in the North American Free Trade Agreement (NAFTA). This particular wage impact of trade policy is not captured by any of the models measuring trade and investment flows, since the downward pressure on wages occurs with no cross-border movement of goods or capital.

I conclude the paper by exploring alternative trade policies that could potentially preserve (or reduce only slightly) the net gains from trade while mitigating the negative impacts on less-educated workers.

Basic Framework

If we accept that not every individual is made better off through increased trade, then how do we compare various policy options (with more or less trade liberalization) to each other? In fact, this question is harder for economists to address than one might think. Economic theory long ago declared itself incapable of comparing the satisfaction one person receives from a dollar of income to the satisfaction of another person from the same dollar. That is, economists cannot rank the social welfare of two different situations that are identical except that a dollar has been transferred from one person to another. Strictly speaking, then, economists do not possess the theoretical tools to declare unequivocally that free trade, which will tend to reduce the incomes of some workers while raising the incomes of others, is a better policy than protectionism. This judgment can only be made by assuming explicitly that the loss of a dollar in income to a garment worker is exactly offset by the gain of one dollar or one dollar and one cent to a manager. Even when politicians and economists tout the export-led creation of high-wage jobs, they do not usually argue that the same individuals who lose their jobs to imports will succeed in getting the export jobs.

It would certainly be possible to link trade policies more directly to redistributive schemes.

A redistributive plan that truly compensated trade's "losers," however, would be costly and is not feasible in the current austere political context. A program such as Trade Adjustment Assistance, which is a transitional program rather than a compensatory one, now serves only a small fraction of eligible workers and is perennially under attack. Meanwhile, the entire social safety net of welfare, unemployment compensation, and food stamps is shrinking as congressional budget-cutters search for social programs to cut. Free-trade economists have been much more forceful in their advocacy of rapid and unencumbered trade liberalization than in pressing for serious income redistribution domestically.

David Richardson describes trade's uncompensated losers as a "philosophical" problem, but essentially dismisses the issue by noting that, "Lots of otherwise desirable trends leave some people with lower relative income."[2] But there are several reasons why it is important to pay attention to the distributional consequences of trade policy. First, the magnitude of the gross losses and gains are large relative to the net gains. In other words, losers lose a lot and winners win a lot, while the net gains to society are relatively small. Second, the redistribution of income resulting from trade liberalization is regressive: The relatively rich gain at the expense of the middle class and poor. Whether or not this polarization of incomes is a problem depends on one's point of view. But in the present context of dramatically widening gaps between the incomes of the rich and the rest of society, most people would agree that further increases in inequality strain the social fabric. It is also quite possible that the losers outnumber the winners, even if the dollar value of total gains exceeds the dollar value of the losses. Finally, trade liberalization can lead to permanent and sizable disruptions in people's lives. Our current measurement techniques do not capture the true social costs of these disruptions.

David Richardson compares the inequality generated by trade to education: Education, he argues, "makes those who participate in it better off compared to those who choose not to, and may lead the former to fill jobs that would otherwise be available for the latter, imposing absolute losses, too."[3] Leaving aside whether most workers can choose to participate in trade-induced downsizing or not, Richardson has to work hard to make the argument that many people suffer absolute income losses as a result of other people's education. Education is much more likely to affect relative income rankings (by sorting job applicants) than it is to reduce incomes absolutely. Certainly, other people's educational attainment does not disrupt lives in the way that a factory closing does. Furthermore, government funding of education (including primary and secondary schools) is likely to close income inequalities, not widen them.

The impact of trade policy on people's incomes and lives is more aptly compared to building a highway through a residential neighborhood. Some commuters will clearly benefit and jobs will be created, while some residents will lose their homes, and the property values and quality of life of others will be diminished by traffic and pollution. Generally, the government compensates those whose homes are razed, and even so, building a highway occasions lengthy and heated political battles. Why then is it so surprising that trade policy is not warmly embraced by those it affects adversely? And why have economists been so unsympathetic to the disruptions caused and losses imposed by trade liberalization?

How Big Are the Gains from Trade, and Who Gets Them?

Rising trade volumes and growing wage inequality have brought renewed attention to this question of winners and losers. Economists have produced a number of theoretical and empirical studies. At first glance, these studies appear to offer starkly conflicting results, with the authors loosely falling into two camps: those who believe trade matters (as a contributing factor to growing wage inequality) and those who believe it does not. In fact, there is more agreement than disagreement within the ranks of economists, and over time the common ground has expanded. A consensus is emerging that trade has contributed between 10 and 30 percent to the growth in wage inequality over the last fifteen years, with some estimates higher than 50 percent. The strongest disagreement is not over the empirical findings *per se,* but rather over the appropriate adjectives with which to characterize the findings. Economists' assessments range from "no impact" or "very small" to "moderate" and "substantial."

One of the reasons why the literature on trade and wages has been so confusing and at times contradictory has been that it has focused on ranking contributing factors to growing wage inequality (or falling non-college wages). My view is that it is not particularly important to know whether it is trade or technology that accounts for a larger proportion of wage decline. Clearly (as many economists have pointed out), trade, technology, declining unionization, and changes in educational quality have all played roles and have interacted with each other along the way. A more interesting project is to assess the role of each as fully as possible and to propose policy solutions that address the problem of declining wages. As Edward Leamer has pointed out, identifying technology as the sole or main suspect leads to "a very passive response."[4] Gary Burtless is one of the few economists who has admitted that recent work suggests that "benefits of trade protection to the unskilled could be sizable."[5]

The Right Yardstick

The relevant comparison is not between trade and technology; rather, we should compare the impact of trade to the net social benefits it brings. Paul Krugman and Maurice Obstfeld estimated the cost of existing trade barriers in 1984 at 0.26 percent of GDP, a figure that would probably be lower in today's substantially more open economy.[6] Free trade agreements with Canada, Mexico, and Israel, as well as the most recent round of the General Agreement on Tariffs and Trade (GATT), have cut both tariff and non-tariff barriers. Thus, the gains from eliminating all remaining trade barriers is less than a quarter of a percent of GDP. Recognizing that this measure of the potential gains from additional trade liberalization looks "disappointingly small," as one economist put it at a Brookings conference a few years ago, some economists have evoked higher, but as-yet-unquantified, "dynamic" benefits of trade to bolster their arguments about the urgency of the free-trade agenda. These phantom benefits have not been demonstrated empirically and so far exist mainly in the imagination of economists.

Even the conventional gains from trade (sometimes called the "static" gains) are often assumed rather than shown empirically. During the NAFTA debate, for example, the computable general equilibrium models used to measure the impact of NAFTA generally *assumed* that there would be sizable efficiency gains. Press reports then trumpeted this figure as a "finding" of the model.

It is important to note that there can be dynamic *costs* to free trade (or dynamic benefits to trade protection) that are not measured by conventional models. It could, for example, be socially efficient for temporary trade protection to allow an industry to retain key workers and maintain capital equipment during a period of disequilibrium in currency markets. In another scenario, well-designed trade protection could provide enough confidence in the size of the domestic market to spur needed investments, leading to faster productivity growth and gains to consumers.

The public can perhaps be excused for its skepticism over the gains from trade, given the slowdown in productivity and output growth since the early 1970s—a period that roughly coincides with trade liberalization and rapid growth in the volume of global trade and investment flows. Many other relevant policy and social changes also occurred during that period, but economists who want to make the case for either trade or technology as contributors to wage inequality should also be prepared to explain why the gains from trade and technology are not reflected in more rapid aggregate growth.

Replacing the Revenue Generated by Tariffs

Finally, economists' obsession with the inefficiency of trade barriers misses a crucial point. Economists compare an economy with tariffs to one without any such barriers and conclude that the barrier-free economy allocates its resources more efficiently. This comparison ignores the fact that tariffs (and "auction quotas") generate government revenue. The proper comparison, therefore, should be between an economy with tariffs and one with an alternative revenue-generating mechanism, such as a sales or income tax. Of course, any such tax will also "distort" economic activity and create some inefficiency in a pure market model. It is that distortion that should be compared to the distortion imposed by tariffs. The tradeoff could also be expressed in terms of the public debate by explicitly identifying which social services would be cut, which taxes raised, or how much the budget deficit would have to increase in order to compensate for the lost tariff revenue in any trade liberalizing measure.

During the debate over GATT, the last-minute requirement imposed by the Congressional Budget Office that Congress find $13 billion worth of revenues to replace the projected loss of tariff revenues almost brought the legislation to an impasse. Free-trade advocates railed against this requirement. If the gains from trade, however, were as enormous as was often implied, it should not have been so excruciatingly difficult to cover the lost revenues.

In fact, our society has come to view all the redistributions of income caused by trade liberalization as somehow natural and right: Losers must simply grit their teeth and gracefully accept their losses for the overall good of society, while the winners hold onto their gains and express outrage at any attempt to tax away any portion thereof. But the losers are getting restless, and this particular "understanding" may have reached its limit.

A Framework for International Trade and Investment

A review of the empirical literature suggests that the negative income effects of trade are large (on the order of 4 or 5 percent of wages for non-college-educated workers), while the net social gains are small, probably less than 1 percent of GDP. The theoretical case in favor of free trade is weak in the presence of uncompensated income effects that are large relative to net social gains. I conclude that the political and economic case in favor of unfettered free trade has not been made. It does not follow from this consideration of the evidence that we should stop trading or rush to erect trade barriers; but it strongly suggests that we should slow down the "free trade juggernaut," the ongoing project to eliminate all remaining trade barriers as quickly as possible. The trade debate should also open up to include more options than free trade versus no trade.

Most of the mainstream economists and analysts who have weighed in on this debate—even those who find that trade has had a large or significant impact on inequality—have concluded that no trade protection is warranted in response. This unanimity on policy prescription is not always a direct and logical outcome of research, but rather reflects norms within the economics profession.

In another context, Paul Krugman has written: "If a policy change promises to raise average income by a tenth of a percentage point, but will widen the wedge between the interests of the elite and those of the rest, it should be opposed. If a law reduces average income a bit but enhances the power of ordinary workers, it should be supported."[7] Economists like Krugman should be urged to hold changes in trade policy up to the same scrutiny as other policy changes. If our current trade policies are shifting jobs out of the manufacturing sector, undermining the bargaining power of workers, and imposing a large burden on less-educated and less-affluent workers, then we should question whether we must continue those policies indefinitely.

Similarly, it is important to view recent changes in international trade and investment policies in a broad social context, not as marginal adjustments to already low tariff rates. Clearly, businesses see policies such as NAFTA and the pending Multilateral Agreement on Investment (until 1998 under negotiation in the Organization for Economic Co-operation and Development) as crucial to their abilities to reorganize production across national boundaries. While such reorganization may in many cases be motivated by the desire to achieve market access, it often is aimed at taking advantage of cheap labor.

In any case, businesses have not hesitated to use mobility-enhancing trade rules to whipsaw workers at the bargaining table. As early as 1992, 40 percent of corporate executives polled by the *Wall Street Journal* (September 24, 1992) admitted that it was likely or somewhat likely that their company would shift some production to Mexico within a few years. Twenty-four percent of the executives polled said their companies were likely to "use NAFTA as a bargaining chip to keep wages down in the U.S."

Since the implementation of NAFTA in January 1994, these expectations have been fulfilled. In a report prepared for the NAFTA Labor Secretariat's Commission on Labor Cooperation, Cornell researcher Kate Bronfenbrenner documents numerous examples of employers using the possibility of relocating production to Mexico under NAFTA as a threat during wage negotiations or union organizing campaigns.[8] Some employers posted a large map of North America with arrows pointing from the current plant location to Mexico. Others provided statistics to workers detailing "the average wage of a Mexican auto worker, the average wage of their U.S. counterparts, and how much the company stood to gain from moving to Mexico." ITT Automotive in Michigan parked tractor trailers loaded with production equipment labeled "Mexico Transfer Job" in front of a plant where a union campaign was under way. Clearly, labor-management relations and the balance of bargaining power between workers and employers are affected by trade flows and trade rules. This effect comes on top of the two more easily quantifiable effects studied more intensively by economists: the relative wage impact that results from sectoral shifts in production and the downward drag on labor markets from chronic trade deficits.

One of the obstacles to clear thinking on this issue is that mainstream economists tend to see trade policy as bipolar: trade or no trade, tariffs or no tariffs. In fact, the present trade debate in Washington is more about rules and the framework of international trade and investment than it is about tariff levels. Current trade policies "protect" some national parties and expose others to new and sometimes destructive forms of competition. Business interests are embedded in most aspects of current trade law, while labor and environmental concerns are relegated, at best, to relatively toothless side agreements (as in NAFTA).

We must continue to press for a link between freer trade and minimum labor and environmental standards. In other words, in order to enjoy continued access to overseas markets, governments should be expected to enforce some internationally agreed-upon standards. This would mean negotiating a core set of standards and then allowing governments to impose sanctions against goods produced in violation of these standards. Currently, GATT allows countries to impose sanctions against goods produced with forced labor, but does not address other labor rights or environmental standards. NAFTA contains very stringent protections against violations of intellectual property rights, but has much weaker provisions on labor and the environment.

Most proposals for incorporating labor standards into trade agreements focus on the following core labor rights: freedom of association, right to collective bargaining, restrictions on child and prison labor, prohibition against racial or sexual discrimination, minimum standards on workplace health and safety, and a "decent" minimum wage. International environmental standards are somewhat more difficult to identify but might include a right to know (about public environmental threats), the right to a safe workplace and living environment, and possibly a long-term plan to phase out the use of certain toxic chemicals.

The modest U.S. proposal to establish a working party on trade-linked worker rights in the World Trade Organization (WTO) met with fierce opposition and only lukewarm advocacy in the first WTO ministerial meeting in Singapore in December 1996. In the absence of progress in the multilateral arena, critics of current U.S. trade policy are pressing for change in several crucial areas. One change would be for the United States to use its own trade laws (Section 301, the Generalized System of Preferences, and the Caribbean Basin Initiative, for example) more aggressively to enforce stronger trade-linked protection of worker rights. Other changes would encourage corporate codes of conduct with outside monitors. This could also lead to a labeling initiative rewarding companies that respect core labor rights and produce goods in an environmentally responsible manner.

In addition to pressing hard for incorporating labor and environmental standards into trade agreements, the U.S. government should take steps to reduce the trade deficit. As the research reviewed here shows, much of the negative impact of trade on wages comes from the large and chronic imbalance of imports over exports that the United States has experienced in recent years. We should consider the use of targeted, temporary trade restrictions (tariffs or auction quotas), which are allowed under the GATT Balance of Payments exception clause.[9]

The rhetoric of "free trade" somewhere along the way got mixed in with pro-business investment rules and intellectual property rights protection. All other issues are labeled "social" or "non-trade" and put firmly on the back burner. If the imperative for free trade can be kept in perspective relative to such social concerns as equality and democracy, maybe we can have a more open and intelligent debate over the kind of trade policy we want and need relative to the kind of society and economy in which we would like to live.

Notes

1. Wolfgang Stolper and Paul Samuelson, "Protection and Real Wage," *Review of Economic Studies* 9 (November 1941): 58–73.

2. David Richardson, "Income Inequality and Trade: How to Think, What to Conclude," *Journal of Economic Perspectives* 9, no. 3 (Summer 1995).

3. Ibid.

4. Edward E. Leamer, "Trade, Wages and Revolving Door Ideas," National Bureau of Economic Research Working Paper No. 4716, 1994.

5. Gary Burtless, "International Trade and the Rise in Earnings Inequality," *Journal of Economic Literature* 33 (June 1995).

6. Paul Krugman and Maurice Obstfeld, *International Economics: Theory and Policy,* 2d ed. (New York: HarperCollins, 1991).

7. Paul Krugman, "Technology, Trade and Factor Prices," National Bureau of Economic Research Working Paper No. 5335, November 1995.

8. Kate Bronfrenbrenner, "The Effects of Plant Closing or Threat of Plant Closing on the Right of Workers to Organize." Report submitted to the Labor Secretariat of the North American Commission for Labor Cooperation, 1997.

9. See Robert E. Scott, "Trade," in *Reclaiming Prosperity,* ed. Todd Schafer and Jeff Faux (Armonk, NY: M.E. Sharpe, 1996), pp. 245–61, for a more detailed proposal.

B. Education

21

Schooling, Learning, and Economic Growth

Mark R. Rosenzweig

Rising inequality and sluggish growth in the United States and the lack of sustained economic advancement in many low-income countries of the world are major challenges for economists and policy-makers. Many believe that investment in education is a key instrument both to improve growth and distribute widely the proceeds of growth. The exact nature of the relationship between productivity growth, education levels, and income inequality, however, is actually little understood, and the worldwide evidence is mixed. The historical experience of contemporary industrialized countries and the recent experience of newly industrializing countries in Asia appear to suggest that investments in schooling are critical determinants of economic growth. These economies invested heavily in schooling as their economies grew at rapid rates and now are characterized by high average levels of schooling and widely shared prosperity. On the face of it, schooling appears to be a worthwhile investment indeed. However, the recent experience of many other countries presents a mixed picture, suggesting that schooling is not a sufficient condition for economic growth. For example, many countries with relatively high levels of schooling compared to their level of development in the 1960s, such as the Philippines, Sri Lanka, Ar-

gentina, Costa Rica, Cuba, and Uruguay, did not subsequently achieve high growth rates over the next twenty-five years.[1]

One way to achieve a better understanding of the interrelationships among schooling, growth, and inequality is to consider the fundamental issue of how schooling affects productivity. There is emerging evidence that schooling does not always have payoffs, and just where and when schooling does augment productivity suggests some answers to our puzzles. One long-standing hypothesis is that schooling augments productivity by enhancing the ability to learn, which implies that where profitable learning opportunities exist, schooling is most productive. In this view even if such desiderata as basic macroeconomic stability and unfettered markets are in place, if markets and technical processes have been stable for some time, or if new technologies are introduced that actually simplify work tasks, the true returns to schooling will be low. The corollary is that where opportunities to exploit learning arise, the absence of schooling can impede economic growth and those who have invested in schooling reap rewards while those who have not share less of the growth dividends.

In this essay, I review new evidence from around the world pertaining to the hypothesis that schooling augments the ability to learn outside the classroom and thus enhances productivity where learning has payoffs in the economy. The purpose is to obtain more fundamental insights into when and where schooling investments have high returns. In contrast to most of the studies of the "returns to schooling" that rely on wages and earnings data, I restrict my attention to direct measures of the productivity of workers and/or enterprises. As is well known, wages, even if they are earned by most workers in an economy and even if markets are unregulated, are not always good measures of worker productivity at a given point in time. For example, earnings also may reflect costs of unmeasured self-financed investments in on-the-job training and/or effort-eliciting incentives when there is imperfect information.

To test the hypothesis that schooling enhances general learning skills also requires that attention be restricted to activities that require skills that are not taught directly in schools. There is not much value in assessing whether trained medical doctors practice medicine more productively than those who did not attend medical school or if classes in auto repair produce more skilled automobile mechanics. Indeed, the conventional wisdom that in poor countries the returns to schooling are highest for the lowest schooling levels suggests that it is basic skills rather than task- or occupation-specific skills that have the highest payoffs in such contexts. But as will be seen, the appropriate level of schooling depends on the nature of the change affecting the economy.

To meet the twin criteria that productivity be measured directly and the activities examined represent those for which there is no specific in-school training, I review studies of the productivity of harvest workers in the Philippines, the effectiveness of contraceptives used by U.S. women, the profitability of African manufacturing firms, changes in the new seed use and profitability of Indian farmers during the "green revolution," and the determination of the cognitive development of U.S. children.

My review suggests that general investments in basic schooling will not always pay off. In particular, such investments will not have high returns where learning opportunities are scarce, such as where technology is stagnant and uncomplex, where the returns to learning are inhibited, and where forces that would ordinarily require changes in economic practices are stifled. In contrast, the evidence suggests that the returns to schooling will be high where there are such challenges as new tasks to master. By inference, these settings include "in-transition" economies experiencing a change in economic regimes, economies newly opened to novel technologies or competitive practices, and economies experiencing home-grown rapid technical progress. In such settings, growth performance is impeded if a significant proportion of the labor force lacks appropriate learning skills, and this group will fall behind those who do. The view that schooling augments learning skills, which appears to be supported by some evidence, thus suggests that schooling is an important complement to growth and development policies and has important distributional consequences but is not itself an engine of growth.

Defining Learning

While there are many ways to define learning, a useful economic framework is one in which learning entails the acquisition of better information on the most appropriate set of inputs in a production process. If discrepancies between optimal and actual input levels are significant, then there are incentives to learn and rewards for those who learn the fastest. Information on "best practice" may come from external sources such as manuals or help lines. It also may be acquired by experimentation. Such learning by doing enables individuals or firms to determine the optimal use of a new production technology. To the extent that learning leads to input use that is closer to the optimal and takes place over time, learning is "signaled" by the increase in profits or efficiency or in the reduction in costs—learning thus is observable in productivity change.

An example in which learning is important is where a new production process becomes available but the optimal use of the process is initially not known perfectly. In this context, there are two ways schooling may affect the production *cum* learning process. First, those with more schooling may through superior access to information have a better idea than the less educated of how to use a new technology prior to actually using it. Second, the better educated may obtain more information from each use of the technology compared with the less educated—those with more schooling may learn faster. In either case, if the more educated begin a new production process with more information or learn more efficiently as they utilize it, they will have greater output or profits in any stage of the technology adoption process than the less educated. The greater the gains from mastering the new process, the higher must be the returns to schooling. Conversely, if mastering the new technology is trivial, because the technology is very simple, or information on the technology is disseminated easily, the returns to schooling are small. Likewise if there are no new techniques at all. Thus, for example, in "traditional" agriculture in which best practices have not changed for many generations, school-ing would not be expected to provide a high return.

The two routes by which schooling increases the profitability of a new and complex technology have different implications for the relationship between schooling and the dynamics of new technology profitability. If schooling does not enhance learning but only increases access to external information, schooling and experience are substitutes—in that case the returns to schooling decline with experience, and are only high when the production process is relatively new. Conversely, if schooling enhances learning, but the more educated do not begin with any prior informational advantage, then at low levels of experience, schooling and experience are complements. The returns to learning by doing increase at a faster rate for the more educated technology adapters when schooling enhances the ability to learn.

Schooling Returns and Task Complexity

The first implication of the hypothesis that schooling augments information or learning ability is that the returns to schooling should be higher where there is greater scope for misusing an input or where tasks are sufficiently complex that substantial learning is required to execute them efficiently. Conversely, where tasks are simple and easy to master—such as on an old-fashioned assembly line—schooling should have little influence on productivity. One example of a set of simple tasks is that associated with agricultural operations such as harvesting or weeding that are still the predominant activities of many low-income countries. Because many of these operations are paid by piece rate, it is relatively simple to infer actual worker productivity and to assess if schooling affects productivity.

Many data sets based on surveys of rural households do not describe the types of payments received by workers. One data set that does is based on a survey of 448 households in Bukidnon in northern Mindanao, the Philippines, collected in four rounds in 1984–85. In this setting, most agricultural workers are paid by piece rates sometime during the year, so that piece-rate workers are typical workers. Based on information on the piece-rate daily wages, schooling and height for 170 harvest workers aged 21–59 observed over four crop seasons, one can look at the relationships between the daily piece-rate wage and worker height, net of schooling effects, and the piece-rate wage and worker schooling level, net of the influence of worker height. The results are very clear: While taller workers are more productive—a six-inch difference in height is associated with 9.3 percent more harvest output—there is no significant relationship between productivity and schooling, net of height. Increasing schooling years from none to fourteen, the entire sample range, increases worker output by only 3.3 percent. Evidently, in an economy in which the principal tasks are routinized and mechanical, such as in harvest work in Bukidnon or on many traditional manufacturing assembly lines, there may be payoffs to physical stamina, but raising the level of schooling would not augment incomes. And, not surprisingly, average schooling years in the Bukidnon economy is low, only 5.2 years.

Another study by Howard Pack and Christina Paxson also suggests that the scarcity of skilled workers does not necessarily imply that school investments would have high payoffs (but rather the opposite). The study is based on estimates of cost functions for manufacturing firms in three sub-Saharan African countries—Ghana, Kenya, and Zimbabwe. These firms exist in non-competitive environments and generally have little exposure to new technologies. The estimates are based on cost functions that incorporate variables measuring exposure to new technologies with variables characterizing participation in foreign markets. The authors find that the schooling levels of owners or managers bear little relationship to the total factor productivity of the firms, although the effect of schooling in reducing costs, given output, is enhanced in firms that export a higher share of their output and must keep up technologically in an internationally competitive environment subject to technical progress.

While the African manufacturing data and the Philippines harvest-worker data suggest that the absence of new techniques of production is a reason for the low returns to schooling, such returns are not necessarily augmented by the introduction of new technologies that are relatively simple to use. Novelty is not a sufficient condition for schooling to provide an advantage. An important example of this is the new technology that was associated with the "contraceptive revolution" of the 1960s. Mastery of the new contraceptives—the pill and IUD—does not require substantial abilities on the part of the user. In the case of the IUD, after insertion by a doctor the user can do little to affect its contraceptive efficiency. The requirement to take a pill every day also is relatively easy to understand. In contrast, a traditional contraceptive method—the rhythm method—is complex and requires a basic understanding of human reproduction and an ability to decipher information that is person-specific. This author and Paul Schultz used the 1973 U.S. National Survey of Family Growth to estimate a "reproduction" function in which the effects of the duration of use of different contraceptive methods on women's conception rates were estimated.

Our results show that a woman's schooling level is not significantly related to her knowledge of the pill or IUD. Only 9.6 percent more college-educated women reported that they knew how to use the pill or IUD than did women with only a high school education. In contrast, 38 percent more college graduates than high school graduates reported that they understood the rhythm method. The use-effectiveness of the pill and IUD was no different across high school and college graduates. However, while among high school graduates the rhythm method was completely ineffective, among college graduates the method was 93 percent as effective as sterilization, and more effective than the use of the pill or IUD.

The Indian Green Revolution and the Returns to Schooling

New or sophisticated technology and high returns to schooling are thus not necessarily linked, as seen in the contraceptive revolution. The introduction of new technologies can, however, raise the returns to schooling if the new technology increases rather than decreases the gains from learning by increasing the potential for the misuse of inputs. The "green" revolution exemplifies a case of an increased premium on learning or information acquisition. The new, high-yielding imported seed varieties that were the engines of growth of the green revolution were potentially more productive than the traditional seeds but significantly more sensitive to the use of such inputs as water and fertilizer. Typical yield curves from experimental plot data relating output per hectare for traditional and high-yielding varieties at different levels of fertilizer intensities indicate that the returns to the optimal allocation of fertilizer are higher for the new seeds. Given the high costs of fertilizer,

farming profitability critically depended on input allocations.

Thus, at the onset of the green revolution, learning about the appropriate allocation of inputs with a new technology was a challenge that had large potential payoffs to farmers formerly engaged in "traditional" farming practices, and the continuing introduction of new seeds every few years should have permanently raised the returns to skills in information decoding. What did happen to schooling returns?

The green revolution experience in India has two important characteristics that make it possible to identify the relationship between schooling returns and technical change via learning. First, the fundamental "engine" of growth is clearly identifiable. The green revolution has a clear beginning—the importation in the mid-1960s of new hybrid seed varieties of wheat, rice, and corn (and later sorghum) that were substantially more productive than indigenous traditional seed varieties, but also more sensitive to inputs.

A second important characteristic of the green revolution is that the potential enhanced productivity of the new seed varieties varied across India precisely because of the sensitivity of the new seeds to water and soil nutrients. There were substantial variation in productivity growth over this period in different states. For example, crop productivity rose 2.5 times from 1961 through 1981 in Punjab and threefold in Karnataka but by less than 10 percent over the same period in Kerala and Madhya Pradesh. Not all of these differentials are due to differences in climate and soil; the growth in productivity reflects, in part, initial capital assets and investments, including those in schooling, although the correlation between initial 1961 schooling levels by state and subsequent yield growth was slightly (insignificantly) negative.

Andrew Foster and this author exploited longitudinal data describing farm production in 2681 rural households across all of India in 1971 and 1982 to estimate the relationship between agricultural technical change and the change in the returns to schooling. Our results indicate that the returns to primary schooling, but not above primary, rose significantly in high-growth areas. For example, the estimates suggest that in Kerala, which had high levels of schooling in the mid-1960s but which experienced little subsequent growth because of the lack of suitability of the environment for the new seeds, the profit differential was only 11.4 percent between schooled and unschooled farmers. In contrast, in Karnataka, which had average estimated rates of technical change, the schooling profit differential was 17.9 percent, and in the Punjab, with the highest estimated rate of technical progress, profits for farmers with primary schooling exceeded those of unschooled farmers by 39.2 percent. Thus, in the absence of new relevant technologies such as in Kerala, schooling investments had low payoffs in terms of economic growth. But, where technical change required new and complex farming practices that substantially affect profitability, schooling investments had high payoffs.

Another implication of the role of schooling in realizing the potential of technical change is that in those environments experiencing the same rates of exogenous technical change, those areas with relatively few farmers with primary schooling at the onset of the green revolution should have experienced less growth than initially high-schooling areas—initial schooling levels should have mattered for subsequent performance given the same growth potential. By how much did initial low levels of schooling in areas of India actually impede growth where

such growth was possible? As noted, one cannot use the relationship between initial schooling levels by state, for example, and actual state-specific rural growth rates to infer anything about the role of schooling in agricultural growth. This is not because schooling did not differ across areas of India in 1961—there were substantial differences. For example, the proportion of households with primary schooling was 0.6 in Kerala but only 0.2 in Bihar, both of which were low-growth states, while the proportions were also 0.6 in Punjab and 0.25 in Karnataka—both high-growth states. There is little relationship between initial schooling and actual growth performance because the potential for growth associated with the green revolution depended on soil and climate and these were unrelated to initial schooling levels.

To assess therefore whether and to what extent initial schooling levels affected realized productivity, one needs to look at the relationships among schooling, growth potential, and realized productivity gains. Counterfactual experiments based on the Foster-Rosenzweig structural technology estimates imply that if Kerala, a state with initially high levels of schooling, had had the same high rate of exogenous technical change as did a state such as Maharasthra in the 1970s, yield growth in Kerala in that period would have been more than doubled. In a low-schooling state with a moderate growth potential due to more favorable natural endowments, such as Bihar, however, increasing technical change to the same level as in Maharasthra would have only increased yields by 4 percent. The estimates thus suggest that where learning payoffs are high, low-schooling levels can substantially constrain growth, but further investments in schooling, such as in Kerala, would have yielded a low payoff (in terms of green revolution crop productivity) not because schooling levels were already high but because of the absence of learning opportunities.

The distributional implications of the seed-based technical change were also clear. First, in high-growth areas, more-schooled farmers shared more of the growth returns than did low-schooled farmers. Second, those rural households without access to land—the landless—benefited only indirectly from the increased demand for labor arising from the use of more productive seeds. The schooling payoffs to these principally manual workers were not increased. Indeed, the evidence indicated that the enrollment rates of children in farming households increased at a much faster pace in high technical change areas than did those of children in households without land. Schooling and income inequality thus grew in high-growth areas, across farm and non-farm households, and income inequality grew, at least initially, between the schooled and the unschooled among farmers. These results thus suggest that in high potential growth settings, a more equitable distribution of production assets and schooling and a higher overall level of schooling would have raised growth levels and distributed the gains from growth more equally.

Learning by Doing and the Role of Schooling

The estimates of the relationships between contraceptive method efficacy and schooling and between exogenous technical change and the profitability of schooling do not shed light on the question of whether schooling facilitates learning or instead improves access to external information sources. To answer this question it is necessary to examine more closely the time paths of productivity change, which presumably reflect changes in the proximity of actual input use to its optimal allocation as information is acquired over time.

For my research with Foster, we used a three-year national panel of Indian farm households surveyed in the initial years of the green revolution (1968–71) to quantify the time paths of the effects on profitability of farmers' experience with the high-yielding seed varieties (HYV). Their estimates showed that learning how to effectively use the new seed varieties was an important barrier to their profitability and contributed to profit differentials among farmers with different schooling levels. Learning curves for the new seed varieties were quite steep, with high and declining returns to experience.

I used the information on the growth in farmer experience with the new seeds and on seed profitability to focus on the role of schooling in enhancing technology adoption. Three conclusions emerged: First, profits among farmers with no prior experience with HYV seeds, regardless of their schooling, were on average negative. This indicates both the novelty of the new seeds and the costly consequences of departures of initial input allocations from their optimal levels. Second, more-schooled farmers did not have an initial advantage in HYV profitability. Schooling had virtually no effect on HYV profitability when farmers had no prior experience with HYV seeds. Third, the profitability of the new seeds rose more rapidly with experience for the schooled farmers than for those without schooling—an additional acre of prior HYV use as of the second year of the survey had an 18 percent greater effect on the per-acre profitability for farmers with primary schooling compared with farmers with no schooling. These results thus suggest that schooling enhanced the ability of the farmers to learn from observations about optimal use of the new technology but was not associated with advantageous initial access to external sources of profit-relevant information.

Learning Externalities and Optimal Schooling Interventions

In assessing the growth and income distributional consequences of schooling, it is important to take into account the possibility that the benefits from schooling spill over to others. In that case, targeted strategic investments in schooling can be cost effective. Survey data from the Philippines and India, reported by Foster and myself, for example, indicate that farmers believe that their neighbors are important sources of information on input use. Because more-schooled farmers were the first to use the new seeds, consistent with the hypothesis that schooling increases the profitability of such seeds, farmers with low levels of schooling but who lived in villages where other farmers were more schooled benefited from their neighbors' superior informational skill. The slowest rate of adoption is by an uneducated farmer with uneducated neighbors, who reaches complete specialization in HYV cultivation only by the fifth year. However, the same uneducated farmer with educated neighbors reaches full specialization in the fourth year, and by the third year the proportion of his land devoted to HYV seeds is 25 percent higher than that of uneducated farmers with uneducated neighbors. The estimates suggest that over a five-year period the cumulative profits of a farmer with no schooling is 4 percent higher if his representative neighbor had completed primary schooling rather than no schooling.

Thus, when schooling is more universal the speed of technology adoption is accelerated and growth occurs at a more rapid pace. However, the evidence also suggested that schooling, unless subsidized, would be at less-than-optimal levels by each of the farm households, since each household does not take into account the benefits to his neighbors of his own schooling. Subsidization of schooling in the context of new technology adoption in which there are high returns from learning and learning spillovers would appear warranted as indicated by the experience in the early stages of the Indian green revolution.

Another spillover effect of schooling can occur within households and across generations. In a 1994 study, this author and Kenneth Wolpin used the U.S. National Longitudinal Survey of Youth, a panel survey of young men and women age 14 through 21 in 1979, to estimate the effects of a mother's schooling on her child's cognitive achievement, as measured by a test administered when the child was between the ages of five and eight. In particular, they exploited the fact that in the 1990 round of that survey, 23.4 percent of mothers who had at least two births continued their schooling after the birth of their first child. The data could therefore be used to answer the question of whether test scores improved across the first and second children for mothers who added to their schooling between births compared with mothers who did not.

The results from that study indicate that the achievement test score of a child would be 9.7 points (10.6 percent) higher if the mother had a college education rather than a high school education. This effect is not trivial and suggests that formal schooling enhances mothering skills, skills that are not directly taught in the classroom. Moreover, the additional achievement of the child from increased maternal schooling represents an intergenerational externality—the child reaps benefits from the mother's schooling. If mothers do not completely take this benefit into account when making their schooling investments, there is again a justification for schooling interventions. In this case, the increased schooling investment contributes to long-term, sustained growth, but again only if the increased capacities to learn can be productively exploited.

Conclusion

The empirical findings discussed in this essay suggest that where learning has payoffs, whether from the introduction of new technologies or from changes in the rules of commerce and trade, schooling can have large payoffs and schooling investments respond to those opportunities. Where there are groups with low levels of schooling in such settings, however, overall growth will be impeded; inequality will widen; and, to the extent that such groups face barriers to reaping the returns to schooling investments, such inequality in schooling and incomes will persist over time and generations. There is no evidence that schooling investments, in the absence of learning opportunities, are profitable, unless such investments themselves induce innovation. The principal lesson to be drawn is that the justification for general investments in schooling requires knowledge of the precise character of the anticipated changes in technology or capital investments. Neither the measurement of earnings differentials across schooling groups nor forecasts of aggregate capital investments are sufficient for formulating successful education strategies aimed at achieving higher growth rates with shared prosperity.

Note

1. The research reported was supported in part by grants from the National Science Foundation, SBR93-08405, and the National Institutes of Health, HD30907.

22

How the United States Can Develop a World-Class Education System

Marc Tucker

Perhaps we should start by asking what prevents our students from performing at world-class levels now. Surely the candidate list would include the following:

1. *Few students have any incentives to take tough courses or study hard.* Unless one expects to attend a selective college—a very small fraction of our students—it makes no sense to take tough courses or to study hard. A high school diploma will get any student into more than half of the colleges in the United States. And many entry-level jobs require no more than a high school diploma, if that. A high school diploma can be had almost everywhere if one attains a seventh or eighth grade literacy level, attends school with some modest regularity, does not cause too much trouble, and turns in one's homework most of the time. This is not true in the countries of northern Europe or in the industrial powerhouses of Asia, where taking tough courses and working hard to get good grades pay off for virtually all students, not just a small minority. In those countries, the standards against which they will be judged are clear and high, and how they do on their exams, the grades they get in their courses, and the recommendations of their teachers are typically very important, whether they want to be an auto mechanic or a brain surgeon.

2. *Teachers and other school professionals who do what is necessary to help their students achieve at high levels are not only not rewarded—they are frequently punished for their effort.* Any organization that is serious about achieving its stated aims rewards those staff members who regularly contribute to success and provides real consequences for those who repeatedly fail to do so. Our education system does just the opposite. Loyalty, responsiveness to those in authority, and the ability to maintain order are rewarded in promotions. Seniority and the taking of courses unrelated to the requirements of the work are rewarded in compensation. Teachers who are widely recognized for their achievements are frequently ostracized by their colleagues. Teachers whose dedication leads them to stay late on the job, come in early, and work on the weekends are likely to be in trouble with their unions. Principals who succeed in spite of the central office are honored for a moment and then sidelined as soon as the spotlight has moved elsewhere. Some fine, dedicated educators rise to the top, but the system favors timeservers and politicians, not people who make the waves needed to produce dramatic gains in student achievement.

3. *We expect very little of most of our children.* It is startling to see how little we expect of

our youngsters in comparison to what is expected of children of the same ages in Europe and East Asia. Almost alone among industrial nations, we estimate the ability of youngsters when they are five or six years old and then assign them to ability groups in which they are typically stuck for the rest of their life in school. This is the most vicious form of tracking the author knows of in any nation, because the effective denial of opportunity to achieve occurs earlier and with fewer opportunities to reverse it than in other nations that have milder forms of tracking. Most industrial nations expect far more of youngsters in the bottom half of the distribution than we do, and most of those youngsters rise to those expectations. Years of research show what common sense suggests—that young people capable of performing at far higher levels rarely rise above the levels expected of them by the adults to whom they are closest.

4. *Our schools use an early twentieth-century form of industrial organization never designed to produce quality results.* We call our teachers professionals but treat them like blue-collar workers; then we complain when they organize industrial unions. The United States is almost unique in the world in having large local school district bureaucracies that combine the worst features of bureaucracies with few of the benefits of local autonomy. From the point of view of the professionals in the school, the central office has all of the brakes and none of the motors. That is, it is full of people who can say "no" but no one who is in the habit of saying "yes." The central office controls all the money, sending only pocket money to the school itself. It determines the curriculum, organizes the professional development, hires and deploys the staff, and makes all the rules. Yet no one in central except the superintendent has responsibility for student achievement. The people with the "motors," the people who are actually responsible for providing the services that should enable students to achieve, are in the schools, not the central office. Deprive them of control over curriculum, pedagogy, professional development, and everything else of consequence and it is quite unreasonable to hold them accountable for student achievement. So no one is responsible. This system was installed in the 1920s, not to insure high-quality results, but to enable the country to build a mass production education system that would ensure minimum quality with high rates of efficiency. It is no more suited to the modern requirement for high quality than the industrial management systems rejected in the 1980s in the search for quality in the business world.

5. *In the classroom, the shinbone is not connected to the kneebone, which is not connected to the thighbone.* In those nations of Asia and Europe where achievement is highest, it is assumed that one begins by being clear about what standards of student achievement must be met, creating an assessment system matched to the standards, and then designing a curriculum that will enable the students to reach the standards. Not so in the United States. We have never believed in explicit standards for student performance. We have certainly believed in testing, but few people can tell you what the standard is to which most standardized, norm-referenced tests are set (in the sense of telling you just what one has to know and be able to do to succeed on the test). Until recently, the idea of teaching to the test was heresy. So neither the student nor the teacher were shooting at a clear target; there were no tests designed to assess whether the students were reaching that target; and there were no curricula designed to enable students to reach the targets that were not set.

6. *Outside of school, young people have far less support than they used to. Some have almost no support at all.* It is well known that the United States has the highest rate of child poverty among the industrialized countries. The recently passed welfare reform legislation is likely to make matters worse, at least in the near term. It has not always been this way. Less than a quarter-century ago, the distribution of income in the United States compared favorably to that in most other industrialized nations. Now, many schools take in youngsters who have no home to go to or whose single parents are unable to care for them or are unable to provide three meals a day, the most basic health care, or a warm place when it gets cold. But poor children, however miserable their plight, are not the only worry of the modern school. Because of the steady drop in real wages over more than two decades, millions of American families have both parents working the equivalent of two or more full-time jobs in order to bring in the income that one wage earner could have brought home a few years ago. In most cases, these families simply cannot afford high-quality care for their children when they are at work, and they are often too tired to do much with their children when they finally get home. There are many families with relatively high incomes in which both parents are working because they want to, in which the parents spend very little time with their children compared to the time their parents spent with them. And there are many more teenage unmarried women with children than there were only a few years ago. All this adds up to far less time available for parenting than was available previously. The schools are reaping the consequences of these trends in children who come to school malnourished, who are afraid of being beaten or driven from their homes, who have no place to study, who must work every hour outside of school to support their family, who are angry at a world that does not appear to love or value them, who do not know the names of the colors when they first arrive at school, and who are convinced by the time they reach their teens that they will die a violent death before they emerge from their teens. To say that these children are not "ready for school" is to shade the truth beyond recognition.

7. *There are great inequities in the financing of schools.* Despite great reform efforts in the 1970s, public education is little if any improved with respect to finance equity. Critics of public education often respond to this point in two ways, first by claiming that, overall, Americans spend more on education than most other Organization for Economic Co-operation and Development countries and second by claiming that the evidence shows that differences in school finance are not well correlated with school achievement outcomes. It is true that OECD statistics show the United States in the upper reaches of spending on education. But this is very misleading. OECD officials have pointed out to me that European countries that appear to spend less on primary and secondary schools do not include expenditures on interscholastic sports, or for food (because they send the students home for lunch) and their students almost always use public rather than school transportation. According to these officials, the United States would rank in the lower half of the range on school expenditure if the rankings reflected these facts. So overall spending on the schools is lower than among our competitors. But that average masks enormous inequities among and within the states. And the dollars, unequal though they may be, are not the greatest source of inequity. One of the greatest influences on the achievement of any one student is the in-

come and educational attainment of the families of the other students in the class and school. "Local control" of public education in the United States is mainly a means of permitting relatively wealthy people to create school districts with other relatively wealthy people and to exclude people with less wealth. In this way, the wealthy can be sure that a very low rate of taxation will produce schools with very high rates of expenditure, and their children will attend school only with other children who can contribute more to the education of their own sons and daughters than poorer children could. This kind of local control of education finance is mostly unknown among the nations with high and uniform rates of academic achievement. In most countries, the level of school expenditure is set by the national or provincial government. The observation from the critics that we should not worry about the inequities just described because finance cannot be closely correlated with academic achievement defies common sense (and, I would guess, their own behavior as parents when it comes to choosing neighborhoods and schools for their own children). Because many other things affect achievement, one would not expect a close correlation. But only a fool would prefer to send his children to a public school with a leaky roof, no science labs or instructional technology, fifteen-year-old textbooks, and sub-par teacher pay rather than a school with an inviting interior, electron microscopes and a small astronomical observatory, a fine library, and very competitive teacher pay.

8. *The United States has the worst school-to-work transition system in the industrialized world.* Somewhere in the neighborhood of half of those students who enter high school go on to some form of post-secondary education. Fewer than a half of those students enter a selective institution. Fewer than a half of those who enter four-year and two-year institutions with the declared intention of getting a degree or certificate do so within five years. Given these statistics, it is very safe to say that somewhere between half and two-thirds of our students enter the labor market with no better than eighth grade literacy and no vocational skills at all. The market for people with this skill profile is declining very fast. The School-to-Work Opportunities Act was intended to address this problem, but it is not clear that the majority of programs developed under its aegis are focused on giving young people marketable technical skills, nor is it clear that employers are involved in ways that could sustain the development of such skills or the kinds of non-technical work skills (e.g., the ability to work well in groups or to solve problems effectively) that are essential in the modern workplace.

The core challenge facing American education is no different from the challenge that has faced American business and public administration in recent years: to make major improvements in productivity and the quality of its products and services. Because the demand for highly educated and trained labor has exploded in recent years and because the future for individuals who have no more than the seventh or eighth grade level of literacy that was sufficient in the past will be increasingly bleak, the schools must produce a vast improvement in the quality of student performance without increasing the total cost very much. In economists' terms, productivity must greatly increase. Business has accomplished this by introducing technology, winnowing out unneeded layers of management, giving to people on the front line many of the duties and responsibilities formerly held by the indirect staff and by management, upgrading the skills of those on the front line so that they could do the job at much higher levels of quality, giving the people on the front line the authority and responsibility to figure out how to get the job done and then rewarding them when it is done well (that is, treating them like professionals), figuring out what the core competence of the firm is and farming out those aspects of the work that can more efficiently be done by others, and so on. The proposals that follow are partly designed to be specifically responsive to the problems identified in the first part of this essay, but they are also framed in the recognition that considerable progress toward world-class schools can be made by borrowing some ideas from those firms that have done the best job of improving productivity and quality in their own domains in recent years.

The Argument for Standards-Based Reform

Imagine a civil engineer in a county office. The county needs to replace a bridge. The engineer can design the bridge and ask for bids, giving the contract to the low bidder. Or the engineer can specify the load the bridge must bear, the distance it must span, the time it must last, and so on, and then ask for bids. Hands down, the latter method works best, because it produces much better ideas and lowers costs. Education policy and administration is made in the first way, each layer telling the next lower layer how to do the job. No one has agreed on just what the performance standards are, but everyone is busy doing something (each with a different idea about what the object of the game is). Suppose we built our bridges in education in the second way—by making the standards for student performance clear and then letting the people closest to the students figure out how to get them there. Then, just like the engineer, we can count on getting better ideas and lower costs.

Here is what we have to do to make such a system work.

1. *Build an American qualifications system.* A qualifications system is a nested set of standards, arranged in a progression, so that an individual can first reach a foundation standard of skills and knowledge and then progress to higher or more specialized standards. National qualifications systems of this sort are emerging in many nations. They typically start with a series of progressively more demanding academic performance standards for young people as they proceed through the school years and then incorporate more vocational skills later on. Some national systems stop at the level of the skills required for front-line supervisors; others continue into the full range of professional and managerial roles. Most qualifications systems state the qualifications in terms of performance requirements rather than course requirements. Stated in that way, the standards leave it up to the individual how he or she acquires the necessary knowledge and skill to pass the assessment and elicits the maximum innovation from those who provide the education and training. The typical qualification is not tied to a specific age or level of the provision system. One can meet the standards for the foundation qualification or any of the technical or vocational qualifications at any age. The only thing that matters is whether one can demonstrate that one has the requisite skills and knowledge. Because the qualifications system is universal throughout the nation, it becomes a universal language for communication about skills and a reliable basis for planning one's education and training program, one's career, an educational institution's program, a course, a firm's training program, a hiring plan, a promotion policy, and so on. Colleges in one part of the country can count on students coming from another part of the country having met

the entry-level standards for college work at their institution. Employers can count on candidates for employment having the skills their certificate says they have. The records of many providers—from primary schools to colleges and job training programs—can be judged by individuals and government and other funders against a common set of standards.

Many states are on their way to having statewide academic standards of some sort, usually pegged to three or four grade levels in three or more subject areas. Few of these standards are performance standards, in the sense that they are precise about what kind of performance will meet the standard. They usually are content standards that specify what students should know, not performance standards that specify how well they must demonstrate what they know. The standards issued by the teacher subject-matter societies are also content, not performance, standards. As is to be expected, the standards of each state vary significantly in rigor and are sufficiently different from one another on a variety of other dimensions that the performances of students in different states cannot be compared.

New Standards™, a national program of which the author is co-director, is a consortium of seventeen states that has developed integrated, internationally benchmarked performance standards for mathematics, science, English language arts, and applied learning at the elementary, middle, and high school levels. Matching performance assessments are available in English language arts and mathematics now, and thanks to a recent grant from the National Science Foundation, development of matching assessments in science is under way. "Applied learning" refers to the generic skills required for success in high-performance workplaces, such as the ability to work well in a

group and to solve complex, real-world problems effectively. The New Standards assessments are designed to provide a means of nationally assessing individuals against the standards. This is a crucial point, because the experience of other nations is that the lack of incentive for our students to take tough courses and study hard could be reversed if standards like those produced by New Standards were in place and employers and post-secondary institutions relied at least in part on the matching assessments to assist them in their hiring and admissions decisions. The form of the New Standards performance standards and examinations is also deliberately designed to model the kind of instruction that would enable students to achieve the standards, thus providing a powerful means of improving—not just measuring— student performance.

The National Assessment of Educational Progress, sponsored by the United States government, was designed to describe the trends in elementary and secondary student performance in key subject areas. It does this by sampling students with assessment instruments, parts of which are administered to each student in the sample. Thus, while NAEP cannot be used to incent individual students to perform at high levels (because no individual student gets a score), it is an ideal instrument for tracking the progress of the nation, a state, or a large school district toward the national standards.

The National Skill Standards Board (NSSB) is chartered by the Congress to develop a national system of occupational skill standards. Its plan for doing so is to divide the national economy into fifteen broad clusters, further divide each cluster into up to six concentrations, and then further divide each concentration into an unlimited number of specialties. Voluntary partnerships are being created to develop certificates for individuals who meet the common standards for the cluster and the standards for one concentration. The voluntary partnerships will be empowered by the NSSB to authorize other organizations to award specialty certificates in its name, under specified conditions.

Finally, the National Board for Professional Teaching Standards (NBPTS), launched in 1987, was created to award certificates to school teachers meeting high standards of skill and knowledge in areas in which they teach. The Board recently awarded its first certificates and is expanding its offerings.

Clearly, these separate elements could and should be welded together into a powerful national qualifications system. The performance standards developed by New Standards on the base built by the subject-matter societies and the states could be used as the point of departure for the student performance standards that are held in common by New Standards, NAEP, and the NBPTS. NAEP could then be used to track state and national trends in student performance against the standards. New Standards could be used as a high stakes assessment to drive improvement in the system and to incent individual student performance. The NBPTS could be used as the nation's method for driving up the quality of teaching, with assessments designed to measure teachers' capacity to get students to the new student performance standards. If these elements were in place, the NSSB could develop occupational standards and matching assessments that stand squarely on the foundation knowledge-and-skill standards for students coming out of high school just described.

The keystone of the new national qualifications system would be a new and much higher standard for high school graduation. Imagine that we identified those nations whose high school students do the best in science, mathe-matics, and their native language. Imagine further that we found out what they expect of the great majority of their sixteen-year-old students. Suppose that we then offered a certificate to every student in the United States who meets that certificate standard (adding to it a requirement that they also demonstrate a high level of competence in applied learning). And then we tell every school in the United States that it has only one job: to bring all but the most severely handicapped students up to that standard, no exceptions and no excuses.

In one stroke we would drive a stake through the idea that we can expect very little from most of our students, that it is all right to give some students an "A" in science courses in which no science is taught, that we are doing a favor to many children who are given "A"s just for showing up, doing little work, and not causing much trouble. The high school level performance standards developed by New Standards are set to such internationally benchmarked standards. The New Standards examinations are designed to assess whether students have met these standards.

The whole system would provide very powerful incentives to people of all ages to take tough courses and study hard. Neither employers nor postsecondary institutions would continue to be satisfied with high school diplomas that signify little more than time in the seat. Beyond the foundation academic skill certificates required for high school graduation, employers would be much more likely to rely for their hiring and promotion decisions on certificates that attested to actual occupational skills and knowledge acquired than on passing grades in courses taken, the contents of which are very unclear. Certifying competence, not time in the seat or courses taken, will motivate students everywhere to acquire the needed competence.

2. *Modernize the organization and management of American education.* The delivery level of the American primary and secondary education system is the school. Think of everything else—the state policy-making apparatus, the state department of education, the local school board, and the central office, whatever intermediate education offices there might be between the state and the local levels—as "central." The job of central is to set the targets or standards for student performance, raise the money needed to operate the system and equitably allocate at least 95 percent of those resources to the schools, and put in place strong incentives for the professionals in the schools to produce steady gains in student performance as well as real consequences when they fail to do so. Central must also arrange to have technical assistance and other services available to the schools should they want it and make sure those services are fully responsive to the needs of the schools as the schools see those needs, monitor the system to track student performance against the standards and the satisfaction of all parties with the performance of the system in all its aspects, and dispense the rewards and administer the consequences. Central might also be responsible for developing a cadre of professional staff from among which the schools can select the people to work in their school.

The schools, then, are responsible for deciding whom to hire, how to deploy them, what materials will be used, methods of instruction, how to order the school day, how much time to allocate to each academic subject, how to develop the necessary staff skills, and so on. The school, in short, decides how it is going to use the available resources to get its students to the standards. Each school might have its own school board, a group of parents and faculty who meet from time to time to set broad policy on the matters just discussed. If it does, then it is the board that receives the rewards and is subject to the sanctions of central. If it does not, then it is with the principal that the buck stops. The principle in either case is that authority is lodged with the individual or group that will be held accountable for the results. Results, in this system, are always king. Central defines, monitors, and rewards them. The schools produce them or fail to do so and reap the rewards or consequences.

In this system, large central staffs are no longer necessary. The line supervisory staff is very small, and the distance between the principal of a school and the CEO of central is very short. There is a small staff at central to keep the standards up to date, decide on the measures of customer satisfaction to be used, administer the performance assessments and satisfaction surveys and analyze them and publish the results, distribute the resources to the schools, and manage the incentive system. Everything else, from curriculum consulting to school repair and maintenance, from textbook purchasing to instructional computer systems and services, is defined as services. And all these services can either be run out of central, recovering their costs not through the budget but through purchase decisions made by the schools (which would have the option of buying those services elsewhere, on the open market), or they could be disbanded altogether and provided entirely by the market.

Why call it "central?" Because in New Zealand, this role is played by the national government for the whole nation. Each school in New Zealand has its own school board, which reports directly to the national ministry of education. In Victoria, Australia, each school also has its own school board, but in this case, the board reports directly to the state department of education.

So, in Victoria, the role of "central" is played by one state in a federal system. In Edmonton, Alberta Province, in Canada, the role of "central" is played by a large district (about 200 schools). In the United States, one can imagine school districts throughout a state operating this way. Or one can imagine that all the schools within a state become public charter schools, and the state department of education becomes "central" for all these schools. Either way, whether "central" as described here is the state or the district, layers of bureaucracy disappear, lines of authority emerge clearly and cleanly from the chaos, services actually serve rather than constantly obstruct, and the incentives for school professionals to perform at high levels become positive instead of negative or perverse, as they are at present.

If the state becomes "central" and each school has its own school board and that school board reports to the state, then all schools would be funded from the state's general revenues. That would in one stroke equalize state funding of schools and lodge the responsibility for the schools exactly where the constitutions of most states say it should be—with the state. State allocation formulas would be based on the characteristics of each student, so handicapped and limited English-speaking students would bring more money to the school in which they enrolled than students who were not handicapped or limited English-speaking. In that way, the state could give an incentive to schools to enroll students who are more expensive to educate.

State assumption of full responsibility for school funding, however, would only work if the state is prepared to considerably increase overall funding of public education. Absent that, the funds allocated to relatively wealthy districts would have to decline to the same degree that funds allocated to relatively poor districts increased. There would be more equity, but it would come at a terrible price, just as happened in California as a result of the combined effects of the Serrano decision requiring funding equity and Proposition 13, which limited the revenues that could be raised through property taxes.

In this imagined world, the state allows parents to choose to send their children to any state-funded school they wish that has a place, and the schools would be required to enroll student bodies on a non-discriminatory basis. Schools experiencing strong demand could expand; others might be forced to contract or even close. The state would provide transportation for the students within reasonable limits. Thus, there would be plenty of tough competition among these public schools and many could be expected to go out of business as others sprang up in their place. In this way, the public would get all the advantages of a private voucher system without any of the disadvantages. These schools would still be public. Poor children would not be left to fend for themselves as private schools skimmed the cream. You can think about this system as one made up only of charter schools, but in this charter system, performance against common standards is all that counts. This would not be a charter school system whose touchstone is freedom from regulation, but rather a system in which the regulations are focused on the only thing that matters: results.

3. *Make resources available to build curriculum materials, instructional programs, and instructional technology, and provide professional development designed to get students to the new performance standards.* Changing the standards will not help unless what students are taught and how they are

taught it change greatly. To be sure, some, but not many of the materials and instructional programs that are now available will fit the new standards, and it will be hard to weave what does fit into an effective program. Many millions of dollars will be needed to make a great variety of materials and techniques available as flexible resources to teachers, who can then choose what they want and add their own twist to come up with a program for their school that, in their judgment, will work for their students. The educational publishing industry is poorly capitalized, highly fractionated, and therefore unable by itself to make the kinds of expenditures needed to develop the quality and range of materials and techniques that will be required. Only government has the requisite resources. But when the prototype materials are in fact available, the educational publishing industry will be able to produce, market, and sell them to the schools.

Instructional technology is a special problem. American schools' purchases of computers and modern telecommunications equipment have increased steadily since the mid-1980s, but very little of the computer software that has been purchased has been tightly linked to the core curriculum, certainly not to a curriculum driven by the kind of standards proposed here. Instead, the computers and their associated software have been used mainly to support computer literacy, drill and practice, and enrichment. These tools, however, can potentially provide very powerful supports for the curriculum that will be needed to get students to demanding standards. Their capacity to simulate very complex systems; to access virtually unlimited raw data about almost every conceivable phenomenon; and to measure, store, analyze, and graphically display data in real time could all result in great improvements in the quality of student achieve-

ment and the productivity of our schools. But this outcome will also depend on substantial pump-priming investment by government, in the same way and for the same reasons as the needed investments in curriculum and instruction.

It will also be necessary to help teachers acquire the knowledge and skills needed to get their students to the new targets, using the new standards, assessments, materials, technology, and techniques. This, too, will require a substantial initial investment by government. But only an initial investment. It is widely believed that school districts underinvest in staff development, but this is not necessarily so. The average investment by private industry in formal staff training averages about 1.5 percent of payroll. In the best firms, it comes in at 3 to 4 percent. The largest fraction of these expenditures are accounted for by the cost of the time of the people being trained. When I have calculated school district expenditures on the same basis, I have found, for the districts checked, that expenditures on staff development come in on the order of twice the expenditures of private industry, not counting the expenditures on salary increments tied to courses taken and degrees received by teachers as they advance up the pay scale. The problem is not the amount spent but the way in which the funds are used. Under the management scheme described above, the money for staff development will be in the school's budget, not in central's, and school faculties will have very strong incentives to invest heavily in acquiring the specific expertise needed to execute their plans for improving student performance. In this way, the money that is now wasted on professional development will be used in a far more efficient way to help teachers acquire the knowledge and skill they actually need to do a better job.

4. *Use the qualifications to frame a powerful*

system for the technical and professional preparation of the front-line workforce. Any student who meets the new standards for high school graduation should qualify for immediate admission to a non-selective college or could go on into a program designed to prepare the student for the college entrance examinations required by selective colleges. But many students will not want to go on to a four-year college, selective or non-selective, preferring instead a shorter program, offered by a specialized vocational school, a technical college, or a community college, designed to prepare them for a rewarding career that does not require a bachelor's degree at the entry level. State funding for such programs should be contingent on the institution offering programs designed to prepare students for examinations matched to the industry standards endorsed by the NSSB or comparable state standards. As a matter of state policy, institutions whose role is mainly the provision of vocational education and training should be governed by representatives of industry; all programs offered by these institutions to get students to these new standards should be governed by industry committees; and the examination of students for the certificates signifying that they have met the industry standards should be done by industry representatives. The states should also require that all programs leading to these skill certificates include a specified minimum component of time at the work site in a structured training program designed to complement the classroom instruction and contribute to the development of the skills and knowledge required by the industry standards. It is only by including industry in the development of the standards, in the governance of the provider institutions and the programs and in the examination of the students that industry will gain enough feeling of participation in the whole workforce development system to be willing to offer the worksite-based training slots on which the success of the whole system depends.

5. *In communities that are home to large numbers of children from low-income families, expand facilities that can meet the after-school needs of children where necessary, build better bridges between them and the schools, and make sure all schools serving large numbers of low-income children have close ties to public health and social service agencies that enable them to more easily and flexibly meet the needs of those children.* The challenge of reducing poverty among children is beyond the scope of this essay, as is the challenge of increasing the time available for parents to spend with their children. But there are things that our education system can do to ameliorate the effects of these problems on the most severely affected young people. For many poverty-stricken students, the Family Resource Center solution embraced by Kentucky as part of the Kentucky Education Reform Act will make a significant difference at a modest cost. These centers, located at schools enrolling high proportions of low-income students, have a room set aside that is staffed at all times of the school day with a representative of the many local agencies that serve children and their families, from youth services and juvenile justice officers, to public health officials and the representatives of the welfare program. Responsibility for staffing this room is rotated among the agencies. All of these people are knowledgeable about the services offered by the other agencies and the procedures required to determine eligibility and to access those services. Parents and children can come to a center on an emergency or routine basis to sign up for all the services for which they are eligible at one time, often using a single universal form to which all the participating agencies have agreed.

When this form of outreach is combined with a serious and ongoing effort to coordinate the work of these agencies in the most severely affected school enrollment areas at the highest agency levels, the lives of these young people can become, for the first time, tolerable, and they may, for the first time, be able to take advantage of what the school has to offer.

For some children, this will not be enough. These are the children who need a safe refuge after school, sometimes in the evening or on weekends and have none now. In some communities, the modern version of the settlement house is serving this need well, but in others these institutions are struggling or not present at all. In many cases, they need to be strengthened or developed anew, and in most communities, new ties need to be forged between these institutions and the schools, often facilitated by co-location. The details are unimportant, but the commitment to meet the needs of these youngsters is crucial.

The list of eight obstacles that stand in the way of world-class schools is no more exhaustive than the list of five solutions is a complete catalogue of all the good ideas for improving the schools. But both lists are strategic. In my judgment, if we accomplished 80 percent of the tasks laid out in the description of the five proposed measures, the United States would have a decent shot at being among the ten nations in the world that do the best job of educating its young people. If we also found a way at the same time to reduce the proportion of our children living in poverty from more than 20 percent to something on the order of 5 percent, there is no reason the United States should not lead the list.

23

Transition from School to Work: Black, Hispanic, and White Men in the 1980s

Avner Ahituv, Marta Tienda, and V. Joseph Hotz

Introduction

Recent years have witnessed a resurgence of interest in the transition from school to work both because it marks a critical threshold in the progression to adulthood and because there is mounting concern in policy arenas over the plight of youth who enter the workforce ill prepared to perform basic job tasks. Although many studies underscore the deficiencies of high school education for subsequent labor market experiences, most analysts focus exclusively on *post-secondary* school work experiences and ignore or downplay the investment value of work experience acquired *prior to* leaving school. This oversight is surprising because virtually *all* adolescents experience at least one episode of employment before leaving school.

Accordingly, we assess the importance of ignoring work experience during periods of school enrollment by examining variation in the timing and character of initial labor market encounters for a nationally representative cohort of black, Hispanic, and white young men ages thirteen to sixteen in 1978.[1] We address several questions. First, how sensitive are conclusions about the school-to-work transition to variation in criteria used to define first job experience? Second, do black, Hispanic, and white youth follow similar pathways from school to work? If not, in what ways do they differ? Finally, what individual, familial, and market factors shape alternative pathways to employment? To address these questions, we (1) chart ethnic differences in the timing and industry sector of first jobs using alternative criteria to define "first job," (2) examine the sequence and combination of work vis-à-vis school activity, and (3) evaluate the determinants of pathways from school to work using a multi-state dynamic model. We demonstrate that ignoring employment during school not only misses key differences in the labor market stratification processes of minority relative to non-minority youth, but also raises questions about the pivotal effect of early labor market experiences on disadvantages during adulthood. Conceptually, we offer a more in-depth examination of early work experiences by analyzing the *pathways* to first employment. As life-course students have proposed, this concept refers to the *sequencing* of events that have implications for future transitions and outcomes. In this application, pathways depict the sequence and combination of school, work, and military states from ages fifteen to twenty-eight, during which time the majority of youth complete the transition from school to work. We document three distinct pathways that differentiate racial and ethnic origin: Hispanics leave school early and begin working early in their life course; blacks stay in school longer without working, and often use military service as a bridge between the two; and whites combine school and work over a protracted period, thereby accumulating labor market experience while raising general skills.

The remainder of this essay proceeds as follows. The next section describes the data and presents descriptive results characterizing race and ethnic variation in the transition from school to work. The third section traces race and ethnic differences in full-time employment to group variation in family background and early investments in work experience and educational attainment. We conclude by summarizing key findings and discussing the theoretical and practical importance of more detailed scrutiny of early work experiences.

Data and Descriptive Results

We analyze the National Longitudinal Survey of Youth (NLSY), a national probability sample of 12,686 individuals aged 14 to 21 as of January 1, 1979, who were re-interviewed annually for over a decade. Central to our analysis of youth employment is the operational definition of a youth's first job. We use alternative constructions to demonstrate the importance of considering the different ways adolescents enter the labor force. Therefore, definitions of first employment vary according to the following criteria: *school departure,* whether the sample includes all youth (regardless of school enrollment) or only those who have left school, and

military service, whether the definition of work includes or excludes military service. We measure school departure as being out of school for at least six months.

To characterize all possible activities in the school-to-work transition, we include youth from ages 15 to 28, the last age observed for our sample. The six mutually exclusive states we examine are: (a) exclusive school enrollment; (b) simultaneous school enrollment and part-time work; (c) part-time work; (d) full-time work; (e) military service; and (f) idle. Within this scheme, full-time work is more than thirty-five weekly hours and more than forty weeks per year and indicates completion of the transition from school to work.

Timing of First Employment

Several general conclusions emerge from our findings on the timing of first employment:

1. Consistent with many prior studies, we find that the vast majority of initial labor market encounters occur while youth are attending school. The percentage of young men who work by age 17 ranges from 70 (for blacks) to 83 percent (for whites), with Hispanics between this range. Yet, if work during school enrollment is not counted, only between 16 (black and white) and 26 (Hispanic) percent of 17-year-olds held a job.

2. If all employment spells are considered, white youth enter the labor market three to four months before blacks of the same median age. Furthermore, there is an employment gap of up to 14 percentage points at age 16, when 62 percent of whites held a job, compared to 48 and 59 percent of black and Hispanic youth, respectively. By age 18, when most youth should have completed high school, the black-white gap narrows to 9 percentage points, as approximately

94 percent of white youth had worked, compared to 85 percent of black youth. Such racial and ethnic differences dissipate by age 21, however, when over 96 percent of all youth reported some work experience.

3. If work during school is considered, by age 17, higher shares of whites (83 percent) have entered the labor market than either Hispanics (79 percent) or blacks (70 percent). However, if the definition of employment is restricted to school leavers, at age 17, 26 percent of Hispanics worked, appreciably higher than that of whites and blacks—17 and 16 percent, respectively. Moreover, Hispanic youth maintain this lead over whites through age 19 if military experience is included as work, and through age 23 if it is excluded. Thus, a third conclusion is that generalizations about the timing of labor market entry (and thus the acquisition of work experience) depend crucially on definitions.

4. If military service is counted as employment, there is little or no racial or ethnic variation before age 19 because military service requires high school completion or its equivalent. However, noteworthy differences begin at age 19 when there is a 6 percentage point increase in the share of blacks who had "worked," compared with an increase of only 3 percent points for whites and Hispanics. These results demonstrate how military service fills a gap in work experience for black youth who have completed secondary school.

Industrial Profiles

An analysis of the industrial distribution of young men's first jobs further illustrates the sensitivity of conclusions about early work experiences to definitional criteria. Our findings show that retail industries, which frequently offer flexible schedules, were the modal employment sector for male teens. Between 23 percent (for blacks) and 43 percent (for whites) of in-school youth hold their first jobs in one of the four retail categories—general, auto, food sales, and restaurants. Fast-food and eating establishments are particularly important ports of entry, employing almost 20 percent of all in-school white and Hispanic youths, and 13 percent of blacks.

There are, however, pronounced racial and ethnic differences in these entry-level employment patterns. Retail establishments are clearly the dominant ports of entry for all youth, but provide higher shares of entry-level jobs for whites than for blacks or Hispanics. Services for professionals (e.g., janitorial and auxiliary support) provide first jobs for higher shares of minorities than non-minorities. For example, 18 percent of black and 10 percent of Hispanic, but only 4 percent of white youth, secured their first jobs in health and education service industries. Similarly, among in-school youths, 10 percent of blacks and 7 percent of Hispanics, but only 4 percent of whites, held first jobs in public administration service industries.

These industrial profiles change if the definition of youth employment is restricted to post-school employment. For example, the share of youth whose first jobs are in manufacturing is roughly 15 to 16 percent of post-school employment, but about 10 percent of in-school jobs. These definitional differences also narrow the racial employment disparities. For example, the white-black employment differential in health and education services falls from 14 percentage points to roughly 5 points. Finally, nearly 12 percent of young out-of-school blacks were in the military compared to 6 percent of whites and Hispanics. Summary calculations confirm these definitional impacts. Using an index of dissimilarity (ID) for comparisons, nearly one-quarter of young black or white men would have to change industries to eliminate racial differences in the industrial profile of first jobs based on the most inclusive definition of employment. Still, these variations in the timing and character of first jobs leave many unanswered questions about the sequence of activities during adolescence and young adulthood, especially whether these differ by race and Hispanic origin. We address these issues next.

Pathways from School to Work

The transition from school to work includes high school graduation for most youths, college attendance or military service for a subset of high school graduates, and, most importantly, increasing commitment to the labor force from early to late adolescence and into young adulthood. The actual sequencing of activities does not follow an ordered progression because many youth combine school and work, some withdraw from school without completing a grade, while others withdraw from school and return after testing the labor market. Nevertheless, there are two general phases after high school: college and/or military service (ages 19 to 22), and full-time employment (ages 19 to 26, depending on whether youth entered college and/or military service).

The vast majority of youth work while they are enrolled in high school and/or college. At ages 13–14, virtually all youth are enrolled in school full time, but a tiny share (1 to 3 percent) have begun to work part time. By age 25, only between 5 and 7 percent of young adults are pursuing formal schooling, a vast majority of which is in tandem with work. During middle adolescence (e.g., age 15), about 20 percent of white and Hispanic youth work part time while

being enrolled in school, as do 15 percent of black youth. But by age 25, full-time employment is the modal activity of all young men, though there is substantial race and ethnic diversity in the shares of youth this age who work full time. Nearly 75 percent of young white males, but only 65 percent of Hispanics and 61 percent of blacks, are employed full time or are in the military at age 25. Minority youth complete the transition from school to work later than whites, irrespective of whether they prolong schooling (blacks) or enter the labor market early (Hispanics).

Overall, the age-specific activity distributions portray distinct racial-ethnic pathways from school to work. These distinct pathways result from differences in the timing of school departure, differences in the likelihood of military activity, and differences in the prevalence of idleness. The modal Hispanic pathway involves early school departure coupled with early labor market entry. Through age 19, the proportion of out-of-school Hispanics who are working or in the military far exceeds that of other groups. For instance, at age 18, 26 percent of Hispanics are in nonschool activities compared to approximately 19 percent of whites and blacks. Over half of white and black youth are in school at age 19, while the majority of Hispanics have already left school. Hispanics become employed full time earlier than whites and blacks, but they do so at the *expense* of schooling. Furthermore, their full-time employed advantage is lost by age 25, when whites overtake them based on the share employed full time.

A second pathway, most typical of black youth, involves prolonged schooling without work experience. Young blacks are more likely than either whites or Hispanics to not work while in school. To illustrate, among in-school youth at age 17, 32 percent of blacks were not working compared to 21 percent of Hispanics and only 17 percent of whites. Yet, 74 percent of enrolled white youths worked compared to 62 percent of blacks. By prolonging their schooling, young blacks delay the transition from school to full-time employment.

A third pathway, typical of white youth, involves an extensive overlap of school and work activities, especially after age 16. White adolescents combine work experience with schooling at younger ages than either blacks or Hispanics, and this pattern continues through early adulthood. At age 17, nearly three out of four in-school white youth work, which is 10 to 12 percentage points more than Hispanics and blacks, respectively. At age 21, only one in three white youth are still in school, among whom over 90 percent work. And, while lower shares of blacks and Hispanics are enrolled at this age, even lower shares (approximately 70 percent) work. Thus, the pathway of white youth, combining early work experience with formal schooling, has the advantages of both the black and Hispanic pathways and may be pivotal in understanding the origins of racial and ethnic labor market stratification.

One final noteworthy racial and ethnic difference in young men's pathways from school to work is the incidence of idleness. Although this category may include a wide range of informal and/or illicit work activities, and even incarceration, it nonetheless represents youth who are absent from the formal, paid labor market. Several issues warrant emphasis. First, this group is sizable: At its peak ages (20–24), it includes up to 12 percent of young black men. Second, at any age minority men are appreciably more likely to be idle than non-minority men. For example, at age 24 only 6 percent of white men are idle, compared with 12 percent of blacks and 9 percent of Hispanics. Third, idleness increases during late adolescence, peaks during early adulthood, and falls after age 24. These age-specific profiles suggest slower exits from idleness for young minority men, particularly blacks.

One interpretation of these findings is that group membership defines distinct pathways from school to work. However, it is conceivable that the distinct pathways result from group differences in characteristics. If minority group status does not directly produce the alternative pathways from school to work, which individual and family background characteristics are conducive to an optimal pathway involving minimal episodes of joblessness, maximum human capital accumulation (both formal schooling and work experience), and a timely beginning of full-time employment? Why do Hispanic youth appear to fare better in the labor market than black youth, even though they achieve lower average levels of education and withdraw from school at faster rates? More generally, does the propensity to combine school and work help explain the race and ethnic differences in labor market outcomes for young men? To address these questions, we turn to a multivariate analysis that models the school-to-work transition as a dynamic, multi-state process.

Determinants of School-to-Work Transition

Empirical Specification

Economic and sociological perspectives of the labor market, while differing in their emphases, have common grounds that are essential for modeling the school-to-work transition. Both perspectives acknowledge the value of skill acquisition early in life; both appreciate that school and work choices are driven by future economic expectations and circumscribed by budget and resource constraints; and both recognize that labor market conditions determine the range of opportunities for acquiring early work experiences. Accordingly, we model the school-to-work transition as a function of four types of influences: (1) *budget and resource constraints,* defined by family socioeconomic background and parent absence; (2) *early achievements,* including progress in school (grade completed) and developed ability based on test scores; (3) *labor market opportunities* that are governed by location and cyclical changes in the local economy; and (4) *ascribed traits,* namely race and Hispanic origin, foreign birth, and birth cohort.

Specifically, early achievements and developed aptitude are conducive to prolonged school attendance. Thus, early scholastic achievements should reduce the likelihood of becoming idle or withdrawing from school prematurely, depending on family background. We measure early achievements and aptitude using highest grade completed in each prior year and Armed Forces Qualification Test (AFQT) score. Higher AFQT scores are associated with prolonged school enrollment and exclude the least able from military service.

Family background and parent absence, our indicators of budget and resource constraints, influence the transition from school to work because they provide the financial resources and social incentives for investing in human capital. A vast sociological literature has established a strong association between parental and offspring's educational attainment, hence youth reared in more affluent families should prolong school departure and avoid idleness compared to youth from disadvantaged families. Well-educated parents may both appreciate and convey to their children the benefits of more schooling, and they may also have the financial resources to avoid excessive early employment. We therefore expect well-educated parents to encourage youth to prolong school, even in tandem with work. A single-parent household often implies insufficient parental supervision, greater psychological stressors, and less-structured lifestyles, all of which, in tandem with financial difficulties, often truncate educational careers.

Labor markets affect school to work by changing the opportunity structures for youth and thereby influencing employment decisions. A vast literature shows that youth employment is highly sensitive to changes in aggregate demand. For example, high unemployment rates may translate into negative signals of worsening job opportunities. In turn, these negative signals may encourage youth to prolong schooling as a way of increasing their employment prospects when the economy improves. Moreover, given the differential responsiveness of Hispanic, black, and white youth to cyclical variation in unemployment, the effect of unemployment on youth's school and work choices may vary by race and ethnicity. As proxies for these changes in the demand for youth labor, we use annual county growth in total employment, manufacturing and services, and average county income per worker in manufacturing and services. Unemployment rates are measured at the state level.

The mean family income of white youth is nearly double that of blacks, and 60 percent greater than that of Hispanics. Among parents, Hispanics have the lowest educational achievements, approximately three to four years less than whites, and two to three years less than blacks. At age 14, nearly one in three blacks and one in four Hispanics resided in a mother-only household, compared to less than 10 percent of whites. We expect that youths in single-parent families will work full time earlier and that this effect will differ for whites, blacks, and Hispanics because of differences in family structure.

Minority and non-minority men also differ in the years of school completed by age 18, the end of the first phase of the transition from school to work, and age 24, when most youth have completed the transition. Our findings show that Hispanics withdraw from school at earlier ages than either blacks or whites and average half a year less formal schooling than whites at age 18 and 1.3 fewer years by age 24, when black men average about half a year more school than Hispanics. From a human capital perspective, these educational differentials imply that young adult minority men will be disadvantaged in the labor market vis-à-vis their white age counterparts, and that Hispanic youth are the most educationally disadvantaged. Differences in developed aptitude, measured by AFQT, confirm this white advantage, but show a modest Hispanic advantage over blacks.

Empirical Results

Our quantitative results not only refute the hypothesis that Hispanic and black youth were more likely than white youth to be working part or full time relative to attending school exclusively, but they indicate exactly the opposite. That is, minority youth are less likely than statistically comparable white men to work part or full time relative to exclusive school attendance. Surprisingly, minority men also are less likely than their white statistical counterparts to participate in military service relative to full-time school attendance. And young black men are less likely, and Hispanics as likely, as whites to combine work and school. Finally, young minority men are less likely to be idle than statistically comparable whites relative to pursuing school exclusively. Thus, the higher minority idleness rates arise because they are more likely to reside in resource-poor families and face limited job opportunities. The general lesson from the multivariate analyses is that the *distinct race and ethnic pathways we observed arise largely because of group differences in socioeconomic composition.* Whether these unequal outcomes can be rectified with policy instruments remains to be seen.

That the hypothesized effects are statistically negative (rather than zero) warrants further explanation. Substantively, the consistently negative effects of race and Hispanic origin on the various activity states imply that minority men are more likely than their white statistical counterparts to be enrolled in school at any age. This may at first blush seem counterintuitive, but it is entirely consistent with other studies that show lower drop-out rates for minorities relative to statistically equivalent whites, as well as evidence that minority youth are more likely than whites to experience age-grade delay.

Further support for this interpretation and ethnic pathways is afforded by estimates for family background and the AFQT scores. For virtually all activities, higher levels of parental education lower the odds of exclusive work relative to exclusive school attendance. The notable exception is school and work, which is statistically indistinguishable from exclusive school attendance based on the effects of parental education and family income. This indicates that parental education is a powerful force influencing human capital formation, including moderate labor market experience. Moreover, for whites the relationships are stronger.

Group-specific estimates qualify this interpretation in several ways. First, family background characteristics do not influence the school and work choices of Hispanic youth. Although the very low educational thresholds of Hispanic parents may be partly responsible for this finding, the small sample size is also a contributing factor. Second, for both black and white youth, higher levels of parental education slow the rate of entry to full-time work relative to full-time school attendance. Third, for white youth, father's education discourages part-time employment relative to exclusive schooling, but increases the odds of military activity. Finally, for both black and white youth, parental education (father's education for whites and mother's education for blacks) lowers the odds of idleness relative to exclusive school.

The most consistent and statistically significant effects on the transition from school to work correspond to the AFQT score. For all youth, higher AFQT scores were associated with delayed part-time or full-time employment relative to exclusive school attendance. Youth with higher AFQT scores were more likely to combine school and work relative to full-time education, and were less likely to be idle. However, youth with higher AFQT scores were *not* more likely to enlist in the military relative to remaining in school full time. Thus, the AFQT may help exclude the least able from the military, but not to select the most able. Yet, AFQT scores do appear to channel the most able into formal schooling, often with work experience. Group-specific estimates generally support the powerful influence of pre-market skill on pathways from school to work. For Hispanics, higher AFQT scores lowered the odds of part-time work and idleness relative to full-time schooling, but increases in AFQT scores did not alter the odds of full-time work or military service relative to exclusive schooling. Black youth had similar results, except that higher AFQT scores delay full-time work relative to exclusive school attendance. In contrast to white youth, higher AFQT scores did not increase Hispanic or black youth's odds of combining school and work, which appears to

compound labor market success for young adults and may hold a key to understanding why race and ethnic wage inequality has been growing.

Conclusion

To recapitulate, the general questions motivating our empirical research focus on racial and ethnic differences involve: (1) the timing of school departure and labor market entry, (2) the nature of the early work experiences, and (3) the determinants of alternative pathways to full-time employment. An implicit assumption pervading the literature on youth employment is that early labor market activity is desirable both because it signals youth's awareness of adult activities and because these experiences may provide valuable information about the consequences of premature school withdrawal. Prior research shows that both the timing and the nature of early work experiences differ by race, but there is limited evidence about the experiences of Hispanic youth. Our research therefore fills an important void by broadening the race and ethnic spectrum, by questioning whether conclusions about the advantages and disadvantages of early work experience depend on the definition of first employment, and by examining the correlates of seemingly different pathways from school to work.

For example, we consider the implications of ignoring military service and jobs while at school. This is important because assessments of the returns to experience are distorted by failure to consider early work activities. We demonstrate that analyses restricted to out-of-school youth ignore non-trivial amounts of work experience, which not only is relevant to subsequent labor market success, but also is crucial for understanding the underpinnings of racial and ethnic income and employment inequalities. Specifically, restricting the definition of youth employment to post-school experiences masks important processes undergirding racial and ethnic stratification during adolescence. Surprisingly, however, our multivariate analysis indicates that minority youth are more likely than statistically comparable white men to prolong school, and less likely to be idle. In addition, Hispanic youth are as likely as white youth to combine school with work. Thus, the multivariate analysis revealed that the distinct race and ethnic pathways arise largely because of group differences in family background characteristics. These socioeconomic characteristics influence school and work choices that undermine the early accumulation of human capital, which has a profound impact on adolescent employment and the transition to full-time employment.

The group-specific results point to one important factor that undergirds the distinct pathways we found. That is, the transition from school to work among the more able whites (based on AFQT) entails the optimal strategy of prolonging formal schooling while acquiring work experience. This strategy has the added advantage of raising human capital essential for long-term returns, while providing the benefits of early work experience. Specifically, *the*

school-to-work pathway of white youth involving acquisition of early work experience and prolonged enrollment in school appears to be pivotal in racial and ethnic labor market stratification.

Although we have shown that the characterization of the school-to-work transition is sensitive to the definition of work, to the importance of military service, and to whether work experience is acquired while enrolled in school, we have not considered whether there are, in fact, any lasting economic effects of early work experience. However, in other research we found that not only do early work experiences have persistent effects for young men, but that differences in these returns, coupled with the differences in the labor market conditions that whites, blacks, and Hispanics faced in the 1980s, accounted significantly for the diverse pathways taken by these three groups in the transition from school to work.

Note

1. This research was funded by the Russell Sage Foundation and the National Science Foundation (SBR 96-01995). Institutional support was provided by the Population Research Center of National Opinion Research Center and the Center for the Study of Social Inequality at the University of Chicago.

C. Labor Market Policies

24

Wages and the Service Sector

Lester Thurow

If broadly shared prosperity across the American workforce is to be restored, the key to unlocking this new pattern of prosperity will be found in the service sector. According to the 1996 Economic Report of the President, private services provided 98 percent of the economy's employment growth in the past twenty-five years, 94 percent in the last nine years, and 104 percent in the last five.

While service wages vary widely, from some of the economy's highest wages in industries such as investment banking or entertainment to some of the economy's lowest wages, average hourly wages in the goods-producing sector are 30 percent above those in the service sector. Service activities such as transportation, communications, and utilities with hourly wages 19 percent above those in the goods sector are more than counter-balanced by other activities such as retailing, with hourly wages just 46 percent of those in the goods sector. Much of the growth in service employment is statistical rather than real since many service sectors such as retailing have been splitting what were full-time jobs into several part-time jobs. According to the Department of Labor, services are the nation's biggest employers of part-time (accounting for 74 percent of total part-time employment) and contingent (temporary, on-call, or contract) workers. With the shift to part-time work comes lower wages and large reductions in the fringe benefits (pensions, health care, paid vacations, and holidays) that are an important part of a good job, along with reduced training, skills, and career ladders.

While services output has grown two and a half times in real terms since 1970, the source of rapid employment growth is to an even greater extent to be found in low, or in some years even negative, productivity growth rates. Over the past twenty-five years, the average rate of growth of output per worker has been just 0.7 percent per year in the service sector. Not surprisingly, if output per worker is low and only slowly growing, wages will be low and falling behind those in other sectors while employment opportunities are growing rapidly.

Put simply and bluntly, broadly shared prosperity cannot be restored for most Americans unless the service sector undergoes some major structural changes. It needs a new structure of employment and remuneration that will lead to a very different pattern of productivity growth.

This clearly can be done. In continental Europe a very different pattern of employment and remuneration in services explains much of the difference between their patterns of earnings distribution (only small increases in the wage gap between the top and bottom quintiles and few if any workers with falling real wages) and America's rapidly widening differentials and falling real wages for many. (The exact number with falling real wages depends upon what one believes about the exaggeration of inflation in our statistical indexes but not even a 1 percentage point per year adjustment would bring the numbers with falling real wages close to zero.)

Services also explain much of Europe's better productivity performance. With service wages near those in manufacturing, continental Europeans simply run a much more capital-intensive service sector with much higher rates of investment. And as a result, services have a much higher rate of growth of productivity. A Swiss ski resort, for example, operates with a very different capital-labor ratio than an American one. Tickets are sold electronically, lifts operate automatically, the lift attendants who are responsible for safety watch more than one lift, and resorts are organized from the perspective of reducing the need for labor. In America, wages are so low that it does not pay to make the necessary labor-saving investments.

But there is a price to be paid. Services also explain much of Europe's failure to create new jobs. With much higher productivity growth in the sector and little growth in part-time workers, service employment grows much more slowly than in the United States, even though output growth has followed the American pattern—albeit with a time lag that is now rapidly narrowing.

Higher productivity growth could have been offset with macroeconomic policies that lead to higher overall economic growth rates but this did not happen. Europe's macro-policies have been even more restrictive than those in the United States. As a result, productivity rises in pace without output growth and there is no need to add new employees.

Nevertheless, continental Europe clearly demonstrates that it is possible to run a profitable, high-wage service sector with the career ladders and skill development found in other industries such as manufacturing.

Before proceeding to analyze the service sector, it is important to understand that services are not a normal sector of the economy, statistically speaking; the service sector is what might be called a "garbage" statistical category. Statistical agencies carefully define agriculture, mining, construction, and manufacturing and then everything else not meeting those definitions is dumped into a statistical category called "services." The result is a sector without any common denominators. Services include high-tech, capital-intensive activities (such as nuclear power plants) and low-tech, labor-intensive industries (such as dog walking). It includes some of the country's most skilled workers (medical doctors) and some of its least skilled workers (janitorial services). There are even goods-producing activities (kilowatts of electricity) to be found within it.

With out-sourcing and the use of temporary workers, activities that used to be included in other sectors are now included in services. Usually this shift is a process for sharply cutting wages and fringe benefits. The implicit social contract that limits wage inequalities in "core" activities does not apply to out-sourced activities or temporary workers who are not really on the team.

The policy changes that would be required to produce the European pattern of service provision are clear. They would begin with laws requiring identical wage and fringe benefit packages for full-time and part-time workers and for temporary or contract workers and regular workers. This would quickly convert services away from part-time, temporary, and contingent workers to an industry of regularly employed full-time workers. Other industries would quit out-sourcing simply to get lower-paid service workers. Part-time, temporary, and contingent workers are cheap today principally because they do not have to be given standard compensation benefits. If firms had to give the same fringe benefit packages regardless of a worker's status and the same wages for the same work, the service sector would quickly shift to what would become cheaper (per hour) full-time workers. Compensation per employee would rise.

As an example, if President Clinton's universal health reform package had passed in 1993, it would have pushed many service firms back toward more full-time employment, since the health care costs that would have had to be covered by the employer would have been much higher for part-time workers than for full-time workers.

To raise productivity to cover the costs of this extra labor compensation, firms would provide more training or undertake more capital investment to cut the unit labor costs of the services they supply. They could also go out of business or raise prices to the consumers, but as we shall see later, neither of these two other options are likely. Having to operate with a more skilled, full-time workforce would cause turnover to become more of a handicap (costlier) and force firms to think about career ladders and other inducements (the opportunity for promotions and higher wages) to reduce turnover.

With a more stable full-time workforce, a more egalitarian implicit social contract would emerge and force some additional wage equalization with the firm. It is much easier to treat those officially off the team harshly than it is to treat harshly those that are officially on the team. Firms who have tried two-tiered wage structures (the airlines a decade ago) for regular employees quickly found that they sociologically did not work. An attached workforce simply has to be managed and paid differently than an unattached workforce.

While it is true that low wages are a sign of low productivity and that low productivity operations can only pay low wages, if one is seeking to identify cause and effect, the direction of causation does not always run from low productivity to low wages. Consider those years when measured service productivity was falling in the United States. How could that be happening? Technology was not disappearing or retrogressing. If wages are falling, it is profitable for companies to move to lower-cost, lower-productivity, labor-intensive methods of production. The guard at the parking lot gate becomes cheaper than the automated fare-collecting machinery.

Conversely if service companies were forced to operate with higher wages, they have to reorganize their production processes to justify those higher wages, pass on the new higher prices to their customers, or go out of business. The experience of continental Europe where social legislation, social solidarity, and unions force service wages near those in manufacturing indicates that companies do not go out of business (there are few if any services that are available in the United States but not available in Europe) and that few even raise their prices (service prices relative to other prices are not in general more expensive than those in the United States). Most find it profitable to make the investments necessary to move to high-productivity, more capital-intensive, labor-saving forms of production. If the European wage structure were imposed on the American service sector, its productivity would quickly rise to European levels. What would happen would be very similar to what occurred in manufacturing when Henry Ford dramatically raised the wages of his auto workers even though he had no shortage of people willing to work in those factories. Then and now it would have ripple effects that would lead to a very different wage structure.

Both of these policies (fringe benefit and wage policies that reverse today's incentives to hire part-timers, temporaries, and contingent workers and wage policies that narrow the wage gap between services and manufacturing) would, of course, cause an enormous reduction in service employment. This is both necessary if the wage structure in services is to rise and become more egalitarian and good for the long-run health of the economy. With a higher rate of productivity growth in services, the non-inflationary growth rate of the economy, and with it real wages, could presumably accelerate.

While the service sector, like the rest of the American economy, could use a lot more investment in skills, it is important to note that skill training by itself will not lead to the desired results—a more broadly shared economic prosperity. If macroeconomic policies were not simultaneously adjusted to accelerate economic growth and if the incentive structures of sectors such as services were not altered, additional skills by themselves would simply push wages down faster. When the data show wages falling for males at all education and skills levels, the supply of skills is already moving outward faster than the demand for skills. To accelerate the outward movement of the skill supply curve in such a situation is simply to increase the divergence between demand and supply and to make wages fall even faster. Skill training has an important role to play in a more broadly shared prosperity, but only after faster growth and different incentive structures have been put in place.

While social legislation could alter private incentives so that the service sector would contribute to a broadly shared prosperity, this will not happen by itself in the marketplace. As the incentives are now structured, services can only lead the economy toward a more inegalitarian structure of wage and employment opportunities in the future as they continue to be an increasingly larger percentage of total economic activity.

25

A Thirty-Five-Year Perspective
on Workforce Development Programs

Garth Mangum

Vantage Point

Where one stands usually depends upon where one sits, and the reader is warned that this essay is a very personal perspective. After being involved as a Senate staffer in the first year of the 1962 Manpower Development and Training Act (MDTA) and its first few amendments, as well as the beginnings of legislative consideration of the Economic Opportunity Act of 1964; becoming director of the President's Committee on Manpower later in that year, where one of many issues was developing the administrative structure of the new spate of manpower and antipoverty programs; leaving government to be involved in some of the early evaluations of those programs; being at one point a member of a National Advisory Council on Vocational Education; serving at George Shultz's request on a task force recommending labor policies to the incoming Nixon administration, which were later incorporated in the Comprehensive Employment and Training Act (CETA); spending some years at the University of Utah running a program that trained at the master's degree level program operators at the state and local level in many areas of the nation; working with Senator Orrin Hatch on the formulation of the Job Training Partnership Act (JTPA); serving

for several years on a State Job Training Coordinating Council and writing many books about what started as manpower policy, later becoming known as employment and training programs and now workforce development policy, I have never been known as a caustic critic of those efforts with which I was involved. Neither do I consider myself a major architect of the programs. Hundreds have played more critical roles in the unfolding thirty-five-year drama. This personal history merely alerts the reader to the vantage point from which the following observations emerge.

Observations

No policy is without precedent. One could begin with the history of vocational education or of 1930s work relief programs, the Employment Act of 1946, the growing demand for post-secondary occupational preparation after World War II, or many other events. But 1962 represents the growing recognition that a second chance at more formal preparation for work would become increasingly essential. That need has intensified over these thirty-six years so that, on the average, the only people who maintained their real earnings over the period from the early 1970s to the mid-1990s were those with a college education, and only those with graduate degrees, again on the average, actually experienced real increases in their standards of living. That was the leading edge. But at the rear of the column were those who had entered the working world underprepared, who were at risk of doing so, or had become displaced from reasonably satisfactory but tenuous positions somewhere up the line. They have been the targets of programs that have never been funded at any level capable of serving more than a small margin of those eligible but have made significant contributions to the well-being of most of those who have been involved. Who has and who has not profited, how much and why, is the controversy toward which these comments are addressed. Despite the drastic changes that have occurred in the U.S. economy over the last one-third of a century, the experience of these workforce development programs has been remarkably consistent.

Bipartisanship

Among the observations from my vantage point is recognition of the consistent role of bipartisanship. It was as easy for Republican Senators Jacob Javits and Winston Prouty as it was for my Democratic boss, Senator Joseph Clark, and the brand-new young Democratic senator, Edward Kennedy, to believe in and support MDTA. To the liberal, it meant opportunities for the disadvantaged, to the conservative it meant preparation for the responsibilities of self-reliance. CETA was very much a bipartisan creation between the Republican Labor Department and the Democratic Congress. The Reagan administration Secretary and Assistant Secretary of Labor for Employment and Training wanted to kill CETA without replacement. JTPA was substituted through an alliance be-

tween the Republican Senate, the Democratic House, and the sub rosa involvement of a "kitchen cabinet"–level Labor Department staff. The final act was the personal intervention of Senator Hatch with White House staff director Edwin Meese to get the Labor Secretary overruled. The compromises necessary to save the employment and training program included ending public service employment and stipends. Without essentially changing the membership of local governing bodies, the chairing role was shifted from local elected officials to private employers. Governors were promoted from merely overseeing the rural "balance of state" to a dominant position in governing the program.

Continuing bipartisanship in a more negative mood, in 1993 the Clinton administration changed the name and took over President Bush's Job Training 2000 proposal of 1992, and Republican and Democratic proposals were made but never acted upon to devolve employment and training responsibility totally to the states in 1995–96 through federal block grants.

Brevity

Another constant throughout the thirty-five years has been the brevity of training. Among the first amendments to MDTA were successive lengthenings of program authorization to allow longer training times and the availability of remedial basic education to support it. Yet, despite the authorization for up to 104 weeks of training—what could have been more than long enough to obtain an associate's degree and even make major inroads on a baccalaureate—the average training length for adults has fluctuated between twenty and thirty weeks or more; youth have averaged about 15 weeks—no more than one week for each year of their age. During the 1980s, there was a period of flirtation with job search training, a process which, if done well, can speed the return to work but can only help people find jobs commensurate with the skills they already have. But in pursuit of cheap training, a few days or weeks of job search assistance seemed an easy answer. The reason is obvious: If eligibility exceeds funding twentyfold, local administrators are in no position to say no to the many in order to provide meaningful training to the few. JTPA added another pressure toward brevity: it eliminated subsistence payments, without which not many of the poor can undertake lengthy training. Yet both occupational choice and training outcomes are determined largely by program length.

"Creaming"

A related constant has been complaints of "creaming." Whatever the eligibility criteria prescribed by the Congress, the most aggressive and most competent are the most likely to become aware of the program opportunity and be at the front of the applicant line. Recruiters and program operators are unlikely to reject those eligibles in order to beat the bushes for those with more formidable barriers—and the employers who are the ultimate determiners of program success are even less likely to insist that they do so. The only defenses are to narrow eligibility requirements and reward or punish selectivity accordingly.

Related to that forward selectivity has been the tendency to abandon innovations designed to better enable the system to serve the disadvantaged in order to return constantly to the mainstream. Examples are the abandonment by the Labor Department once it gained total domination under CETA of two contributions of the Department of Health, Education, and Welfare during its dual administration of MDTA. One

was the Area Manpower Institutes for the Development of Staff (AMIDS), designed to train state and local vocational training staff to relate effectively to the unfamiliar new disadvantaged training population. Another was the almost but not-yet-total abandonment of the separately administered skills centers separately designed and operated to serve the disadvantaged population. Many of their innovations such as open-entry, open-exit access and individualized and modularized curricula have been adopted by mainstream institutions, but the willingness to start with a disadvantaged population from where they are and bring them step-by-step forward until they can compete in the mainstream has too often been abandoned in favor of merely paying an eligible trainee's tuition to compete with all other enrollees in ongoing vocational or technical education courses.

Current advocacy of training vouchers is one more step along that road. Displaced but experienced workers may know what they want to learn and where to find it, but those who do can hardly be classified as disadvantaged. Counseling and guidance with considerable handholding are essential to the transition from disadvantagement.

Outcomes

All of that led to a constancy of result throughout the thirty-six years. There was considerable consternation at the end of the 1980s when national JTPA evaluations showed that women profited substantially; men had positive outcomes that were too small to be statistically significant; but youth were worse off for having enrolled. There were many reasons for protesting the structure of the evaluation and disputing the results, but despite weaknesses in methodology, these results did not surprise old hands in the employment and training game. Women had experienced greater gains than men since the initiation of MDTA. Most enrolled women were pursuing full-time employment after being out of or only sporadically in the labor force. The program provided not only training but a priority access route to jobs. More of the earnings increase was from steadier employment than from higher wage rates. Most of the men had already been in the labor force, and many were really displaced workers who had fallen under the poverty incomes necessary for disadvantaged eligibility after some period of unemployment. For the latter, even retraining was unlikely to offset the loss of seniority wages. These losses would have to be offset against the earnings gains of others for a lower average gain for men. Aggregate statistics also obscured anomalies such as the period in Michigan when MDTA program dropouts did better than program completers because the training was undertaken during a period of automobile factory layoffs and the dropouts were those who were recalled to their former positions. Similarly, youth programs throughout that history often were described as "aging vats" where young people were parked until they either went back to school or became old enough to become better employed. There were always some successful youth programs but they were never run-of-the-mill. Note that youth programs are still primarily for work experience rather than skill training, though they have become enriched with some basic remedial education in recent years. Average enrollment durations have been around fifteen weeks throughout. The vaunted gains for Job Corps always have been generated by the minority who remain in residence long enough to make a substantial difference in their conduct as well as their skills.

Budgetary Consequences

The drumbeat of publicity about negative evaluations throughout the 1980s could not but lessen enthusiasm for adult employment and training programs and create the conviction that "nothing works" for out-of-school and at-risk youth. Amendments to JTPA in 1992 insisted that disadvantaged enrollees have other identified employment barriers than merely low incomes in order to qualify for JTPA and also prohibited job searches unaccompanied by skill improvement. But that only demonstrated the concern of the friends of employment and training. Greater animosity was demonstrated by the recisions of already appropriated but as-yet-unspent budgets following the 1994 election.

Program Results

Congressional reactions to JTPA did not necessarily reflect what was going on in the programs, however. It is useful to contrast the recent experience for disadvantaged adults and youth with the record for dislocated workers and a few comments concerning Job Corps.

Title II-A Disadvantaged Adults

In the Title II-A program enrolling low-income adults, demographic characteristics changed little between program years 1990 and 1995, except that the female proportion grew from 58 to 68 percent, perhaps reflecting increased pressures to move Aid to Families with Dependent Children (AFDC) clients into employment. The proportion of single parents enrolled rose from 34 to 46 percent. High school graduates rose from 49 to 56 percent, but that was way behind population proportions and those with post–high school education declined from 24 to 21 percent.

AFDC recipients rose from 28 to 35 percent of enrollees (41 percent if general assistance and Supplemental Security Income recipients are included), and those who were not in the labor force prior to enrollment climbed from 20 to 35 percent. Though the 1992 JTPA amendments required that at least 65 percent thereafter should have had at least one specific barrier to their employability in addition to having a poverty income, that was true of 87 percent in program year 1995 (PY95) and 57 percent had two or more such barriers. For instance, 58 percent were deficient in basic education skills; 35 percent lacked significant work history (contrasted with 19 percent in 1990); 14 percent (up from 9 percent in 1990) had been convicted as public offenders; and long-term AFDC recipiency was up from 12 percent in program year 1990 to 16 percent in program year 1995.

Not only had funding been declining, at first in constant dollar terms and then in current dollar terms, but training costs had been rising, consequent both to less-qualified trainees and longer training durations (up from twenty-four weeks in the late 1990s to thirty-four weeks in program year 1994). As a result, the number of adult enrollees who received JTPA services beyond mere assessment declined from 307,935 in program year 1990 to 162,120 in program year 1995. Despite worsening employability characteristics of the enrollees and more rigorous definitions of placement, program operators take considerable satisfaction in the fact that they have been able to maintain a placement rate of 63 percent and a follow-up employment rate three months after termination of 66 percent. Average hourly wages at placement rose from $6.08 to $7.25 over those same years, a pace somewhat faster than inflation. As might be expected, the sex, age, race, ethnicity, educational attainment, basic skills, disabilities, and welfare

Table 25.1

Type of JTPA Services Provided as Proportions of Total Enrollment, 1982–95 (in percent)

Service Provided	1982	1987	1991	1994	1995
Classroom training	48	34	44	59	61
Work experience	29	8	6	5	6
On-the-job training	12	24	15	14	9
Job search and other assistance	11	34	35	22	24

status of the enrollees all affected the placement wage in the directions that would be expected. On-the-job training resulted in a higher placement rate, but classroom skill training produced the highest placement wage rate, with basic skills and work experience achieving lower results in both categories.

That being the case, the changing mix among program alternatives, after diverging in the mid-1980s, has been moving in a promising direction (see Table 25.1). After falling into some disfavor because of its length and cost, classroom training has returned to predominate. On-the-job training still meets employer resistance and is not popular among JTPA staff. Relatively few adults are lacking in work experience. Job search training is highly useful for the already skilled who are years from their last job search and for those with newly acquired skills, but it can find only unskilled jobs for the unskilled.

Whatever satisfaction might be taken in JTPA placement rates is dampened by examination of placement wages. An hourly wage of $7.25—the program year 1995 average Title II-A placement wage—would result in a full-time, full-year income of $15,080, approximately the poverty threshold for a family of four. Multiplying the mean weekly wage of the program year 1994 terminees by fifty-two weeks results in an annual income of $13,624, approximately the poverty threshold for a three-person family. Relying on program year 1994 data, 41.4 percent of JTPA Title II-A terminees had no dependents at the time of enrollment; 20.9 percent had one dependent; 20.6 percent had two; and 17.1 percent had three or more. Those relatively small family sizes are important to JTPA's antipoverty role because annualizing the gross weekly earnings of those terminees would have brought 75.7 percent above the two-person poverty line, 58.6 percent above the three-person poverty line, but only 31.0 percent above the four-person poverty line.

Considering that only two-thirds of terminees were placed into jobs upon termination, only one out of five Title II-A terminees would have been able to achieve annual earnings at or above the four-person poverty line of $15,141. Probably because of the lack of stipends, JTPA Title II-A had become a successful program for single persons with no one else to support and single parents receiving cash public assistance. Of those program year 1994 terminees who were less than 65 years of age, 43.5 percent were parents in one-parent families; 30.0 percent were individuals who were not part of a family; 8.3 percent were non-parent family members; and only 18.2 percent were parents in two-parent families. The basic problem, as already noted, is the relative brevity of the training duration, an indicator of the levels of the occupations for which training is offered—an issue to which I return.

Title III Dislocated Workers

It is instructive to compare the participant characteristics and results for Title III dislocated workers to the above disadvantaged adults. Title III terminations fluctuated between 164,000 and 188,000 during the early 1990s and then rose sharply to 266,401 for program year 1995. Males outnumbered females 54 to 46 percent for the latter year. The ages were about the same as for the Title II-A enrollees, but about three-quarters were non-Hispanic whites compared to one-half for Title II-A. Unlike the II-A family sizes cited above, 36.4 percent of Title III terminees were parents in two-parent families; 29.4 percent were not members in a family; and 21.5 percent were non-parent family members. Only 11 percent had less than a high school education; 47 percent were high school graduates; and 13 percent had college diplomas. By definition, all had been in the labor force with over half making more than $10 an hour at the time of displacement. Nearly half of the dislocated worker enrollees as contrasted with about 10 percent of disadvantaged adults engaged in neither remedial education nor skill training, concerning themselves primarily with job search assistance. However, once entering training, the number of hours spent was about the same for both groups. Of those trained, the average duration was only 223 hours. Title III terminees experienced a higher placement rate—64 to 68 percent—and an even higher retention rate—69 to 74 percent—during program year 1991 through program year 1995. Their placement wages were substantially higher, climbing from $8.46 an hour in program year 1991 to $10.18 in program year 1995, rising to $10.81 in the latter year when contacted three months later.

Data on most dislocated worker programs reflect a population that has been steadily employed and needs primarily to be restored to that status. They are anxious to return to work to support their families, not to spend time in school. Less than one-third of Title III program participants were poor or near poor. Since many participants had substantial skills, local project operators have emphasized short-term, low-cost assistance designed to get them back to work without additional training. Two-thirds of enrollees receive job search assistance, which often lasts no more than a few days. Nevertheless, skill training seems to have paid off for those who received it. In program year 1994 when 188,000 were enrolled, those trained had a placement rate at termination of 76 percent and a wage recovery rate of 93.6 percent compared to 63 percent and 86.2 percent respectively for those Title III participants not retrained.

Title II-C Disadvantaged Youth

It is not surprising that JTPA youth programs cannot compete with those results. Title II-C year-round youth terminees declined from 257,503 in program year 1991 to 130,116 in program year 1995 and, of course, must have continued to decline as funding fell. The Title II-C terminees were composed of a more heavily minority population—38 percent were non-Hispanic white, and three-fourths were not high school graduates. Still, despite their youth, one out of five in program year 1995 were single parents; 31 percent were welfare recipients; and 42 percent had received food stamps. Two-thirds were not in the active labor force and had no significant pre-enrollment work history; 71 percent were basic skills deficient; 28 percent were pregnant or parenting youth; and one out of nine was a public offender. Only 113,563 of the 130,116 program year 1995 youth terminees had received any service beyond objective assessment. Of those, one-half were provided with basic skill training during their enrollment; a quarter underwent some skill training; and a similar portion obtained some work experience. Four out of five were involved in the program

for no more than 500 hours with an average training duration of 330 hours. Not surprisingly, only about one-third entered employment at termination, and a little over half were calculated to have attained employability enhancements of some type such as improved basic skills or a General Education Diploma. Only 2 percent of those previously out of school returned to school, while 15 percent were in school and remained. Average hourly wages for those entering employment rose from $5.07 in program year 1991 to $5.81 in program year 1995, but this only matched the rise in the Consumer Price Index over the same period.

Although the existing JTPA law allows local administrators to offer participants a wide variety of services, the summer youth employment program funds primarily work experience. Most enrollees work thirty-two hours a week at government agencies, schools, or community organizations for seven weeks at the federal hourly minimum wage. The law requires local sponsors to assess the reading and math skills of participants and to allocate at least some funding to teaching the "three Rs." The summer and year-round youth programs are designed to offer work experience and earnings as an incentive to stay in or return to school, as well as a source of needed income. Requirements for inclusion of basic remedial education were introduced in 1986 and then intensified after the devastating reports of the early 1990s. About half of the summer youth enrollees receive academic enrichment as well as work experience. Half of the year-round enrollees receive basic skills training, and 25 percent receive job skill training, thereby raising the total employability enhancement rate from 39 percent in 1990 to 54 percent in 1994. Nevertheless, the limited time spent in either remedial education or work experience could hardly be expected to substantially improve the learning and earning experience of youth confronting major barriers to employment.

Job Corps

Space does not allow substantial review of the Job Corps experience. Suffice it to say that a willingness to invest substantially and at length in the rehabilitation of severely disadvantaged youth has been the source of over three decades of plaudits for the Job Corps. Despite its continued high cost per participant—$15,300 per trainee in 1993 compared to $3,700 for each JTPA youth enrollee—the program remains the least-changed survivor of President Johnson's Great Society antipoverty efforts. However, in the harsher atmosphere of the 1990s, this program too has been subjected to more critical analysis, though it has not yet suffered budget cuts. The program's high costs throughout its history have been attributable primarily to the use of residential facilities to remove severely disadvantaged youth from their presumably debilitating environments.

Some Job Corps instructional techniques have been praised as models in instructing youth and adults who failed in or were failed by the school system. Training programs are open-entry and self-paced, allowing students to enter at any time and progress at their own pace. Each Job Corps center offers basic education, vocational skills training, personal and vocational counseling, health care and recreational activities, as well as room and board. Students can stay as long as two years but the average is only eight months, pulled down by a high dropout rate. The latter issue relates to one of a rising crescendo of complaints about Job Corps. A General Accounting Office study noted that, though 59 percent of Job Corps enrollees obtained jobs and another 11 percent continued on to further education, half of the jobs were low-skill, low-pay jobs unrelated to the training provided. That was consistent with the fact that 22 percent had dropped out before obtaining any significant training; 40 percent had been engaged in vocational training they had not completed; and only 36 percent had completed their vocational programs. Forty percent of center funds, it was lamented, were being spent on those who did not complete their assigned vocational training. However, GAO also found that those who completed their vocational training were five times more likely to obtain a training-related job than those who did not, and training-related jobs paid 25 percent more than others.

None of these complaints is new to those familiar with the Job Corps history and evaluations. The dropout rate has always been high, a consequence of the combination of the backgrounds of the youth, their distances from home, and the training discipline involved. In recent years there has been growing concern that the discipline has not been tight enough, leading to some unfortunate incidents in the centers and their surrounding communities. The Job Corps gains have always been attributable to those who stayed long enough to make a difference in their lives.

Shall We Rejoice?

What should one conclude concerning the results of over one-third of a century of second-chance workforce development programs? Was the $2,165 per adult participant, $2,108 per youth participant, $7,378 per adult who entered employment, and $4,764 per youth positive termination (job placement, school enrollment or military enlistment) in program year 1994 a worthwhile investment? First, there are reasons to think that the cost per adult participant is higher and the cost per adult who entered employment lower than those official figures. But taking those costs at face value, let us compare the costs to the results. Going in, 51 percent of disadvantaged adults in program year 1995 had not worked for over twenty-six weeks; 14 percent earned less than $5.99 per hour, 32 percent between $6 and $7.49, 24 percent between $7.50 and $9.99, and 13 percent $10 or more for an average hourly wage of $7.25. But full-time, full-year employment at that average wage would just bring a four-member family to the federal poverty line. That phenomenon too has a long history. MDTA and CETA also brought their average participants from deep in poverty to its upper edges.

A major factor is training duration. A study of classroom training under CETA in the 1970s demonstrated that those whose training duration was less than twenty weeks experienced only one-sixth the gains of those few who trained for more than forty weeks. It was not surprising, therefore, that during the late 1980s, when the average training duration had shrunk to less than twenty-four weeks, a comparison between the subsequent earnings of adult JTPA participants who had not necessarily been trained and a control group who had not been enrolled in JTPA but might have been enrolled elsewhere, showed only modest gains for adults and negative returns for youth whose enrollment was even briefer.

However, even though the average duration of JTPA training lengthened from twenty-four weeks during the 1980s to thirty-four weeks in the 1990s, the program suffered from the same forces that widened the earnings advantages of college graduates over those with less education and training and dictated that only those with post-graduate training were, on the average, able to keep their real incomes from declining. Those completing JTPA classroom training during 1993–94 found a positive relationship between training duration and placement and retention wages, but the margin was by no means as great as it had been under CETA.

Unfortunately, only 5.4 percent of JTPA participants were enrolled for over 1,600 hours where they could average above $8 an hour. Interestingly, the consistent increase in average wages with enrollment duration does not prevail for either on-the-job training nor basic education, supporting the view that subsidizing on-the-job training under JTPA buys a job but not training. Neither does it hold true for Title III where the degree of convergence of the skills and experience of the dislocated worker with labor market need is the determining factor. The number of youthful trainees engaged in any long-term training under JTPA has been too few to measure the differential results.

But time as such is not the telling factor. It is what is done in the time allocated. There are successful programs in addition to the Job Corps for out-of-school and at-risk youth, but they require more commitment and investment than is generally found in run-of-the-mill JTPA youth programs. The school-to-work movement has concentrated on the in-school population and largely ignored those already on the outside. The few programs that had demonstrated success with at-risk and out-of-school youth have been characterized by at least a year's enrollment duration; integrated combinations of basic education, skill training, and on-the-job experience; and had visible connections to jobs of promise, mentoring by respected adults, opportunities for high-profile community service, and the possibilities of further educational advancement upon demonstrated success. These youth have shared decision-making responsibilities within their programs and gained a greater sense of empowerment than that available through antisocial activities. There is no reason to expect success with lesser commitment.

Conclusions

There is little reason to doubt the worth of the 36-year investment in remedial skill training for disadvantaged adults. It could have been done better, but the evidence is that the investment has paid off as well as any human capital investment. James Heckman has estimated that the average mainstream investment in human capital pays off at a rate no greater than 10 percent. Robert LaLonde has concluded from his review of the evaluation literature that MDTA and CETA, and by implication JTPA, have raised the annual earnings of their participants by $1,000 to $2,000. With costs of $7,368, as in program year 1994, it would only be necessary to increase the annual earnings of those placed by $737 in perpetuity to equal the rate of return from college education and employer-sponsored training. The perpetuity is the challenge because the durability of the earnings differential is a debated unknown. The struggle is to keep up with the race between education and the job market. As noted earlier, between 1973 and 1993 only the college educated were able, on the average, to avoid deterioration of their real earnings and only those with education beyond the baccalaureate have enjoyed real increases in their living standards. Yet ten occupational categories have accounted for half of all occupationally specific training through-

out MDTA, CETA, and JTPA: clerk or typist, secretary or word processor, electronic assembler, machinist, custodian, nurse's aide, salesperson, licensed practical nurse, accounting clerk or bookkeeper, food service worker, and computer operator. These were a substantial step forward for most enrollees during the 1960s and 1970s. They enjoy little wage advantage today. Giving a meaningful second labor market chance to a disadvantaged adult in the 1990s and beyond requires at least two years of intensive preparation. That need not be accomplished in one jump. It may mean a period of full-time classroom training followed by on-the-job training continuing on to full-time work while completing the process with part-time schooling. It may also involve a combination of JTPA and Pell Grant support.

When the time limits of the 1996 welfare reform take hold, an addition of public service employment or subsidized private employment to the working and learning mix probably will become essential. Given the lag in the value of the federal poverty threshold, no wage short of 150 percent of poverty should be considered an acceptable program objective for an adult enrollee, allowing a family to reach the median income with 1.5 full-time jobs, however divided. For youth, the alternative objectives must be a return to full-time schooling or a series of workplace learning opportunities leading to a similar result. For over twenty years, American workers have had to run faster and faster in order to stand still in living standards. There is no reason to think that trend has subsided. Our thirty-five years of workforce development experience should have taught us something about how to do it.

26

Public Labor Market Policies for the Twenty-first Century

Christopher T. King, Robert E. McPherson, and Donald W. Long

Working and Living in the New Economy

The U.S. economic landscape at the end of the twentieth century is shaped by three major forces: internationalization, the "third industrial revolution" generated by microelectronics and information technologies, and rising customer expectations and demand volatility. Changes of this magnitude call for markedly different public labor market policies.[1]

The Changing Workplace

Employers are adjusting to these economic forces in a number of ways. Management practices such as contingent work, contingent pay, and contracting out have emerged. Contingent workers now comprise as much as one-quarter of the civilian workforce, and the temporary staffing industry has accounted for nearly 10 percent of employment growth since the early 1990s.

Management structures have flattened and career ladders have been truncated while the incidence of internal labor markets, with their favorable characteristics—advancement opportunities, earnings gains, buffering from external market forces, long-term stability and security—has diminished considerably. Employers are looking *outside* their organizations for workers with the desired skills rather than developing them from within, jettisoning workers with obsolete skills in the process.

Market pressures for rapid product changes, broader product lines, and more flexible production are leading firms to emphasize "core competencies," cross-functional work teams, new forms of employee participation, and external sourcing. Employers are looking for workers with broader skills, skills which are increasingly cognitive/thinking and interpersonal in nature rather than physical. All of these pressures increase the demand for skills, education, and training.

Changing Industrial Relations

The new economy is also marked by greatly weakened unions and dated industrial relations systems. To the extent that workers and their unions are in a weaker position, so are the policies and institutions they have supported.

The Changing Workforce

We are also experiencing important changes in the makeup of the nation's workforce. On the one hand, participation in the labor force has reached an all-time high and workers' educational attainment has increased markedly. On the other, new workers are increasingly drawn from the ranks of immigrants, never-married women, and minorities, groups whose average education and basic skills often need enhancement. Moreover, important population groups are being bypassed by economic progress altogether, most notably minority males, whose participation in work, school, and training is frighteningly low but whose incarceration rates are intolerably high.

Changing Family Structures

Along with these other changes has come a dramatic rise in single parenthood as well as an increase in the number of households with two parents in the workforce. Both situations place added stress on work and family as well as on the surrounding institutions, especially schools and dependent care providers.

Investments in workforce development bring forth improved economic growth and progress over time. It is in the interest of government, employers, and workers to share in financing them. Now, unfortunately, when global competition has raised the importance of workforce development to our economic well-being, employers appear to be offering less training and government is pulling back from its commitment. Markets traditionally produce too few public goods such as training and do so inefficiently, so government—especially the federal government—must intervene to ensure that workforce education and training are provided and provided well.

Labor Market Policies of the Past: A Cursory Review

Public labor market policies traditionally have been poor, neglected relatives in the nation's economic policy family, viewed more as social welfare than economic policy. Our past policies—ranging from labor exchange and job training to occupational and technical education and various welfare-to-work efforts—can be characterized along the following lines.

Public Labor Market Policies Have Been Largely Ad Hoc and Reactive

Most federal education and training initiatives have been devised in response to the immediate needs of particular subpopulations or geographic areas.

These Policies Have Been Oriented Almost Exclusively to the Supply Side of the Labor Market

Very few connections have been made to the demand side, to employers who actually control jobs. Too often, employers have been sought after as a source of employment as the final step in the service process, not at its front end or on an ongoing basis.

Public Labor Market Polices Have Featured "Second-chance" Programs

Rather than offering a comprehensive array of services for all, these policies have focused largely on the unemployed and/or the economically disadvantaged. Though well intentioned, these programs more often than not have further stigmatized the very individuals they were trying to help.

Labor Market Policies Have Been Seriously Underfunded

Since 1960, federal expenditures on all forms of workforce development have never exceeded 0.85 percent of gross domestic product or 2.4 percent of federal budget outlays. More to the point, real federal workforce spending per civilian labor force member peaked in the late 1970s at less than $250 and has hovered in the $50–60 range since 1984.

Labor Market Policies Have Been Fragmented, Categorical, and Poorly Coordinated

Our education, training, and employment "system" features confusing, duplicative delivery systems for multiple programs that serve overlapping populations and support competing bureaucracies. Not surprisingly, these programs lack strong champions in either Congress or the administration.

Public Labor Market Investments Are Characterized by Relatively Modest Returns

Modest investments, not surprisingly, have produced modest returns, though as Garth Mangum shows in his essay, the rates of return on federal employment and training expenditures are comparable to those of other human resource investments. The fact that one-time expenditures of $2,000–3,000 for multiply disadvantaged persons (e.g., JTPA) fail to produce dramatic improvements in their career earnings trajectory should not be much of a shock. Experience with severely disadvantaged youth in the Job Corps, human capital development for welfare recipients, and other programs suggests that substantial investments yield sizeable returns.

U.S. Labor Market Policies Have Suffered from Bipartisan Neglect at the Federal Level for Two Decades

For brief periods, notable individuals have served as articulate spokespersons for U.S. Labor market policies, but for the most part,

national leaders have been willing to let funding erode and policy responsibility devolve to states and localities, despite indications that many of them lack the capacity or willingness to take them on. The nation's labor market policies have pushed responsibilities to ever-lower levels, ultimately offloading them onto those individuals least able to control their economic destinies. The 1996 welfare reform initiative, the Personal Responsibility and Work Opportunity Reconciliation Act, is a disturbing example of this phenomenon.

Our Public Labor Market Policies Lack the Broad-based Constituency That Characterized Past Approaches

Our public labor market policies operate largely without the support of the political coalitions that were once the dominant forces behind the war on poverty, civil rights, and other socioeconomic movements. General public dissatisfaction—with public education and employment and training programs and with this country's growing wage and income inequalities—may spur the forging of new coalitions built on issues of economic competitiveness as well as disparities in earnings and wealth, but right now public labor market policies lack organized constituencies.

Public Labor Market Policies and Shared Prosperity

Public labor market policies must operate in concert with the nation's macroeconomic policy, as stated in the Employment Act of 1946 and reinforced by the Humphrey-Hawkins Act of 1978, to achieve maximum growth, low inflation, and full employment, which in today's world can only be achieved through global competitiveness.

At the same time, labor market policies must ensure that the fruits of successful global competition are shared with *all citizens*. This leads inevitably to considering the high-skills/high-wage strategies detailed in the 1990 report, *America's Choice,* by the bipartisan Commission on the Skills of the American Workforce. Public labor market policies must work to ensure that both jobs *and* earnings are equitably shared. To do so, they must work on both the supply and demand sides of the market and effectively connect the two.

Broad and Necessary Supportive Policies

A number of policies must be in place if our labor market policies are to function well and meet the goal of shared prosperity. Among the more important of these are:

Renegotiating the Social Contract

This must come first, and given the dramatic changes outlined above, the new version is likely to look quite different. The old implicit social contract emphasized long-term commitment between a worker and a single employer for career advancement, wage increases, and employment security. It stressed a commitment by employers, government, and unions to support workers by various means. The new contract must be pacts between workers and multiple employers with the government in a supportive role. Further, it must be cast more in terms of employability security and access to lifelong learning opportunities.

Providing for Dependent Care

Providing improved mechanisms for the care of young children and the elderly is also essential. Securing dependent care—now the term of choice—for their children and parents has become one of the major issues affecting workers' on-the-job performance. For children, such care affords quality early childhood development opportunities.

Providing Universal Health Insurance

Health insurance is one of the most expensive employee benefits. It is also one of the benefits workers seek first and worry about most. Numerous proposals have been made to address the need for and financing of health insurance (reviewed by Karen Davis in this volume).

Extending Fully Vested, Portable Pensions to All Workers

Retirement and pension institutions and policies need revamping, a process already under way, but with undue emphasis on *individual* responsibility. Whatever other changes are needed, pensions should be vested and portable for all workers.

Ensuring a Strong, Independent Worker Voice

As the 1994 report of the Commission on the Future of Worker-Management Relations demonstrates, the United States is unique among its major trading partners in the weak role labor unions play in the workplace. Public labor market policies would have significantly improved prospects if workers and their unions had greater participation in managerial decision-making, as they do in high-performance work organizations adopted by some leading employers.

Enforcing Existing Anti-Discrimination Policies

If economic prosperity is to be shared equitably, policies prohibiting discrimination in workplaces, schools, unions, and other entities must be strictly enforced. Higher education and enhanced occupational skills mean nothing if those possessing them cannot gain access to jobs.

Supply-Side Policies

As indicated earlier, policies must address both the supply and the demand sides of the market to ensure an equitable sharing of jobs and earnings through the promotion of high-value-added strategies. Key policies on the supply side include:

Investing in Education and Skills Training

Investments in human capital make up the very foundation of supply-side labor market policies. Our goal should be to provide at least fourteen years of publicly supported education and training to all Americans.

Moreover, much of that education should relate to work. As our colleague Bob Glover often says, "Education may be preparation for life, but much of life is work." Our decentralized public education system needs reforms of the sort detailed by Marc Tucker in this volume. We should emphasize post-secondary, non-baccalaureate skills training for occupations that pay enough to support families well above the federal poverty line. In addition, training should focus on skills appropriate to broad occupational clusters, not narrowly defined occupations. Nor should training be tailored to the unique needs of individual employers. We must design education and training to include the kinds of skills that will enable all Americans, with periodic public and private assistance, to achieve productive working lives.

Training must also encompass the key workforce competencies required by employers, including organizing and managing time and resources, utilizing interpersonal skills, processing and communicating information, understanding complex relationships, and using computer technology. Learning itself is perhaps the most important general skill of all in a highly dynamic world.

Ensuring Workplace Readiness

Workplace readiness skills comprise the generic skills, behaviors and attitudes needed to survive in the modern workplace. They encompass personal behaviors (e.g., punctuality, willingness to accept responsibility, self-esteem, and general appearance). Rather than provided separately, these skills should be addressed as an integral part of the workforce development process beginning as early as the middle-school years.

Providing Job Search Training

Many individuals are employable but lack the skills to find a job. Particularly true of youth with no labor force experience and women who have been out of the labor force caring for families, it is also the case for many dislocated workers who spent years in the same job. Job search training (e.g., résumé preparation, interviewing, networking, and techniques for using labor market information) provides the skills to seek and secure good jobs. Because such training does not augment individuals' hard skills—their occupation-specific knowledge and skills—it can boost work effort and reduce unemployment, but is unlikely to lead to sizeable long-term increases in earnings.

Supporting Those in Training

Federal grants and student loan guarantees must expand to ensure "free" public education (and/or training) through grade 14. When we moved into the industrial era, public education escalated from primary school to grade 12. But a high school diploma no longer suffices for economic success, either individually or nationally.

Demand-Side Policies

Important labor market policy elements on the demand side include:

Ensuring Fair Compensation

It is important to raise the federal minimum wage to restore the levels of economic self-sufficiency provided thirty years ago. The employment displacement effects of increasing the minimum wage appear to have been overstated, and full-time workers should be able to support their families at least at the federal poverty level. Also, to the extent that wages alone fail to accomplish this, tax policies (e.g., the Earned Income Tax Credit) should ensure that workers' disposable earnings will support them and their families. A single earner working full time should be able to attain economic self-sufficiency. Two earners—one working only part time—should be able to support a four-person household, freeing the half-time earner to support children's school activities, assist aging/infirm parents and meet other pressing family needs. Such thinking formed the basis of the Clinton administration's initial plans for welfare reform.

Requiring Proportionate Employee Benefits

Employers should be required to provide access to and proportionate financing for workers'

fringe benefits, and temporary employment agencies should also be obligated to meet these requirements.

Developing Strategies for Public Job Creation

Funding for public service employment was eliminated from the federal budget in 1981, while public works projects such as those of the 1930s were abandoned years ago. Yet, as recent welfare reform policy debates clearly show, there are many groups in the population unable to compete for private-sector employment for whom public job creation can play an important role. It is equally clear that our vast unmet infrastructure needs could be addressed *at least in part* through such strategies. Public job creation is not inexpensive, but neither is the alternative. As Eli Ginzberg, Richard Nathan, and William J. Wilson demonstrated in this volume, public service employment can be a useful component to a high-value-added, full employment strategy.

Connecting Policies

Several measures, best viewed as connecting policies, are necessary to bridge supply- and demand-side policies. These include:

Providing Labor Market Information

The importance of providing workers and employers ready access to reliable information about labor markets (e.g., career opportunities, wages and working conditions, available workers, vacancies, employment projections, and training outcomes) cannot be underestimated, especially after we move to more market-oriented mechanisms. Working within well-established federal-state partnerships, the federal government should ensure continuing improvements in this area (e.g., the American Labor Market Information System project).

Nor will information alone be adequate to our needs. Many voucher proposals now circulating assume that all individuals are equally capable of using information wisely in making career choices. While this may be true for well-educated, experienced workers, it is not for many others. Career guidance and counseling also are essential for labor market policies to be successful.

Offering Labor Exchange and Job Matching Services

Since the 1930s, the U.S. Employment Service has offered labor exchange and job matching services to help labor markets function more smoothly. Still important, these public services now compete with temporary agencies and private placement firms for market share. This service should be strengthened, and new alignments—possibly including public and private ventures—must be explored.

Adequate Funding

While "throwing money at problems" is rarely the answer, in the labor market policy area we have failed to approach even a reasonable scale. We do not need to reach adequate funding levels overnight but can approach them incrementally. To this end, federal funds should properly be considered the "driver," not the bank of first and last resort. States—which historically have failed to ante up even when federal/state matching rates approached 2:1 (e.g., welfare-to-work efforts of the 1990s)—and localities must become equal partners in finance as well as policy development and implementation.

In sum, labor market policy must shed its traditional associations with social welfare policy and become a fully integrated component of economic policy, addressing both the supply and the demand sides of the market. It must do so in ways that respond to the dramatic global and social shifts that have changed our economic landscape so radically.

A System for Implementing New Labor Market Policies

As is clear from our earlier discussion, it is time to replace our fragmented, program-by-program approach with one that is systematic and stable. This can only be done by making a national commitment to build and fund a single, integrated labor market system that responds to the needs of both its customers—employers and workers. This new system would not only prepare individuals for work but also help them make the transition from school to work and provide further training throughout their working lives. Clearly, such a system depends on the mutual reinforcement of public and private policies. It must:

- Be flexible and highly responsive to changing labor market conditions as well as customer needs.
- Be customer oriented, operating out of a services-first philosophy rather than devotion to cumbersome eligibility processes.
- Offer multiple points of contact, and give access to the same information and services regardless of where or how customers contact the system.
- Recognize employers as critical customers, and develop ongoing relationships with them by providing quality solutions to their human resources problems. As a

quality supplier of human resource services, an integrated system engages employers on economic rather than social welfare grounds and thereby helps workers gain access to high-skill, high-wage jobs typically not available to them.

- Provide universal access to information and services to all individuals regardless of their labor market status, income, or age and treat them as the lifelong learners they must become for the nation to be competitive in the global marketplace.

- Operate within an explicit, well-articulated accountability framework. Process and outcome components of accountability must be balanced while near-term measures of performance promote attainment of longer-term goals and objectives. The shift to integrated services also demands that accountability be systemic rather than programmatic in nature, relying on a series of core, overarching measures of performance. Moreover, financial incentives—including staff compensation—must be tied to performance. The accountability system must be designed to promote continuous improvement.

System Structure

The structure of this new system has five features that distinguish it from earlier approaches. First, it requires a three-tiered set of national, state, and local labor market boards, with shared responsibility for policy-making, planning, overseeing and evaluating the delivery of all labor market services. State boards would develop policies and a system consistent with the national board's, while local boards would operate within the national and state frameworks. At each level, representatives of employers, workers, and the general public would come together as partners to plan, set performance expectations, allocate resources, determine incentives policies, and evaluate results.

These labor market boards would function much like corporate boards of directors, not directly involved in day-to-day administration and service delivery but held accountable for results. They would be appointed by the appropriate elected officials at each level of government and structured to ensure local representation on state boards and state and local representation on the national board. Employers would have majority representation on state and local boards, but a plurality (say, 40–45 percent) on the national board. Service providers, including education and training institutions, would not be allowed membership on local boards, but they would be encouraged to participate in planning and evaluation activities, serve on advisory committees and offer their input.

At all levels, these boards should have staff separate from and independent of any administering agency or vendor providing labor market or workforce services. The national and state boards would be quasi-governmental entities while the local workforce boards would be private, not-for-profit entities chartered by state government.

Second, rather than flowing categorically and supporting separate administrative and service delivery mechanisms, funding for labor market services would flow through these boards to the appropriate administering agencies and, at the local level, to service providers. Funding as well as service delivery should be integrated.

Third, the new delivery system and the services it offers would be supported by multiple funding sources. Federal funds now supporting "second-chance" programs would be augmented by state and local funds. Further, the new system would operate on the assumption that employers and many individuals can and are willing to pay for quality labor market services. Over time, diversified funding should result in state and local delivery systems that are less dependent on federal funding and more responsive to the needs of employers and workers in the markets they serve. At the same time, the intergovernmental nature of the system would provide a stable infrastructure that could accommodate any increases in federal funding in response to changing economic conditions, shifting national priorities, or the special needs of a particular geographic area.

Fourth, local boards would be required to design service delivery systems that respond to the labor market needs of employers and workers in their labor market areas. At a minimum this would include building a centralized capacity to develop, market, and sell services to employers and establishing a network of career development centers offering comprehensive labor market information and services to all local residents—students considering their education and career options, unemployed workers seeking jobs or additional training, and incumbent workers wanting to upgrade their skills, change jobs, or ea. n more money.

To be truly universal, the local system must provide ready electronic access to information and services. Employers should be able to obtain information, list job openings, screen applicants' résumés, and schedule interviews without leaving their desks. Individuals seeking assistance should be able to get labor market information, administer their own needs assessments, register with talent banks, apply for jobs, and review the track records of competing service providers via computers in their homes, in schools, libraries, or shopping malls.

Finally, the local delivery systems should be designed to ensure objective assessments of individuals' service needs. To meet this requirement, these assessments must not be done by potential service providers. Assessments are probably best done in career development centers that determine eligibility, provide labor market information and career counseling, and work with individuals to mutually develop and finance their career development plans. The centers should not also provide developmental services such as education and skills training. Only after their needs are independently assessed and career plans jointly negotiated should individuals be referred to education and training providers for services. Not only does this approach ensure that individuals' training and education needs are considered independently of the services offered by providers, but it also ties resources to individuals rather than to vendors, as has been the case in the past. This approach transforms individuals seeking assistance from passive clients into effective, well-informed consumers and simultaneously forces providers to compete for students and funding. Poor performance becomes self-correcting.

Management Infrastructure

Making such a delivery system operational requires a strong, supportive management infrastructure (e.g., planning, contracting, and performance management), two elements of which are critical. First, the new system's service capability depends on the ready availability of labor market information and must include accurate and timely data on labor supply and demand as well as service and performance information on education and training providers.

Second, the linchpin of the new delivery system is an automated eligibility determination, case management, and reporting system. Such capability is absolutely essential to providing seamless services, particularly in cases where individuals need longer-term, intensive services and qualify for support from several different funding sources. Such an automated system also gets the paperwork out of case management, counseling, and reporting, freeing professional staff at the career development centers to do their jobs.

This new delivery system must also be driven by a national system of industry-based standards for certifying the technical and professional skills of those broad occupational areas requiring less than a four-year college degree. Because these skills standards forge a link between public workforce services and the performance expectations prevailing in the wider labor market, employers must play a major role in their formation to reflect their education and skill requirements. These standards must be used to guide all relevant public education and training efforts.

Financing the New Public Labor Market System

With the exception of those making the transformation to high-performance workplaces or shielded somehow from the pressures of intense competition, employers appear less willing to make long-term training commitments to their employees. Those employers who invest in training tend to do so disproportionately for their managerial and professional employees and limit their commitments to core employees, who in many cases constitute a decreasing portion of their total workforce.

If employers are training less at the same time that lifelong learning has become the essential ingredient of employment and income security, the question arises of who will pay for workers' continuing education and skills development.

Who Pays?

In the current climate of fiscal austerity—one likely to extend well into the next century—financing at levels adequate to build the necessary infrastructure and provide labor market services for those unable to pay their own way will not come from the federal government alone. Employers, workers, and state and local governments will have to share the cost.

The new system could be financed in large part by employers and individual workers through a payroll training tax not unlike the unemployment tax that has long funded the federal-state employment security system and benefit payments for unemployed workers. Rather than having two separate taxes, one supporting training and the other unemployment benefits, it would be preferable to fully integrate unemployment insurance services in the new labor market delivery system and levy a single training tax. This tax, the benefits it provides, and the labor market services it supports should be maintained outside the unified federal budget.

Revenues generated from the training tax would be used to help finance the development and operation of the new labor market delivery system, provide unemployment benefits, and fund individual training accounts. This new tax should not supplant the federal government's current financial commitment to workforce development. There must be a continuation of federal general revenues to support the new labor market system. These resources are particularly important for financing access to labor market services for individuals who are unable to pay for the education and training they need to secure productive employment.

However, much like the shared funding responsibilities in other federal-state systems, states should be required to match the federal funding commitment as a condition for receiving the money. In turn, local governments should also match their formula allocations of federal and state workforce dollars, not necessarily dollar for dollar, but these commitments must be large enough to get the attention of state and local partners. Past initiatives fully funded by the federal government have not succeeded in developing effective partnerships at either level.

Finally, some labor market services could be financed in part by its customers, especially where employers and individuals seek specialized services. Individuals seeking more intensive services might pay out of their current incomes, individual training accounts, or from grants and scholarships.

Where Does the Money Go?

Building the Delivery Infrastructure, Including the Essential Management Support Systems

First, we have to make the necessary investments to develop and maintain the delivery infrastructure. We must respond to employers' needs by building the capacity—independently or through joint ventures with private or private not-for-profit entities—to market and sell employer services in local labor markets. Further, such services must be formally linked with career development centers, local education and training institutions, and other labor market entities to better meet employer and worker needs.

Financing Individual Career Plans

Some resources should be reserved for those unable to pay for needed labor market services but should be available only through career development centers where individuals access labor market information, undergo assessment, and receive career counseling. A mutually negotiated career plan should be developed before the resources to implement that plan are committed to individuals. These resources can only be used to purchase services from certified education and training providers. Ongoing case management and counseling services will ensure that those referred make satisfactory progress toward completing their career development plans. While this approach resembles a voucher, it is not in the conventional sense.

Compensating Private-Sector Training

Public labor market policies should complement those of the private sector. To the extent that the private sector addresses worker training, the public sector may not need to. At a minimum, we suggest continuing favorable tax treatment for firms that invest in their employees' further education and training. In addition, employers who aggressively train their workforces—front-line as well as managerial employees—should be federally chartered as "learning organizations" for their industries. These firms would qualify for reimbursements for training workers they subsequently lose to other employers. Industry associations may offer an efficient vehicle for designing, offering, and reimbursing such training, especially for small and mid-size employers not likely to make significant training investments on their own. However it is implemented, we suggest this initiative begin with high-skill, high-wage firms that have completed the transformation into high-performance work organizations.

Providing Matching Grants to Employers Making the Transition to High-Performance Workplaces

Funding much like that now available through state-financed customized training programs should be provided to employers that commit to becoming high-performance workplaces. These should be dollar-for-dollar matching grants to provide incumbent workers with the knowledge and skills required to remain employed. This "preventive" approach makes a great deal more sense than our current practice—paying unemployment benefits to those laid off and eventually funding their retraining even as we absorb the full cost of educating and training new workers to replace those just laid off.

Investing in System-Building Research and Development

Finally, a renewed effort should be made in building this system through research and development financed by all levels of government. Federally financed R&D in the 1960s and 1970s yielded enormous returns through its small dissertation grants program and institutional grants to institutions of higher education to support a regional R&D and technical assistance network, among other mechanisms. Only marginal improvements have been supported since these efforts were abruptly terminated in the early 1980s. Rejuvenated congressional interest in R&D should be expanded to building and supporting better workforce development delivery systems as well. Federal investments in R&D should be matched at the state and local level.

Conclusions

Our existing array of public labor market policies responds to an increasingly outdated view of labor markets and focuses almost exclusively on the supply side of the market. Reactive rather than proactive, they have failed to position the country for continued growth in a more competitive, knowledge-intensive global economy.

New workforce development policies must be rooted in the realities of present and future labor market conditions and framed to promote *learning* in the broadest sense rather than old-style employment and training programs. These new policies alone, however, will not bring about broadly shared prosperity. They must work in tandem with fiscal and monetary policies and must also be "nested" in industrial relations, education, health, and other complementary policies that promote safe and secure environments for workers and their families.

Further, these policies must be adequately funded and fully implemented. The United States must commit to an integrated workforce system that involves all of the major beneficiaries of a competitive workforce as partners to plan, manage, and finance this new system.

The costs of inaction are enormous. We cannot afford to relegate such policies to the backwaters of economic policy. To do so leaves us picking up the tab again and again in the form of reduced productivity and a shrinking economic pie, higher incarceration costs, and growing poverty and inequality.

Note

1. The authors acknowledge the invaluable contributions of our colleague Bob Glover, research assistance of Shao-Chee Sim, and administrative support from Diane Janes-Tucker, Karen Franke, and Sasha Waid, all at the Center for the Study of Human Resources. A special thanks goes to Liza Hallman for editorial assistance.

27

Public Service Employment: A Look Back and a Look Ahead

Eli Ginzberg

President Roosevelt and his closest adviser on social welfare policies, Harry Hopkins, decided early into the New Deal that the best way for the federal government to respond to the appallingly high unemployment and underemployment rates—about one out of four members of the labor force unemployed and around another one out of six underemployed—was to provide work relief for all men as well as some women and young people who needed a job. Compared to our British cousins who relied on the dole, the New Deal's approach to work relief at something approaching market wage rates had much to commend it, though one quickly must add that the nation's economy was lagging when World War II broke out in September 1939.

By 1943, after more than a year as an active participant in the war, the U.S. unemployment rate dropped below 2 percent, which most experts defined as "over-full" employment. In my two-thirds of a century as a participant observer and labor market researcher, I believe that it is correct to claim that the only time that the U.S. economy operated at full (even over-full) employment was during the two war years of 1943–44.

It is worth noting that many, probably the majority, of the senior economists working in Washington as World War II drew to an end were seriously concerned that with demobilization about to start, the country faced the danger of a very high level of unemployment, about 10 million, such as it had confronted toward the end of the depressed 1930s.

But this pessimism must be put alongside the 1945 hearings in which Congress deliberated about passing the "full employment act," an action that it finally failed to take because of uncertainty over whether the federal government could deliver on such an ambitious goal. In 1946, Congress passed the Employment Act of 1946, which obligated the federal government to operate the economy at as high a level of employment as it could sustain.

The highly successful conversion of the economy from war to peace and the modest levels of subsequent unemployment, despite the tremendous adjustments that peace brought in its wake, kept manpower policies from being placed on the public agenda until the 1960 election campaign, when John F. Kennedy used as a slogan, "Let's get the economy moving again," a reference to the fact that the Eisenhower era had suffered three short recessions that had pushed the unemployment rate up to around 6 percent in 1960, with no decline in sight.

In 1996, I wrote on my intimate interactions

as the chair of the successive congressional committees and commissions to advise the administration and Congress about the policy implications of the 1962 Manpower Development and Training Act (MDTA), which was superseded in 1973 by the Comprehensive Employment and Training Act (CETA), with intermittent additional legislation during these two decades.

Employing the Unemployed, which I edited in 1980 when CETA was still active but beginning to fail, contains the contributions of nine experts, each of whom dealt at some length with a major facet of the sizeable federal effort, that together with MDTA involved total outlays of about $85 billion over two decades to provide training and public service employment (PSE) to improve the job and income prospects of vulnerable unemployed persons. Over the two decades, Congress targeted the following groups for special assistance: skilled workers, many of whom presumptively lost their jobs because of automation; minority and other disadvantaged persons; and Vietnam veterans that experienced difficulties in getting and holding a job.

Looking ahead to 2030, I will limit my retrospective assessments of PSE to the following major points. For those who seek to learn more—and in more depth—about PSE, I strongly urge them to read *Employing the Unemployed*. But I assume sole responsibility for the emphases that follow:

1. It should be noted that the initial 1962 legislation stressed "manpower development and training" and failed to include any direct mention of employment or PSE in its title. In fact, while MDTA was being drafted, I pressed Secretary of Labor Arthur Goldberg to seek White House support for a PSE provision to balance the training effort on the assumption that, with an insufficient number of total jobs, there always would be people at the end of the queue; thus, more training opportunities probably would result only in a shift among those at the end of the queue. Goldberg tried to win White House support for PSE but failed.

2. The reason for his failure was closely linked to the split among the political leadership. The dominant Kennedy team favored a macroeconomic approach to stimulating the economy via expenditure and tax policy. The "structuralists," including several Republican congressmen, favored the "training" approach. And with the fears of "automation" unsettling many in both parties, it appeared sensible and politically more feasible to seek new legislation that would expand training and retraining opportunities for the unemployed.

3. In the mid-1960s, the National Manpower Advisory Committee (NMAC) first considered PSE, but with the economy expanding and unemployment declining, the NMAC did not press the issue. In 1969, Labor Secretary George Shultz proposed amending MDTA to include a PSE dimension, but Congress failed to act. The following year, Congress acted but President Nixon vetoed the legislation, stating that he wanted "no part in reconstructing the leaf-raking jobs characteristic of the New Deal." Six months later, however, he signed the Emergency Employment Act of 1971 that provided $2.2 billion over a two-year period for direct job creation to assist, among other priority groups, Vietnam veterans being released from active duty. By the late 1960s, organized labor strongly supported PSE, a position that it maintained throughout several legislative initiatives of the 1970s.

4. CETA was passed in December 1973 in response to the onset of a severe recession but was amended the following year by the addition of 300,000 PSE jobs available to anyone unem-

ployed for seven days. In short, Congress now saw PSE as an anti-recession measure.

5. PSE came into its own under President Carter, who allocated about half of his $20 billion stimulus package to expand PSE to about 725,000 jobs. Many of his economic advisers questioned whether PSE was the best way to stimulate the economy, and many others, concerned with accelerating inflation, saw dangers in such additional spending. But Carter held firm, and Congress went along, although not for long. Even with PSE commanding the largest part of the $10 billion outlay for CETA in the late 1970s, Congress became increasingly aware of the fact that it provided jobs for no more than 0.8 percent of all jobs holders; to make matters worse, the media continued to report on waste, mismanagement, and fraud. CETA began to lose ground with the Democrats in the face of worsening inflation and budgetary stringencies before Reagan's 1980 election.

Although the new president was in favor of eliminating all employment and training efforts, he agreed to a much reduced program that had no room for PSE. The question to examine is what explains the radical shift between Carter's early enthusiasm for PSE and Reagan's determination to liquidate it. The oversimplified answer is twofold: Carter looked to PSE to reduce the slack in the economy. In 1981, the new administration was still working overtime to moderate the severe inflationary pressures. Further, there was a growing belief among Democrats and Republicans that PSE was not the answer to expanding employment opportunities for the difficult to employ. PSE cost too much and accomplished too little.

Isabel Sawhill and Laurie Bassie's chapter titled "The Challenge of Full Employment" in *Employing the Unemployed* summarizes the antecedents to the Full Employment Act of 1978 (Humphrey-Hawkins), during which Congress long debated the proposed legislation's goals, as well as failed to specify the policies and programs required to realize the substantial goal of reducing unemployment by 1983 to 3 percent for adults and 4 percent overall. In addition, the legislation looked to reduce inflation to 3 percent by 1983, balance growth, realize gains in productivity and total income, improve the balance of trade, and balance the budget! It would be difficult to identify another piece of federal legislation that promised so much and accomplished so little.

It may be helpful to report on a "private" negotiation that I carried on for the better part of a year with my colleague and friend, Arthur F. Burns, who served as chairman of the Federal Reserve Board in the mid-1970s at a time when he recognized the emergence of inflationary pressures. I promised to do my best to moderate the recommendations of the National Commission for Manpower Policy, which I chaired, for greatly enlarged manpower appropriations if Burns would come out in favor of the federal government as the employer of last resort. In a speech at the University of Georgia at Athens on September 19, 1975, Burns said: "Nevertheless there may be no way to reach the goal of full employment short of making the government the employer of last resort. This could be done by offering public employment— for example in hospitals, schools, public parks, and the like—to anyone willing to work at a rate of pay somewhat below the federal minimum wage." It is highly unlikely that the present Federal Reserve Board chairman would agree with his distinguished predecessor.

This brings us to the third theme that we identified early, specifically how thinking and policy on PSE has been affected—some would say undermined—by the revisionist views among economists in academia and government, and particularly members of the Federal Reserve Board. Oversimplified, the argument goes something like this: Until the end of the 1960s to early 1970s, mainline Keynesianism guided macro-policy in most advanced nations. President Nixon stated early in his first administration, "We are all Keynesians now." But if we were all Keynesians at the beginning of the 1970s, there were few left at the end of the decade, because of more sophisticated analyses by academic economists—who saw growing flaws in the earlier simplistic view that, in the face of underutilized economic resources, the government needed only to increase public spending or lower the tax rate or both—as well as the growing demonstration in the latter 1970s that more public spending could result in accelerating inflation, rather than adding to total and per capital real output.

By the start of the second half of the 1990s, academia's views had changed again: The theory of rational expectations, despite its propounder, Robert Lucas, having been awarded the Nobel Prize, is no longer firmly entrenched, and Milton Friedman's monetary theories also have been marginalized. But on the other side, the Fed has until recently been operating on the conviction that the nonaccelerating inflation rate of unemployment of 6 percent (plus or minus) requires maintaining the growth of the U.S. economy at around 2.5 percent per annum, no matter how many people remain unemployed or underemployed.

Lester Thurow of MIT, in a 1996 *American Prospect* article, called for a reassessment of our currently entrenched macroeconomic policy of limiting U.S. growth to 2.5 percent per annum. He argues, with considerable cogency, that we are still fighting the war on inflation, not recognizing that it was won long ago. He

then points out that one must add to the number of reported 7.5 to 8 million unemployed (or a 5.7 percent unemployment rate) another 5 to 6 million persons who are not working but who are not counted in the labor force, and another 4.5 million who would prefer to work full time. In addition, there are 8.1 million American workers in temporary jobs (2 million of whom work on call) and another 8.3 million self-employed "independent contractors" who also are looking for more work and better jobs. Finally, there are another 5.8 million "missing males" between 25 and 60 who can be found in the off-the-record economy and among the homeless. In short, the U.S. unemployment rate is not the reported 5.7 percent, but, according to Thurow, closer to 33 percent!

Thurow goes on to attribute the long-term stagnation of wages and income for all except the best-educated segments of the labor force to this overhang in numbers seeking jobs, more work, and better pay.

I accept several of Thurow's assumptions and conclusions. We have a much larger proportion of people seeking regular jobs than suggested by our below 5 percent reported unemployment rate. The Fed probably is wrong to assume that a growth rate greater than 2.5 percent per annum would reinvigorate inflation. The employer community has been well positioned these last years to restrain wage rates and has taken advantage of its power to do so. So far so good. But I question Thurow's thesis that our macroeconomic policy should be informed by his calculation that one-third of our 133-million-person labor force requires government intervention to assure them improved job access.

Further, neither Thurow or any other economist has a convincing explanation for the serious retardation in U.S. productivity since the early 1970s, without which we have at best an imperfect explanation for the retardation in the rate of growth in real wages and income. And I would add one more cautionary note: nobody really knows how the longer-term impacts of the accelerating internationalization of the world's economy—with its combined impacts of intensified capital movements, export-oriented growth policies, and factor price equalization—are affecting the U.S. economy and labor market, as well as the economies and labor markets of Western Europe, East Asia and Japan. Admittedly it is difficult to acknowledge that we are in less control of our economy than we would like to be, but I believe it is preferable to acknowledge that we are flying half-blind than to fool ourselves into believing that we know how to solve our most serious labor force problems.

We come now to the fourth and last segment of my overview of PSE, focusing on the period between now and 2030.

Thirty-two years out is a long way off. In reverse, it would take us back to the Johnson administration. The best we can hope to do looking that far ahead is to note some of the more important aspects of PSE that should be placed on the nation's agenda, taking 1998 as our point of departure.

First and foremost, we need to start a dialogue that will lead to political action to place PSE on the nation's agenda. I have long been distressed by the fact that Americans are unable to face up to the gap between their deeply held belief that all capable adults should work to earn a living and the continuing shortfall of jobs to make working a reality for all.

Putting PSE back on the nation's agenda is a first major step, but we must acknowledge the host of complex administrative and income transfer issues that must be dealt with if PSE is to succeed. The federal government should be the employer of last resort, but all other levels of government, as well as non-governmental sectors, need to participate in the administration and execution of the program. An effective PSE program can succeed only to the extent that we address such problems as what types of minimum income transfers must accompany low-paying jobs, as well as such supplementary supports as who will care for young children or perform other chores for women who currently face major responsibilities in and out of the home and a shortage of time. We also need to learn from our repeated efforts to reform welfare.

I have no easy or ready answer for what the nation should do to find constructive answers to the gross imbalances between concentrations of unemployed and underemployed persons in rural and urban areas where there is little or no prospect of economic renewal or a prospective expansion of private-sector employment. But we have no real option but to put the issue on the nation's agenda and at least start to grapple with it.

Ours is an increasingly service-sector-oriented economy, with about three out of four jobs in service occupations. This means that most of our PSE experience, especially going back to the New Deal, is at best marginal. We need to think long, hard, and constructively as to how we can mount and operate an effective, ongoing PSE effort focused on "personal" and "community" services.

Next, we need to recognize that our nation is expanding the effective adult working life of most citizens from around forty to sixty years as a consequence of increasing life expectancies and the control of chronic illnesses. Therefore, we need to begin now to experiment with alternate patterns of work to encourage more women to remain home with their young children and extend their working years into their sixties and seventies, either full or part time.

And men also could gain from flexibility and adjustments in their lifetime patterns of work. We have a few years before the first of the baby boomers reach 65 (2011), but it is none too early to start experimenting with more flexible work hours.

There is one front on which we cannot afford to procrastinate. We know about the social pathologies affecting young people who grow up in urban slum areas, particularly the violence that afflicts so many minority males. While we need to avoid simplistic responses to our mounting crime rates, we should agree that young people who grow up with little expectation of qualifying for a regular job that will enable them to be self-supporting heads of families are urgently in need of assistance to provide them the education and skills required to become self-supporting. These youths could obtain PSE jobs until they are able to move into the private economy. Only an obtuse, insensitive society would use taxpayers' money to build more jails rather than develop effective PSE programs.

And it would be a mistake to focus exclusively on young minority males. The nation understandably is concerned about the large number of out-of-wedlock teenage mothers. It takes no great stretch of the imagination to appreciate that many of these young women see their future as very bleak and therefore conclude that they have little to lose and probably something to gain by opting for motherhood. A society that wants to reduce illegitimacy must provide skill acquisition and self-supporting work to many of the young women who now choose motherhood outside of marriage.

The issue of immigration, both legal and illegal, is back on the nation's political agenda, and the odds are overwhelming that no matter what decisions are made in the near future the issue will reappear on the nation's agenda between now and 2030.

In sum, what are the challenges to PSE in the third of a century which lies ahead? First and foremost is to persuade the citizenry that our democracy cannot afford to keep PSE off the national agenda. Macroeconomic policy will not provide jobs for all who want and need to work. But placing PSE back on the national agenda is the beginning, not the end, of multiple challenges of providing reasonable work opportunities at reasonable earnings to reasonably large and diversified groups of citizens from adolescents still in high school to prematurely retired pensioners who would prefer to continue to work. An effective PSE program is not the only challenge that the United States needs to meet and resolve before 2030, but it is surely among the most important, considering that most Americans believe that a citizenry that supports itself through work is the best guarantor of the continuing vitality and viability of American democracy.

28

Public Service Employment: Lessons from U.S. Experience in the 1970s

Richard P. Nathan

This essay concentrates on experience with public service employment (PSE) in the 1970s under the Comprehensive Employment and Training Act (CETA). It is fitting that the lessons recounted should follow the broader analysis by Eli Ginzberg. It was Ginzberg, as chair of the National Commission for Employment Policy, who had the idea for the research on which this essay is based and arranged for its support. The research was conducted over five years in four rounds of field observations from mid-1977 to December 1980. Academic field analysts in forty locations in thirty-two states assessed the economic, fiscal, programmatic, and institutional effects of the CETA-PSE program, which rose rapidly both in spending and enrollments in this period, peaking at $4.1 billion and 755,000 jobs in April 1978. Unlike almost any other federal domestic program, PSE experienced sudden death syndrome in 1981, the first year of the Reagan presidency. In fact, the CETA-PSE program was so unpopular at that time that even if a new liberal administration had been elected, the PSE program would probably have been severely cut.

Why? It cost a lot of money. Labor was getting restive. Stories about frivolous, wasteful, and in some cases fraudulent uses of PSE funds were getting wide play. In *Fortune* the author was blunt:

> It has wasted billions of dollars on ill-defined and hastily executed relief programs. And the slackness of its management has been an invitation to widespread fraud and abuse. As a result, a sizable number of Congressmen and even some White House officials have come to think it is time to scrap major portions of the program and start all over again.[1]

More than that, however, the PSE program changed its purpose and focus in the period of our study. In the late 1960s, the emergence of PSE—really its re-emergence from the mid-1930s—was as a countercyclical policy instrument. The public employment program (PEP) was enacted to help relieve the recession that began in 1969. Presidents Nixon and Ford (especially Ford) built up federal funding for PSE as unemployment rose. Later, President Carter stepped up the pace of PSE in response to the recession that began in mid-1974, which was largely brought on by rising energy costs associated with the Arab oil embargo.

However, as unemployment receded in 1977,

PSE did not. It did, however, shift to a structural rationale that required participants to be low-income, disadvantaged, and long-term unemployed. As this happened, not surprisingly, the politics of PSE changed as well. The lessons of this experience are pertinent today because of a renewed interest in the potential of PSE as a way to reduce welfare dependency.

The recently enacted national welfare act ratchets up both the rhetoric and the requirements to place working-age, able-bodied, poor family heads in jobs as an alternative to welfare. This, of course, is not a new goal for welfare policy. For fifty years, politicians have tried different national and state strategies to create incentives, opportunities, and requirements for people to choose work over welfare. The 1996 welfare reform law created state block grants for welfare, another in a long series of attempts to replace welfare with work, although this law is particularly severe compared to past legislation. In effect, politicians have thrown up their hands. Welfare has failed, they are saying, so the states should take over and try to do a better job. In the process (and in a way that is *non*-devolutionary), the 1996 law imposed strict work requirements, even stricter than similar welfare laws enacted in 1967, 1971, 1976, and 1988. *The beat goes on!* Under the 1996 block grants, all able-bodied family heads on welfare must work after two years, and after five years—if they have not become self-sufficient through work—they are to be removed from welfare anyway, with relatively few escape hatches. This law, called the Personal Responsibility Act (PRA), supersedes the 1988 welfare reform, which can be viewed as a *"mutual* responsibility act." Title II of the PRA (the Job Opportunities and Basic Skills [JOBS] program) provided services to facilitate work and self-support;

however, this authority and funding was eliminated in the 1996 law.

The pertinent economic concept here is "signaling" in the labor market. Out of frustration, this signaling is being made stronger as if to say, "Time and again, we told you [the welfare system] to stress work and you have not done it, so now we are requiring it—*really requiring it."* To emphasize the point, the name of Aid for Families with Dependent Children (AFDC) was changed to the Temporary Assistance for Needy Families (TANF) program. It is in this context that we need to ask how much of a role PSE can play in giving substance to this stronger political signaling. An analysis of the law and the available research does not provide much comfort.

When CETA-PSE changed its form in the late 1970s, it lost its luster. The structural version of PSE that existed from 1978 to 1980 had a very weak political constituency. As an antirecession tool, the conclusion of our research was that PSE worked pretty well. Displacement was minimal, primarily because politicians and government managers did not want to lock PSE employees into civil service, union, or essential jobs for fear they would have trouble laying off these workers when the federal money stopped. And of course the money would stop. For one thing, the recession would end. For another, federal funding is notably unreliable; it can end or change abruptly. Our research revealed much smaller displacement effects of PSE compared to econometric studies by George Johnson and others.

Our field research, which examined a sample of jurisdictions accounting for approximately 10 percent of all PSE participants, was done in four observation periods, in all of which the job creation effect of PSE was found to exceed 80 percent.

Our researchers also conducted a complementary statistical analysis of the job creation impact of PSE, which involved pooled time-series data on thirty large cities for the period 1970 through 1979. In the years following the build-up of PSE focused on structural unemployment (1978 and 1979), this research showed that each dollar of PSE spending added over 70 cents to wage and salary outlays.

When PSE shifted to its structural form under President Carter, its attraction to local officials was reduced because the workers involved were less employable than the recently displaced unemployed workers hired under the 1974–77 CETA-PSE. In recognition of this, it was specified that up to one-third of PSE jobs should be assigned to non-profit groups providing social and community development services.

A detour is appropriate here to comment on this shift of PSE to non-profit organizations. Non-profit groups like to think of three sectors—private, public, and non-profit or "independent." When all of the jobs in hospitals, churches, universities, museums, the arts, recreation, social services, and community development are put together, they constitute an appreciable chunk of the labor force. Although there are limited employment data for non-profits, a recent analysis indicates that non-profits accounted for 16 percent of all non-government jobs in New York State in 1995. Nationally, the proportion is probably lower.

As I got into the subject of devolution and non-profit sectors, I made some intriguing discoveries that heavily influenced my research on the management challenges faced by state governments. First of all, I do not think the independent sector is usefully viewed as a sector. In the functional areas of interest for our research (notably human service programs and community development), services performed by non-profits are in effect

extensions of government and it is appropriate to use the term "non-profitization" (not privatization) to describe it.

In short, most social services today are *not* performed by governments. They are performed by non-profit groups—for example, drug treatment; child care; employment and training; health clinics (including mental health clinics); foster care and services for children, families, youth, the elderly, abused women and children; and much more. The same is true of community development, where community development corporations have proliferated (and I think this is a good thing) with the aid of intermediary organizations such as the Local Initiative Support Corporation, the Enterprise Foundation, and the Neighborhood Housing Service.

Altogether, spending by tax-exempt organizations (under Section 501(c)3 of the Internal Revenue Code) accounts for about half a trillion dollars annually, or about 8 percent of GDP. (Note that if New York State is typical, the labor market share of non-profit jobs could be almost twice as large as its share of total national economic activity.) As stated earlier, I do not think it is useful to lump all of this activity together. The social-serving and community development groups highlighted here account for at most 10 percent of Section 501(c)3 spending, about $50 billion, which is still a big deal. It has to be emphasized that these groups are different from other non-profit types such as churches, universities, museums, and hospitals. Non-profit social-serving and community development groups receive *much less* of their money from charitable contributions and fees. What distinguishes them relative to others in the "non-profitization" category is that they receive a very high proportion of their revenue from government. In effect, they are agents of government, providing services that used to be provided by state and local governments and in some cases and places still are.

These groups have grown for a number of reasons, some of which involve practical politics. Local politicians and government managers apparently decided this was a good way to accomplish three things: to insulate themselves from the fickleness of the flow of federal and state aid, to avoid civil service and union rules, and to save money. If services are contracted out, presumably you can control them more easily and buy them more cheaply.

Unfortunately, there is a rule of political science: *Things often do not work out the way you expect.* This law of unintended consequences may be the only true law. In the PSE case, it applies very well; non-profitization has created its own politics. The lobby groups for the affected functional fiefdoms care about and need to protect the fiscal flows that pay for their "non-profitized" services. This makes it harder than might be expected to turn off these services even when federal and state grants are reduced or materially changed, as is now the case in many areas of social and urban policy.

Another political point needs to be added here. The *prattle* by conservative politicians that non-profit "charitable" groups can take over social functions where federal and state aid is being reduced is just that, prattle. The non-profit groups involved in this work, as just stated, are heavily dependent on public aid. They cannot take over anything. In fact, the people who run these organizations (many of whom are heroes—wonderful entrepreneurs who put government money streams together creatively) often do not know how much public money they receive because it comes in so many forms. There is some philanthropic giving to these groups, but it is a sliver of what they get. Rich people prefer other groups and causes

when it comes to big money. If we want to ask what the potential is for PSE, clearly it is enlarged by the fact that in recent years more and more social and community development services have been contracted out to non-profit groups. As a result, is there more hope now for PSE? I think the answer is yes, but we need to be careful.

We need now to put together the areas of potential supply for PSE jobs. There are three main categories. We can extend public services provided by public agencies and workforces—cleaning up parks, adding corridor monitors and teachers aides in schools, filing in police stations, picking up litter in parks and along highways. A second group of opportunities, as already described, involves allocating PSE funds to non-profit groups who provide social and community development services. Still other opportunities (the hardest ones to classify) involve the use of PSE workers in situations where government activities have been privatized. Nonetheless, this third area helps to make an important general point that "public" service has come to involve boundaries that are increasingly blurred. Government has changed a good deal more than most people realize; we now have a *"contractual state."* To add to the complexity, both governments and non-profits contract out activities (mostly "hard" tasks like records management, data handling, catering, and maintenance) to private companies. In the welfare field, there is further talk of privatization under state welfare block grants whereby private companies such as Lockheed will bid to run state welfare systems. A *New York Times* article said,

> Selling Federally subsidized management systems to welfare departments was a separate and much bigger business, the province of

huge information-technology companies. Now the separation has vanished, and the welfare-to-work crevasse is suddenly a canyon. Sheer scale puts the big companies in command.[2]

In the health field, hospitals and other health facilities are being converted from non-profit to private status.

To sum up, PSE can be used:

1. In the public sector to augment existing agency missions and carry out marginal tasks—that is, tasks that are desirable but not sufficiently valued to be publicly funded.
2. In non-profitization areas where social services and community development activities have been heavily contracted out to non-profit organizations.
3. In the work of profit-making organizations that have close ties to government, notably in the health sector—hospitals, nursing homes, hospices, clinics, and so on.

This is the supply side for PSE jobs. The other side of the equation is of course the demand side—how many people need such jobs. Eli Ginzberg's essay in this volume includes a thoughtful discussion of the potential demand of PSE. Ginzberg concludes, "We have a much larger proportion of people seeking regular jobs than suggested by our below 5 percent reported unemployment rate."

Prior to 1996, federal welfare laws included the authority to assign welfare workers to public and quasi-public (work-for-your-welfare) jobs called "community work experience," abbreviated as CWEP, and often referred to as "workfare." This in contrast to PSE where the wage is more explicit, although the distinction between the two job-creating approaches can be oblique. Studies have found CWEP is not all it is cracked up to be. Research by the Manpower Demonstration Research Corporation (MDRC), the Rockefeller Institute, and others on the logistics of transporting, training, and supervising workers in these settings casts serious doubt on how much can be achieved because CWEP is so expensive and hard to administer. Even if we wanted to restrict PSE and/or CWEP to the welfare population, we are talking about numbers (probably over a million family heads) that exceed what was achieved under PSE in 1978–79 and far exceed what has been achieved with CWEP.

I often find myself in the lonely position of being a social scientist interested in management as a field of applied study. Politicians blithely opine on how PSE is a preferable alternative to welfare because it can produce a double social utility plus a happy feeling of self-esteem on the part of PSE participants. But the management challenges involved are formidable; even with the best of intentions and the most serious commitment, the results of previous efforts do not provide much comfort. It is possible that there will be a new and stronger commitment to the PSE and CWEP routes to welfare reduction in the future, but until this happens, I find the lessons of the CETA-PSE experience to be chastening about the potential of PSE.

Work on this essay was completed three months after President Clinton signed the welfare block grant law. That law eliminated provisions that had been carefully crafted in 1988 with the active participation of then-Governor Clinton and others to create the JOBS program as a component of the Family Support Act. The Family Support Act of 1988 was explicit in spelling out the tasks and providing money for putting welfare family heads to work, including, for example, child care, transportation, training, education, counseling, and so on. Ironically, eight years later, the 1996 national welfare law signed by President Clinton abolished the JOBS authority, giving welfare recipients the message, as in the Nike ads, "Just do it." The block grant authority is broad enough so the funds provided can be used for many work and work-facilitation purposes, which includes explicit authority for CWEP-type jobs, PSE, and work by welfare family heads for community service organizations.

One possibility for supplying PSE-like experiences for welfare family heads (that is, what is for now the TANF population) is that the states will use welfare block grants and other funds (federal and state aid) to provide work instead of welfare. This, for example, is the strong theme and presumably exclusive purpose of Wisconsin Governor Tommy Thompson's "Wisconsin Works" approach. His program seeks to abolish welfare payments and only pay people for work performed. However, I am hard pressed to see how this can be done on a national scale given the number of jobs needed just for those in the TANF population alone who are affected by the two-year and five-year cut-offs. But we shall have to wait and see.

There is, of course, always the possibility that the national government will modify the new welfare law and provide explicit PSE authority and more money for job creation for the welfare population and for other populations when the next recession occurs, especially if it is deep. Ordinarily, American government legislates incrementally, adding to what went before. Implementation is the short suit of American government; legislation is our long suit. Legislating is always happening, mostly at the edges of existing law. It is unusual for non-incremental change to occur, as was the case

with the 1996 welfare block grant. At some point in the near future, in response to the next recession, it would not surprise me if the national government added additional PSE and/or CWEP funding to the 1996 welfare law. The president has already indicated areas where he favors adjustments to the new law even as it is being implemented by the states. My guess is that when the next recession occurs, people who do not like the 1996 welfare law will see the jobs angle as the best one to use to change it. These are conservative times in the country on social issues, a point that needs to be kept in mind in thinking about welfare and social policy options.

Taking another detour here, years ago when we did a study of the revenue sharing program, the *New Yorker* magazine said of revenue sharing that the governors supported this program, "or whatever the federal government is calling money this year." People who engage in the dance of domestic legislation are savvy people. In the present period, what governors and other public officials will call money in the social sector is likely to be money for jobs. Such a program (whether PSE, or CWEP, or some hybrid form) enacted in a period of economic downturn could be made more palatable politically if it is not just for people on welfare, but also includes eligibility and funding for some recently unemployed people, as was the case in the 1970s. Again, we found then that the countercyclical component of CETA-PSE worked pretty well. A structural program is harder to operate, but in light of the extensive "non-profitization" that has occurred, many non-profit social-serving groups need and prefer having PSE workers, even those with limited experience and job skills. With decent supervision, these groups can use these funds to good effect to achieve additive public and community service purposes. Government agencies as sponsors of new PSE projects are more choosy, but their role too can be important, especially if funds are provided for project supervision. At the outset of a countercyclical PSE program, its job-creating effect may not add to total employment in the nation (although it would be redistributive), but over time, once established, PSE would have a net job-creation impact in the labor market.

To conclude, my special interest in management becomes important if the jobs route to the next round of welfare reform puts greater em-phasis, as many have argued it should, on job creation. If (and this is a big if) we do the job right, there is a sizeable potential demand. It is not too early for analysts and advocates to be thinking about delivery concepts and mechanism for a new PSE program.

Notes

1. Juan Cameron, "How CETA Became a Four-Letter Word." *Fortune*, April 1979, 112–14.

2. Nina Bernstein, "Giant Companies Entering Race to Run State Welfare Programs," *New York Times*, September 15, 1996, p. 1.

29

Employer Training: The High Road, the Low Road, and the Muddy Middle Path

Anthony P. Carnevale and Donna M. Desrochers

As our economy continues to evolve, American employers and workers are experiencing a new set of challenges fueled by surging technological innovation, growing international trade, deregulation in domestic markets, and fundamental changes in the nature and structure of work. In response to these changes, there have been two primary paths taken, oftentimes characterized as the "low road" and the "high road" to the new economy.

The low road to the new economy continues along the historic path of mass production, emphasizing downsizing, outsourcing, "deskilling," and other methods to improve productivity by slashing labor costs. While low-road strategies result in short-term productivity gains, they reduce the nation's long-term economic competitiveness, living standards, and income equality. The low road emphasizes the dark side of the current economic transition, encouraging the evolution of hollow institutions with no long-term viability and desperate wage bargains in a race to the bottom levels of global living standards.

The high road harnesses the American future to the positive energies evident in the current economic transition—the growing value of investments in human capital. The high-road path

relies on highly skilled employees who can react quickly to changing technology and market requirements. It presumes longer-term investments in educational preparation and lifelong learning—on and off the job.

A minority of elite American employers have taken the high road. High-road strategies are difficult in the current institutional framework. They presume shared power, mutual commitments between employers and employees, and longer-term investment horizons that are not encouraged by current market forces. Only dominant firms can afford to train employees, commit to employment security, and provide full benefits and high wages.

Wherever wage and benefit differences are small, low-road employers can bid away skilled workers with marginal wage increases. As a result, training, full benefits, and high wages tend to be found together in employer organizations with technological, size, regulatory, or other barriers to entry.

Absent alterations in the current institutional incentives, the American economy—and most workers—will never find the high road. An elite corps, less than 20 percent of all workers, will continue along the high road. They will have job security, training, the latest technology, and will be involved on the job.

A substantial share of American workers, the 40 percent that do not receive education or training after high school, will "make do" along the low road at the contingent periphery of increasingly dynamic labor markets in the new economy. Without changes in policy and market incentives that encourage an equal opportunity to learn, uneven access to good schools and lifelong learning will only force more Americans onto the low road, driving an already deepening wedge between the learning-haves and the learning have-nots, substituting an exclusive meritocracy for more traditional forms of economic elitism.

The rest of us, as much as 40 percent of the workforce, will continue to slog along the "muddy middle path" between the high road and the low road. These workers will get some form of education or training after high school but will never catch on with employers who will fully train, equip, or include them in their core workforce.

The High Road: Skill and the New Workplace

The high road is not the easy path. The most prominent difference between the old and the new workplace is the increasing intensity of competitive forces on the high road to the new economy. No longer is it enough for a business to compete solely on the basis of price for generally standardized goods or services. Today's global customers and suppliers are linked by an ever more complex web of standards that, while still including price, extend to quality, variety, customization, customer service, timeliness, and continuous innovation.

In order to meet new competitive requirements at the least cost, high-road employers are turning to information technologies—our old friend the computer in its various disguises. The new technology works to increase efficiency and quality standards more than labor-intensive methods, enables more consistent quality control, promotes continuous innovation, customizes with a few keystrokes, and provides a user-friendly customer interface. Information technology increases skill requirements most among non-supervisory workers, because it is more widely distributed than previous technologies. In a study of American manufacturing institutions, it was revealed that companies that raised the proportion of non-supervisory employees who use a computer by as much as one-third would increase overall productivity by 5.4 percent.[1]

New performance standards and new technologies encourage high-performance organizational formats that expand worker autonomy, thus increasing skill requirements. For example, in the old economy, quality was determined by checking for defects at the end of the line. In the new economy, higher quality standards tend to be built into the production process, requiring more worker involvement and skill up and down the line.

Modern work organizations are constantly adapting to new technology and changing work formats. Employers who empower their employees with new technology and flexible work formats also need to enable them with skill. More than half, about 53 percent, of all companies provide training on the job as a result of the need to adapt to changes in technology and work formats. An additional 26 percent of firms train to keep up with computer changes.[2]

High-performance work systems are most successful when training and other complementary work reforms are bundled together, rather than applied piecemeal. Firms with employee assistance plans, wellness plans, total quality management plans, "pay for knowledge" systems, and employee involvement are more likely to train, compared with the average firm. Moreover, the literature on training and integrated high-performance work systems details their powerful performance effects.

The American Market for Career Education and Job Training

In general, job-related skill development and skill enhancement works in a relatively predictable sequence. Success in job markets requires a minimum of educational attainment beyond high school. Education beyond high school leverages access to higher-wage and higher-skilled occupational preparation. The combination of post-secondary education and more specific occupational preparation provides access to elite managerial, professional, and technical jobs. Those who secure managerial, professional, and technical jobs tend to have far greater access to technology, and formal and informal learning on the job that further increases earnings and other career advantages.

The Complementarity Between Post-Secondary Education, Occupational Preparation, Job Training, and Computer Technology

General education, broad occupational preparation, and access to training and technology on the job complement each other in their overall impact on earnings. While real earnings have been flat, the relative earnings differences between those with high school degrees and college graduates have increased between 1979 and 1994 from 13 to 48 percent for men and from 23 to 54 percent for women.[3] Those with college degrees have the best access to elite occupations, especially managerial and professional occupations. Access to elite occupations confers greater access to training and computer technology on the job, which generate higher earnings returns. More than 60 percent of managers and professionals have college degrees, whereas only 20 percent are high school graduates or do not have high school degrees. By occupation, the earnings of technicians and craft and sales workers equal about 60 percent of what workers in managerial and professional jobs earn; relatively unskilled service and blue-collar workers earn about 50 percent of managerial and professional wages; and farm workers earn just over 40 percent of what managers and professionals earn.[4]

Employer-based training has a positive effect on workers' earnings regardless of education level but the returns increase with education level and access to elite occupations. Workers who receive formal company training consistently earn higher wages than do similar workers who only attend school or receive informal on-the-job training. Employees in occupations that pay $25,000 or more per year comprise just over half of the workforce; however, these workers receive 72 percent of all formal training provided by employers (see Table 29.1). Given the current distribution, and gains associated with employer-provided training, it is the elite workers receiving the majority of training who are positioned to increase their earnings while the workers in less-skilled occupations, who are provided with few training opportunities, will continue to stagnate in a hollow of modest earnings.

A portion of the returns to training can be explained by an apparent complementarity between the new technology and skill. Improving

Table 29.1

Workforce Distribution and Incidence of Formal Company Training by Earnings Level and Occupation

Median annual earnings (1991 dollars)	Distribution of the workforce in 1991	Distribution of company training in 1991 (in %)	Occupations included in the median annual earnings levels and percent of training received by each occupation
$0–$10,000	0	0	None
$10,000–$14,999	14.9	5	Services, except protective services (4.7); Farming, forestry, and fishing (.5)
$15,000–$19,999	10.5	5	Machine operators, assemblers, and inspectors (4); Handlers, equipment cleaners, and laborers (1)
$20,000–$24,999	19.9	18	Administrative support (15); Transportation and material moving occupations (3)
$25,000–$29,999	28.2	37	Technicians and related support (5); Sales occupations (13); Protective service (4); Precision production, craft, and repair (15)
$30,000–$34,999	12.8	19	Executive, administrative, and managerial (19)
$35,000 +	13.7	16	Professional specialty (16)

skills to adapt to the new technology rewards the people who use the new technology. Those who use computers on their job consistently earn more than people with the same education level but who do not use computers on their jobs. Moreover, the earnings premium for computer use increases with the education level of the employee—from about 15 percent for high school dropouts to almost 30 percent for college graduates.[5]

The Substitutability Between Education and Job Training: Education Signifies Ability and Training Improves Ability

According to available evidence, about 60 percent of annual job openings correspond to some form of institutional education degree or specialized training beyond high school, although, the strength of the match varies. The match is strongest among management, professional, and technical jobs and weakest between service and production jobs.

In some cases, there are many more people with degrees and certifications than jobs. For example, there are more management, law, and economics degrees each year than there are annual openings in these fields. Yet, in these cases, and many others, post-secondary education and training is indirectly useful in accessing many types of entry-level jobs by signaling to employers the ability of applicants to benefit from further on-the-job training. In these cases, general education or training credentials substitute for a more stringent analysis of potential employees in employer hiring practices and for job-specific training.

Post-secondary graduates not working in their field have acquired general skills that make them more productive than workers with less education in the same job. At the same time, the fact that as many as one in three workers with college degrees and four of five people with less than four years of college report they do not need or use their education or training in their current job, suggests a mismatch between the quantity and distribution of degrees and available jobs.[6] Better information on learning outcomes and job requirements would result in better matches between individuals and available jobs, reducing costly inefficiencies in school-to-work transitions for both employers and individuals.

While the most powerful wage premiums accrue to workers who are able to utilize training on the job to complement pre-employment educational and occupational preparation, employer-provided training can substitute for missing educational preparation. Informal on-the-job training is the largest source of training for those who do not go beyond high school. In fact, workers without high school degrees who get formal training by their employers earn more than high school graduates without such training; furthermore, workers without high school degrees who receive formal training from their employers earn more than high school graduates who are trained but did not receive their training from their employers.

Although employer-based training can substitute for educational preparation in a particular job, it has less durability than broader educational preparation. Much the same is true for job-specific vocational preparation in schools, especially in high schools. Employer-provided training and vocational training are effective substitutes, but the value of both degrade quickly absent the leavening effects of early education; both require long-term access to learning—general and job specific—for sustained career adaptation.

The Dynamic Relationship Between Learning on the Job and Education

The central dynamic in our skill development system is a two-way street between school and work. Schooling prepares people to learn on the job. Conversely, changing educational and occupational requirements tend to evolve from incremental changes in skill requirements at work and are passed back and integrated into school-ing over time. Initially, small changes in skill requirements are learned informally, and then incremental changes on the job accumulate until they affect a sufficient number of employees to justify formal training programs. Ultimately, changes on the job can grow into new skill requirements that need to be integrated into the educational and occupational preparation system. While every acorn does not become an oak, job-based skill changes may eventually create whole new occupations and professions. In a market-based system of skill acquisition such as our own, efficiency improvements in the transmission of job-based skill requirements into formal training and educational programs can result in substantial increases in the rate of economic and technological adaptation.

The Unique Role of Employers in the Education and Training System

Employers play a pivotal role in our job-related education and training system. Employers create and design jobs, thereby determining the demand for pre-employment education and training. Employers use education and training provided by others and also are major training providers. Employers are second only to four-year colleges and post-graduate programs in the training of workers to qualify for their jobs. Employers are the primary source of training to improve skills in a current job. The earnings effects of employer training are equally impressive. Employer training to help workers qualify for their jobs can substitute for inadequate education, and retraining provided by employers increases earnings more than retraining in schools.

Closing the "Training Gap"

Employer-based training expenditures are difficult to measure, given the lack of establishment data on firm costs and the number of workers trained per establishment. However, the estimated formal training costs range between $30 and $44 billion, or 1.2 to 1.8 percent of payroll.[7] It was estimated that firm expenditures on formal training in 1991 equaled $63 billion; however, including informal on-the-job training, estimates could be much higher. In comparison, the investment by U.S. businesses in structures and equipment during 1991 totaled $731 billion, more than ten times the amount spent on formal training. An analysis of formal training expenditures in 1991 estimated that firms with formal training programs spent, on average, $344,885 over two years, with the average cost per worker trained equal to $1,206.[8]

Over time, the proportion of workers who need training has risen slightly: Although the proportion of workers indicating that they needed training to qualify for their job rose, the increase in workers who needed skill improvement training once on the job was greatest (6 percentage points) between 1983 and 1991. Companies have responded to the increase in the demand for training. Over the same period of time, there was a 2 percentage point increase in the number of workers who received company training to qualify for their job and a 5 percentage point increase in the proportion of workers receiving skill improvement training from their employers. The increase in the proportion of workers participating in skill improvement training was driven mainly by the rapid expansion of company programs designed to provide this training. Employers have also responded to the training needs of their workers by increasing financial support for employees who enroll in training courses provided by educational institutions. Employers have more than doubled their financial backing for qualifying training courses since 1983 and in 1991, two-thirds of workers had their tuition fully paid for by their employer when they enrolled in training courses offered by schools.[9]

Although employers have made gains in providing training for their workers, the proportion of workers receiving company training remains low. For the American economy to take the high road in a global economy—producing quality products with a skilled workforce—additional employer investments in training will be needed. These investments will have to extend beyond the current realm of training, reaching core workers in addition to elites, as well as workers in small companies that are not afforded the same opportunities as their counterparts in large corporations. Just less than half of companies with fewer than fifty employees offer formal job skills training whereas nearly all companies with at least 250 employees offer similar training.[10]

Future training needs also are determined by changes in employment patterns. Given the varying incidence of formal training by occupation, such occupational shifts will affect the number of workers who will need training in the future. A conservative estimate of the cost of future training needs in 2005, based upon the incidence of occupational training in 1991 and the projected increase in jobs by occupation in 2005, yields an estimate of $78 billion. The "training gap"—or increase in expenditures of $15 billion above the estimated 1991 spending level of $63 billion—that must be closed reflects a projected increase in overall formal training of 23.8 percent. The projected slowdown in the incidence of training (the 1983–91 increase was 59.3 percent) reflects the projected slowdown in employment growth. By occupation, the greatest increase in the need for training is projected in the professional specialty, technicians and related support, and administrative occupations.

Given that the preferable training strategy is to increase the number of workers who receive training, the actual "training gap" surpasses the estimated $15 billion. If the number of training incidences were to increase to 50 percent of the workforce in 2005, the "gap" would be closer to $80 billion and employers would need to spend an additional $65 billion, just to "keep up," to train additional workers. All totaled, the training resources needed in 2005 could be as large as $143 billion.

Policy Implications

Policies for encouraging employer-based training should emphasize strengthening the complementarity between learning on the job and schooling. Policies that encourage a greater focus on the complementarity between employer-provided training and schooling encourage the highest earnings returns for individuals, provide a broader base of human capital development for sustained adaptation in increasingly volatile labor markets, and improve efficiencies in the transmission of skill changes from workplaces to schools. While employer-based training and narrow vocational preparation can be effective substitutes for schooling in a particular job, their value degrades over time, and skills are less transferable from job to job.

Subsidies or tax incentives for employer training will work best and avoid unnecessary regulatory burdens if they reward employers only for training that is accredited by educational organizations. Employer subsidies regulated by educational organizations will ensure the highest returns to individuals, encourage collaboration between employers and schools, and avoid regulatory burdens otherwise necessary for a company to receive employer training subsidies.

Employer subsidies should be targeted on young, non-supervisory, and educationally disadvantaged workers, all of whom have the least access and can benefit most from employer-based training.

Subsidies targeted to adults for lifelong learning should also be expanded. The tax code should make job-related education deductible both when it applies to a current job and when it provides education or training for new jobs. Eligibility for federal higher education grants and loans should be expanded to include adult learners enrolled in career-related courses and in degree programs.

Policy also should encourage more collaboration between employers and the schools in order to improve the transmission of information on emerging skill requirements. Ultimately, our interest should be in creating dynamic networks of employers and educators. Effective networks rely on real-time information and involvement rather than fixed standards. Creating skill standards can be helpful. Standards should be flexible and market driven. No attempt to create "one-size-fits-all" labor market standards can possibly capture the complexity and dynamism in labor markets. We should create a market for standards and not standards for markets. Our ultimate goal is to create processes and relationships to transmit skill information that is always partial and never finished.

Jobs Matter

Training does not create high-wage, high-skill jobs. High-wage, high-skill jobs create demand for education and training. Ultimately, a high-road strategy with human capital investments at its core succeeds or flounders on the basis of the general availability of high-skill, high-wage jobs. If human capital investments outpace the corresponding increase in good jobs, we will only end up with a lot of very smart workers chasing a lot of very dumb jobs.

Notes

1. Sandra E. Black and Lisa M. Lynch, "How to Compete: The Impact of Workplace Practices and Information Technology on Productivity," Working paper, U.S. Department of Labor, Office of the Chief Economist, September 1996.

2. Harley J. Frazis, Diane E. Herz, and Michael Horrigan, "Employer Provided Training: Results from a New Survey," *Monthly Labor Review,* May 1995, Tables 3 and 4, pp. 7, 9.

3. Committee for Economic Development, *American Workers and Economic Change,* Washington, DC, April 1996.

4. National Commission for Employment Policy, *Declining Job Security and the Professionalization of Opportunity,* Research Report No. 95–04, Washington, DC, May 1995.

5. Lawrence Mishel and Jared Bernstein, *The State of Working America, 1994–95.* (Armonk, NY: M.E. Sharpe); analysis of Alan Krueger, "How Computers Have Changed the Wage Structure: Evidence from Microdata, 1984–89," *Quarterly Journal of Economics,* February 1993.

6. U.S. Department of Labor, Bureau of Labor Statistics. "How Workers Get Their Training: A 1991 Update." Bulletin 2407 (Washington, DC: U.S. Government Printing Office, August 1992).

7. Office of Technology Assessment, U.S. Congress, *Worker Training: Competing in the New International Economy,* OTA-ITE-457 (Washington, DC: U.S. Government Printing Office, September 1990).

8. David Knoke and Arne L. Kallenberg. "Job Training in U.S. Organizations," *American Sociological Review* 59, August 1994.

9. U.S. Department of Labor, Bureau of Labor Statistics, 1992.

10. U.S. Department of Labor, Bureau of Labor Statistics, "BLS Reports on Employer Provided Training," Press Release #USDL 94–432 (Washington, DC: U.S. Government Printing Office, September 1994).

D. Health Care

30

Health Care for Low-Income People

Karen Davis

Health and the economic well-being of families are interrelated. Physical or mental disability undermines the capacity of a child to learn and an adult to work; serious illness in a family—whether that of a child, spouse, parent, or grandparent—can require a worker to drop out of the labor force to care for those who are incapacitated. Similarly, poverty and lack of education can pose barriers to preventive health care, early detection of disease, and proper treatment of chronic conditions, leading to preventable illnesses, disability, and premature mortality. Poverty can also be a threat to health because it is a factor in living in unsafe neighborhoods with greater rates of accidents, air pollution, lead poisoning, substance abuse, and violence. Low-wage jobs tend to pose greater risks to health—for example, by exposing workers to toxic substances and job-site injuries—and rarely convey health benefits that help families obtain needed health care. Not surprisingly given these risks and interrelationships, most measures of health status are inversely related to income, and growing poverty and income inequality have important health implications.

Investment by government in better health care and better health conditions in jobs and communities can contribute to economic growth and worker productivity. This essay primarily focuses on the importance of financial access to health care in reducing inequality in the use of health care services and improving the health of particularly vulnerable populations. Enactment of Medicare and Medicaid in 1965 as part of the Great Society represented a commitment by the federal government to assuring health care and opportunity for the most vulnerable Americans: elderly and disabled people and low-income families. As a direct consequence, differentials in access to health care and health outcomes across different income groups narrowed markedly in the ten years from 1965 to 1974.

Unfortunately, over the last twenty years the restructuring of the American economy has undercut these gains. The proportion of the population without health insurance, after falling from one-third of all Americans in 1965 to 11 percent in 1976, began to rise, reaching more than 15 percent of the population today. Employment-based health insurance, in particular, has steadily eroded. Even those with employer-financed coverage have experienced an erosion in real benefits and a shifting of premium costs to workers. Health benefits for retirees have declined as well, increasing the health and economic insecurity of older adults, especially early retirees under age 65. Competitive pressures on employers to cut costs have led to the promulgation of managed care plans for working families, where a focus on lower costs may be detrimental to quality and access to care.

Medicare and Medicaid are also coming under increasing attack. Expenditures have spiraled upward as health care costs in an unregulated, noncompetitive health care system have grown. In addition, Medicare has borne the additional demands created by an aging population and advances in health care technology that have brought increased life expectancy and quality of life to 39 million currently covered elderly and disabled Americans. Medicaid has expanded from 22 million people in 1975 to 37 million today—mostly as it has been expanded to cover more low-income children and women. These rising expenditures have strained federal, state, and local government budgets and led to proposals to slow spending and restructure the programs. States are rapidly enrolling Medicaid beneficiaries in managed care plans. Proposals to "privatize" Medicare with vouchers to purchase private insurance or managed care coverage or replacement of comprehensive benefits with a combination of medical savings accounts and catastrophic coverage are getting serious attention.

These forces are segmenting the health care of different groups of Americans. Those who are uninsured are most at risk—for failure to receive needed care, risk to their health and productivity, and financial ruin that major illness or injury can bring. But access to care and health security varies increasingly across the insured population. Medicaid beneficiaries and lower-wage workers are directed toward managed care plans without adequate quality standards or enforcement. Increasingly, only higher-wage employees can afford free choice of physicians and hospitals through a traditional health insurance plan. Even Medicare, built on social insurance principles, may be increasingly segmented, with different care available to those who are well-to-do and those who are sick and poor.

The growth of managed care and the push for a reversal of comprehensive health insurance coverage are a natural reaction to the uncontrolled growth in health care costs. But relying on market forces to foster competition through managed care plans without quality and performance standards and governmental oversight runs the risk of widening the gaps among different groups of Americans. Lower-income and minority Americans, especially low-wage workers and their families, run the risk of falling outside the health care safety net, with serious health, social, and economic consequences for the entire society.

This course is not inevitable and is within our power as a nation to change. While President Clinton's proposal for universal health insurance failed to muster support, the nation continues to need a national policy that guarantees access to health care for all Americans and removes the fear of financial hardship and inferior-quality health care that a market system can inflict. Building consensus on such an approach and making some concrete practical steps toward its fulfillment should be an important component of our public policy for the twenty-first century.

Uninsured in America

Today 44 million Americans are without any form of health insurance coverage, up from 32 million in 1988. The proportion of Americans who are uninsured has grown steadily: 17.4 percent of all Americans under age 65 were uninsured in 1995, compared with 15.2 percent in 1988. Since Americans move on and off of coverage depending on their employment and eligibility for public programs, a larger number are uninsured over a period of time. Over a twenty-eight-month period, 67 million people were uninsured at least one month. Over two-thirds of those were uninsured at least six months.

Most uninsured people have modest incomes, and the vast majority are in families headed by workers. Twenty-eight percent of the uninsured have incomes below the poverty level, and another 32 percent are near-poor (between poverty and twice poverty). Eighty-five percent of uninsured children and adults are in families where the family head works full or part time. While there are many reasons why people are uninsured—related to health status, unemployment, or age—the inescapable fact is that low income is the predominant risk factor. Americans are uninsured because they cannot afford health insurance coverage and, if working, their employer does not pay for coverage.

Not surprisingly, minorities are hardest hit. Hispanic and Asian-Americans are more likely to have jobs in the retail trade, service, and agricultural sectors that do not provide health insurance benefits. Thirty-five percent of Hispanic-Americans are uninsured, as are 22 percent of African-Americans. Uninsurance rates are also high among Asian-Americans: 23 percent of Asian-Americans are uninsured, including 38 percent of Korean-Americans.

Since health insurance coverage is linked to employment, those outside the labor force—the unemployed, early retirees, and disabled—are also at high risk of being uninsured. One-fourth of all non-working adults under age 65 are uninsured. Public programs cover those with long-term disabilities, but only after a two-year waiting period, in the case of Medicare, or after stringent income and asset eligibility requirements are met, in the case of Medicaid. Half of the unemployed are either currently uninsured or have been uninsured at some time in the last two years.

Perhaps the most seriously at risk are those between the ages of 55 and 64. While older adults are less likely than younger people to be uninsured, they are more likely to be in fair or poor health, to face high individual health insurance premiums when coverage is available at all, and to risk financial hardship if they incur major medical expenses. Three million Americans between the ages of 55 and 64 are uninsured, and almost 1 million are doubly vulnerable—they are not in good health and have no health insurance coverage. Poor, older adults are particularly at risk: 28 percent of adults ages 58 to 63 with poverty incomes are uninsured, compared to 5 percent of those with incomes above twice the poverty line.

The consequences of being uninsured include failure to get preventive care, inadequate maintenance of chronic conditions, and adverse health outcomes. Those who are uninsured are less likely to get needed medical care and more likely to postpone care and wait until medical needs become an emergency. Thirty-four percent of the uninsured report failure to get needed care during the year, and 71 percent postpone needed care.

This failure to receive proper care takes an economic toll in terms of preventable hospitalization, disability, and mortality. It also inflicts financial hardships on those who are sick, and heightens emotional stress on families during a time of serious illness. For society as a whole, preventable disease and poor health inflict high "indirect costs" as well as direct costs due to lost work days, premature deaths, and lowered productivity. Estimated indirect costs of chronic disease came to $234 billion, with 4.5 million years of productivity lost due to sick days and another 24 million years lost due to premature death. Worker productivity is reduced, as workers are unable to work either because of their own illness or the necessity of caring for sick family members. Health is an extremely important determinant of early exit from the labor force; it accounts for almost all of the two-to-one difference between the fraction of black versus white middle-aged men out of the workforce. Women, particularly, feel the brunt of caring for a disabled child, spouse, or parent, and they are often unable to work themselves because of this caregiving responsibility.

Employer Coverage

The principal way most Americans receive health insurance is through employment. Today 72 percent of the employed workforce has employer health insurance coverage from their own or a spouse's employer. Employer-provided health insurance, however, has begun to decline. By 1995, only 64 percent of the under-65 population (including children and non-working adults) had employer-sponsored insurance, down from 69 percent in 1988. This reduction is due largely to the changing nature of where people work and a smaller share of premiums paid by employers. Workers have moved away from industries with relatively generous sponsorship of family coverage to industries less likely to provide health insurance at all, and with much less generous premium coverage. Younger workers with children, in particular, are more likely to work in the service sector, where health benefits are less common.

Retiree health coverage is eroding even more rapidly than worker coverage. The proportion of retirees ages 55 and over currently receiving health benefits from their prior employers declined from 44 percent to 34 percent from 1988 to 1994. The decline in coverage results from a combination of factors, including lower coverage of workers during their working years (and thus no option of retiree coverage), reduction in

offering retiree coverage, and an increasing share of premiums shifted to retirees. For lower-income older adults without employer coverage, the cost of insurance is high: Half of those with incomes below 200 percent of poverty pay more than 15 percent of their family income just for health insurance premiums.

The erosion of employer-based coverage has affected not only the numbers of workers and retirees with coverage, but the quality of coverage as well. Workers have faced increasing premium costs, as well as higher deductibles and out-of-pocket costs. The major shift, however, has been the decline in traditional health insurance coverage that gave working families the option of selecting any physician or health care provider of their choice. Today, 75 percent of workers in medium- and large-size firms enroll in managed care plans that require families to seek care from a defined set of physicians and other health care providers. Forty-seven percent of medium- and large-size firms offer employees only one plan, and small firms typically offer one, if any, plan so that most workers do not have a choice among managed care plans with different lists of eligible providers. When workers do have a choice of a traditional health insurance plan, they often must pay a substantially higher premium for this option. As a result, lower-wage workers are much more likely to opt for managed care coverage.

The implications of managed care for quality of care are still not clear. The rapid evolution of the industry, with new and changing forms of organization, have outpaced research on performance. The basic concerns about quality come from the incentives inherent in a capitated (i.e., per person) form of payment to managed care plans. Plans receive the same revenues, regardless of the quantity and quality of health services provided to enrolled beneficiaries. Profits are higher, therefore, when costs are lower—either from increased efficiency or lower quality and limited services. In a world of perfect information and many choices, market forces could lead to the financial failure of low-quality inferior plans. However, information is quite limited; techniques for measuring quality and performance are rudimentary; choices are few; and both employers as purchasers and managed care plans have major incentives to reduce costs regardless of the consequences for quality.

Quality of care may be affected in numerous ways. By linking where patients go for care to their particular insurance coverage, any change in plan often requires changing physician, thus disrupting the continuity of care. Studies show that patients benefit from having a long-term ongoing relationship with the same physician. Studies of managed care enrollees also identify problems with access to needed specialist care, difficulty obtaining appointments, and lower-quality care. Most troubling is recent evidence that managed care works less well for low-income patients, leading to restricted access to services and poorer health outcomes. There may also be system-wide effects of managed care. Studies indicate that managed care plans are steering patients away from academic health centers with advanced teaching hospitals; while more costly, such institutions play a critical role in the testing and diffusion of the latest medical advances.

Medicaid

The federal-state Medicaid program is a major source of health insurance for low-income Americans. Medicaid covers 37 million people—more than one in eight Americans—including low-income children, parents (mostly mothers), disabled people, and elderly people. Without Medicaid, almost half of the poor and near-poor would be uninsured. Indeed, if low-income women succeed in working their way off of welfare and, as a consequence, are no longer eligible for Medicaid, they are likely to become uninsured: Almost two-thirds (63 percent) of women leaving Medicaid are uninsured.

Medicaid has been particularly important in recent years in offsetting some of the decline in employer-based insurance. More than 10 million people, mostly low-income mothers and children, were added to Medicaid coverage over the last ten years through legislative changes that set federal income eligibility standards for children and pregnant women tied to the federal poverty level. Today, among poor families, 76 percent of infants are covered by Medicaid, as are 72 percent of children ages 1 to 5 and 64 percent of children ages 6 to 12. Under current law, Medicaid coverage of poor children ages 13 to 18 will be fully phased in by the year 2002.

Medicaid has markedly improved access to health care and served as a crucial safety net for the nation's most vulnerable populations, caring for individuals who would otherwise have few options to meet their health needs. Gains in access to care for significant numbers of low-income people have translated into important health gains. Although it is difficult to isolate the independent contribution of improved coverage, since 1965, when Medicaid was introduced, maternal mortality has fallen by three-quarters and infant mortality has halved. Age-adjusted death rates are down substantially for leading causes of death amenable to improved medical care. Life expectancy at birth has increased by six years; almost half these gains can be attributed to improved medical care.

Medicaid, however, is currently undergoing strain. The expansion of coverage, increased disability, and rise in conditions such as Human Immunodeficiency Virus disease have placed fiscal pressure on federal and state budgets.

States have turned to managed care as a way of controlling costs. In a short period of time, one-third of Medicaid beneficiaries have been enrolled in managed care plans, often with inadequate quality controls or standards. Some states are planning to enroll their entire Medicaid population in such plans—not just mothers and children, but also those who are seriously disabled and frail. This is largely uncharted territory, and how well managed care plans that have little experience providing specialized services to low-income disabled populations will perform is an unanswered question.

Enactment of a children's health insurance program (CHIP) in 1997 provides matching funds to states to cover low-income children in families with incomes up to 200 percent of the poverty level. States can either expand coverage under Medicaid or establish a new children's health insurance program. This program could cover almost three-fourths of all uninsured children but its success hinges critically on state outreach efforts to enroll eligible children.

Medicare

Medicare is the major source of basic health insurance for the nation's 39 million elderly and disabled population. Particularly striking has been the program's success in improving access to care for low-income and minority elderly Americans. Racial disparities in care for elderly Americans have largely been eliminated, and Medicare was instrumental in spurring the desegregation of medical facilities. Medicare has also contributed to the development of research and innovation through its funding of medical education and more generous allowances for teaching hospitals.

Despite its success, Medicare benefits have remained relatively modest. It covers only half of the health care expenses of older people, both because it requires substantial cost sharing (e.g., a $768 deductible for hospital care in 1999 and 20 percent co-insurance for physician services) and because it does not cover such services as prescription drugs, dental care, and long-term care. Today, older Americans pay 21 percent of their own incomes for health care, and low-income elderly people, even with Medicaid supplemental coverage, devote 30 percent of their incomes to health care expenses.

Given current budgetary pressures, however, the prospects for improving benefits are dim. The rising cost of health care generally, as well as the increase in life expectancy and growing numbers of older people, are causing the program to increase at an 8–9 percent annual rate at a time when policy-makers are trying to contain the growth in the federal budget to a 4–5 percent rate. Various proposals have been advanced to curtail spending, including reductions in provider payment rates and health maintenance organization (HMO) premiums, overall expenditure caps, expansion of enrollment in managed care plans, substitution of current benefits for a fixed voucher or medical savings account combined with catastrophic coverage, and higher beneficiary financial contributions.

Even without legislative changes, increasing numbers of Medicare beneficiaries are enrolling in managed care plans. Currently, 6 million Medicare beneficiaries, or 18 percent of all Medicare beneficiaries, are enrolled in HMOs and enrollment has been growing rapidly. Beneficiary experience to date seems mixed. There is some evidence that relatively healthier beneficiaries are more likely to enroll in HMOs than are sicker beneficiaries. Among those joining, Medicare managed care beneficiaries are more likely to be found at both ends of the spectrum—either very satisfied or very dissatisfied with their care—than are those continuing under traditional Medicare coverage. Medicare beneficiaries enrolled in HMOs are less likely to be very satisfied or confident in their doctors' care and skills than those in traditional Medicare, yet more are satisfied with coverage of costs. Managed care plans offer comprehensive benefits, often with lower out-of-pocket costs to Medicare beneficiaries, and reduce the hassle of filing claims.

Proposals to substitute traditional Medicare coverage for vouchers or medical savings accounts would further segment the Medicare population. It seems likely that only the relatively well-to-do and healthy would be attracted to medical savings accounts combined with catastrophic health insurance coverage that leaves them financially responsible for health expenses of $5,000 or more per year. Since 75 percent of Medicare beneficiaries have incomes under $25,000, this financial liability is unlikely to be either attractive or sound for the bulk of beneficiaries.

These proposals share the limitation that they undermine the social insurance nature of Medicare, in which those who are healthy cross-subsidize those who are sick and those who are well-to-do pay more into the system than those who arc of modest means. Furthermore, they increase the uncertainty of out-of-pocket medical expenses in old age and threaten to undermine the gains in economic security achieved by older people in the last thirty years.

A Multi-Tiered Health System

Those fortunate enough to work for larger firms with generous health benefits and choices of plans and to have sufficient incomes and information to pick higher-quality coverage may continue to receive high-quality health care when needed. At the other extreme, a growing number of Americans (one-sixth of those under age 65) are without any health insurance coverage, and their access to sources of free care is increasingly limited by competition among health care providers to lower costs. Medicaid beneficiaries will increasingly be required to enroll in managed care plans, with as-yet-unknown consequences for quality of care and in an environment where the major priority is controlling costs. Lower-income workers who are fortunate enough to have employer-provided coverage still face financial burdens from required premium contributions and out-of-pocket costs, or they may be required to enroll in managed care plans that impose barriers to needed care. Medicare beneficiaries currently have choices of selecting their own physician or enrolling in a qualified managed care plan with at least minimum quality requirements, but mounting fiscal pressures may also segment beneficiaries into different arrangements with different consequences for access and quality.

All of these trends are the result of the uniquely American system of financing health care in different ways for different population groups, rather than a single universal system available to all. It is in striking contrast to health systems in other industrialized nations that provide comprehensive benefits with little or no out-of-pocket costs, cover the elderly and the non-elderly alike, and devote a much lower percentage of their national economic resources to health care. To argue that the United States is unable to afford comprehensive coverage for all when all other major industrialized nations do so is untenable. It is a reflection of policy choices that shape the U.S. health system— choices that can be changed to assure that all Americans have access to needed health care and that health and productivity of Americans is not undermined by inadequate prevention and treatment of health conditions. If we view health care as an investment and not merely as a budget cost, our present health system is very costly in the long run.

Sharing Economic Prosperity

A national health policy that assures health security for all Americans should have the following basic components:

- Commitment to financing health care for all, with the long-term goal of a single system for all;
- Incremental steps: expansion of public programs to the neediest uninsured;
- Preservation, protection, and strengthening of Medicare;
- Appropriate use of market forces to promote efficiency;
- Establishment and enforcement of uniform quality standards that apply to public and private plans.

Universal Coverage

Inequality in the U.S. health system is a by-product of a financing system that depends on employment, geographic location, income, family status, and age. Workers in larger firms are more likely to have health insurance than workers in smaller firms. Low-income mothers are more likely to be covered in states with generous Medicaid programs than in other states. Mothers with children are more likely to be covered than single adults. Americans over age 65 are typically covered by Medicare; early retirees under age 65 are not.

This patchwork system of health insurance leaves a large and growing number of Americans without any health insurance coverage. The erosion of the major pillar on which the U.S. health financing system is built—voluntarily provided employer health insurance—calls for a major shift in direction. Either all employers must be required by legislation to provide such coverage, or we as a nation must begin to move in the direction of a publicly financed system independent of employment.

The greatest assurance of equity would come with a single universal system of financing health coverage for all Americans. This will require a major change in the sources of financing a $1 trillion health industry, including identifying new tax-financing options. These tax revenues could replace employer-financed premiums, Medicare payroll taxes, and general revenue financing for Medicaid and a portion of Medicare—and would not necessarily represent net new payments. However, "winners and losers" are inevitable in such a major shift, and it will take time to develop national consensus on the best approach and transition to such a system.

In the meantime, efforts should be made to expand health insurance incrementally for those most in need. One approach would be the establishment of a national health insurance trust fund with a dedicated and fixed revenue contribution (e.g., $10 billion from such sources as cigarette taxes or dedication of taxes on for-profit health care providers) that would be used to purchase coverage under managed care plans, Medicaid, or Medicare for high-priority population groups. Uninsured low-income families, the unemployed, the disabled, and older adults, for example, would be candidates for coverage. Coverage would be expanded until annual revenues were used, at which point other eligible families would be placed on a waiting list. Gaining experience with such an approach would clarify the cost of different population groups and the administrative issues involved in offering a menu of choices to available families.

Medicare

Medicare is important to the health and economic security of older Americans. Federal budget pressures and the projected insolvency of the payroll-tax-financed Hospital Insurance Trust Fund portion of Medicare have spawned numerous proposals to restructure the program. These proposals have taken the form of reduced payments to hospitals, physicians, managed care plans, and other health care providers, as well as proposals to increase beneficiary financial contributions through increased premiums or cost-sharing; these latter proposals would provide incentives for beneficiaries to enroll in managed care plans. Other proposals would fundamentally alter the social insurance nature of Medicare, replacing current benefits with vouchers for the purchase of private insurance or managed care coverage, or vouchers to purchase private catastrophic coverage combined with tax-sheltered medical savings accounts.

These changes all run some risk of undermining the adequacy of Medicare, the quality of care available to beneficiaries, and the financial protection that Medicare affords against the high cost of health care for older and disabled Americans. In the short run, oversupply of hospital beds and physicians, especially specialist physicians, creates opportunities for modest tightening of provider payment rates without serious risk of limiting the willingness of providers to participate in Medicare. Over the long run, holding rates paid to hospitals, physicians, managed care plans, and other providers below rates paid by private insurers runs the risk of relegating older Americans to inferior health care.

Increasing financial contributions from Medicare beneficiaries is particularly problematic. Today, even with Medicare, older Americans devote 21 percent of their incomes to health care—over $2,600 per capita. Three-fourths of older Americans have incomes below $25,000—suggesting that further financial contributions are unrealistic. A genuine policy debate on Medicare would weigh the merits of paying more for health care during the working years (through payroll or other taxes) and reducing the costs borne during retirement. At a minimum, Medicaid should be expanded to provide better protection to low-income elderly Americans.

Options to replace Medicare with vouchers raise a number of concerns. Most importantly, they fragment older Americans into different arrangements. Those who are healthy and well-to-do are likely to be able to afford comprehensive coverage and high-quality care. But a limited voucher is likely to reduce choices for modest-income older people who could not afford the difference between the value of the voucher and premiums for comprehensive quality health care coverage. Nor is there evidence that private coverage is more efficient. To the contrary, Medicare's administrative costs average 2 percent of health outlays, compared with 15–20 percent in managed care plans and 30–50 percent in individual health insurance plans.

Retaining a high-quality Medicare program should be a top priority. It is in the interest of working Americans as well as retirees to be assured the health and economic security in old age that Medicare affords. While modest savings can be achieved through further tightening of provider payment rates and further incentives for health care providers to control costs, longer-term solutions will also need to look to additional revenues.

Market Incentives

Market incentives are transforming the American health care system. Large-scale purchasers, mostly managed care plans, are succeeding in getting price discounts from physicians and hospitals—in a largely oversupplied health care industry. Assuring genuine competition under multiple systems of care has promise for making health care more affordable and imposes much-needed restraints on health care costs. Consolidation and instability in the managed care industry, however, raise concerns about realizing this promise.

The incentives in fee-for-service care are to provide too many services at too high cost. The incentives in managed care are to provide too few services at too low quality. Effective competition between both traditional fee-for-service coverage and managed care at least holds the promise of avoiding the extreme of either system. Steps should be taken to preserve the choice of traditional fee-for-service options as well as expanding choice among managed care plans in coverage for working Americans as well as retirees.

Quality and Performance Standards

Choice is only meaningful, however, if systems of care offered to consumers meet quality and performance standards and if information on quality and performance is collected and disseminated to all parties. The National Committee for Quality Assurance is the major nonprofit accrediting body for managed care plans. It has begun, through its Health Employer Data Information System (HEDIS 3.0), to assemble quality and performance indicators on plans. However, currently only about half of managed care plans seek accreditation, and fewer than half voluntarily supply HEDIS data. Requirements that all managed care plans meet minimum quality standards, submit standardized data on quality and performance, and make such data available to the public are minimum safeguards required for the assurance of effective competition and quality. Patients should have the right to appeal denials of services external to the plan and the right to disengage from plans that are not meeting their needs. Physicians should have the right to act as advocates for their patients and assure that they have access to needed specialty care.

These elements of a quality and performance system are a beginning. Further research and methodological development will be required as the United States moves to this new system of financing and delivering health care. But the promise of better care for all is within our reach as a nation, and it should be part of national public policy to assure broadly shared prosperity in the twenty-first century.

E. Industrial Relations

31

Reconstructing the Social Contract in Employment Relations

Thomas A. Kochan

The primary challenge facing labor and employment policy in the next decade is to reconstruct the social contract between the American workforce and employers in ways that address the needs and realities of a modern economy and society. To do so, the country will need to modernize the labor and employment policies carried over from the New Deal era and foster innovations in labor unions, labor market institutions, corporations, and in their relationships. In this essay, I will sketch out an alternative policy framework that I believe would foster the innovations needed, recognizing that the political will to seriously debate—much less enact—this set of changes is sorely lacking today.[1]

The term social contract is often used but seldom defined. I use it to characterize the mutual expectations and obligations that employees, employers, and society at large have for work and employment relationships. The social contract that is under duress today grew up over the decades following World War II in which an expanding economy produced a set of rising expectations and aspirations that carried over to relations at the workplace. While a caricature, the features of that social contract generally included the expectation that wages and earnings would rise in tandem with increasing productivity and prosperity of employers and the economy. Hard work, good performance, and loyalty would be rewarded with security, fair treatment, dignity, and status. Increased tenure with a firm conveyed certain "property rights" to a job—that is, job and income security would accumulate over time with tenure, thereby producing an upward sloping age-earning profile, rising standards of living, and savings for retirement.

Other essays in this volume document the breakdown in the features of this contract in recent years, and therefore, I need not do more than highlight them to set the stage for the analysis to follow. At the macro-level, the economy has performed relatively well in generating new jobs, reducing unemployment, controlling inflation, and improving the competitiveness of American firms in global markets. Compared to historical standards, however, it has performed relatively poorly when measured against improvements in real earnings, income inequality, employment security, and income security for workers displaced due to economic and organizational restructuring. Therefore, improving the quality of jobs and employment outcomes must be a primary objective.

The United States has performed poorly on another dimension of national welfare that does not show up in aggregate economic statistics: It has allowed relationships among business, labor, and government leaders to deteriorate and become more adversarial, thereby reducing their capacity to innovate and adjust to the changing workforce and economy. A critical task for labor and employment policy-makers lies in reconstructing positive relations among these institutions.

But changes in public policy alone are not sufficient. To address the needs of today's labor force and economy, policy changes need to be matched by equally fundamental institutional reforms and innovations involving labor, community, education, and employer organizations. What follows is a sketch of the policy and institutional changes that I believe are needed.

Traditional Perspectives on the Employment Relationship

For more than sixty years, American labor and employment policies have been predicated on a view of work and employment as a long-term relationship involving a large firm competing mostly in an expanding domestic market and one of two types of employees—hourly wage workers or salaried managers—with a spouse at home attending to family and personal matters. However, today's labor force and employment practices vary considerably from this standard picture. The distinction between management and labor is increasingly blurred by the movement to decentralize decision-making and the growth in technical, middle- and lower-level managerial, and professional occupations. The increased labor force participation of women not only has changed the demographic make-up of the labor force but challenges deeply entrenched assumptions about the relationships of work, family, and personal life. The prevalence of part-time work and the growth of temporary,

contract, and self-employed workers, along with the increased risk of permanent job loss, adds further variation to employment relationships.

The New Deal employment policies focused on the domestic economy. The underlying objective of these policies has been to standardize conditions at the high levels Americans expect and thereby "take wages and terms of employment out of competition." However, globalization increased competition and ease of entry into highly differentiated domestic markets, rendering efforts to take wages out of competition difficult, if not impossible. In the absence of improvements in labor force quality, availability, and utilization, this inability to standardize wages leads to both a decline in wages of those lacking the skills needed to provide firms with a competitive advantage on the basis of product quality, technological innovation, and customer service and to an increase in the premiums offered to those who have the skills and abilities needed by firms seeking to compete on these other grounds. Thus, the future of the overall wage structure and income distribution in the United States will be determined by the ability of our policies and institutions to supply a labor force with the skills needed to compete on bases other than wages and labor costs and to encourage American firms to compete on this basis rather than get mired in a fruitless "race to the bottom."

The New Deal labor policies were based on a fundamental premise that continues to be valid and useful in an economy with highly varied employment relationships—that is, the premise underlying collective bargaining has always been that the parties closest to the problems of their workplace are best positioned to shape the terms and conditions of employment that suit their needs and circumstances. This, I would argue, is a first principle to which we need to return if we are to reconstruct a social contract suited to today's economy and workforce; however, to implement this principle in today's economy will require several fundamental changes in perspectives.

First, the implicit model of the standard employment relationship needs to be replaced with a more accurate view of the range of employment settings observed in today's economy. The starting premise must recognize and build on the variations found in contemporary employment relationships. The goal should be to encourage continuous improvement in employment practices and standards in ways that allow flexibility in how the underlying policy goals are achieved.

Second, employment policies should support mobility across jobs and employers. Policies that encourage high and improving employment standards and practices within individual firms and employment settings need to be integrated with policies to encourage mobility so that the costs of job changing are reduced and the costs to employers of hiring and developing new employees are lowered.

Third, the enforcement and monitoring of employment regulations should also build on the variations in employment settings by encouraging the development and maintenance of democratic self-governance among the parties to employment relationships. By recognizing that the parties closest to the workplace know the most about how to adapt broad principles to their particular circumstances and giving them the opportunities to implement those adaptations, we can achieve the goals of national policies both more efficiently and effectively and encourage practices and innovations that move us above the minimum standards required by law.

Finally, the twenty-year record of failed efforts at incremental reforms or negotiated compromises within the existing policy framework suggests a different approach is needed to the design and enactment of labor and employment policies. The marginalization of these issues to the status of "special interest politics" and the inability of the traditional interest groups—labor and business—to negotiate compromise or incremental reforms in the face of mounting problems suggest new participants need to be brought into the process. In short, a broader constituency needs be created that sees an effective and modern labor and employment policy vital to its goals and aspirations. Workers at all occupational levels are an important part of this constituency, and therefore, we need to listen attentively to their voices and bring them into the policy-making process.

The Substantive Challenges

The foundation for a policy that supports renegotiating the social contract in employment lies in the rules governing interactions among employees and employers in negotiating the terms and conditions of employment and their day-to-day administration. Unfortunately, this aspect of American labor law is perhaps the most outdated and ineffective of all components of employment policy. This was one of the basic conclusions documented in the Fact-Finding Report of the Commission on the Future of Worker-Management Relations. The following section reviews the three sets of problems identified by this report.

Failure of Labor Law

A basic tenet of the National Labor Relations Act (NLRA) is that employees should be able to choose whether or not they wish to be represented by a labor union for the purpose of collective bargaining. This is a bedrock principle for labor policy in any democracy and remains as valid and necessary today as it was when first embodied in national policy in the 1930s. Unfortunately, rather than a free choice, the process by which employees gain access to union representation today often resembles a high-pitched, high-stakes battle in which the benefits to the winners and the costs to the losers are very high. Consider the basic facts:

1. The level of conflict as measured by the number of unfair labor practices that occur and the likelihood of legal challenges that extend the time required to complete representation elections have increased over the years, resulting in rising frustrations among workers and unions with these procedures. The reality today is that only a very small number of workers and unions trust and use the election procedures. (In the 1990s, on average, less than 250,000 workers voted in certification elections per year, out of approximately 65 million non-union workers eligible under the law.)

2. The probability that a worker will be discharged or discriminated against for attempting to organize a union increased over the past twenty years. Approximately 25 percent of representation elections result in at least one worker being illegally discharged.

3. Where unions win elections, approximately one-third fail to achieve a first contract as the battle over initial recognition continues into the negotiations process.

These problems could be addressed by improving the procedures and legal remedies that govern organizing and representation elections. Unnecessary delays in elections could be reduced by broader use of injunctions to put workers discharged during organizing campaigns back to work immediately. Challenges to bargaining units could be heard by the National Labor Relations Board (NLRB) after the election is held and the results tabulated. Arbitration of first contracts could be provided where necessary to achieve a fair first contract. Indeed, these are essential starting points for remedying longstanding and clearly documented injustices in the law.

But these changes are only a starting point. Alone, they do nothing to address the following structural limitations of the NLRA: The only way to gain union representation is for workers to convince a majority of their peers that management cannot be trusted (or in plain English, that the employer is a bastard) and that they should risk their jobs to gain representation. If a majority cannot be convinced—or is unsuccessful in overcoming the delays, employer opposition, and workplace tensions that accompany the union recognition and first-contract bargaining processes—no individual gets representation even if up to 49 percent want to be represented. If the workers establish a bargaining relationship they can expect the employer to resist contract improvements to the extent that competitors are not also organized and likely to match the union-negotiated gains.

In fact, the United States has the most rigid and high-cost system of worker representation of all industrialized democratic countries. The risks and costs to workers come in the difficulty any individual has in gaining access to representation under the law. The costs to employers come if they do get unionized and must compete against non-union domestic employers or with firms from a low-wage country.

The result of this limited system and the difficulties workers encounter in using it to address their key interests are visible in numerous worker surveys. About one-third of the non-union workforce express an interest in joining a union. This implies that nearly 25 million workers want to be represented by a union but cannot gain access to representation. Approximately 70 to 80 percent of the respondents to these survey indicate an interest in being part of a process that consults and has significant influence in decision-making but that has the cooperation, not the opposition, of management. The clear and consistent message is that workers want more varied forms of participation and representation than the type promised but not realized in the NLRA.

Given that the primary focus of collective bargaining remains wages, benefits, and working conditions, employers have strong incentives to resist unions and, once organized, must compete with non-union firms that are, on average, likely to experience at least 10 to 20 percent lower wage and benefit costs (in some cases more). While some of these costs to employers are unavoidable, the trade-off between representation and employer costs could be reduced by opening the law up to allow for alternative types of representation in addition to exclusive representation under collective bargaining. Some of these might involve the type of direct employee participation that will be discussed below; however, others could involve a variety of elected or jointly selected workplace councils that involve all employees, worker representation in corporate governance structures, and so on. One advantage of opening the law to these alternatives is that it would encourage the type of institutional innovation in labor organizations called for later in this essay.

Failure of Labor Law to Promote Direct Participation

In response to intensified competition and worker expectations for a voice in workplace affairs, most American employers have introduced one or more types of direct employee representation. Recent surveys find these pro-grams equally likely in unionized as well as non-union workplaces. Employee surveys indicate a high level of interest in having the opportunity to participate directly in workplace decisions affecting their job. The evidence suggests that the broader the scope of the innovations, the bigger their effects on productivity and quality. Yet, the broader their scope, the more likely they are to also violate the NLRA. Thus, the labor law inherited from the New Deal era fails to encourage and support new forms of employee participation that hold promise to improve economic performance and worker welfare.

These limitations could in theory be addressed by eliminating or modifying section 8(a)(2) of the NLRA that limits employee participation in non-union settings. The problem with this type of surgical excision is that it would not only leave the other problems with the law unaddressed, but also would make it more difficult for workers to gain independent representation since one of the most effective union avoidance strategies an employer can mount is the promise of an employee participation program. Thus, any easing or elimination of the restrictions on employee participation needs to be accompanied by increased opportunities for workers to choose the forms of participation and representation that best suit their circumstances and needs. As will be noted below, opening up labor policy in this way would also foster the institutional innovations needed to improve the effectiveness of workplace regulations.

Increased Regulations, Declining Enforcement

A third problem relates to the range of regulations governing specific workplace issues or practices. The number of regulations has grown; the number of claims brought before enforcement agencies has increased, even as staffing levels and other resources have been kept flat or declined; and the number of members of the labor force that are either excluded de facto for lack of resources or de jure for falling outside the definition of a "covered employee" renders these legal protections meaningless for large numbers of workers. Thus, an overhaul is needed of both the scope of coverage and the means used to enforce and monitor compliance with these regulations. Recently, the Occupational Safety and Health Administration (OSHA), the Equal Employment Opportunity Commission (EEOC), and the Department of Labor's regulatory agencies all announced initiatives to encourage alternatives for resolving problems and increasing compliance. OSHA, for example, encouraged state and regional experimentation with self-governance programs in which inspections and penalties were reduced in workplaces that implement comprehensive safety and health programs that include employee participation. The EEOC and the Department of Labor are experimenting with voluntary mediation and arbitration to resolve claimed violations of employees' statutory rights. But all of these efforts risk violating labor law by encouraging employee participation on working conditions covered under the NLRA. Safety, for example, is a mandatory subject of bargaining. Labor-management committees in non-union settings that make effective recommendations on safety issues would likely violate NLRA's section 8(a)(2).

Similar problems are likely with the expanded use of the alternative dispute resolution (ADR) to resolve workplace disputes involving statutory rights. Most experts agree that ADR works best when it is part of a comprehensive workplace justice system that includes internal grievance and appeal procedures that often involve employee committees to hear complaints and recommend resolutions. Again, these processes, which more and more firms are implementing to address the diverse workplace conflicts, run afoul of the NLRA's restrictions on employee participation in non-union settings.

A second challenge to the use of ADR and workplace self-governance procedures is that individual workers are at a significant power disadvantage in addressing safety concerns vis-à-vis their employer. Civil rights advocates, women's groups, and union representatives have voiced this critique with particular passion. To the extent this is a problem, the obvious solution is for unions and/or other advocacy groups to provide representation services to individuals and groups that require it. This is both a challenge and an opportunity for labor organizations. Again, however, it will take the reforms in labor law proposed above to permit this new type of representation.

Lagging Changes in Labor Markets

So far, the changes in labor policies and regulations suggested focus on relationships inside the firm. Yet increasingly, workers' economic security and advancement are determined by their ability to move across jobs and employers. Wage inequality has risen dramatically in response to increased premiums firms place on education and skills with new technologies, work practices, and behavioral attributes. Permanent job loss has increased relative to temporary layoffs and spread to a broader range of occupations, therefore increasing the importance of policies to support mobility without large losses in earning power and income security. This, in turn, increases the importance of lifelong learning and human capital development and maintenance.

Given these new realities, labor market policies need to lower inter-firm costs to both individuals and firms. This implies the need to decouple provision of health insurance coverage from individual firms, increase the portability of pension benefits and other retirement savings plans, modify unemployment insurance coverage to cover employees with shorter employment durations with single employers, and to extend benefits to employees who invest in training or retraining when making a transition between jobs. Indeed, it may be time for a detailed and comprehensive look at labor market policies to ask how they might be reformed to accommodate a more mobile and transient workforce.

Complementary Institutional Reforms

Full-service Unions

I have argued elsewhere for "full-service" unions—representative institutions that provide the full range of services discussed above, including individual representation and labor market service of workers over the course of their careers regardless of where and for whom they work, support and training for direct employee participation, collective bargaining, and representation in corporate governance. The changes in policy discussed above would both create a market and a need for this array of services. Existing union and professional associations, perhaps along with new employee organizations, would compete for members. In this way, workers might regain control over

whether or not and by what type of organization they will be represented.

Employer Networks

Organizational theorists and management consultants predict that the organization of the future increasingly will have features of a network—an entity that has seamless boundaries linked to numerous other organizations and institutions in its supplier, customer, and contractor network. This would pose significant challenges to employee relations. The biggest effect would blur authority relationships and increase uncertainty over who should manage the workforce and insure compliance with employment regulations in settings that mix employees and contract workers, consultants, and others in the same work environment. Evidence from the petrochemical industry demonstrates that contractor relationships can cause a host of problems and risks, including increased safety risks that result from labor relations tensions and conflicts, lower levels of training and experience associated with short-term employment relationships, and gaps in supervision resulting from the desire to avoid co-employment liabilities. While clarifying the rules over the responsibility of different employers is a necessary first step in insuring that workers in these settings obtain the legal protections, ultimately effective management of these relationships requires coordination among the participating organizations.

Greater coordination among employers also is needed to overcome a classic market failure with respect to training and employability. No individual employer has an incentive to train workers in the skills needed to maintain their external marketability, yet collectively all firms, as well as employees and the overall economy, would benefit if workforce skills were maintained in this fashion. Thus, employer networks that pool resources and establish common skill standards for different occupations will be needed if the labor market of the future is to function efficiently.

Professional Networks

If employees are to change jobs and firms frequently, human resource professionals will need to work together with educational, labor, and labor market professionals to smooth these transitions and lower their costs to both employees and employers. Common training programs, occupational standards, and pooled benefit and pension plans that move with employees will all need to be common features of future labor markets. To achieve this, human resource professionals need to reverse the trend of the past two decades, which saw them look inward to top executives to set their professional agenda. They must engage labor union representatives, community organizations, education institutions, and social service agencies in constructive dialogue aimed at creating the networks to support a more mobile workforce and fluid labor market. But given the polarization between business and labor, such networks are difficult to create and sustain, unless the agenda is so inconsequential as to avoid the tough issues separating these parties. This is another cost to the current stalemate and polarization between workers and employers that must be overcome if we are to foster the innovations needed to update the social contracts governing contemporary employment relationships.

Human Capital and the American Corporation

The legal rules specifying that the goal of the American corporation is to maximize share-holder wealth grew out of an environment in the early part of this century when it was necessary to pool large amounts of finance capital to build the large-scale companies capable of serving the expanding mass markets. Thus, the owners of finance capital became the primary "residual risk" bearers and the most powerful beneficiaries of the firm's success. If we are to renegotiate the social contract in employment, we may need to open up a debate over the goals of the corporation, its governance structures and processes, and particularly over the role of human capital as both a critical asset and a residual risk bearer. In many cases today, the human assets are the firm's most critical resource, yet both employment and corporate laws, and the ideologies that support them, deter employees and their representatives from participating in corporate governance and shaping corporate practices to achieve mutual gains or more equitable tradeoffs and distributions of rewards to all the stakeholders who bear residual risks of corporate failure. This is perhaps the most controversial idea raised in this paper, but one that I believe deserves a place on the policy agenda if we are to update the full range of institutions that influences the nature of social contracts in employment relationships.

Conclusions

The above discussion suggests there is no single new social contract that meets the needs of the economy and the labor force of the future. Thus, the challenge lies in providing the parties to employment relationships with the tools to renegotiate their relationships to suit their needs. For those with sufficient skills and labor market power this might be done on an individual basis. For many, however, who prefer or depend on collective efforts, it will require labor and employment laws outlined here.

This is a tall order, and one that presently lacks a significant political constituency. It includes several changes favored by labor and opposed by management and vice versa, and ideas that neither party favors and both perceive as threats to their interests. But this is what is needed to break the political logjam that has been reinforced by years of failed effort at incremental reforms within the prevailing legal structures. Nevertheless, there is little reason to believe significant change will be forthcoming in the short run. Instead, a more realistic hope might be that encouraging experimentation at the grassroots level with new approaches to the issues facing employers and workers will create the empirical basis for policy and institutional innovations when the pressures to do something can no longer be avoided.

Note

1. Support for this work was provided by the William and Flora Hewlett Foundation and the Alfred P. Sloan Foundation. The views expressed are solely the author's.

32

Employee Involvement and Representation: Economic and Policy Implications

Paula Voos

Introduction

Today, there is considerable discussion of the need for greater employee involvement in workplace decision-making. This perceived need for greater employee voice reflects a fundamental structural feature of current American society—corporations do not guarantee that employees have many rights or much influence over workplace decisions. This is an anomaly in a society that generally values individual rights and democratic voice. Employee involvement and representation both promise an increased degree of workplace democracy.

Three types of initiatives have been posited as contributing to employee voice:

1. *Employer-provided employee involvement structures.* This includes worker participation/consultation programs of various types, total quality management programs, work-reorganization initiatives such as teams, and other related human resources (HR) innovations.

2. *Institutions that are universal as a matter of law (or available in all workplaces over a certain minimum size or that meet other criteria).* Examples would be the works councils found in many West European countries, em-ployee representation on corporate boards, or more-limited structures such as universally required health and safety or training committees.

3. *Employee representation through independent labor organizations (unions).* In the United States, unions primarily provide representation through collective bargaining and related grievance arbitration systems. This basic form of employee voice is sometimes supplemented through negotiated employee involvement, teams, health and safety committees, and periodic union-management consultation.

Continuing growth in U.S. income inequality in the 1990s and declines in the standard of living for those in the bottom 80 percent of the income distribution have led many to ask how we can promote a rising and more broadly shared standard of living, and ultimately a more democratic and stable society. Do employee involvement and representation contribute to these goals, and if so, which initiatives are most promising? This question and the implications for public policy are the focus of this essay.

Economic Considerations

A variety of claims have been made about the economic effects of employer-provided involvement, universal workplace institutions, and collective bargaining. What summary judgments are reasonable about whether these alternatives promote a rising and more broadly shared standard of living?

Employer-Provided Involvement Programs

A variety of employer-provided employee involvement programs have been implemented in the past twenty years. The growing consensus about the economic effects of these programs is aptly summarized by Casey Ichniowski et al.:

> A collage of evidence suggests that innovative workplace practices can increase performance, primarily through the use of systems of related practices that enhance worker participation, make work design less rigid, and decentralize management tasks. A majority of U.S. businesses have adopted some innovative work practices. However, only a small percentage of businesses have adopted a full system of innovative practices.[1]

That is, organizations adopting a holistic, systematic bundle of practices—variously termed a "high-commitment" or "high-performance" work organization—have the largest positive gains. There is consensus on some of the practices that are part of this bundle: a non-authoritarian management style, movement of decision-making downward in the organization, more flexibility in internal work organization through teams or other flexible work practices, regular labor-management information sharing, increased employee training, and enhanced job security.

There is less consensus, however, on the needed accompanying compensation practices—with some seeing contingent and flexible compensation in the form of gainsharing, profit-sharing, and even traditional non-union "merit pay" as essential elements of the bundle. Others emphasize the need for a "positive reward system" that de-emphasizes the negative motivators used in mass production systems (fear of discharge or punishment, individualistic incentives such as piece rates) and instead gives employees security in the form of an adequate, non-contingent compensation package, with gainsharing, other group incentives, or pay-for-knowledge used as "add-ons" to motivate performance.

In short, research to date reveals that management-provided employee involvement programs usually make small contributions to enhancing economic performance, but holistic high-performance initiatives have larger positive effects. Very little systematic attention has been paid to the impact of employee involvement on the distribution of income. This is because these programs are neither intended to be, nor have been evaluated as, vehicles of income redistribution.

Institutions That Are Universal as a Matter of Law

The economic implications of legally required institutions such as works councils or health and safety committees are less clearly understood, although again most discussions assume that they have negligible impact on the distribution of income.

Many observers of German works councils have argued that they have positive effects on economic efficiency at the enterprise level. Councils increase the flow of information in the firm, aid in the diffusion and implementation of advanced production practices, facilitate trust, and encourage economic upgrading as a competitive strategy. While they also have costs (e.g., slowing decision-making), most European managers report that, on balance, councils benefit employers, although econometric studies have not managed to substantiate a statistically significant impact of councils on productivity. Recent economic criticisms of the "German system" have been aimed at its social welfare provisions and legal regulation of employment—not at works councils themselves—indicating that both labor and management view councils as beneficial.

Health and safety committees typically are evaluated in more limited terms: Do they succeed in making the workplace safer and in reducing the cost of workplace mortality and morbidity? Many Canadian provinces and some states require employers over a certain size to establish joint health and safety committees, providing a legal guarantee of a minimum degree of worker participation in this area of crucial importance to employees. There is evidence that employee participation through committees does improve health and safety compliance, reduce workers' compensation costs, and thus provide an economic benefit to society as a whole.

Employee Representation Through Independent Labor Organizations (Unions)

Unions raise wages and benefits of represented employees. In the United States, virtually all important benefits (pensions, health insurance, paid vacations) were initially brought to non-managers by collective bargaining, and unions continue to shift compensation toward benefits. Unions have worked to make income distribution more equal; contemporary studies demonstrate that unionization reduces the inequality of wages among workers with similar skills and increases the share of the economic pie enjoyed by labor as a whole. This is particu-

larly true in sectors characterized by monopoly profits or other economic rents. The continuing decline in union representation since the early 1970s has been one factor contributing to growing income inequality.

Unions traditionally have been able to raise wages and improve benefits by standardizing them across competing employers, forcing firms to compete on the basis of quality, customer service, and productivity—rather than low wages, long hours, unsafe work, child or prison labor, or other strategies that depress the standard of living. This has been called "taking wages out of competition," and it requires labor organizations that reach across competing employers. Other compensation-increasing practices have included productivity bargaining (the explicit trading of productivity-enhancing work practices or participation in "continuous improvement" programs for higher compensation) and union apprenticeships and other systematic training programs.

Labor unions raise wages and benefits at a relatively small cost to economic efficiency—all recent estimates of the cost are less than 1 percent of GNP. These estimates of static "welfare loss" do not include the positive economic effects of labor organizations. Unions reduce the turnover of employees and thereby enhance the retention and accumulation of skills, encourage employer-provided training, and improve health and safety on the job. There is little evidence that unions generally harm productivity—rather, in many sectors they are associated with higher productivity, especially where there is a constructive labor-management relations climate. Higher skill formation and retention, more capital per worker, productivity bargaining, and more management attention to efficiency in the context of higher labor costs all accompany collective bargaining.

Given all these effects, it is reasonable to view unions as having a small positive effect on economic efficiency (or at worst, no effect) at the same time they reduce inequality and hence promote a wider sharing of economic prosperity.

Combinations of the Three Types of Initiatives

In the United States, because of the absence of workplace involvement structures that are universally required by law, the most common combination is that of collective bargaining and employee involvement programs. There are a number of reasons to believe that where unions support high-commitment or high-performance workplace initiatives and are involved in designing and operating the involvement process, these efforts are likely to have greater potential for enhancing economic performance. Since employee involvement itself has positive effects on efficiency (with little effect on the distribution of income) and since unions tend to reduce income inequality (with a small positive or no effect on efficiency), the combination might reasonably be expected to promote both greater equality and a rising standard of living.

Considerations Related to Employee Voice and Democracy in the Workplace

Employer-provided involvement, universally required workplace institutions, and union representation provide different types and different degrees of workplace democracy. American unions have focused largely on providing a degree of representative democracy in the workplace—of employee input through bargaining—affecting employee compensation, treatment of individual employees in disciplinary situations, and work rules or practices. Works councils, or

legislated provision for employee representation on boards of directors, provide alternative avenues of representative democracy in some other industrial nations, typically in conjunction with collective bargaining.

In contrast, the employee involvement movement and most of the associated programs provided by employers focus on providing a degree of participatory democracy or direct involvement of workers in the decisions that affect their working lives. Teams, quality circles, total quality management plans, and so forth do not typically involve workers in making decisions on compensation or the fair treatment of individuals.

Individual Rights Related to Workplace Democracy

Whether it is representative or participatory, democracy is made real through a series of rights and responsibilities. Freedom of speech, freedom of association, habeas corpus, and other individual rights clearly are necessary for real democracy—individuals in American society can criticize the existing government and organize associations to change its policies because in doing so they are not likely to be accused of a crime and placed in prison. Similarly, individual rights in the workplace are crucial for employee voice.

Consider the typical set of rights accorded employees in a union workplace as opposed to a non-union workplace (see Table 32.1). Clearly, union workers enjoy greater freedom of speech (and more freedom to criticize management or existing work practices), greater freedom of association (including the crucial right to caucus on what workers want from any existing participation process), and more freedom to meet openly with independent experts on workplace issues or with union representatives; they also

Table 32.1

Democratic Rights in the Workplace

Democratic Right	Non-Union Workplace	Union Workplace
Freedom of Speech	**Limited**	**Substantial**
	The ease of discharge under employment-at-will and firm control over pay and promotions can create an environment of self-censorship.	The contract limits favoritism in pay or promotions; workers cannot be fired for speaking up because of "just cause" provisions in contracts.
Freedom of Association	**Uncommon**	**Standard**
	Participation programs usually lack right of caucus for workers and provide limited means of employee input into meeting agendas or overall program operation.	Workers use the union to discuss what they want from participation programs; input into program operation, meeting agendas, and caucuses are more common.
		Unionism is a result of freedom of association; democracy determines union leaders and policies, including the position on involvement itself.
Freedom of Assembly	**Limited**	**Standard**
	Workers have no right to meet with outside experts or union representatives in non-work areas and may be discouraged from meeting with each other at work.	Meetings in non-work areas are often possible by agreement; otherwise workers can meet in the union hall.
	Non-union workers have the right to strike but in reality it is difficult to exercise that right.	A clear right to strike exists within rules on timing, pickets, primary disputes, etc. Management, however, has the right to permanently replace strikers.
Rights When Accused	**Uncommon**	**Substantial**
Know the charge; Present evidence; cross-examine witnesses	Rights are only as given by management, and management usually decides the outcome.	Grievance arbitration systems have these rights, including representation by the union and a final decision by a neutral party.
Have legal representation; Neutral judgment; (judge [civil] or jury [criminal])	Employees may not know the allegation or the person making it. No lawyer or union representative is typically present.	

have greater guarantees of just treatment when accused of violating workplace rules. If an employee involvement process is in place, union workers typically enjoy more influence over the entire involvement process and more rights in that process. Finally, unions grant workers the opportunity to initiate employee involvement (explaining the greater prevalence of health and safety committees in the union sector) and provide some protection against the unilateral discontinuation of programs or committees by management.

Progressive non-union companies unilaterally instituting high-performance work reorganization try to assure employees of some degree of free speech and fair treatment (sometimes through alternative dispute resolution [ADR] or peer review). Still any neutral observer would view the typical resulting procedures as providing "softer" rights (that is, fewer or less clearly defined and enforceable rights) than exist in a typical union company. For instance, ADR procedures usually cover a limited range of rights provided by U.S. law (like freedom from discrimination) whereas the "just cause" provisions of union contracts ensure that employees cannot be disciplined or discharged for anything other than a valid reason. Virtually all non-union employers have retained control of compensation decisions.

Individual employee rights also are relevant for the operation of works councils, legally required health and safety committees, training committees, or other universal involvement structures. Free speech, freedom of association/assembly, and protection against unfair dismissal are needed to increase the effectiveness of such universal institutions and ensure that they expand workplace democracy.

Public Policy Implications

What does this discussion suggest about the highest priorities for public policy on employee involvement and representation, given the need to simultaneously promote and encourage a wider sharing of prosperity? I would advocate (1) providing everyone with the individual rights needed for the successful exercise of democratic voice in the workplace, (2) insuring that all employees participate in certain workplace decisions (especially regarding health and safety), and (3) promoting widespread union representation through enhanced organizing and bargaining rights.

Employee Involvement

Employee participation in health and safety is especially important and legislation should insure the existence of health and safety programs utilizing employee involvement in all workplaces. Beyond this reasonable minimum, public policy should encourage both more extensive involvement and more comprehensive high-performance initiatives. The Commission on the Future of Worker-Management Relations, of which I was a part, made a number of constructive proposals to reform labor law toward this end, including a clarification of the legality of most such current programs in the context of a continued ban on employer-dominated labor organizations, a reduction in the scope of the supervisory and managerial exclusions from coverage (to facilitate teams and the movement of decision-making downward in the organization), and the authorization of pre-hire agreements (encouraging labor-management partnership).

Additionally, legislation enhancing the free-speech rights of individuals in all workplaces would vitally aid employer-provided employee involvement initiatives—both by providing the individual liberty necessary for the successful functioning of participatory democracy and by removing a barrier to their establishment. National legislation guaranteeing a just or good cause standard of dismissal for non-probationary employees also would promote involvement. While other rights (see Table 32.1) also would be beneficial, removing the barriers to free speech is the logical first step to giving employees more voice.

Most importantly, public policy should reaffirm workers' rights to choose union represen-

Table 32.2

Priorities for Reform of Conventional Labor Law

Return choice to employees, and make the process less bureaucratic
- Certify based on authorization cards where there is a "supermajority."
- Hold representation elections in other units quickly by hearing challenges after the election.

Reduce unfair labor practices
- Require that the National Labor Relations Board applies for injunctions to return workers to work where there is prima facie evidence of unlawful discharge.
- Increase penalties for unfair labor practices.

Encourage bargaining
- Make it illegal to permanently replace strikers (encouraging compromise).
- Provide final and binding interest arbitration for first contracts (encouraging compromise).

Make information and access more equal
- Increase union access: malls, parking lots, non-working areas of the job.
- Allow union supporters to speak at any "captive audience" meetings held by the employer.

Expand coverage of the law and its protection of workers
- Update the definitions of supervisor and manager to insure that only those with full supervisory or managerial authority and responsibility are excluded from coverage.
- Ensure that no one is excluded because of participation in group decision processes, such as work teams.
- Reaffirm and extend protections of individuals against discrimination for participating in employee involvement processes or for drawing on the services of an outside labor organization.
- Grant supervisors the right to remain neutral in organizing campaigns.

tation, because collective bargaining gives employees a way to effect changes in the workplace—involvement, health and safety committees, higher compensation, more security, or whatever. Union representation gives employees the individual rights in the workplace that are crucial for effective participation. It also gives employees as a group some degree of independent power. Alone, or in conjunction with employee involvement, union representation is the one form of employee voice that would contribute to a more equal sharing of prosperity and reduction in income inequality. Collective bargaining is particularly suited to a political environment suspicious of government-mandated universal solutions.

For all these reasons, my top policy priority would be reform of labor law that would encourage collective bargaining by making it not only *possible,* but actually *easy* for employees

to organize. Conventional reform, of the type detailed in Table 32.2, is necessary but not sufficient for this purpose. Such conventional reform would re-empower employee choice in stable employment situations, but would do little in other emerging employment situations with less stable employment practices. Reforming labor law to provide for increased opportunities for occupational, market-wide labor organizations in situations with many small employers, and considerable inter-firm mobility (whether or not employment is formally contingent) is increasingly important. While a variety of legal changes might be useful, the most promising ones would facilitate consultation between employers and employee representatives where a significant number, but not a majority of employees, designate a labor or other organization as their workplace representative. Such meet-and-confer rights for "minority" or "members-only" labor organizations would have to be carefully drawn to coexist with the U.S. practice of exclusive bargaining rights for labor organizations that have demonstrated majority status.

Nonetheless, encouraging individuals to join labor organizations that have some ability to represent them before they achieve majority status with a group of employers would greatly facilitate market-wide occupational or associational organizations.

None of these public policy initiatives are likely to be politically easy to implement. Legislation encouraging employee involvement in health and safety is probably least daunting given that a number of states now require such committees in firms over a certain size. Tom Kochan persuaded me that works councils or similar encompassing institutions of workplace governance would need to emerge incrementally before national legislation in the area is feasible. Americans fundamentally value individual liberty, so national "good cause" legislation has a wide potential constituency; at present, however, there is no major political movement for such legislation.

Given the current low levels of union representation, many despair of passing legislation promoting collective bargaining. While such pessimism is understandable, it seems to me that a law promoting collective bargaining is at least as feasible as the major alternatives. Labor history is replete with examples of labor movements that have surmounted legal environments that are less hospitable to organization than that of the United States today. If we do not provide legal means whereby employees can exercise the human impulse to mutual aid and mutual self-help, then we are likely to face a more militant labor movement, rather than no labor movement whatsoever. Frustration over labor law reform is one factor contributing to the current shift in the AFL-CIO toward an activist, socially-conscious, innovative movement that emphasizes organizing—within or without the law. If we want to promote a stable, democratic society, with a rising and broadly shared standard of living, then it would be wise to offer employees improved legal channels for achieving union representation.

Note

1. Casey Ichniowski et al., "What Works and What Doesn't," *Industrial Relations* (July 1996): 299.

F. Corporate Governance

33

Financial Market Barriers to High-Performance Work Organizations

Eileen Appelbaum and Peter Berg

Introduction

As companies find themselves competing in markets characterized by differentiated products, high standards of product quality, rapid development of new products, and quick delivery of finished goods, improvements in productivity and reductions in costs depend critically on the nature of the production system and on human resources. The decision to transform the basic organization of production from a system based on the principles of mass production and Taylorism to one with an entirely different organizational logic may be critical to the ability of the United States to maintain a strong presence in manufacturing and producer services, particularly in traditional industries. In the 1990s, production capacity is as much a matter of investment in work organization and worker skills as it is of additions to the capital stock.

This essay examines in some detail a dramatic set of developments in corporate finance in the United States during the 1980s—developments that paralleled, in time at least, considerably more experimentation with high-performance work systems. These new financial matters include developments in corporate control, the shareholder revolution, and the economic theory of agency. The thesis of this essay is that, as a result of

these changes, financial markets have played an increasing, and detrimental, role in discouraging companies from making the large investments necessary to transform the production process.

It is by no means certain that the strategies associated with the adoption of high-performance work systems will win out in the United States over those focused more narrowly on immediate cost containment and downsizing. In contrast to the neoclassical economic assumption that the most efficient uses of technology and organization are both available to firms and easily achieved, a more dynamic theory suggests that firms' choices are affected by management structures, organizational systems, and company strategies, which are shaped, in turn, by the institutional framework within which firms operate. Most important are the financial system, which affects the firm's ability to modernize or invest in new technology and in such intangibles as work reorganization and training, and labor market institutions, which govern skill acquisition and employment relations. As we argue in this essay, financial market constraints loom larger in the 1990s as a barrier to innovations that may be essential to high-value-added production in high-wage economies. As experience with transformed work systems has increased in the United States and elsewhere, it has become apparent that these processes hold out the greatest promise for enabling plants in high-wage economies to exploit their proximity to the domestic market and compete in their home markets against imports.

More importantly from a social perspective, a country whose firms adopt more innovative work systems can hope to maintain a broad manufacturing capability, though manufacturing employment may continue to shrink. Increasingly, as even some plants in less industrialized economies adopt innovative work systems, worldwide standards are being set for quality and customization that exceed the capability of mass production systems. Nevertheless, major changes in work organization and human resource practices have been slow to diffuse.

The innovations required to transform production systems entail large up-front investments. Reorganizing generally involves modernization of physical plants—more equipment, more technologically sophisticated equipment, and new logistical designs of the work site; in addition, initial investments in training of front-line workers may be several times the 1.5 percent of payroll typically expended for training in U.S. firms. Firms need access to financial resources available over long time periods to undertake the innovations required to move from mass production to more flexible production systems. Since access to these investments are critical, financial markets play an important role in organizational change.

The Increasing Influence of Financial Markets on Business Strategy

The decades following World War II were an era of inexpensive financing for U.S. corporations. Banks were highly regulated; households were relatively restricted in their investment opportunities; and institutional investors—insurance companies and pension funds—mainly held long-term corporate bonds. Companies financed industrial investment through retained earnings or stable long-term debt instruments.

Following the managerial revolution in the early decades of the twentieth century, companies were evaluated on how well they met managerial agendas. Companies that set and achieved appropriate strategic goals with respect to markets, mix of products, sales and revenue growth, and return on investment enjoyed access to bond and equity financing, as well as to the banks and insurance companies that were their major sources of finance capital. As managers worked their way up in the corporation, they accumulated knowledge of the firm's internal operations and learned to manage relations with the board of directors to retain power and control over the company's strategic agenda. Control of large organizations rested not with the shareholders, but with professional managers with little ownership stake in the company. Shareholders were effectively powerless. Large corporations were safe from takeovers, and oligopolies sheltered the largest companies from product market competition and the almost exclusive pursuit of profit maximization.

While managers in these corporations generally enjoyed the perquisites attendant upon employment in firms buffered from intense product market competition and with highly developed internal labor markets, managerial capitalism frequently was anything but benign in its treatment of front-line workers. In non-union companies, the treatment of lower-level workers ranged from paternalism to despotism. In unionized companies, labor-management relations could generally be characterized as adversarial. The hierarchical organization typical of these companies produced numerous opportunities for what is often referred to as "managerial opportunism." The history and culture of managerial control are cited frequently as important obstacles to the transformation to more participatory and flexible production systems. Nevertheless, corporate managers enjoyed a great deal of flexibility in defining the goals necessary for viability, which generally included the growth of sales and revenue and increased control over the firm's markets. And in the decades following World War II, many successful companies, including some that were unionized, shared their gains with workers.

As long-term company employees, top corporate managers were encouraged to pursue these strategic goals by the low capital costs made possible by regulated financial markets. As a result, shareholders seemed generally content, and the strategic goals of top corporate officials and process-oriented goals of plant and middle managers were in rough alignment. Growth in sales, revenue, and market share were important outcomes by which managers at both corporate levels were judged.

It was not until the late 1970s and early 1980s, when changing competitive conditions and an overvalued dollar undermined the ability of U.S. manufacturing firms to achieve sales and revenue growth and the deregulation of U.S. financial markets provided increased opportunities and incentives for hostile takeovers and shareholder activism, that investors were able to contest the power of professional corporate executives.

A number of changes in U.S. financial markets set the stage for this increase in shareholder influence. Deregulation of financial markets in the 1970s and the growth of mutual funds and uninsured money market accounts increased competition for these savings. Interest rates on bank deposits rose, as did rates that banks charge borrowers. The largest borrowers, especially well-managed corporations with stellar reputations, ended relationships with banks or other financial intermediaries and borrowed directly through financial markets. The customers of banks now are primarily smaller or weaker businesses, and much bank financing consists of variable rate, short-term loans.

The separation of ownership from management control in U.S. companies was challenged in the 1980s by corporate takeovers, which became a significant force for disciplining firms whose strategies were focused on the survival of the organization but did not lend themselves easily to present value calculations. Firms that were deemed to have deviated from the principal of maximizing the present value of the firm often became the targets of hostile takeover bids.[1]

Institutional investors also emerged as a much more important influence in the 1980s. Mutual funds, through which individuals pool resources and purchase stocks, joined pension funds and insurance companies as major holders of corporate shares. Many institutional investors look to trading as a way to increase returns. This, together with changes in technology that have made it easier and cheaper to trade shares, has increased the volume of stock trading dramatically since the early 1980s. One result is that institutional investors have been able to exert much greater pressure on corporate managers to place shareholders' value ahead of other stakeholders' interests.

Finally, the influence of financial institutions on corporate strategic decisions has been reinforced by changes in the way compensation of top corporate officials is determined. In an effort to more closely align management goals with shareholder value, corporate boards have tied an increasingly large proportion of official pay to the company's stock performance. This provides top managers with a strong incentive to consider the effects of organizational restructuring on share prices.

The implication of these developments is that the creation of shareholder value—as measured by rising share price—has become a key performance measure for corporate executives and the firm's access to capital markets. The success of a firm's organizational plans increasingly is determined by Wall Street's response to the initiative and by its effect on financial indicators. Unfortunately, Wall Street appears to favor downsizing over other, more uncertain, and more difficult-to-evaluate approaches to restructuring.[2] This raises questions about sustainability and diffusion of innovative production systems that have high up-front costs and long-term payoffs. Even such firms as Xerox, which was among the earliest U.S. adopters of high-performance work systems, carry out mindless downsizings and across-the-board cuts in staffing to the applause of institutional investors and Wall Street.

Corporate Control

Changes in corporate control—takeovers or the threat of takeovers—emerged in the 1980s as an effective means of holding corporate managers accountable to shareholders and assuring close adherence to the principle of maximizing the present value of a firm. One study found that corporations that were most successful by the standards of the managerial revolution—companies with high cash flow and low debt or with long-term employment relationships with their workers—were most likely to be taken over. Corporate raiders used junk bonds to finance leveraged buyouts of these companies, earning huge returns on small initial outlays and saddling the takeover targets with substantial, often unmanageable, debt. Leveraged buyouts appear to have been driven by the desire for quick financial gains and to have ignored the firms' strategies designed to achieve long-term payoffs to investments in technology or employees.

Institutional Investors and Shareholder Power

Deregulation of the U.S. banking system in the late 1970s increased alternative investment opportunities for households and put pressure on institutional investors—pension funds and insurance companies—to increase their returns by substituting stock for long-term bonds. From 1981 to 1988, the stock holdings of institutional investors grew at an average annual rate of 14 percent. Increasingly, institutional shareholders assure that the gains, which companies previously shared with suppliers and employees, are appropriated by shareholders. They exert this pressure in two very different ways: by threatening to sell shares (and depress share prices) and, where they hold large blocks of stock, by directly influencing corporate managers.

Despite the fact that stock ownership, which has been fragmented in the United States since the early decades of this century, is now becoming more concentrated in the hands of institutional investors, these investors do not behave like their German or Japanese counterparts. Institutional investors are more likely than individuals to engage in short-term trading practices. According to Michael Jacobs, Director of Corporate Finance in the U.S. Treasury in the Bush administration:

> In many cases, current earnings are a poor proxy for the long-run prospects of the com-

pany, which is why relying too heavily on them can produce valuations that misrepresent a firm's true economic worth. Obviously, weak earnings can signal problems ahead. But to the extent that the market inappropriately reads weak interim results caused by long-term investments as discouraging news about the future, it will penalize the stocks of companies that are truly investing for the future. And to the extent that corporate officers care about the value of the company, seeing the stock price decline will make them more hesitant to commit resources to strategic initiatives with distant payoffs.[3]

The problem is not that financial markets are naive or deliberately take a short-term perspective—it is that high-performance work systems require high up-front costs (that are easy for financial analysts to measure) in order to yield long-term uncertain potential payoffs (that are difficult for financial analysts to evaluate).

The hurdle set by financial analysts or institutional investors may be even more difficult to surmount. The lack of relationships between companies and most institutional investors that is typical of the U.S. financial system creates uncertainty among the investors about the corporate plans (e.g., CEOs may be reluctant to share all the details of their competitive strategy). Financial hurdles also increase the risks related to investors' inability to monitor corporations closely, as well as their desire for liquidity. As a result, the cost of capital as calculated by Wall Street, with adjustments for perceived risk premiums, may be higher than the cost of capital as calculated by the firm's managers. Of course, some investments in training and work reorganization will be judged profitable by this criterion and will be undertaken. In particular, this will be true of firms in which these types of organizational changes are already well established, so that payoffs in the form of higher earnings are readily apparent. But the rate of return required by Wall Street is likely to lead to the rejection of many more projects and to increase the difficulty of undertaking such investments for firms just beginning the process of change.

As institutional investors began to demand more accountability from their agents—top corporate managers—poor stock price performance was seen as the result of bad management that was entrenched and unaccountable to shareholders.

Perhaps the clearest indicator of the increase in shareholder power in the 1980s can be seen in the change in the price-to-earnings ratios (p/e). Corporate managers following a strategy of using retained earnings to finance innovations prefer low p/e ratios, which permit relatively low dividend payout rates that are acceptable stock yields (i.e., dividend-to-price ratios) when the p/e ratio is low. Most shareholders, by contrast, prefer high p/e ratios, which put upward pressure on dividends in order to maintain stock yields. Thus, as shareholders exert greater control over their companies, the share of profits distributed as dividends increases. The proportion of after-tax corporate profits distributed as dividends was 44 percent in the 1960s, 45 percent in the 1970s, 60 percent in the 1980s, and 72 percent in 1990. This left fewer resources for investment in innovative equipment, training, and work organization.

CEO Pay

Changes in the structure of compensation of top executives at large corporations are a clear manifestation of shareholder activism. Throughout the 1980s, the composition of executive pay shifted from a more fixed to a more variable structure linked more closely with shareholder value, not return on equity or other traditional measures. This shift in the compensation structure has a negative effect on the ability of companies to invest in continuous innovation. They now have individual incentives for personal financial success, and their incentives to innovate have weakened.

Thus, in many U.S. corporations, the interest of shareholders in a high share price now takes precedence over the traditional interest of managers (and employees, suppliers, and communities) in the survival of the company, which clearly has important implications for corporate restructuring, for the adoption of innovative workplace and human resource practices in individual firms and, more broadly, for the ability of the United States to maintain and build its productive capacity.

Implications for Organizational Restructuring

The pressures of pursuing shareholder value as the primary measure of organizational success have made it more difficult for companies to introduce innovative work systems. Managerial capitalism was less hostile to the stakeholder view of the firm, which is more central to high-performance work systems than is the newer agency theory of the firm. One result of the recent organizational alignment around the goals of financial markets has been the decentralization of authority through the ranks of management. Companies are reducing levels of management hierarchy, creating flatter organizational structures and giving managers and operating units more discretion to make decisions. As Michael Useem points out, however, this is not done to create a high-performance work system:

In no case was the acknowledged motive [of a leaner and flatter organizational chart] to empower the workforce, to give managers greater control over decisions, or to improve the quality of work life. To some managers these were of course laudable byproducts of the decentralization. But the organizational alignment was result driven, not process driven. The actions were not taken because management believed in decentralization for its own sake. . . . The steps were instead simply a derivative of management's commitment to increase shareholder return.[4]

In making these changes, however, top managers reduced their ability to monitor and control the decisions of managers lower in the hierarchy. To overcome this, corporations established a new system of control that linked managerial success at all levels of the organization to financial performance results. In this environment, making long-term innovative investments in workforce training, reorganizing the production process, and expanding the job tasks of shopfloor workers become more difficult. Although plant and operating unit managers may have more authority to make decisions, they are constrained by the strict financial performance-driven restructuring, that leaves little room to incorporate the interests of other stakeholders, such as local unions and employees. Reducing the number of employees immediately lowers costs and increases the value of the company. There are examples of share prices rising simply because a company announced its commitment to downsizing.

It often is assumed that downsizing is an effective way to raise productivity. However, a 1994 study by Martin Baily, Eric Bartelsman, and John Haltiwanger contradicts this assumption. Using plant-level data, these analysts examined the relationship between manufacturing productivity growth during the 1980s and plant-level employment changes. They show that productivity growth is affected more by plant-specific factors, such as management and worker skills, than by simply cutting employment.

While the performance effects of downsizing are mixed, the effects of downsizing on innovative work systems and the implementation of performance-enhancing strategies clearly are negative. Large cuts in personnel not only demoralize a workforce, but can also restrict the communication among employees who feel their resources and jobs are threatened. Employees may hunker down and try to protect their department or area against further cuts. Rather than sharing ideas across departments and taking risks, employees become overly cautious and reticent. In the process of downsizing, the company also may lose employees with extensive firm-specific knowledge. None of these factors are consistent with performance-enhancing strategies that rely on open communication, trust, and highly skilled and organizationally committed workers.

A strategy responsive to the concerns of financial markets and shareholder value and one based on creating performance-enhancing work systems rest on different principles and emphasize different performance priorities. While financial markets view shareholder wealth as the only valid measure of performance, performance-enhancing strategies are designed to affect broader performance measures, including quality, market share, revenue, and time-to-market—all of which are related to long-term company survival. Moreover, to be effective, performance-enhancing strategies require the participation of other company stakeholders (employees and/or local unions) who are most interested in wages, working conditions, employment security and the survival of the company.

Strategies for maximizing shareholder value and those for adopting innovative work systems both focus on the elimination of waste as a means to increase performance; however, the two approaches emphasize different methods. Innovative work systems eliminate waste by empowering workers to make more decisions and developing the mutual trust and high commitment necessary if workers are to continuously improve the process. This process-oriented approach treats human resources as a special strategic resource to increase productivity and efficiency by increasing the breadth and depth of their skills, reorganizing their jobs, and increasing their responsibility.

Financial restructuring, on the other hand, tends to view human resources as one input among many. Labor essentially is a cost to be minimized through downsizing or repressing wages, not a resource to be developed.

Conclusion

Financial markets are pressuring companies to concentrate single-mindedly on maximizing shareholder value—to the exclusion of all other performance goals, even including survival of the firm. The advocates of agency theory reject the idea that a corporation has any interest in its own survival or that managers have any legitimate goals apart from their obligation to maximize the wealth of the company's shareholders, whose agents they are.

As we have shown, this strategy can have a negative effect on efforts to restructure the work process. A key component of the public debate about high-performance work systems is the recognition that shareholders are merely one group with a stake in the corporation. Corporate laws separate the ownership of shares of stock from the ownership of property. Owners of a few shares of stock in a company are not entitled to the ordinary rights of property ownership—the rights to possess, use, and exclude others, as well as manage and control the company. In addition, shareholders are exempt from the liabilities usually associated with ownership.

Employees, like shareholders, bear the risks of investing in the corporation. Shareholders who have invested in a company's stock get their piece of the corporate pie only if there is something left after all the expenses are paid. Thus, they bear the risk that nothing will be left for them. They have an interest, therefore, in monitoring management to ensure that corporations are efficiently managed and that these residual gains (profits) are maximized. Economic theory says that companies are likely to be more efficiently run when corporate managers are accountable to those who bear such risks.

But employees invest and bear risks as well. Most employees invest in skills and knowledge that are specific to the company. Their potential payoff is in the form of wages that are higher than what they can earn in a job at another firm—but only if the company prospers. Because they bear risks in the same way as shareholders, employees are equally motivated to see that the firm's resources are used efficiently and that the firm prospers.

Like shareholders, employees make investments in a firm and take risks. Unlike most shareholders, however, employees' livelihoods can be severely threatened by poor investment decisions and bad management. Shareholders, after all, rarely have more than 2 or 3 percent of their holdings in any one company. And it is easier for investors to sell their shares when they see that a company is poorly managed than it is for workers to change jobs. In most cases, laid-off employees with years of experience are unable to find other jobs at their previous wages. Decisions in which they had no part essentially wiped out their investments in skills and knowledge. This is not only unfair but an inefficient use of society's resources.

As stakeholders in the corporation, employees' incomes depend on the corporation's profitability and its ability to employ them. Workers should have the same rights and opportunities as shareholders to hold managers accountable. Indeed, their knowledge of the company and its customers may make them better suited than more distant shareholders to monitor management's decisions and assure that they serve company interests.

We believe workers' rights to representation, like those of shareholders, should be legally mandated in the rules of corporate governance. Specifically:

- Employees should have a voice in decisions that affect the viability of the company. We propose that a significant proportion—perhaps a third—of corporate boards of directors be elected by employees.
- Because employees invest in firm-specific skills, they should participate in decisions about training. Training committees composed of employees and managers should decide both the content of company training and who gets it. Employee participation within a high-performance work system can bring new ideas to bear on how to increase everyone's returns on investments.

By expanding corporate governance to include employees, who clearly have a stake in the enterprise, investments in the work process and the skills of the workforce would be much more likely to occur.

Notes

1. Jacobs, for example, provides an excellent example of how information asymmetries may cause corporate in-

vestments in intangibles—training, research and development, or other expenditures that are not capitalized under U.S. accounting practices—to be misconstrued by shareholders as a decline in the company's prospects. This then causes shareholders to adjust their valuation of the stock downward when they calculate present value and to behave in a myopic fashion even though they have acted on calculations of the firms' long-term profit prospects.

2. Corporate executives also "game" the system—what Jeffrey Pfeffer of Stanford University refers to as "management by denominator." One example is Kodak's 1988 decision to transfer its data processing operation—including $1 billion of computers and other equipment, as well as 700 employees—to IBM's books. With little or no change in efficiency as economists measure it, Kodak succeeded in boosting return on assets and revenue per employee as Wall Street measures it. Analysts applauded Kodak for downsizing and becoming leaner. Other companies that have made similar decisions include General Dynamics, McDonnell Douglas, Sears Roebuck, and Bethlehem Steel. Xerox signed a ten-year contract with EDS (General Motors' data processing subsidiary) in 1994 estimated at over $4 billion. Of the 6,000 people working at Coca-Cola headquarters in Atlanta, Georgia, 2,000 are leased employees. This includes administrative staff and information systems professionals leased from the Talent Tree company and building maintenance and cafeteria workers leased from other contractors.

3. Michael T. Jacobs, *Short-Term America: The Causes and Cures for Our Business Myopia* (Boston: Harvard Business School Press, 1991), pp. 36–37.

4. Michael Useem, *Executive Defense: Shareholder Power and Corporate Reorganization* (Cambridge, MA: Harvard University Press, 1993), p. 84.

34

Restoring Broadly Shared Prosperity:
A Business Perspective

Thomas J. Usher

I am grateful to contribute to these essays on restoring broadly shared economic prosperity, the concept of which was a creation of the Industrial Revolution and stemmed from the ability of the basic industries in this country—steel, coal, automobiles, rubber—to provide a large number of high-paying jobs to a workforce that was not highly trained or college educated and included many members of minority groups.

The increase in economic inequality that characterized the 1980s, as well as the current decade, has corresponded with, and was caused by, in part, the decline of these same basic industries and the loss of hundreds of thousands of well-paying jobs. This broadly shared economic prosperity cannot be restored unless and until our basic industries are able to again supply large numbers of these higher-paying jobs to the non-college-educated portion of the population.

A number of years ago, Charley Wilson, former head of General Motors and Secretary of Defense in the Eisenhower administration, attracted a good deal of ridicule for allegedly stating, "What is good for General Motors is good for America." (He actually said, "What is good for America is good for General Motors and vice versa.") Well, to paraphrase Charley Wilson, what is good for the steel, coal, automobile, rubber, and other industries is good for America, if you believe, as I do, that this country needs more better-paying jobs that can be filled by ordinary Americans who have the basic ability to read, write, and do simple mathematics but who are not college graduates and who will not necessarily find employment in the high-technology companies.

It is interesting to note that while a number of papers in this volume recognize that one of the causes of increasing economic inequality has been the great decline in the number of manufacturing jobs, few of them, if any, consider the possibility of reversing this trend by strengthening manufacturing industries and thereby increasing the number of these jobs.

Indeed, some of the papers in this volume propose that the cure for increasing inequality is to increase the power of labor unions. This approach puts the cart before the horse and ignores the basic reality that labor unions may redistribute wealth, but do not create it. The object of governmental policy should be a strengthening of those industries that provide high-value jobs, as opposed to efforts to encourage redistribution in industries that provide mostly low-paying jobs.

Movie critics are predicting that the biggest movie hit of the summer will be *The Titanic*. Many of you may be aware that the percentage of the first-class and second-class passengers on the Titanic who were saved was much higher than the percentage of third-class passengers. A number of contributors to this volume, if asked to re-order the developments of the Titanic, would have insisted that spaces on the lifeboats be distributed more equitably. Fair enough. But it misses the point. Recognizing that the Titanic carried only half the number of lifeboats needed, I would have insisted on more lifeboats.

With that thought in mind, I would like to talk about some things that U.S. Steel, in partnership with the United Steel Workers of America, has done to increase the number of lifeboats and what the government must do to help USX adopt a high-value strategy and increase the number of high-paying jobs it provides.

And, in doing so, I suspect that John Sweeney, president of the AFL-CIO, and I might find many points that we agree upon.[1] Competitiveness and economic growth are not management or union interests but national interests.

It is, however, appropriate for someone who worked as a management employee for U.S. Steel all his life to speak from management's perspective.

The steel and mining industries are bedrocks of the labor movement. Fairly or unfairly, U.S. Steel carries the legacy of Andrew Carnegie and Henry Clay Frick and the still bitter memories of the tragic Homestead Strike of 1892, even though Carnegie never worked a second for U.S. Steel, and the company did not even exist until 1901.

Ah! But what a company it was when it was formed in 1901—the world's first billion-dollar corporation, with 149 facilities, 168,000 employees, and a capacity of about 9 million tons a year. Today, ninety-six years later, we have four steel mills, 20,000 employees, and produce 20 percent more steel. That is quite a testimony

to employee and equipment productivity, and quite a challenge to labor-management relations.

And, while it is probably human nature to remember some of the unpleasant aspects of labor-management relations that occurred in the early days of the industry, it is only fair to mention that there were quite a number of progressive actions as well.

U.S. Steel, for example, was the first company in the nation to establish a safety department (that was in 1906), and we coined the term, "Safety First." In 1911, we introduced the first company-paid pension plan, and in 1912, we introduced the first eight-hour workday, only to rescind it a year later at the request of the workers.

Significantly, U.S. Steel, in 1937, was the first company to recognize the steelworkers' union and to sign a company-wide contract with them. In those early days, both we and the union more or less viewed labor relations as a battleground where there were winners and losers. This problem was compounded because steel was such a dominant factor in the national economy; hence, prolonged labor strife was deemed unacceptable, and U.S. presidents did not hesitate to intervene. President Truman actually seized the mills during a 1952 strike, and President Kennedy had a famous confrontation with our chairman, Roger Blough, in 1962.

The practical result was that the union would not allow management to win a short strike, and presidential politics would not allow us to win a long one. So, we entered a twenty-five-year period of no strikes, when we agreed to cost-of-living adjustments and other increases that were too expensive, out of line with reality, and unrelated to productivity improvements. Added costs could not always be passed along in the form of increased prices to our customers.

This continued until foreign competition

made it impossible for us to continue to pass through added expenses. That was when it became apparent that the too-rich contracts were not only detrimental to the company, but also to our customers, the nation, and—in the long run—our employees.

A painful restructuring of the industry took place in the late 1970s and early 1980s—a restructuring necessary for the company's survival but one viewed in many quarters as cruel and heartless. Throughout the industry, hundreds of facilities were closed, hundreds of thousands of steelworkers lost their jobs, and plant communities were severely affected. Many companies went bankrupt. Everyone suffered.

For U.S. Steel, the situation boiled over in 1986 with a bitter, acrimonious strike that lasted six months. It was our first strike in twenty-five years and was the longest in industry history until the current Wheeling-Pittsburgh strike broke that dubious record. The 1986 strike was undoubtedly the low point in our modern labor-management history. All sides were bloodied; nobody won; and everybody lost—we, the union, the employees, the plant communities, and our customers.

Amidst the debris of the strike, we discovered another disquieting fact: we were not all that vital to the national economy any longer. In effect, we had a strike and nobody cared—and nobody missed us. Our customers had gone elsewhere, and we had to fight very hard to get them back. This was a real eye opener for us. We suddenly realized that we had a major rebuilding job to do with our customers, our employees, and our shareholders.

It was a turning point in our relations and attitudes toward our employees and the union, and in theirs toward us. We all came to understand that if we were to survive into the next century, things had to change. One approach to change came at our Mon Valley Works in Pittsburgh. Shortly before the strike, we had launched a quality improvement program there called Appliance Product Excellence (APEX). The program was aimed at improving our product quality for the critical appliance market.

The strike, however, intervened, and the issue grew larger—the plant's very survival was at stake. So, to reintroduce the program and to address the now larger issue of survival, we laid out the issues at a plant-wide meeting to which all plant employees and their spouses were invited. The meeting and the subsequent involvement of our employees at all levels of the plant processes stimulated a rapid, full-scale renewal of the APEX effort in the Mon Valley. Shortly thereafter, this approach was introduced to our Gary Works in Indiana. Key stimulation came when the employees heard a warning from Ford purchasing executives that the plant must immediately improve its lagging quality performance or face the loss of its Ford business.

One of the more noteworthy APEX activities in the early years at Gary involved a team of veteran, hourly employees that visited automotive customer plants to assist in solving problems involving our steel. This quality team ultimately submitted its own application to the USA Today Quality Cup competition in 1992 and became the first winner of that prestigious award.

Throughout all of this, APEX was and is largely a plant effort—not so much a headquarters-driven directive, but a locally initiated empowerment undertaking that quickly moved to other locations throughout the U.S. Steel system. Along the way, it dropped its initial emphasis on the appliance market and APEX came to stand for "All People, All Process, All Product Excellence"—a total quality system that includes all product lines and employee disciplines.

From the low point of the 1986 strike, empowerment activities have become an integral feature at the plant level, blurring the once sharply defined divisions between management and union employees that prevailed at U.S. Steel prior to the strike. Detailed communications about the competitive circumstances at each operating location have been a mainstay in improving the situation. Problem-solving teams have spread and flourished. Large-scale training efforts in such areas as environmental control have been undertaken. Continuous improvement training has been widespread, with significant successes at each of the operating locations.

It is reasonable to say that the improved relationships and the various achievements have reflected a heightened attitude of mutual respect by all parties involved. Increasingly, our management people have adopted an approach suggesting that employees be treated with the same respect and fundamental decency with which they themselves would wish to be treated. In return, the employees have reciprocated. We try to foster an environment best illustrated by the slogan, "Manage as if you're the worker; work as if you're the boss"—the Golden Rule philosophy of labor relations, if you will.

In any event, the last ten years have shown us what it is possible to achieve when all—regardless of employee status—have the same goals. Just last month, a reporter toured one of our facilities and had dozens of private conversations with individual employees. He came out amazed. He said: "I cannot tell who's the manager and who's the union worker. They're all saying the same thing." Andrew Carnegie and Henry Clay Frick would not recognize the place today.

Now, this did not come about unilaterally. To make it work, both the company and the union had to exhibit good faith, cooperation, and flexibility. Trust had to be earned on both sides, and this did not happen without a few rough patches here and there. But it did happen, and now everyone knows that they are stakeholders in what we do and how we perform. As an example, we now tie a portion of each employee's compensation to the performance of the business. When the company does well, the employees receive profit-sharing above their regular pay. No profits, no sharing. It works, and it makes a difference.

Now, we and the union still have a lot of areas of disagreement. We will still continue to vigorously present our position. I suspect the union will do the same. We will not agree on a lot of things. But we can disagree as honorable people. We can disagree and still treat one another with dignity and respect. However, we must never slide back into the bad old days of winners and losers. It is a matter of survival, and to survive, we all need to win.

Now, the question is how do we keep winning? What external forces affect our ability to be profitable and competitive? What outside forces affect our ability to "grow" our business in hopes of providing a greater number of well-paying jobs and thus contributing to the restoration of broadly shared prosperity? Remember, competitive means globally competitive. Make no mistake, we are in a world market with world-class competition. Also, recognize that U.S. Steel today is the lowest-cost steel in the world, and yet we still need to import 20 percent of our needs. We should be building more capacity today.

When you think of forces that encourage or restrict growth, you inevitably think of the policies of the federal government. So let me list a few of the things that our friends in the White House and Congress could do to help increase our competitiveness.

I believe higher rates of economic growth are possible without increasing the rate of inflation. In order to better complement these new growth-rate possibilities, the government needs to modify several of its policies in the areas of budget and tax, regulatory reform, and trade.

First, balancing the budget. A large federal deficit has the effect of reducing national savings and keeping interest rates higher than they would be otherwise. By decreasing the federal deficit, the federal government would increase the savings rate. As the savings rate increases relative to capital investment, the balance of payments deficit will fall. However, any balanced budget package should include both spending cuts and a tax-related growth component, including a reduction in entitlement spending and reform of the corporate tax structure to encourage investment. One example of a tax modification that is necessary is repeal of the alternative minimum tax (AMT).

The AMT discourages firms from making capital expenditures in new plants and equipment and is particularly unfair to capital-intensive industries such as steel. With the current system, the only way a capital-intensive firm can work its way out of AMT liability is to slow its capital outlays and some companies may even be forced to shut down U.S. plants because of the negative effect of the AMT. If you are an AMT taxpayer, your ability to recover capital investment takes longer than in any industrialized country in the world. The money we have paid in AMT over the past few years would have gone a long way to building a new steel mill that would have provided hundreds of those high-paying jobs we have been discussing.

In the area of regulatory reform, government regulations raise operating costs. While many are good, unnecessary regulations divert resources into compliance, without necessarily adding anything to output. The benefit from reducing regulation is that it would lower the cost of capital, permitting greater investment and increased productivity.

The Clean Air Act is an example of overreaching federal controls. It is important for Congress to allow the benefits of the Clean Air Act Amendments of 1990 to be fully obtained before changing the underlying standards. Unfortunately, the Environmental Protection Agency is proposing to change national ambient air quality standards for both particulate matter (soot) and ozone (smog) without scientific consensus that such changes are necessary to improve human health. A tighter ozone standard produces no demonstrated improvements in public health but imposes substantial costs on society.

Many scientific questions and uncertainties also surround the EPA's proposal to change the current particulate matter standard. The EPA's own panel of independent scientists has urged the agency to implement a targeted research program to address the unanswered questions surrounding the potential health effects of particulate matter before changing the standard. As a practical matter, a more stringent particulate matter standard will significantly increase the number of areas throughout the country requiring regulatory control programs. Because of these substantial uncertainties, EPA should retain the current standard until it obtains the data and performs the research necessary to develop scientific consensus for a more stringent standard.

Global climate change is a subject much discussed these days. In 1996, the Clinton administration committed the United States to a legally binding agreement to reduce post-2000 greenhouse gas emissions. Scientific data and economic experience, however, argue against precipitous, potentially counterproductive action. The treaty now being negotiated has serious problems. It rushes toward economically damaging steps in spite of significant scientific uncertainty about the existence of a serious global warming problem, and even if global warming is taking place, is it good or bad? The treaty almost certainly will force the United States to significantly reduce energy use, which would affect both the economy and lifestyles. The treaty does not commit developing countries, such as China and India, to any emissions controls at all, making the treaty ineffective and creating a huge competitive disadvantage for most U.S. businesses.

As the treaty currently is structured, the United States bears a disproportionate burden, and thousands of our manufacturing jobs will be exported to nations with lesser controls. The long-term nature of this issue allows time for better understanding before taking premature costly action. Congress must provide careful oversight of the nation's global climate policies and seek ongoing improvement of the scientific understanding of possible global warming.

Reclamation of brownfield industrial sites—areas that once housed factories but now are vacant—is another area where regulatory actions should be re-examined. There are hundreds of these industrial sites in the urban areas of our country that remain vacant because of fear of environmental problems. The companies that own them are afraid to enter the bureaucratic nightmare of environmental cleanup, yet they cannot sell them because lenders and potential buyers are fearful of trailing environmental liabilities. These sites are in prime locations with good infrastructure—good access to railroads, highways, waterways, municipal services, and labor markets—and are in areas that desperately need new jobs and new opportunities. Yet, they sit vacant with fences

around them, contributing nothing to the community tax base.

Federal regulatory barriers to brownfield development should be examined in light of the successes of states such as Pennsylvania and Illinois with proactive development programs. States such as these are out in front on this matter and look at environmental remediation issues in a practical manner. Certainly, environmental problems ought to be addressed, but these and other states require remediation that is appropriate to the future use of those areas. Clean them up to meet those less stringent standards, consistent with the intended use of the site.

Restoring the nation's brownfield sites to productive use would go a long way toward providing new jobs and restoring prosperity to ordinary Americans. Federal regulations should promote the reuse of industrial sites.

Trade barriers, inadequate laws, or weak enforcement of existing laws are still a major threat to competitive U.S. industries and jobs. In its annual review of unfair trade practices, the Clinton administration said that while progress is being made, Japan and forty-five other nations still have trade barriers costing U.S. businesses and farmers billions in lost sales annually. In particular, the steel industry and its workers face an ongoing struggle against dumping and foreign subsidies. A recent Department of Commerce investigation of unfair trade cases filed by domestic steel producers found that flat rolled steel products from twenty-two different countries had average dumping margins of 37 percent.

A lot of foreign steel that is in the U.S. market today could be produced domestically, but steelmakers are reluctant to add expensive capacity without more assurances that they will not be harmed by unfair trade practices. Of all the trade policy issues, the vigorous enforcement of our trade laws, and, where possible, their strengthening, should be top priority.

My final area of government policy to be addressed is not a federal one, but a local issue—our public schools. All of us, privately and as corporations, pay enormous taxes to support the public school system. I'm a product of the public schools and have been a supporter of the concept. Consequently, I wish I could say that we are getting our money's worth from them, but in most cases, I fear we are not.

My corporation hires a number of young people right out of high school for entry-level jobs. We are looking for people with basic skills in reading, language, mathematics, computer usage, and so on. We will train them for specific skills needed for the job, but we need people who at least have some proficiency in the basics. They are more difficult to find than you might imagine. We give applicants a rather simple test requiring them to complete sentences, do basic math problems, and perform other general skills. It is a test that a junior high school student who has been paying attention should easily pass. Unfortunately, about half of the high school graduates who take our test do not pass.

I hasten to make two points. The first is that the test is appropriate to the job that the person is applying for. The second is that we do ultimately fill the jobs with qualified people, although it takes longer. The heartbreak is that there are young people graduating from high school today who literally cannot read their diplomas.

If money were the answer, we would have solved the problem long ago. Though our children rank well below those of other developed countries in math and science test results, the United States ranks second from the top in education spending expressed as a percentage of the gross national product. In absolute terms we spend about $6,000 per pupil for primary and secondary education, compared to $3–4,000 in other industrialized countries such as Germany, Britain, and Japan. So, money is not the problem and throwing more dollars into the pot is not the answer.

It seems there are several things we could do to improve our schools. One is to restore discipline, and by this I do not mean installing metal detectors at the front door. I mean giving teachers the right to an orderly classroom and the right to impose discipline without worrying about violating some unruly student's right to be a jerk. Local principals and classroom teachers need the right to control their own environment.

Another area is increased parental involvement. Students always do better when the parents are involved. Parents and teachers should be allies, not enemies.

Last, I think we should be open to new approaches to education because what we have now is not working. Charter schools, school vouchers, back-to-basics curriculums, school choice, special education—all these are hot-button topics that enflame passions on both sides of the issues. But we should overcome our knee-jerk reactions to these initiatives and be willing to try new approaches—and not just for a select few children. The issue here is children's education, not adult employment, and we should not lose sight of that. The message, then, is please educate our kids. That might help the country more than anything else we have talked about.

Note

1. John Sweeney was a participant in the program where Tom Usher presented this paper.

G. Communities, Regions, and Rural and Urban Areas

35

Justice at the Gates of the City: A Model for Shared Prosperity

Ernesto Cortes, Jr.

In ancient Israel, at the gate of every city there was a political institution, the municipal court, that made economic decisions for the city and its inhabitants. The guiding principal behind this institution was "mishpat," or justice. For the decision-makers of this institution, justice was not an abstraction, but a concrete reality; it meant that no one was denied the wherewithal for a dignified life. Justice in ancient Israel, in other words, meant that prosperity would be shared by all.[1]

Equity in the distribution of the costs and benefits of economic change (i.e., shared prosperity) ultimately requires political institutions guided by a sense of justice for all. Consequently, political institutions and the moral vision that guides their development are important issues in the debate on how to restore broadly shared prosperity in America.

America's Growing Prosperity Gap

During the last twenty-five years, the economic security of virtually all families—particularly those whose incomes depend upon work—has been gradually eroded by a combination of forces affecting the labor market and the economy.[2] Over the same period, these forces have also generated enormous prosperity: corporate profits have risen and the real wealth and assets of the top 5 percent of the population have increased significantly. Given the recent deterioration of our public life, the institutions that control economic decision-making are now dominated by the interests of an increasingly narrow band of people (i.e., the top 5 percent of wealthholders). As a result, the mechanism that once enabled a reasonably equitable distribution of the costs and benefits of economic change—that is, a vibrant public life connected to strong intermediate institutions—no longer exists. Consequently, those at the bottom of the income distribution have been made to absorb a disproportionate share of the costs of economic change without receiving any of the commensurate benefits. One of the most important causes of declining incomes and rising poverty among working Americans is this inequity in the distribution of the benefits and costs of economic change.

If we are serious about restoring broadly shared prosperity to the United States, we must take action to reverse the deterioration of our public life and its institutions, especially those community-based institutions (i.e., labor unions, schools, churches, and other voluntary associations) that were the foundation of civic culture and historically have buffered working families from the worst effects of a changing economy. Only through the revitalization of such institutions can working people acquire the power to negotiate with politicians, corporate leaders, and other decision-makers and thereby restore the balance in power that enables prosperity to be shared.

Triumph of the Market Culture

The changes in the economy are reflective of the broader changes in the rest of society—in institutions, families, politics, and public discourse. A society that not very long ago cultivated relationships, conversation, and reasonably vibrant public forums, now cultivates disconnected, self-absorbed, narcissistic individuals. More and more we are yielding to the materialistic, self-centered values of a commercialized and commodified society that has embraced the hegemony of the market imperialists. As a result, more and more of us are living according to individual preferences, needs, and desires without any regard to the common good.

The market is an important institution; it generates wealth, allocates resources, and engenders efficiency and innovation. But the market—despite its important societal roles—has no regard for, and is often inimical to, the common good. In other words, the market is amoral and myopic; it is effective in the short run, but is often incapable of effectively reflecting long-term values, visions, and interests. The market left to itself is incompetent in dealing with issues of equity with respect to the costs and benefits of economic change. As Arthur Okun says, if given the chance (if left unrestricted), "the tyranny of the dollar yardstick" will "sweep away all other values and establish a vending machine society."[3] This dimension of the market is why he argues that although the market has its place, it must be kept in its place. Unfortunately, the recent decline in incomes for working people and the great prosperity experienced by a favored few are evidence that the tyranny of the market has already taken hold.

In his article "The New Society of Organizations," Peter Drucker paints a bleak future, devoid of community, in which multinational corporations become the new Leviathan, conducting our public lives for us, standing as the only entities capable of staving off Hobbes's "war of all against all," in which life becomes "nasty, brutish, and short." Drucker finds himself unable to answer his own questions: "Who will take care of the Common Good? Who will define it?"[4] We must have answers to those questions if we intend to reverse the trends of the last quarter-century—that is, if we intend to prevent the market culture from continuing to grow at the expense of working families.

The Industrial Areas Foundation

Currently, both the state and the market reflect the interests of the dominant culture, which seems intent on squeezing out any space for a vibrant civic culture. The market has rendered human beings into customers, and the state apparatus has reduced us to clients or service recipients. Neither one has allowed any space for the development of an active citizenship. Given the choice between the bureaucratic state apparatus or the market culture, ordinary people are left without any institutional mechanism through which to understand and fight for their interests, and therefore without any way to deal effectively and collaboratively with the new economic forces currently wreaking havoc with their lives.

Founded by Saul Alinsky and currently directed by Ed Chambers, the Industrial Areas Foundation (IAF) is the center of a national network of broad-based, multi-ethnic, interfaith organizations in poor and moderate income communities. These organizations work to renew local democracy by fostering the competence and confidence of ordinary citizens to reorganize the relationships of power and politics and restructure the physical and civic infrastructure of their communities. To that end, the IAF provides leadership training for more than forty organizations representing over 1,000 institutions and one million families, principally in New York, Texas, California, Arizona, New Mexico, Nebraska, Iowa, Louisiana, Maryland, Tennessee, Washington, Oregon, Massachusetts, and Pennsylvania.[5] The IAF also has a training relationship with the Citizens Organizing Foundation of the United Kingdom.

Local IAF organizations, such as Communities Organized for Public Service (COPS) in San Antonio, are funded by the membership dues of community institutions, mainly churches and schools. In some communities, however, other voluntary associations are dues-paying members, such as the American Federation of State, County, and Municipal Employees (AFSCME) in Baltimore, Maryland. Dues pay for the salaries of senior organizers, and a contract between each local organization and the IAF to train and develop leadership. In addition, funding for special projects, including regional seminars and the Alliance School initiative, is provided by private foundations.

In short, the primary mission of the IAF is to teach people to ask and to answer Drucker's questions about the common good. The IAF organizations function as mini-universities where thousands of people learn how to define their own interests and negotiate them intentionally with the interests of others and thereby develop a more concrete understanding of the common good. This understanding emerges through ongoing negotiations that lead to collaborative action and thereby generate empathy, trust, reciprocity, and solidarity.

More specifically, the IAF teaches ordinary citizens to build broad-based organizations to fill the vacuum left by the deterioration of the mediating institutions of their communities—families, neighborhoods, congregations, local unions, local political parties, neighborhood schools, and other civic associations. It teaches them to rebuild damaged institutions, fashion new ones, and enter into the public relationships of democratic politics. It teaches them the skills of listening, respecting differences, arguing in good faith, negotiating, compromising, and holding themselves and others accountable for their commitments. In rebuilding civil society, the IAF provides a potential model for stemming the seemingly inexorable expansion of the market culture to ensure that the market culture, despite its benefits, does not continue to grow at the expense of working families and of the civil society that is requisite for a vigorous democratic culture.

One of the most dangerous consequences of current trends in wages and incomes is the deteriorating effect they have had on our social fabric. Due to the decline of the intermediate institutions that historically have embodied this social fabric, there is much misplaced anger, resentment and fear among working people, who are distracted from their real difficulties by such issues as immigration and welfare. (Organizing in communities in the southwest, the IAF has discovered that often these feelings are related to people's sense of powerlessness in the changing economy, as Harvard professor Michael Sandel asserts in *Democracy's Discontent*.)[6] Further dividing different socioeconomic and ethnic groups and polarizing the political system, elected officials and candidates for public office exploit these misplaced sentiments by attacking issues in isolation. Ultimately, voters support mean-spirited, divisive initiatives without much forethought (e.g., Proposition 187 in California that denied illegal aliens certain public services). This deterioration in civil society makes it increasingly difficult to develop the unified political constituency necessary to effectively address the current economic challenges facing working families.

Politics, Community, and Organization

The IAF recognizes that problems such as poverty and unemployment are not simply matters of income. They are a crushing burden on the soul, and people who suffer under their weight often view themselves as incapable of participating in the civic culture and political community. The kind of development that enables a civic and political sense of self to emerge requires connecting people to networks, relationships, and institutions that make collective action possible and meaningful. Connecting people in such a manner creates the conditions necessary for the development of politics—politics that is about listening, deliberation, narrative, and engagement, which then leads to the development and transformation of the human spirit.

The development of such politics is going to require institutions that teach people that politics is not about polls, focus groups, and television ads, but about engaging in public discourse and initiating collective action guided by that discourse. In politics, it is not enough to be right or to have a coherent position; one also must be reasonable and willing to make concessions, exercise judgment, and find terms that others can

accept as well. Politics is about relationships that enable people to disagree, argue, interrupt, confront, and negotiate, and, through this process of conversation and debate, to forge a consensus or compromise that makes it possible for them to act. The practical wisdom revealed in politics is the equivalent of good judgment and praxis—action that is both intentional and reflective. In praxis, the most important part of action is the reaction that provides the basis for the evaluation and the sustained reflection. The reflections provide the material for the telling, re-telling, and reinterpretation of the story, which enables the story to endure and provide the grist for continuous learning. As Hannah Arendt has said: "No remembrance remains secure unless it is condensed and distilled into a framework of conceptual notions, within which it can further exercise itself. Experience and even stories which grow out of what men do and endure, of happenings and events, sink back into the futility inherent in the living words and the living deed unless they are talked about over and over again."[7]

In *The Presence of the Past,* Sheldon Wolin describes our birthright as our political identity.[8] Echoing Aristotle's idea that we are political beings—that a part of us emerges only through participation in public life—Wolin emphasizes our capacity to initiate action in collaboration with other human beings. Such action often has an element of public drama. But in the IAF, political action is more than drama. It combines the symbolism of active citizenship with real political efficacy, creating the opportunity to restructure schools, revitalize neighborhoods, create job training programs, increase access to health care, or initiate flood control programs.

In addition to tangible improvements in public services, such politics recreates and reorganizes the ways in which people, networks of relationships, and institutions operate: It builds real community. But when people lack the organizations that enable them to connect to real political power and participate effectively in public life, these social relationships disintegrate. We learn to act in ways that are not responsive to our community. There is neither time nor energy for collaboration; there is no reciprocity, no trust—in short, no social capital.[9]

To reverse the current dissolution of our community, we need to rebuild our civic culture through investments in those institutions that enable people to learn, to develop leadership, and to build relationships—to become, in Jefferson's phrase, "participators in the affairs of government." The IAF has found that when people learn through politics to work with each other, supporting one another's projects, a trust emerges that goes beyond the barriers of race, ethnicity, income, and geography. We have found that we can rebuild community by reconstructing democracy.

Congregation and University

The IAF organizations are primarily a federation of associations, organizations, and congregations—that is, institutions of faith that are agitated by the Judeo-Christian tradition and the values and vision of a free and open society. In this context, "faith" does not mean a particular system of religious beliefs, but a more profound affirmation that life has meaning that is transcendent.

The root of the word religion is "re-ligare," which means to bind together that which has become disconnected. The best elements in our religious traditions are inclusive—respecting diversity and conveying a plurality of symbols that incorporate the experiences of diverse peoples. Congregations convey traditions that connect people in the present and hold them accountable to past and future generations. These institutions—churches, synagogues, mosques, and temples—are connected to networks of families, neighborhoods, schools, and other voluntary associations. Unfortunately, they are virtually the only institutions in society that are fundamentally concerned with the nature and well-being of families and communities.

Religious faith, history, and tradition are important because they embody the struggles of those who have gone before—their struggles both to understand and to act. Reflecting on these efforts, one learns not to take oneself too seriously and to recognize the limits of what can be accomplished in a lifetime or in a generation. Traditions—to the extent that they are meaningful and useful—provide a framework for dealing with ambiguity, irony, and tragedy.

Fundamentally, IAF organizations are the "mini-universities" of their communities. Like universities, these broad-based organizations provide arenas in which a wide variety of people with multiple agendas and traditions can engage in constrained conflict, opening the historical contradictions within and among our traditions to inquiry and reflection.

Leadership

IAF leaders—ordinary people from all walks of life—begin their development in one-on-one conversations with a skilled organizer. These conversations represent an exchange of views, judgments, and commitments. IAF organizers see themselves as teachers, mentors, and agitators who constantly cultivate leadership for the organization. Their job is to teach people how to form relationships with other leaders and to develop a network—a collective of relationships able to build the power to enable them to act. Leaders initially learn politics through conversation and negotiation with one another. As they develop a broader vision of their self-interest, they begin to recognize their connections and their responsibilities to each other and to the community.

Organizing people around vision and values allows institutions to address specific concerns more effectively. Beginning with small, winnable issues—fixing a streetlight, putting up a stop sign—they move carefully into larger arenas—making a school a safe and civil place for children to learn. And then to still larger issues—setting an agenda for a municipal capital improvement budget, strategizing with corporate leaders and members of the City Council on economic growth policies, developing new initiatives in job training, health care, and public education. When ordinary people become engaged and shift from political spectators to political agents, when they begin to play large public roles, they develop confidence in their own competence.

Power and the Iron Rule

Most people have an intuitive grasp of Lord Acton's dictum about the tendency of power to corrupt. To avoid appearing corrupted, they shy away from power. But powerlessness also corrupts—perhaps more pervasively than power itself. IAF leaders learn quickly that understanding politics requires understanding power.

A central element of that understanding is that there are two kinds of power. Unilateral power tends to be coercive and domineering. It is the power of one party treating another as an object to be instructed and directed. Relational power is more complicated. Developed subject-to-subject, it is transformative, changing the nature of the situation and of the self. The IAF has spent fifty years teaching people to develop such relational power, mastering the capacity to act, and the reciprocal capacity to allow oneself to be acted upon.

Relational power is both collectively effective and individually transformative. The potential of ordinary people fully emerges only when they are able to translate their self-interests in issues such as family, property, and education into the common good through an intermediary organization. Each of the IAF's victories is the fruit of the personal growth of thousands of leaders—housewives, clergy, bus drivers, secretaries, nurses, teachers—who have learned from the IAF how to participate and negotiate with the business and political leaders and bureaucrats we normally think of as society's decision-makers.

Guided by the Iron Rule, "Never do for others what they can do for themselves," IAF organizations have won their victories not by speaking for ordinary people but by teaching them how to speak, act, and engage in politics for themselves.

At its heart, managing change does not so much depend upon the physical capital of tools and factories, the financial capital of money and assets, or even the human capital of accumulated knowledge and skills, as it does upon the social capital of communities. The capacity to innovate, to readjust, and to maintain common efforts in the face of uncertainty depends upon the trust and mutual commitment among those who do the work of our society—front-line workers, managers, entrepreneurs, researchers, technicians, engineers, owners, shareholders, bondholders, families, employers, teachers, bankers, and many others.

There is no single "method" or "recipe" for dealing with the complexities of our new economic world. That is why intermediary institutions are so vital in devising strategies: Only through the real conversations and relationships—the social capital—on which these institutions are based can the interests of particular communities be translated into real, effective action on behalf of working families. And certainly, the work of rebuilding intermediary institutions through conversation and action is, indeed, replicable.

The IAF Record

In organizing communities around the well-being of families throughout the United States, the leaders of the IAF have reached a number of conclusions about what it will take to reduce inequality.[10] In particular, we believe that redistributing resources to support individuals earlier in their lives is critical to sustaining a civil society in this nation.[11] Our organizations have found that resources invested in public education, after-school programs, preventive health care for children, summer work experiences for adolescents, college scholarships, and similar strategies greatly improve the chances of those children when they become adults. Decades of experience have allowed our organizations to see the adults these children have become. They are now leaders in their community and in our organizations.

The cornerstone in our efforts to support individuals earlier in their lives is the Alliance Schools Initiative, which is a relatively recent strategy developed by the leaders of the IAF. As described by Frank Levy and Richard Murnane in *Teaching the New Basic Skills,* this initiative is a strategy for increasing student achievement through the kind of school restructuring that can only be created and sustained through the work of a broad-based collective constituency of parents, teachers, administrators, and community leaders.[12]

Alliance Schools create a core constituency of advocates that is able to build the relationships necessary to change the culture of schools and the communities they serve. In Alliance Schools, parents, teachers, school administrators, and other community leaders learn how to work together to mobilize people and resources to carry out initiatives that improve their schools and neighborhoods, such as after-school programs, in-school health clinics, learning opportunities for adults, and innovative curriculums—to mention only a few. These initiatives support learning directly in a variety of ways, but most importantly, they transform the attitudes and expectations of students, parents, teachers, administrators, and entire communities. In short, leaders (i.e., parents, teachers, administrators, and community members) develop confidence in their ability to act together to bring about positive change, which in turn creates higher expectations for success among all school stakeholders, including students.

Relative to schools of similar socioeconomic status that received equal amounts of supplemental resources, not only has student attendance increased at the Alliance Schools in Austin, but as Levy and Murnane outline in the September 11, 1996, edition of *Education Week,* these schools increased student achievement as well. While it may be too broad, our interpretation of this information is that resource transfers—particularly in terms of education—will improve the health of the nation only to the extent that there is an organized constituency prepared to operate differently with those supplemental resources. To put it bluntly, money matters. Increased resources are necessary; we must have equity and adequacy in public school finance. But in addition we must restructure and reorganize schools to create the community of learners that enables parents, teachers, school principals, and the other relevant stakeholders to work collaboratively to improve our schools, which is what the Alliance School model of reform creates.

But for all the strategies that we have tested and have found successful, the one strategy upon which the success of all others depends is organizing a broad-based constituency for change. Every successful IAF strategy, including the Alliance Schools Initiative, is a testament to the power of a constituency organized for change. Yet, organizing is the strategy that most progressives talk about the least.

Imagine what would happen if, in seventy-five congressional districts, each candidate attended a meeting with 2,500 to 3,000 organized, registered voters—each committed to turning out at least ten of their neighbors on election day. What if at those public meetings each candidate was asked to make specific commitments to support several elements of a carefully crafted human development agenda, a commitment to extended day enrichment programs for all children, universal health care, a family wage, long-term job training, affordable housing—important elements in any serious effort to reduce inequality and the decline of real wages. Imagine that the agenda had been forged through a year-long process of house meetings, small group meetings in churches and schools—meetings where people's private pain could be transformed into public action. Imagine the new leadership that would be developed through such a process. Imagine the dignity of working people and their families as they collectively forged a powerful role in the governance of their communities and their country. But more importantly, imagine the trust, reciprocity, and solidarity that would emerge—and has emerged—with this type of strategy. Imagine the revitalization of schools, congregations,

and communities as people take responsibility for the vitality of these institutions. Imagine the hope that would be engendered as people began to feel confident about the competence of these institutions to solve their problems. This campaign of conversation would have created a broad-based constituency with ownership of the agenda, a constituency committed to doing the public business and follow-up work necessary to hold the candidates accountable for their commitments.

The IAF has an organizing strategy for making this happen. It is called "Sign Up, Take Charge." Sign Up, Take Charge is a voter education, registration, and turn-out strategy that mobilizes voters around a specific agenda and seeks commitments of candidates in support of that agenda.

The Power of Reinvigorated Social and Political Institutions

The organization of a broad-based constituency for change is possible because the IAF has been doing it on a smaller scale for over fifty years now. The IAF is now the center of a national network of organizations that has produced real results. These results demonstrate the power of reinvigorated social and political institutions and have become the core of a renewed human and community development agenda.

Employment and Work: Long-Term Job Training Strategies

The organizations of the IAF have a proven track record in devising innovative labor market strategies to combat the seemingly intractable forces of the global economy. Much of the organizations' work over the last several years has focused on high-skill/high-wage training strategies first developed by Communities Organized for Public Service (COPS) and the Metro Alliance in San Antonio. Project Quality Employment through Skills Training (QUEST), in marked contrast with most federal training programs, confirms the evidence that effective skills development for high wages cannot be done in a few weeks (every QUEST graduate completes at least a year of training). Project QUEST has graduated 543 participants, over 80 percent of which are now employed in high-skill/high-wage jobs. Other QUEST graduates—forty-five at last count—are currently pursuing higher education (beyond the associate degree level) full time. Synergy, sponsored by Allied Communities of Tarrant in Forth Worth and modeled after Project QUEST, has graduated and placed fifty participants in career-track jobs that pay a minimum of $10.50 per hour. Synergy expects another seventy-five participants to graduate in early 1998. In Dallas, WorkPaths has graduated 213 participants and expects another sixty to graduate in early 1998. WorkPaths has begun working directly with companies and training providers to train participants in general skills, certified for particular industries. In the Lower Rio Grande Valley, Valley Initiative for Development and Advancement (VIDA) has graduated over 200 participants, including over a dozen welders that now work at a local shipyard. This particular shipyard worked with the local community college for two years to develop a training program, but could not come to an agreement on either curriculum or cost. VIDA completed negotiations and began training workers within two months of entering the conversation between the college and the shipyard about creating a training initiative.

These initiatives have done much more than train and place hundreds of low-wage, under-employed and unemployed people who otherwise would not have had an opportunity for high-skill/high-wage careers. More importantly, they have provided tangible justification for public investment of time, money, and energy in an economic development strategy that pays off for ordinary families. They have demonstrated several important, though historically disputed, facts:

- High-wage opportunities exist in even traditionally low-wage urban sectors and regions. Active, publicly supported economic development efforts can find, exploit, and in some cases even create these opportunities for the overall benefit of the community.
- Low-wage, underemployed workers can obtain high-wage, high-skill occupations given the opportunity and support.
- Long-term investments justify their costs. Professor Paul Osterman's evaluation of Project QUEST found that while participants required almost $11,000 each for eighteen months of training, they increased their earnings by $4,500 to $7,000 per year as a result. In other words, Project QUEST returned its investment within two to three years with the increased earnings of San Antonio's citizens.
- The high-skill/high-wage initiatives justify public investment in job training and other labor market interventions at a time when such investment is under attack from ideological conservatives who argue that the labor market will correct itself if "left alone." All the initiatives report that businesses have approached them with training and recruitment needs.
- The initiatives demonstrate the success of collaboration among community and

business leaders who often have been at odds. In San Antonio, COPS and Metro Alliance recruited the leadership of banker Tom Frost, who—two decades ago—had been the target of a major action.[13] In Dallas, the Dallas Citizens Council, the traditional circle of major corporate power brokers, provided the business leadership for WorkPaths.

- The initiatives serve as models of publicly driven economic development strategies that provide benefits to communities and their families, the taxpayers at large, and employer and business constituencies. As such, they provide important alternatives to public economic development strategies that serve narrower interests, such as tax abatements and public construction of entertainment facilities.

Living-Wage Strategies

The IAF's Baltimore organization, Baltimoreans United in Leadership Development (BUILD), and the American Federation of State, County, and Municipal Employees (AFSCME) organized the Solidarity Sponsoring Committee in October 1994. The new organization developed legislation and helped local officials to understand their interest in higher wages for city workers, explaining to them the numerous social costs of poverty. The City of Baltimore no longer supports a system that keeps Baltimore families in poverty. Because of BUILD's work, Baltimore now requires companies to pay their workers a "living wage" for all work done under city contracts. All workers employed by city contractors will make a minimum of $6.10 per hour. Over a four-year period, the rate will climb incrementally to $7.70

per hour, a wage level that will raise a full-time worker's family of four above the poverty line. Inspired by the living-wage bill in Baltimore, IAF organizations have since put together numerous other effective strategies aimed at persuading local governments to rethink their approach to economic development.

San Antonio's COPS and the Metro Alliance, as well as Austin Interfaith, are all fighting for living-wage initiatives in their communities. Thus far, their strategies have been primarily connected to tax abatements. Austin Interfaith recently negotiated a commitment from Samsung, a tax abatement recipient, to pay its entry-level manufacturing workers at least $7 an hour. The organization is now working with the city and the county to establish a policy that would require tax abatement recipients to pay workers a living wage. Similarly, COPS and the Metro Alliance are pressuring the City of San Antonio to refuse tax abatements to corporations that do not pay a living wage. The current struggle is over tax abatements for hotels along the city's Riverwalk—a prime tourist destination. In the short run, the organizations have convinced the city to contract with an independent economist for a cost-benefit analysis of the hotel proposal. In the future, COPS and the Metro Alliance will work to establish as city policy a commitment to invest only in living-wage jobs. They have already persuaded the San Antonio Independent School District School Board to declare a moratorium on school district tax abatements.

The Alliance Schools

It is a familiar truism that the best antipoverty strategy is an education strategy. It is also a fact that support for public schools has weakened to previously unimaginable levels. As the leaders of the IAF network of organizations developed their vision of reforming public education (embodied in the 1990 paper "Communities of Learners"), they came to understand the necessity of developing schools as community institutions.[14] If schools were to prepare our children to attain high levels of achievement, all stakeholders—teachers, parents, community leaders, administrators, public officials—would have to be held accountable for effective, directed collaboration. They connected these parties in the Alliance Schools Initiative, which, as described above, is a partnership committed to fundamentally changing the way that schools and communities work together for student achievement.

In 1993, the leaders' broad-based, statewide constituency brought the Texas legislature into the partnership, which then set aside $2 million for the Investment Capital Fund (ICF) and established an open grants competition to fund schools committed to reform, local control, and local accountability for results. In 1995, the legislature accorded the ICF permanent status in the Texas Education Code, and in 1997, it increased funding for the ICF to $8 million for the biennium. With a membership of 140 schools—and a plan to grow during the coming biennium—the Alliance Schools Initiative continues to garner national, state, and local acclaim for its success in making its vision of schools as public institutions a reality.

To date, the record of the Alliance Schools Initiative is impressive. From 1993 to 1996, twenty-five of the original twenty-seven Alliance Schools experienced a 20.4 percent increase in the number of students passing *every* section of the Texas Assessment of Academic Skills test (TAAS). In addition, seventy-one of the eighty-nine Alliance Schools in Texas (79.8 percent) reached or surpassed the state's attendance average in 1996.

Citizenship

Many of the IAF organizations have begun to implement strategies for engaging legal residents in citizenship; over 15,000 families have been connected to our organizations over the last two years. In Southern California, Texas, and Arizona, IAF leaders are working closely with immigrant communities to guide families not only through the legal process, but also through the development of a more robust concept of what it means to be a citizen in an open democratic society. IAF organizers work closely with the new citizens to connect them to the institutions that will allow them to negotiate the turbulence of the market and the state. Without that connection, their new citizenship would only allow them access to further abuse at the hands of the traditionally powerful. By developing the leadership skills of potential citizens as they go through naturalization, the IAF organizations are working to realize a collective vision of citizenship that extends far beyond the official naturalization ceremony.

Taken together, these concrete accomplishments (and numerous others not listed) represent what is possible for ordinary citizens who have the opportunity to work collaboratively with one another in the political arena. But for this to happen, we have to first go about the business of rebuilding the institutions through which ordinary citizens can practice true politics. Because our political system has failed to address the concerns of working families seriously and effectively, much of our adult population is convinced that politics is largely irrelevant to their lives. And this alienation has impoverished public discourse itself.

The Promise of a New Democratic Politics

One of the most important causes of American poverty, as stated earlier, is that working people are being asked to absorb a disproportionate share of the costs of contemporary economic change without receiving any of the commensurate benefits. A dynamic economy always imposes such costs, and those who are the least powerful—the least articulate, least connected, least organized—invariably bear an inordinate share of the burden. When civic institutions fail to buffer citizens from the market, the effects show up at the bottom line: Real wages for most workers in the United States have been declining since 1973, with the most serious effects visited on the incomes of the less educated. In summary, then, the distribution of the costs of economic change is a matter of politics, not simply economics.

Although the theory of welfare economics implies that the winners (those who benefit from economic change) are supposed to compensate those who bear the costs of that change so that economic growth may continue, in simple terms, today's winners are not compensating the losers. Historically, the balance between the winners and the losers has been maintained somewhat through the social safety net and, most importantly, the implicit social compact that ensured wage and benefit increases during times of economic prosperity. But recently wages have stagnated or declined despite great prosperity, and what safety net existed has been destroyed. Through their positions of power and influence, the winners have developed the capacity to rationalize and legitimize their greed

in the name of the free market. They now completely control those institutions charged with buffering families from the vagaries of the economy. Consequently, it is imperative that those who claim to be concerned about fairness, equity, and stability begin to operate in such a way as to facilitate genuine power-sharing. And equally important, the least powerful members of society must organize themselves and their allies to develop the power necessary to persuade and negotiate with the winners for their fair share of prosperity.

In order for this kind of power-sharing to occur, we must create a public dialogue about revitalizing and renewing our social and political institutions. Only within the context of such a public conversation can we create the intermediary institutions that can serve as a vehicle for teaching and organizing the less powerful.

The rehabilitation of our political and civic culture requires new politics, with authentically democratic mediating institutions—teaching, mentoring, and building an organized constituency with the power and imagination to initiate change. The work of IAF is to establish a public space in which ordinary people can learn and develop the skills of public life, and to create the institutions of a new democratic politics. With organized citizens and strong mediating institutions, our communities can address structural inequalities of the economy for themselves, restore health and integrity to our political process, mitigate the distortions created by organized concentrations of wealth, and—in the end—reclaim the vision and promise of American life.

We must resist the temptation to simply have all of the best policy ideas, without the willingness to work for the realization of those ideas. Regarding the need for a specific policy initiative, Franklin D. Roosevelt is reported to have said something like: "Okay, you've convinced me. . . . Now go out there and organize and create a constituency to make me do it." Unfortunately it seems that too many progressives are still caught up in the "convincing," when what we also need now is the constituency. What we need now are people who are willing to think hard about how to create, sustain, and energize that constituency and connect it to institutions that will challenge and consolidate the power of that constituency. Hopefully, in this way we can restore the vision of the Old Testament prophets in their cry for justice at the gates of the city.

Notes

1. Victor Matthews and Don C. Benjamin, *Social World of Ancient Israel 1250–587 BCE* (Peabody, MA: Hendrickson Publishers, 1995), pp. 122–23.

2. An abundance of research has concluded that wage inequality today is higher than at any time since World War II. See, for example, Frank Levy and Richard J. Murnane, "U.S. Earnings Levels and Earnings Inequality: A Review of Recent Trends and Proposed Explanations," *Journal of Economic Literature* 30 (September 1992): 1333–81; and Janet L. Norwood, *Widening Earnings Inequality: Why and Why Now* (Washington, DC: Urban Institute, 1994).

3. Arthur M. Okun, *Equality and Efficiency: The Big Tradeoff* (Washington, DC: Brookings Institution, 1975), p. 119.

4. Peter F. Drucker, "The New Society of Organizations," *Harvard Business Review* (September–October 1992): 95–104.

5. The IAF is involved in developing broad-based institutions in urban and rural, as well as suburban areas in each of these states. In addition, the IAF is experimenting with metropolitan strategies in Phoenix, Dallas, and particularly Chicago, where such strategies could lead to a new direction in broad-based organizing.

6. Michael J. Sandel, *Democracy's Discontent* (Cambridge: Harvard University Press, 1996).

7. Hannah Arendt, *On Revolution* (New York: Viking, 1963), p. 222.

8. Sheldon Wolin, *The Presence of the Past* (Baltimore: Johns Hopkins University Press, 1989).

9. Social capital is the network of relationships not only among people (as described by James Coleman in "Schools and Communities," *Chicago Studies,* November 1989, pp. 235–37), but also among institutions. Social capital is developed when institutions such as congregations, schools, unions, neighborhood associations, and so forth are not only connected to one another but also organized as a powerful network of institutions around the interests of families and communities.

10. See Ernesto Cortes, Jr., "What About Organizing," *Boston Review* (December–January 1996–97).

11. See Ernesto Cortes, Jr., "Organizing Communities and Constituents for Change," in *Reinventing Early Care and Education: A Vision for a Quality System,* ed. Sharon Lynn Kagan and Nancy E. Cohen (San Francisco: Jossey-Bass, 1996).

12. Richard J. Murnane and Frank Levy, *Teaching the New Basic Skills* (New York: Free Press, 1996).

13. COPS leaders pressured several local business owners to support and lobby the mayor and the City of San Antonio for a new budget that included funding for projects in the poor west side of town. This pressure came in the form of public actions. At Frost National Bank, COPS leaders changed hundreds of dollars into pennies and then back into dollars again, virtually shutting down business at the bank and forcing Tom Frost, the bank's owner, to meet with COPS leaders on the budget issue.

14. Texas IAF Network, "The Texas IAF Vision for Public Schools: Communities of Learners," 1990, unpublished.

36

Access to Capital and Inner-City Revitalization: Urban Policy After Proposition 209

Gary A. Dymski

Introduction: Urban Crisis without Urban Policy

This essay considers whether the urban policy initiatives undertaken by the Clinton administration can appreciably improve the economic circumstances of inner cities in the United States. This administration's principal programmatic initiatives have attempted to stimulate economic renewal and community development by providing support for microenterprise funds and community development banking—that is, by improving access to credit and capital in the inner city. The main conclusion reached here is that these strategies can indeed by effective, *if* they are undertaken on an adequate scale, *if* economic conditions in the inner city do not deteriorate further, and *if* the government simultaneously undertakes other efforts to repair the infrastructure of inner-city communities. These other conditions, however, do not hold: the scale of administration urban initiatives is small, and there has been no serious governmental attention to inner-city deficits in social and physical infrastructure. This situation reflects the attempt by the Clinton administration to assist distressed urban communities while not

violating perceived political constraints on redistribution policy. However, given that market forces are widening the gap between have and have-not areas in cities, this situation amounts to having an urban crisis without an urban policy.

The passage of Proposition 209 in California in 1996, in the same election that brought President Clinton's second term, symbolized these constraints. The Civil Rights Reform Initiative, Proposition 209 on the November 1996 California ballot, provided that no preferential treatment should be given any individual or group in public employment or education on the basis of race, sex, or national origin. As such, this proposition aimed at the root principle underlying U.S. policy toward racial and gender inequality: namely, an individual's race or gender should not in itself be a source of systematic disadvantage in "life, liberty, and the pursuit of happiness." This proposition was approved overwhelmingly at the California polls. On its face, Proposition 209 has a limited scope: it pertains only to public employment and education in California; and even there, its provisions have been blocked by legal challenges. However, as with other propositions debated over the years in California initiative drives, the real impact of

374

Proposition 209 can be found not in its specific provisions, but in the political sentiment this proposition's passage encapsulated: that civil rights law had gone too far in attempting to reduce racial inequality by redistributing income and opportunities.

So enough was enough, was the message of November 5, 1996. Whatever initiatives were designed to turn around the inner-city areas in which minority populations are concentrated must function without large commitments of federal money—that is, without redistributing income or reapportioning opportunities. Ironically, the sentiment crystallized by Proposition 209 was consistent with the thrust of inner-city revitalization initiatives during the entire tenure of the Clinton administration.

To understand this point, a brief overview of U.S. urban policy is in order. The passage of the 1964 Civil Rights Act led directly to programs (including affirmative action) enhancing the opportunities of individual members of disadvantaged classes in U.S. society. It also led indirectly to programs aimed at improving opportunities and services in lower-income areas; while these programs did not specifically target racial inequality, they provided an effective alternative means of attacking systemic racial inequality because of the tight social correlation between race and income inequality. While launched with a rhetorical flourish by Lyndon Johnson (the "war on poverty"), these programs were soon reduced in scope and funding.

During the 1970s and 1980s, corporate disinvestment, together with the rise of satellite cities and decentralized production, have laid waste to inner-city labor markets. The resulting social and economic stagnation in the inner city has been documented elsewhere and requires no repetition here. At the same time, white flight from cities has led to a situation in which redistributive urban programs and efforts to redress racial inequality overlap almost completely. An aggressive urban policy would increasingly involve post-tax transfers from white haves to minority have-nots. As such, urban policy has become ever more politically exposed. Given the choice between political advantage and social need, recent U.S. presidents have taken the path of least resistance.

The Reagan administration dismantled public programs providing for job training, crime prevention, and educational resources in lower-income urban areas. The Bush administration suggested volunteerism ("a thousand points of light") in lieu of government initiative. The Los Angeles uprising in the Spring 1992 electoral season, combined with candidate Clinton's need to attract the urban vote, raised hope of a proactive urban policy. However, after the election the president and his core advisers gave in to Wall Street's demands to shelve plans for fiscal stimulus. In any event, Los Angeles received far more earthquake relief for the 1992 Northridge trembler than it did riot relief. Squeezed between his need to appease Wall Street and "mainstream America" on the one hand, and the urban constituency on the other, the Clinton administration developed urban policy initiatives that target specific problems in stagnant urban economies without setting off fiscal warning beepers. The two urban programs of the Clinton administration, the "empowerment zone" program and community development banking, attack one element of the urban crisis: the shortage of capital in the inner city. Both aim to maximize impact while minimizing fiscal commitment. In this sense, this administration's urban programs already anticipated the impatience with racial-inequality policies embodied in Proposition 209.

But can widespread urban renewal be triggered with "post-Proposition 209" policy tools of this type? The pages below address this question in two stages. First, we delineate the core elements of urban community growth, and contrast the circumstances in struggling inner-city areas with those in thriving suburban areas. Next, we consider how financing mechanisms might bring about renewal in distressed urban communities. This analysis discusses the celebrated Grameen and South Shore Bank cases of capital-led redistributive growth. Finally, we draw some urban-policy lessons from this analytical framework and these cases, and discuss these in light of the political environment symbolized by California's Proposition 209.

Economic Elements of Urban Community

Our point of departure is the raw economic elements of urban and suburban communities. Social reproduction in any urban community requires three elements: robust income flows for local residents and businesses, an asset base with a value that is increasing over time, and an adequate social and physical infrastructure, typically provided and refreshed by public support. When all three elements are present in a community, they are mutually reinforcing; the converse is true when all three elements are absent. If only one or two elements are present, the equilibrium is unstable; the situation will soon shift toward the all-or-none polar situations. How an unstable situation is resolved depends, in turn, on the degree of access to capital and to jobs enjoyed by local residents and businesses.

Consider what happens when income flows are suddenly reduced for numerous members of a stable urban community with an adequate public infrastructure and a robust asset market. This might occur in any inner-city neighborhood where residents have historically held jobs

in local factories and/or in local public bureaucracies. The income starvation creates an unstable situation. Local businesses must either find new customers or make adjustments, and the market for homes will dip unless the area attracts new inflows of residents. In many such cases, asset values have followed income flows downward, and public infrastructure has steadily deteriorated as well. Conversely, suppose asset values drop in a neighborhood that receives adequate public resources and where residents have stable incomes—the sort of situation that occurs when a real estate bubble is burst. In this event, local asset values have often recovered after the passage of a sufficient period of time.

Spillovers in Inner Cities and Suburbs

The three elements of urban economic structure interact because of spillovers generated by market transactions in urban markets. Outcomes in labor markets determine income flows and thus affect asset markets. In effect, employed workers register a demand for assets, such as homes. Conversely, residents who have accrued net worth in their homes can use this to start businesses, to finance educational expenses, and so on—that is, to take steps to increase their income flows. Spillovers also occur within markets. If large numbers of properties are exchanged at high prices, asset values throughout that neighborhood will be positively affected (and vice versa). And the value of any worker's skills will be amplified, in many cases, if that worker is in close proximity on the job or at home to other workers with complementary skills.

The pervasive character of spillovers causes patterns of urban economic prosperity to be uneven. Some areas will flourish as markets generate positive spillovers, which, in turn, encourage more such transactions. Further, urban community development is path-dependent—the history of transactions creates a trajectory of prosperity or stagnation, a cumulative process that is not readily reversed. This history-dependent aspect of urban growth carries historic inequities into the present, and may even amplify them in the future. An implication for urban policy follows: Attempts to intervene in impacted urban areas may have very different levels of success from one location to another, even within the same metropolis.

Changes in the Structure of Production and Financial Intermediation

Two recent shifts in U.S. industrial organization have affected suburbs and inner cities very differently. Structural changes in production and consumption have seriously eroded the effectiveness of traditional fiscal policy in renewing economic growth in inner cities, and changes in the structure of financial intermediation have had a similar effect on the effectiveness of monetary policy. It should be noted that economic globalization has rendered both fiscal and monetary policy less effective than in the past, but the share of inner-city communities in fiscal or monetary expansion has declined as well.

Turning first to fiscal policy, during the early post-war period the inner-city labor force was integrated into primary-sector production; within this labor force, minority workers often were "last hired, first fired." Since primary-sector production is extremely cyclical, inner-city communities experienced large cyclical swings, and the labor-force participation rates and earnings of minority workers were especially procyclical. Further, racial segregation created dense economic interdependencies and cash flows within minority communities. Taken together, these two factors suggest that recessions hit minority communities especially hard, but expansionary fiscal policy produced rapid income gains for workers. Minority communities' internal economic heterogeneity and interconnections, in turn, ensured large fiscal multipliers. And because many factories are located in and near the inner city, "virtuous circles" of expenditure and income sustained many inner-city communities.

In recent years, the sensitivity of inner-city communities to fiscal stimulus has eroded. Fewer inner-city residents are employed in primary-sector manufacturing jobs, so the last-hired, first-fired effect has been diluted. Further, with residential desegregation, the class structures of inner cities have become less geographically integrated, so new spending has smaller multiplier effects. These changes do not mean that fiscal stimulus is now ineffective in inner cities: to the contrary, recent experience suggests that employment and labor-force participation will rise sharply when economy-wide activity is sufficiently robust. The point is, the stimulus required to lift the inner-city economy out of stagnation is much greater than in the past.

Turning to financial intermediation and monetary policy, financial institutions too have redefined their roles in ways that have particularly affected inner-city economies. Deregulation has placed competitive pressures on the financial sector and led financial firms to move toward upscale customers and neighborhoods, leaving lower-income customers behind. With some exceptions, financial intermediaries once served all households and businesses within their market areas. However, these customer bases have now been carved into distinct market segments. The most desirable segments consist of wealthy and middle-income households, which retain access to a wide range of financial services. Customers in this market segment increasingly have their needs met because their financial characteristics are easily measured, standardized, and serviced. They are sold financial services as commodities, impersonally and at low cost. Despite an overall pattern of downsizing and branch closures, financial institutions continue to locate new branches and compete for customers in these more affluent areas. The bottom niche consists of lower-income inner-city households. In the past, many of these households had established relationships with banks and used these relationships to overcome barriers to creditworthiness. However, in the past two decades, formal financial institutions have reduced their services in these communities and raised prices on financial services for lower-balance customers. Lower-income households consequently often cannot afford to maintain accounts.

In effect, banks and other financial firms have shed risks and shifted from an intermediary to a broker role: They no longer create a network of interlocking localized financial relationships, but act as gateways to a set of disembodied financial services. So banks and thrifts no longer are the focal point for integrated, localized savings/investment processes. Instead, they are the localized purveyors of standardized financial services. Some smaller banks retain the older model, but these find it difficult to attract deposits from wealthier households with many savings options. Upper-income households and larger businesses have improved their access to finance even as lower-income households and smaller businesses have seen their financial links erode.

Because of these patterns of banking, lower-income and minority communities experience spillover losses due to redlining and discrimination, branch closures, bank consolidation, and securitization. Externalities in local credit markets lead to the erosion of economic development possibilities in communities populated by critical masses of the unbanked, even as financial infrastructures blossom in communities populated by the wealthy.

These changes reduce the money multiplier and compromise the effectiveness of monetary policy. Fewer households and businesses hold balances with, and borrow from, banks than in the abandoned universal-access system. The customers who banks actively court now have immediate access to the direct credit markets, regardless of the state of monetary policy. Smaller firms and lower-income households still depend on bank credit markets. But the smaller banks that extend loans to these economic units are disappearing in the bank consolidation wave. The loss of financial capacity in minority and lower-income communities implies smaller money multipliers there due to local spillover effects involving housing values, business viability, and job creation. Increased numbers of informal financial firms offering fragmented, costly services cannot duplicate the synergies of the now-dismantled integrated banking system. So monetary policy, never immensely effective in the inner city, is less so today.

Implications for Policy Intervention

There are two key implications of these points for policy efforts aimed at uplifting inner-city economies. First, broad-based demand-stimulus measures—the bread-and-butter of traditional Keynesian policy—will be relatively ineffective, or at least less effective. Rising tides do lift all boats, and tight labor markets do eventually pull in even disaffected workers. But the level of overall stimulus required to significantly improve conditions in the inner city is now higher than before—high enough to challenge prevailing orthodoxy. Urban policies thus should aim at reducing specific institutional impairments in the inner-city economy.

Second, these policies should be undertaken on a scale that will mute and even reverse negative spillovers. In communities lacking all three elements of structural integrity, intervention in two of the three elements is needed. Investment in just one element, at too small a scale, will not overcome the negative spillovers generated by the neglected factors. Taking steps to shore up capital asset values in an area that lacks robust income flows and adequate public investment may fill in some commercial holes, but it will not change that area's character. Similarly, jobs programs without public investment and without any opening of channels to capital flows will be interpreted—rightly—as stop-gap make-work.

If intervention in two elements of the economic matrix does occur, the likely speed of recovery, even given the deployment of adequate resources, depends on which configuration is adopted. The quickest path to recovery involves simultaneously creating labor demand and capital supply, especially if the newly deployed labor works on improving public infrastructure. The slowest two-element strategy involves improving public infrastructure—but not increasing labor demand—while also increasing access to capital. This policy might pay off, but only in the longer run.

This analysis is contrary to many economists' thinking about urban problems today. Many economists interpret inner-city woes as due to blockages or rigidities in the two factor markets—that for labor and that for capital. This supply-side approach ignores the demand for goods and services and blames interference with market forces. Every geographic area can be understood as having a pre-given ideal equilibrium level for its labor and credit markets—these levels, in turn, being set by local residents' preferences and resources. So any inner-city "problem" derives from too little demand or supply in one of the factor markets. Government interference is not necessary; competition will eliminate untaken market opportunities.

A different analysis is suggested here. Markets do not adjust via a simple displacement principle, filling in empty spaces when these emerge. Market dynamics respond positively to prior concentrations of economic activity; because of spillovers, markets work in clusters. So supply or demand deficits in one factor market will spill over to the other factor market and pull it down as well. For example, an inadequate supply of capital will eventually induce a lower demand for labor. Areas lacking suppliers may not get any; those that are mobile may prefer other locations.

Financial Strategies for Inner-City Redevelopment

We now consider specifically whether financing strategies are effective means of intervening in inner-city economies. The last section asserted that the evolution of financial structures now leads them to amplify growth and worsen decay in urban sub-areas. In consequence, lower-income urban communities are increasingly isolated from more prosperous communities. In this new financial environment, low current levels of income, wealth, or human capital within a neighborhood reinforce continued poverty in the future. A lack of capital, in turn, restricts the future access to capital needed to generate the economic growth that can overcome today's poverty.

Problems in Financing Inner-City Growth

Communities and individuals discarded by the formal sector must turn to the growing second-tier sector to meet their financial needs. Check-cashing outlets and money orders are used for cash transactions and payments. The cost of using these facilities generally varies inversely with household economic status. For obtaining credit, the options are fewer. Pawnbrokers have been described as the short-term credit market for the poor; they are more accurately described as the lender of last resort for the financially excluded, since they offer credit only on very onerous terms. Bank credit facilitates the accumulation of new human or physical assets that enhances future income, but pawnbroker credit involves households' decumulation of their stock of assets to meet current income crises.

While the cost of financial services is a large problem in inner-city areas, an equally important problem is these communities' lack of savings and savings vehicles. Without household wealth, local residents cannot engage in the level of investment needed to reverse downward dynamic trajectories and re-ignite growth. This lack of savings results, in part, from discrimination; it also results from these households' unequal access to labor markets, and from financial restructuring and the anemic credit flows in lower-income communities (redlining). In effect, inner-city residents and businesses have inadequate capital assets and lack means of gaining access to capital.

Three Approaches to Improving Access to Capital in the Inner City

The Clinton administration's two programs for increasing access to capital in the inner city are the creation of "empowerment zones" and the

nourishing of community development banks. There are, in turn, two distinct methods of conducting community development banking: the "financing from below" approach and the "greenlining" approach.

Inducements to Mobile Capital: Empowerment Zones

The empowerment zone concept is actually an extension of the "enterprise zone" concept introduced in the late 1970s. The premise is that low-income urban communities are caught in a low-level equilibrium trap in which small amounts of capital and labor are demanded and supplied. The zone program provides incentives for businesses to locate and create jobs in impacted areas; these incentives can range from tax forgiveness to bond-financing subsidies to tax credits. The guiding assumption is that capital is scarce in depressed inner-city areas, and since capital is mobile—and inner-city labor is not—capital must be wooed. The absence of economic activity means the absence of capital, which in turn must be due to the absence of market locational incentives. The zone incentives artificially increase the supply of capital in the zones and hence, by attracting new employers, the demand for local labor. In effect, zone subsidies are designed to shift the labor and capital markets to a higher equilibrium level.

The performance of empowerment and enterprise zones has met with substantial criticism. For one thing, the locational subsidies are scarce and valuable, so it is often alleged that these subsidies are subject to political capture. For another, it is often unclear whether mobile capital has created new jobs or merely relocated existing ones at a net cost to taxpayers. Finally, the higher-skill jobs introduced into these zones have often gone to suburban residents.

Financing from Below: Micro-Enterprise Funds

Micro-enterprise funds improve access to capital by creating mechanisms whereby very poor individuals lacking wealth can acquire assets and undertake entrepreneurial activity. This method of regenerating urban communities is based on the model of the Grameen Bank of Bangladesh. Begun in the late 1970s, Grameen first operated in rural villages in which low-income women lacked access to labor markets, investment finance, and collateral. Poor women were organized into small teams, trained in personal and business skills, and given mutual responsibility for small business start-up loans made to each team member in sequence. This approach has resulted in remarkably low default rates and in marked improvements in the standard of living of poor households.

A modified version of the Grameen Bank, the Good Hope Fund, was initiated in Arkansas under then-Governor Clinton; while this transplant did not touch the very poorest, as does Grameen, its success and that of other U.S. experiments has suggested that micro-enterprise funds could uplift many low-income people, especially women. President Clinton's community-development banking initiative has sometimes been equated with an effort to launch micro-enterprise funds throughout the nation's cities. However, the president's program provides money only to adequately capitalized banks, not to startup community funds, and it insists that the funded banks earn market returns. This hurdle also poses difficulties for micro-enterprise funds. One study of Grameen suggests that its costs equal about 125 percent of its revenues, even after government subsidies for its cost of funds. Any Grameen-type program that works with the very poorest will, to be effective, require a substantial—and costly—training component.

Some structural differences between the U.S. inner city and the Bangladeshi village are also important. The Bangladeshi rural economy allows for factor-market interlinkage, but the U.S. inner-city economy does not—it lacks any equivalent to the labor-absorbing agricultural cycle of the village. The lack of an agricultural cycle, combined with class/race segregation patterns, also creates a problem of insufficient aggregate demand in the inner city. The U.S. urban situation also poses a problem due to the greater capital intensity of U.S. communities, even low-income ones; in consequence, loans will have to be larger—and required baseline payments for rent and food are more substantial than in the Bangladeshi village. Finally, the declining availability of character loans means less credit will be available for entrepreneurs who graduate into small-business status.

Greenlining: Development Banks

The experience of Chicago's South Shore Bank in the 1970s and 1980s offers another model for community development banking. Unlike most micro-enterprise funds, South Shore was chartered as a private (profit-seeking) bank; it aims to "do good by doing well." South Shore Bank achieved fame due to its success in financing home sales in the South Shore housing market at a time when other lenders had pulled out in the wake of this area's rapid racial flux. South Shore's lending strategy was assisted by two factors: first, this area has a large stock of sound housing, since it was once among Chicago's classier suburbs; second, many of the minorities moving in were middle-class households whose wage-earners held stable (disproportionately civil service) jobs. Once South Shore's lending strategy was launched, other institutions were induced to participate. Further leveraging was provided by a "greenlining" strategy—bank officials aggressively sought out long-term deposits and pledged capital from churches' social-concerns funds and activist individuals.

This institution is the prototype for the Clinton administration's community-development banking program—a stable privately owned institution with its own capital base. Generalizing this model poses difficulties, as in the case of the Grameen model. Structural conditions for most inner-city neighborhoods differ greatly from those of South Shore in the 1970s: The stable jobs held by African-Americans then have evaporated for many, and housing stock is often seriously deteriorated. On the other hand, the core elements of this model—private ownership and greenlining—are intriguing; greenlining in particular is a strategy whose potential has yet to be tapped.

Problems and Potentials of Financial Strategies

The programs described here, especially the two financial strategies, are promising. But it should give us pause that large banks have pulled out of areas and products that are no longer directly profitable, and that it is mainly community activists who want to become inner-city bankers in the 1990s. So, what inducements are needed to attract money into inner-city financing vehicles? And can such finance-based strategies be effective in spurring urban revitalization?

The first question poses particular problems because of large banks' withdrawal from inner-city areas. Intermediaries willing to collect, hold, and invest the funds of inner-city residents and businesses in their own neighborhoods are increasingly rare. So generating inner-city financing requires either public-policy sticks or carrots to "tilt" market outcomes. The stick is the Community Reinvestment Act (CRA). The CRA requires depository institutions (mainly banks and thrifts) to make affirmative efforts to meet the credit needs of all portions of their market areas, including lower-income and high-minority communities. Adequate CRA performance must be demonstrated by any depository wishing to acquire another bank or to open new branches. While it has often been honored in the breach, community pressure and ongoing bank mergers have mobilized substantial funds for inner-city assets under the CRA. An obvious step for increasing the supply of loanable funds in the inner city is to extend the CRA to cover non-depository institutions such as pension and mutual funds.

What about carrot approaches? One, suggested by Bob Pollin, is to set lower reserve requirements for banks and thrifts against funds they invest in underserved areas such as inner cities. A second carrot approach is to create a mechanism for securitizing loans made in the inner city—that is, bundling together small loans into securities that are attractive to investors. Securitization requires standardization of terms, underwriting of the extraordinary risks involved, and the establishment of a secondary market. While this is a major undertaking, it is no less than has been done for the mainstream housing market. The Federal National Mortgage Association (FNMA), the key institution in the vast complex of secondary markets that surrounds U.S. housing finance, was sponsored and is underwritten by the federal government. John Veitch and I have suggested a parallel mechanism for securitizing inner-city loans, which we term the Community Development Mortgage Association (Cindy Mae). Cindy Mae would differ from FNMA primarily because it would accept credits carrying higher risk. But these extra risks could be underwritten, as are

Figure 36.1 **Urban Factor-Market Dynamics and Intervention Strategies**

	Insufficient labor supplied in inner city	Labor markets operate efficiently in the inner city	Inadequate demand for inner-city labor
Low level of demand for capital and productive credit in inner city	(culture of poverty)	(lack of entrepreneurial initiative) Grameen	
Capital and credit markets operate efficiently in the inner city	(spatial mismatch, skills mismatch, high return to crime)	"Equal opportunity" and revitalization	(deindustrialization, capital flight, labor-mkt discrimination)
Insufficient supply of capital and productive credit in inner city		(redlining or credit-market discrimination) South Shore	(structural crisis) Empowerment zones

FNMA securities, via a loan-loss equalization fund maintained by lenders, government, or both.

Suppose funds *can* be pushed into the inner city, augmenting the financing available for asset-based activities there. Will these financing vehicles then spark inner-city renewal? Figure 36.1 is useful in answering this question. A diagonal line divides this figure into northwestern and southeastern halves. These two halves summarize two contrasting views of the causes of inner-city economic crisis.

The northwestern half depicts what might be termed the cultural interpretation. This view regards inner-city economic stagnation as due jointly to inner-city residents' failure to supply labor and to demand capital. Skills and spatial mismatches between inner-city workers and available jobs may explain why these workers have low labor-force participation rates, but inner-city residents' reluctance to take lower-wage jobs and their lack of entrepreneurial initiative are also to blame. The situation will improve only when the alternatives to labor-force participation and entrepreneurship—that is, welfare benefits and criminal activity—are made less available and less attractive. A contrasting view of inner-city economic crisis, supported here, points to a different set of factors:

improve only when the alternatives to labor-force participation and entrepreneurship—that is, welfare benefits and criminal activity—are made less available and less attractive. A contrasting view of inner-city economic crisis, supported here, points to a different set of factors: an inadequate supply of capital and credit and an inadequate demand for inner-city labor. This structural interpretation puts the primary blame for the current crisis on deindustrialization and discrimination in markets, not on the behavioral maladies of inner-city residents.

In the terms of our three-element analysis of the urban economy, Figure 36.1's center cell represents a healthy urban economy. Interruptions in income flow due to high unemployment rates push the economy away from the center and toward either right or left. Reversals in asset values push the economy either up or down. How easily the economy can be pushed off its center-cell point—the degree of dynamic instability—depends on the severity of the shock and of the strength of public infrastructure expenditures. For example, a skills mismatch that causes workers in a given community to be unable to supply their labor can be remedied quickly if public education and training programs are strong. If the level of public infrastructure is low, however, then any push away from the center in one direction (for example, due to declining labor demand) will cause further drift from the center in the other direction (toward an inadequate supply of capital). The extreme northwestern and southeastern cells are the perverse stable equilibria discussed above, wherein income flows, asset values, and infrastructure all have collapsed.

Overlaid on Figure 36.1 are the three financial revitalization approaches discussed here. The South Shore and Grameen approaches focus on different types of credit-market failure. The South Shore approach responds to an inadequate supply of capital and credit, while the Grameen approach responds to an inadequate demand for capital and credit. Note that these two diagnoses are not necessarily inconsistent. The empowerment zone, in turn, assumes the problem is both an inadequate supply of capital and an inadequate demand for labor.

The three-factor economic framework developed here suggests that none of these approaches, either in isolation or together, can succeed as an urban policy—that is, as a policy for revitalizing inner cities. For one thing, the problem of scale is of fundamental importance. Turning around outcomes in communities requires a significant investment of resources in whatever dimensions of the economy are being attacked. In the case of financing approaches, which attempt to restore asset values and asset-based earnings, significant programs will have non-trivial costs. As indicated above, "financing from below" is a myth; resource transfers are needed. President Clinton's community-development banking program anticipates the expenditure of a half-billion dollars over five years. This level of expenditure is not adequate to allow for widespread creation and/or support of South Shore-type banks, even given the leveraging of federal monies by the funds of private investors and of financial firms meeting CRA requirements. Further, a widespread Grameen-style program for low-income people would require at least $1 billion annually. This is not to say that neither program should be initiated without substantial federal support. Without it, both programs will be at best demonstration efforts. A small-scale Grameen program will allow some exceptionally motivated individuals to escape the inner city, but will not remake the inner city, and similarly for a small-scale South Shore federal program.

Our three-factor framework also suggests that when urban communities have gravitated toward rest points with triple deficits, a purely financial approach must be supplemented by another urban intervention strategy. Given an adequate attack on asset values via one of the financial strategies outlined here, income flows can be improved by a labor-market program. Increased labor-market earnings will provide markets for budding entrepreneurs and facilitate the stabilization of asset values. As discussed above, a serious effort to improve the public infrastructure of inner-city areas will almost invariably improve income levels as well.

Conclusion

This brings us back to our entry point—Proposition 209. Leaving aside the possibility that numerous supporters were swayed primarily by misleading labeling, the majority vote for Proposition 209, like the inner-city economic crisis examined here, can be given a cultural or a structural interpretation. In the cultural interpretation, "yes" on 209 declares that undeserving minorities should get no help from public programs; those who want to lift themselves up by the bootstraps badly enough will do so. In the structural interpretation, "yes" on 209 represents the white majority's sentiment that scarce resources should not be reserved for minorities. As above, these interpretations are not mutually exclusive; the important point here is that these two readings of Proposition 209 overlap with the cultural and structural interpretations of inner-city economic crisis.

It has been argued here that the differences in inner-city and suburban economies are due primarily to structural forces. So efforts to ameliorate the inner city's crisis must address structural gaps. Operating as if only cultural, not structural, gaps exist will lead to policies that only worsen the inner-city structural crisis. An inner city that is a more punitive environment, with lower levels of public income and infrastructure support, will have even less structural integrity as an economy.

A serious attack on the maladies of the inner-city economy must be mounted on at least two of the three fronts of income flows, asset values, and infrastructure health. As argued here, financial strategies can be part of a successful policy mix, but they cannot stand alone, especially if they are not well funded. This brings us to the dilemma posed by Proposition 209. A low-cost urban policy will abide by the structural message sent by 209's supporters (that is, "don't redistribute scarce resources to voting minorities"), but is unlikely to be effective as economic strategy. Ironically, the failure of a poorly funded strategy could suggest to many that the root problems really are cultural, not structural—preparing the ground for even more disastrous racial conflict. A meaningful attack on the economic problems of the inner-city economy requires a significant commitment of resources. If the resources for this attack are found by redistributing income and program dollars away from other purposes, this aggressive policy approach will run afoul of the political logic of Proposition 209.

There is another way forward. A large-scale inner-city program can be mounted without paying the political cost of redistributing scarce resources if the president is willing to use deficit spending, or a portion of a fiscal surplus, for this purpose. In effect, eliminating the environment of budgetary austerity—which has gone so far as to generate federal surpluses—could go far toward easing the level of political racial tensions as well as clearing the way for an effective assault on inner-city economic problems. Taking this step would not be without economic and political risk. It requires a willingness to confront Wall Street and its talisman of budget balance. It also demands a willingness to call the political bluff of Proposition 209 supporters. If the structural sources of support for Proposition 209 are cut away—if whites do not fear that minorities are getting ahead in a race for a fixed pool of resources—then the only remaining basis for Proposition 209 as a guiding premise of U.S. social policy is a cultural argument that cannot stand up to scientific and ethical scrutiny.

37

The U.S. Rural Economy in Historical and Global Context

William Galston

Although it has been disadvantaged by the dominant economic trends of the 1980s and 1990s, rural America continues to play a vital role in the U.S. economy and society. Today, it is home to 21 percent of the U.S. population, supplies 18 percent of its jobs, and generates 14 percent of its earnings. After decades of decline, the U.S. rural economy showed unexpected economic and population growth during the 1970s. These favorable trends were reversed in the 1980s. Both extractive industries and routine manufacturing, on which many rural areas are heavily dependent, experienced severe recessions in the early and middle part of the decade, and the subsequent revival of production in these sectors was not accompanied by a commensurate revival of employment. Meanwhile, the growth sectors of the national economy—high-tech manufacturing, knowledge-intensive industries, business services—became increasingly concentrated in urban areas.

The difficulties rural America experienced in the 1980s were in large measure the product of vast shifts in the national and international economy. Nonetheless, federal policies also contributed to rural disadvantage. For much of the decade, macroeconomic policies produced currency distortions that impeded rural exports, as well as persistent high real interest rates to

which the rural economy proved vulnerable. Deregulation in transportation and telecommunications wiped out longstanding cross-subsidies to rural areas. Federal spending patterns, particularly in defense, tilted toward metropolitan areas, and the bias of federal rural dollars toward agriculture and current consumption was not conducive to long-term economic growth.

The overall consequence of economic trends and public policies for rural America in the 1980s has been well summarized by Kenneth Deavers: "The recovery that began in 1982 [was] long and fairly strong in terms of compound annual rates of growth in GNP and employment. . . . Nevertheless, in contrast with earlier periods, strong national growth . . . contributed little to improving the relative performance of the rural economy."[1] The elements of this dramatic rural-urban divergence can be measured along a number of key dimensions.

- **Employment.** Between 1979 and 1989, metropolitan area employment grew by 23.8 percent, while rural employment grew by only 10.6 percent.
- **Unemployment.** Between 1979 and 1989, annual rural unemployment rates ranged between 1 percent and 2.5 percent higher than metropolitan rates.

- **Income.** The ratio of rural to metropolitan per capita incomes declined from 77 percent at the end of the 1970s to only 73 percent in 1987, the lowest level since 1970.
- **Wages.** After adjusting for inflation, average annual earnings per job fell 8 percent ($1,700) in rural areas between 1979 and 1989, versus only 2 percent ($450) for metropolitan areas. As a result, the metropolitan/rural gap grew from $5,000 to more than $6,200.
- **Earnings penalty.** In 1974, the ratio of metropolitan to rural earnings was quite similar across educational categories, rising only gradually from 1.08 for individuals with an eighth-grade education to 1.14 for college graduates. By 1986, while the ratio for the eighth-grade educated was 1.18, the ratio for college graduates approached 1.4. In short, returns to education increased much faster in metropolitan than in rural areas.
- **Poverty.** The rural poverty rate soared to 18 percent between 1979 and 1982 and remained stuck at nearly that level throughout the ensuing economic recovery. By 1989, the rural poverty rate was 50 percent higher than for metropolitan areas. Today, 51 percent of rural residents fall in the two poorest quintiles; the comparable urban number is 37 percent.

Not surprisingly, rates for the working poor (the characteristic form of rural poverty) also increased dramatically. In 1979, 32 percent of rural workers earned below the poverty line for a family of four, compared with 23 percent of urban workers. By 1987, the percentage of rural lower earners had risen by 10 points, to 42 percent, versus a six-point rise to 29 percent for urban lower earners. The poverty rate for rural families in which the head of household worked rose from 7.6 to 10 percent during this period, twice as high as the rate for corresponding metropolitan families.

The interaction of poverty and the relative scarcity of critical services such as health care has devastating consequences for many rural residents. According to a 1990 report by the Aspen Institute's Rural Economic Policy Program, "Maternal and infant mortality rates are substantially higher than those in urban areas and are rising at a faster rate. Rural Americans have disproportionately high rates of serious chronic illness, accidents, and disability. But the health care system is not equipped to adequately serve these needs."[2]

- **Population.** While the rural growth rate had exceeded the metropolitan rate by almost 40 percent in the 1970s, it fell to less than half the metropolitan rate through the 1980s. By the mid-1980s, annual out-migration from rural areas reached nearly 500,000, a rate substantially above the annual average for the 1950s and 1960s. More than one-half of all rural counties actually lost population during this period. According to Deavers, in large measure because of the shifts in educational earnings gaps summarized above: "Rural out-migration is not only age specific but education specific. As a consequence, many of the best-trained and most promising young people left rural America during this period."[3]

The evidence suggests that rural population trends during the 1980s were inversely correlated to community size: On average, the smallest towns were hardest hit, and mid-sized communities have come closer to holding their own.

Location continues to affect rural population trends. Given previous research demonstrating the importance of proximity to metropolitan areas for rural county growth during the 1950s, 1960s, and 1970s, it is hardly surprising that adjacency turned out to be so significant in the 1980s. During 1979–88, employment in rural counties adjacent to metropolitan areas grew at more than twice the rate of non-adjacent counties.

In some respects, the 1990s witnessed a reversal of the markedly adverse trends buffeting rural America during the 1980s. The overvalued dollar that impeded exports has been replaced by more sustainable currency valuations. The most recent round of the General Agreement on Tariffs and Trade (GATT) has meant expanded markets and fairer treatment for a wide range of rural American products. The defense budget increases of the 1980s, which shifted rural tax dollars to metropolitan-based contractors, were reversed. New factories appear to be locating once again in rural areas: Between 1989 and 1994, rural counties gained 167,000 manufacturing jobs, while urban areas lost 1,172,000.

The rate of rural population loss appears to have slowed significantly in many areas and in other areas to have reversed. In the aggregate, demographers Kenneth Johnson and Calvin Beale report, rural counties experienced a 5 percent increase in population between 1990 and 1995, with three-quarters of all counties posting gains. Although the majority of farm-dependent counties are still losing population, the rate of loss has slowed. Meanwhile, areas with substantial recreation and retirement development have surged, while rural areas near growing urban areas have continued to show population increases. And a growing body of evidence suggests that the revolution in information technology and telecommunications is beginning to benefit rural America by making small towns and even remote communities more accessible for businesses and attractive for young professionals.

The structure of the rural economy increasingly resembles that of the nation as a whole. Services provide more than half of all non-metropolitan employment, manufacturing slightly less than one-fifth, and agriculture less than one-tenth. Indeed, during the past twenty years the percentage of the rural workforce engaged in farming has been cut nearly in half, and only about five million people (less than 10 percent of the rural population) live on farms.

Notwithstanding some favorable trends in rural America, many significant problems persist. Key indicators such as per capita income and real earnings per job remain far lower in rural counties than in metropolitan areas. (Real earnings per rural job in the early 1990s were significantly lower than in the late 1970s.) The gap between metropolitan and rural college completion rates increased from 6.9 percent in 1980 to 9.5 percent in 1990. Almost one-quarter of all rural counties are persistently poor, with poverty rates in excess of 20 percent since at least the 1960s.

Rural job generation continues at only half the pace of metropolitan areas. Increases in agricultural productivity continue to outpace growth in demand, producing continued downward pressure on agricultural employment.

Rural manufacturing—much of which is routine, low skill, and low wage—remains exposed to international competition. The Asian financial crisis has dealt a heavy blow to U.S. agricultural exports, agriculture-related businesses, rural land values, and farm income. And the nearly one-fifth of rural jobs that depend on government activities may prove vulnerable to continuing pressure to reduce the size and scope of the federal government workforce.

The National/Global Context

These shifting rural trends cannot be understood in a vacuum. American rural society and economy are now exposed, more than ever, to the powerful national and international forces analyzed elsewhere in this volume.

To begin with, the primary products economy is now significantly detached from the industrial economy. In classic business cycle theory, a decline in agriculture and raw materials is soon followed by a serious crisis in industry. Yet throughout much of the 1980s, a prolonged primary-product depression had little effect on the broader economy. Because materials constitute a small, and declining, portion of the GNP of advanced countries, even sharp declines in raw materials output and income have at most marginal overall effects.

This progressive marginalization of primary products is unlikely to be reversed, in part because other countries have increased their agricultural and materials output, but more fundamentally because of the reduced importance of materials as inputs for industrial production. Peter Drucker offers the following examples: Materials and energy constituted 60 percent of the cost of the representative industrial product of the 1920s—the automobile—versus 2 percent for the representative industrial product of the 1980s—the semiconductor microchip. Copper wires with a materials/energy content of close to 80 percent are being replaced in telephone cables by glass fiber with a materials/energy content of 10 percent.[4] While there may be temporal local or sectoral exceptions to these broad trends, rural strategies premised on sustainably rising demand and prices for primary products have no serious chance of succeeding.

The decreasing importance of raw materials has consequences for the entire U.S. economy, not just rural America. In a path-breaking article, Gavin Wright has shown that the rise of the United States to industrial supremacy rested heavily on relative price and supply advantages in non-reproducible natural resources. Since then, the integration of world markets for resources has significantly eroded those advantages. As Wright observes, these resources are now commodities rather than factor endowments.[5] An important issue facing the U.S. economy, then, is whether it can find sustainable sources of competitiveness to replace this vanishing advantage, an issue complicated by the increasing mobility of technology and information.

The second key development is the wedge that has been driven between production and employment throughout traditional economic sectors. This is a familiar phenomenon in U.S. agriculture, where tremendous advances in output have been accomplished with ever-shrinking numbers of producers. There is no reason to expect the increase in agricultural productivity to slow. If anything, biotechnological advances may speed up the rate of increase in coming decades.

Somewhat less familiar, but just as important, is the spread of this inexorable logic of productivity to the manufacturing sector over the past fifteen years. American manufacturing production has risen by roughly half, but manufacturing employment has declined. The much-discussed U.S. productivity problem has been largely confined to the service sector; our manufacturing productivity has risen by more than 2 percent annually since 1982, a rate that has accelerated in recent years.

This trend is also long term. The ratio of blue-collar workers in the total labor force was one in three in the 1920s, one in four in the 1950s, less than one in six today, and likely to be at most one in ten by the year 2010. This decrease, which implies a continuing decline in the absolute number of U.S. manufacturing workers, will coincide with continuing large increases in manufacturing output and exports. Indeed, rapidly rising productivity is a condition for such increases, because without it no industry can hope to remain competitive.

Once again, the implication for rural America is clear. Agriculture, raw materials, and manufacturing will continue to shrink their employment. While recent trends in rural manufacturing offer modest encouragement, there is little possibility that routine production jobs can fully absorb excess rural workers in the future to the extent that they did in the 1970s.

The end of three decades of federal budget deficits has eased pressures on monetary policy and interest rates. But in other respects rural America is unlikely to benefit significantly. As entitlement programs continue their inexorable expansion, pressure for discretionary spending restraint at the federal level continues.

The implications for U.S. rural development programs are clear and sobering. Incremental public funds will be very hard to come by; pressures on (and struggles over) existing resources will persist. As is the case in other areas, demands will escalate for stricter accountability as well as demonstrable results. There is likely to be an expanding market for more efficient, less bureaucratic forms of public-sector activity, a process policy analyst David Osborne has labeled "reinventing government" and that has been pursued by the National Performance Review under the leadership of Vice President Gore.

The need to compete more effectively in the international economy will give an edge to public programs that can be justified as investments in long-term productivity and growth over efforts to promote equity. Rural strategies will have to be defended primarily as contributions to overall national well-being rather than in place-specific terms. But national and local advantage may not converge. For example, human capital investment makes eminent sense as a national strategy, but it cannot succeed in stanching the outflow of trained young people from rural communities unless rates of return to human capital are simultaneously increased in these communities—a goal that may prove far harder to justify in national terms, let alone achieve.

The implication to be drawn from these broad trends is clear: Rural America has entered an era in which innovation may not guarantee success, but status quo policies will ensure failure. The challenge in the years ahead is to shape new strategies responsive to both rural realities and changing national and global circumstances.

Rural Comparative Advantage

To have any chance of succeeding, these new strategies must be built on a realistic assessment of the rural comparative advantage. Early in U.S. history, the development of rural America rested primarily on place-specific resource advantages: land, timber, and minerals. The central rural disadvantage, the obstacle of distance, was overcome in part by natural location factors (such as long, navigable rivers) and in part by publicly guided development of communication and transportation systems. These advantages have not disappeared, but their significance has been steadily eroded by changes in technology, related factors of production, and the composition of final demand.

In the 1960s and 1970s, the primary basis of rural comparative advantage shifted from resources to factors such as cheap land, low-cost labor, relatively relaxed regulations, and weak or non-existent unions. Combined with a new burst of public investment in transportation (the interstate highway system), these advantages spurred a significant expansion of routine manufacturing in rural America. From 1960 to 1980, the rural share of manufacturing employment rose from 21 to 27 percent.

But these advantages, too, have been eroded by economic change. The importance of land costs in plant siting decisions has diminished, and in a global marketplace with fully mobile capital, cheaper labor can be found and employed outside our borders. In the longer term, there is good reason to believe that labor will continue to shrink as a component of manufacturing costs and, therefore, as a determinant of production siting.

During the 1980s, rural America entered its third major phase. The kinds of natural characteristics regarded as "amenity values" by retirees, vacationers, and certain businesses have emerged as the chief new source of rural comparative advantage. (We may speculate that this relative advantage may have been widened by declining amenities in many urban areas.) Rural places with substantial locational assets commanded the lion's share of rural population and employment gains.

There is however a downside. The same characteristics—lower population size and density—that give some rural areas amenity value frequently limit opportunities for development in other economic sectors. Three factors are key: First, lower size and density make it difficult, and in some cases impossible, to achieve significant local diversification, which leaves communities, and even entire regions, highly vulnerable to downturns in their prime economic base. Second, these factors are correlated with larger average distances between individuals as well as between economic activities, which raises costs of communication and transportation. Information is typically harder to get than in urban areas, and transaction costs are higher. The deregulatory wave of the 1980s increased the rural disadvantage in transportation costs. Not surprisingly, rural counties that are adjacent to metropolitan areas did far better than did remote counties during the past decade. Third, successful amenity-based development may eventually erode the original advantage, as population size and density increase and amenity values decline.

As Emery Castle has observed, the financial costs associated with overcoming distance are not a linear function of distance. Technological change and infrastructure development can do a great deal to reduce the costs of geographical distance. Still, he notes:

> The economic welfare of the more sparsely populated areas is linked with, and dependent upon, economic activity in the more densely populated areas. . . . It is not a coincidence that the most prosperous rural areas have close economic links with other parts of the world and the large urban centers.[6]

This thesis suggests that a central challenge for U.S. rural development will be to conceptualize, and put in place, new kinds of linkages between metropolitan areas and remote communities.

Conclusion

Market forces did not adequately promote rural development during the 1980s, and the unchecked market's indifference to issues of geographic distribution was nowhere more clearly demonstrated. Nor, in spite of heroic efforts, was rural civil society able to address effectively the problems with which it was confronted. Churches, communities, and support groups ministered to distress and occasionally warded off worst-case outcomes, but without reversing underlying negative trends. The public sector did no better: In spite of unprecedented spending on programs regarded as "rural," the federal government did little to improve the long-term prospects of rural families and communities.

James Bonnen has argued that U.S. rural policy is a classic example of "government failure." The reason, he contends, is that during the past century the political economy of rural America was institutionalized around key industries rather than communities. For much of the period, this political configuration was not too damaging. But in the crisis of the Great Depression, Congress created rural legislation that for the most part provided selective goods to specific groups, usually agricultural. This evoked a mobilization of agricultural interest groups to defend and expand public benefits to commercial agriculture at precisely the time that this sector was rapidly shrinking in population and output. The result has been the domination of national rural policy by an increasingly narrow and unrepresentative segment of rural America.[7]

Still, it would be premature to give up on the capacity of the public sector to improve rural America, even in the face of the adverse global trends described earlier. Within an overall pattern of stagnation, opportunities for local growth may nonetheless persist. The point is that a sounder understanding of broad developments will create a context in which policy analysts and local decision-makers can more realistically evaluate the odds of success for the options they face. Rural communities need not always "go with the flow," but they should at least understand the nature of that flow.

To summarize:

1. The pressures of international competition will continue to force steady productivity increases in agriculture, natural resources, and manufacturing, driving a deepening wedge between output and employment. Local communities and national policy must turn increasingly toward the substantially non-trade sectors of the economy such as the retiring elderly, tourism, and government activities. This new emphasis is consistent with the shift of rural comparative advantage to a third phase, one that emphasizes amenities rather than natural resources or production costs.

2. Continuing pressure on federal discretionary spending means that large new rural programs are unlikely and that continuing reevaluation of existing programs is inevitable. This is a situation that cries out for innovation in the basic structure of public action. Government programs must increasingly employ cost-effective, non-bureaucratic mechanisms, and they must use public resources to catalyze action in the private sector and in

rural communities.

3. The continuing, perhaps even enhanced, importance of rural linkage to thriving metropolitan areas means that public policy must focus on approaches such as advanced telecommunications that could give rural communities more complete and timely access to information while enhancing their attractiveness as sites for service-sector activities, and it must lower existing barriers to fuller rural participation in the most vigorously growing parts of the economy.

4. The growing importance of size for community survival suggests that organizational change is essential. Small rural communities must break down political boundaries and form new cooperative political units for education, service delivery, and public entrepreneurship—units that more closely correspond to the real scope of contemporary rural economic and social life. Recent trends suggest that only through such consolidation can many of the smallest communities hope to avoid continuing decline and eventual extinction.

5. The progressive globalization of advanced economies has led many analysts to conclude that the skills and cumulative learning of the workforce are the real sources of the "wealth of nations" in the next century. While there is debate as to the rate at which workforce skills will have to improve the basic direction of needed change is clear. It does not follow, however, that what enhances national wealth will necessarily benefit particular regions. There are many reasons for local communities and the federal government to embark on a new partnership to upgrade education and training. But rural communities should be under no illusion that such initiatives by themselves will suffice to create local job opportunities and stanch the outflow of young people from rural areas.

Notes

1. Kenneth L. Deavers, "Rural Development in the 1990s: Data and Research Needs," paper prepared for the Rural Social Science Symposium, AAEA, Baton Rouge, Louisiana, July 28–29, 1989, pp. 12–13.

2. *Search for "The Way that Works:" An Analysis of FmHA Rural Development Policy and Implementation* (Washington, DC: Aspen Institute, 1990), p. 3.

3. Deavers, "Rural Development in the 1990s," p. 11.

4. Peter F. Drucker, *The New Realities* (New York: Harper and Row, 1989), p. 122.

5. Gavin Wright, "The Origins of American Industrial Success, 1879–1940," *American Economic Review* 80:4 (September 1990): 651–68.

6. Emery Castle. "Policy Options for Rural Development in a Restructured Rural Economy: An International Perspective," in *Agriculture and Beyond: Rural Economic Development,* Gene F. Summers et al. (Madison: University of Wisconsin College of Agricultural and Life Sciences, 1987), pp. 16–17.

7. James T. Bonnen, "U.S. Perspectives on the Interest Group Base of Rural Policy: People, Agriculture, and the Environment," paper prepared for delivery at the Aspen Institute, July 1990.

38

Prosperity and Inequality Among America's Cities and Regions

Norman J. Glickman

Introduction

As Ray Marshall's overview stated, the marked increase in income inequality in American society since the 1970s has gained wide public attention. The public and scholarly discussions almost exclusively center on differences among *people*. What are the income differences according to individuals' occupations, the types of industries that employ them, and their skill levels, educational attainment, gender, and ethnicity? While these are indeed proper issues for restoring shared prosperity in our society, they constitute an incomplete set because they do not consider differences in inequality in a *spatial* sense. They ignore differences among and within cities and regions.

Much of the debate about inequality began with Simon Kuznets's important cross-national analyses (in his 1955 and later writings) in which he argued that personal income differentials increase and then decrease as economic development takes place.[1] This hypothesis became known as the "inverted U" (movements from the left-hand side toward point A in Figure 38.1). Later, Jeffrey Williamson extended the notion of the inverted U and applied it to regions: At early stages of economic development, he argued, income and wealth concentrate

in a few regions; subsequently, there is dispersion to poorer regions as development continues.[2] However, since those pathbreaking studies, patterns of inequality have changed. More recent data show that after a decline in inequality at both the personal and spatial levels, inequality again began to increase. These findings are most striking for interpersonal inequality, less so for regions. This suggests that the link between development and inequality may not be as simple and straightforward as some have argued. This controversy also raises questions about future differences among this country's regions. In this chapter, I will examine the trends in personal and regional inequality and attempt to determine whether the recent trends of increasing inequality will continue.

Personal Income Inequality

The data show that Kuznets was correct for most of the last century for the United States and most developed countries. In fact, the distribution of income is among the most stable of all economic phenomena.[3] Over the past 150 years, there have been long periods of relative stability and shorter periods during which there was more substantial change.[4] For example, after the U.S. Civil War there was very high

Figure 38.1 **Economic Development and Changes in Inequality** (The Inverted U)

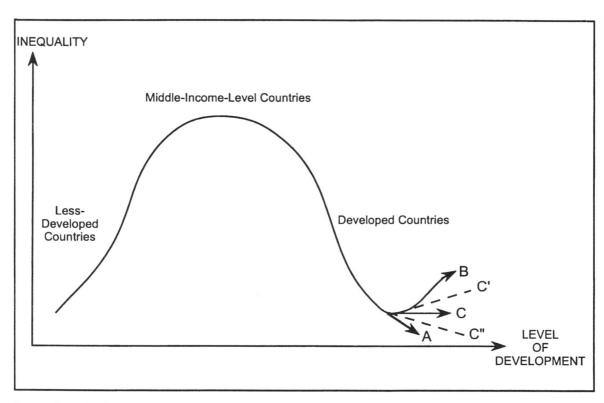

Source: Amos 1988.

inequality (compared with today) and relative constancy in that distribution. For most of the 130 years since the Civil War, the trend of per capita incomes has been toward greater equality. There was a brief drop in inequality after World War I, but inequality increased again during the 1920s. The Great Depression of the 1930s marked the beginning of a sharp decline in inequality through the early 1950s. Inequality was stable for next twenty-five years or so. These events were consistent with Kuznets's **U.**

Beginning in the 1970s, however, income disparities began to widen. The Gini coefficient and other measures of inequality rose sharply, and by the beginning of the 1980s, income in-

equality was higher than at any time since World War II. At the same time, real income growth slowed and the standard of living for most Americans dropped sharply, after more than forty years of nearly constant growth. Inequality then *increased* (moving toward point B in Figure 38.1). This change was inconsistent with the Kuznets's hypothesis and surprised many economists.

The dimensions of the increase in U.S. interpersonal inequality in the 1970s and 1980s have indeed been substantial. During the 1980s, the main economic "winners" were those in the top 20 percent of the income distribution.[5] Simultaneously, the proportion of middle-class families declined, as both lower- and upper-income families increased in number. Since overall income grew slowly, the vast majority of American workers experienced lower real living standards in the mid-1990s than at the end of the 1970s.

Much of the greater inequality was due to the increase in the proportion of families in two demographic groups: two-earner married couples at the top of the income distribution and families with only one low-earning spouse or with no wage earner at all.[6] While real incomes of married-couple families increased by 16 percent, those of single-headed families declined. The number of workers per family, the hours worked per worker, and real hourly earnings all rose for the top decile, but fell for the lowest.

Traditionally, governmental taxing and spending policies helped reduce inequality. In the last twenty years, however, the effect of government has been to make the distribution of income actually *more* unequal than it would have otherwise been.[7]

After relative constancy during the 1970s, there was an income divergence between groups—as defined by age and education—during the 1980s. Inequality within groups (e.g., 25-to-34-year-old high school-educated males) has been increasing since the 1970s and played a key role in the 1980s surge of inequality. For young, less-educated men in particular, the situation became increasingly bleak. Non-college-educated males had much less chance of earning a middle-class income than did their fathers.[8] Women-headed single-earner households were among the worst off in any class.

What caused the increases in interpersonal inequality? Danziger and Gottschalk confess that "no single factor accounts for the many complex changes in the distribution of income."[9] They hold that there are several explanations, all of them partial. Barry Bluestone makes a similar argument, saying that there are several "suspects" in this great "mystery."[10] Some of the most widely-cited causes include changes in technology, shifts in the supply of and demand for labor, deindustrialization, declining unionization, the increase in immigration from poorer countries, the downsizing of U.S. corporations, government deregulation, and changes in tax policy.

Bluestone's answer to the "mystery" is: "They all did it."[11] "That is, all of the factors listed above played some role in the increase in inequality. What is of great policy concern, however, is that in earlier periods, rapid economic growth went hand-in-hand with declining inequality (i.e., inequality was countercyclical). In the 1980s and 1990s, the U.S. economy expanded, yet inequality increased.

Patterns of Regional Inequality

The data indicate that the course of interregional inequality largely followed the inverted U until the 1970s in the United States, the United Kingdom, and other developed countries.[12] The process was not completely smooth, with medium-term periods of increasing and decreasing inequality, but the overall patterns were clear. During the last twenty years, however, there has been increasing regional inequality.

Interregional Disparities

At the beginning of the twentieth century, differences in per capita income across regions were very high. Per capita income in the Far West was about 60 percent higher than the national average, whereas in the Southeast it was about half the national average. As the century progressed, interregional differences declined

Figure 38.2 **Per Capita Income: 1969–93**

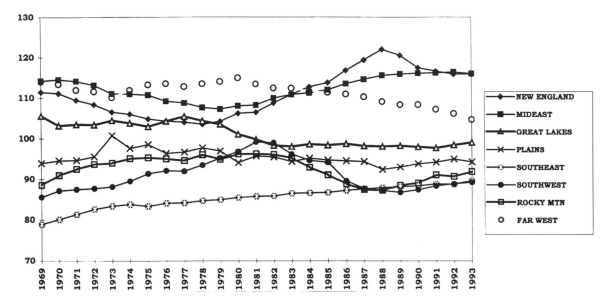

dramatically—especially between 1900 and 1930. By the 1960s, the South had largely caught up with the North and Midwest. During the 1960s, income levels in the South and West grew much more quickly than in the Northeast and Midwest, where old-line manufacturing areas suffered outmigration and job loss. Growth differences between the Sunbelt (South and West) and Frostbelt (Northeast and Midwest) swelled further in the 1970s, as employment decreased and outmigration increased in the latter region. During the 1980s and 1990s, the picture was mixed regarding interregional inequality, although it showed a mostly increasing pattern (Figure 38.2). The high-income New England and Mideast regions experienced rising per capita incomes (especially New England in the 1980s). However, the Far West, another high-income area, lost relative income, while other high-income regions stayed even. At the lower end of the income spectrum, the Southeast continued to gain. The Southwest lost

ground sharply during the "oil bust" of the mid-1980s, although it rebounded a few years later.

The South stood out in a number of ways. Historically, the nation's poorest region, the South's income levels had been gradually rising. By the 1980s, income in the South was about 90 percent of the national average. At the same time, the South had the most unequal distribution of income and the widest divergence of incomes by race.

As the South expanded rapidly, it attracted a number of firms—often branch plants of companies from other regions in low-wage, low-skill industries—because it offered lower labor and land costs, lower rates of unionization, growing local markets, and "pro-business" policies on the part of local governments.[13] However, as Amy Glasmeier and Robin Leichenko show, the growth of the South, though rapid, did not erase serious inequalities within that varied region. In particular, the South's rural areas continued to be the poorest in the country.

These long-term changes in interregional inequality can also be seen in several other measures. The Gini coefficient for the United States, for example, fell from 0.23 in 1900 to 0.07 in 1980.[14] The biggest decreases came during the 1930s and 1940s. There was a more modest decline from about 1950 to 1980 and then an increase during the 1980s. Cindy Fan and Emilio Casetti calculate inequality on a five-year basis and show an increase in inequality beginning in 1975. Amos shows that in 1950, most states were along the declining portion of the inverted U curve, and a few were still on the increasing portion at the left-hand side of Figure 38.1. Over time, as inequality increased, the states moved toward the right in Figure 38.1. Therefore, by 1980, most states were in the upward sloping part of the "new" U.[15]

These long-term patterns are similar to those for interpersonal income inequality. Although the change in patterns was not as abrupt for regions, a "regional U-turn" came into existence in parallel with the interpersonal one. Moreover, there were spatial adjustments in both income and employment growth among large regions that paralleled the changes in interpersonal inequality. There were also changes *within* regions—changes among central cities, suburbs, and non-metropolitan areas.

Intraregional Income Disparities

What happened to inequality within regions? For United States and Europe, there has been greater inequality within countries than between them. Fan and Casetti decompose total U.S. regional inequality into between-region inequality and within-region inequality in an attempt to better explain regional disparity issues; they show that both variables declined between 1950 and 1975 and then turned up again. Of interest,

there is a substantially greater inequality *within* regions than *between* them. The South has by far the greatest level of inequality throughout the four decades analyzed.

Three phenomena are important to consider: (1) overall, systemic inequality increased; (2) the relative importance of between-region inequality grew, as new sources of growth appeared on a regional basis; and (3) after 1975, for the first time since 1950, inequality among high-income states grew. In addition, this took place as manufacturing spread from the traditional core areas to low-cost areas (both within the United States and internationally). Domestic sectoral shifts toward the financial services and high-technology industries meant that regions on the two coasts grew because of their concentrations in those industries. Rapid movements of capital are dependent on the outcomes of the international division of labor. Regions around the globe are quick to feel the differential impacts of new trade and investment patterns.

The highest level of inequality was in the West, South Central, Middle Atlantic, and Pacific regions (where the ratio of the top decile to the bottom was about ten to one). The least amount of inequality was in the West North Central and Mountain states (where there was a seven to one ratio of richest to poorest deciles). The inequality rankings of the regions stayed relatively constant over time (i.e., regions that had lower inequality in the 1970s had the same inequality in the 1990s).[16]

During the past twenty years, metropolitan areas have continued to spread out, with the suburbs and "exurbs," or "edge cities," growing rapidly at the expense of both central cities and rural areas. Suburbs now dominate metropolitan areas in terms of population and employment. The central counties of the Frostbelt's twenty-eight largest metropolitan areas, according to

John Kasarda, lost nearly one million manufacturing jobs and $26 billion in manufacturing employee earnings in the 1980s.[17] The suburbs gained large numbers of these jobs as manufacturing decentralized within regions. In many major U.S. metropolitan areas, the suburbs now have more office and retail space than the central cities. In the largest seventy-four metropolitan areas, I, Michael Lahr, and Elvin Wyly document the widening disparities in income per capita between central cities and the suburbs.[18] For example, the city of Newark had the second lowest level of per capita income while its nearby suburbs ranked first in the nation. Glickman, Lahr, and Wyly's measure of inequality comparing cities and their suburbs confirm that the South's metropolitan areas had the most unequal distributions of income. Over time, increases in inequality of regions have occurred mainly because of declines at the lower end of the income distribution.

One further measure of income inequality is the ratio of the average income in the top fifth of the income distribution to the average income in the bottom fifth. Between 1979 and 1989, fully forty-three of the fifty states showed growing ratios—an indication of growing intrastate inequality. Again, by this measure, the South was the most unequal region.

Not only did inequality change between regions, it grew within them. Decentralization of metropolitan areas and continued middle-class flight to the suburbs widened differences in economic opportunity and demographic composition between different parts of metropolitan areas. Central-city neighborhoods become more racially and ethnically diverse and poorer as suitable employment shifts to the suburbs, even as nearby office districts provide professional jobs for affluent suburban commuters. Moreover, the ratio of city to suburban poverty rates

widened from 1.9 to 2.5 for large metropolitan areas. By 1990, suburban per capita income exceeded city levels in all but one-tenth of metropolitan statistical areas (MSAs), and these exceptional MSAs contained relatively new, actively annexing central cities of the South and West that were surrounded by largely rural suburbs. In the nation's 100 largest metropolitan areas, the dissimilarity index for the poor population, which measures the proportion of the population that would have to move to achieve an integrated spatial distribution, increased from 33 in 1970 to 36 in 1990. In aging industrial metropolitan areas, the segregation of the poor is increasing substantially.

In sum, regional incomes diverged over the past two decades, although not as greatly or uniformly as personal incomes, and average incomes among regions grew more unequal, as did interpersonal incomes within regions. Overall, within-region income inequality was greater than between-region income differences.

Explaining Regional Inequality

As with interpersonal income, several factors explain why regional inequality has increased.

1. *Uneven resource endowments.* Regions begin the development process unevenly, possessing different levels of human and natural resources. Proximity to waterways, for example, has always played an important role in regional development. Resource development—which is also inherently unequal geographically—contributes to income inequality as well. The development of the oil industry in Texas and the rest of the oil patch are good examples of this.

2. *National business cycles.* Although regions' fortunes do not move precisely with the nation's, regional economies are clearly in-

fluenced by what happens to the country's economy. At times, regions follow sharply different courses—as the Southwest did during the oil bust of the mid- to late-1980s when the rest of the country was growing. Inequality increased rapidly in the Southwest during the last half of that decade, while at the same time, the East North Central and Middle Atlantic states were growing rapidly and showed declining income inequality. New England, the fastest growing region during the 1980s, had little increase in income inequality; however, when the early 1990s downturn took place, that region not only lost many jobs, but also increased its inequality. Usually economic growth reduces inequality, while downturns increase inequality over the cycle. However, as noted earlier, the 1980s contained both economic growth and increasing inequality for the nation as a whole.

3. *Demographic factors.* Interregional migration is important in explaining regional inequality. Throughout the history of the United States, migration has brought people from poor areas to greater job opportunities in higher-wage regions; return migration, during later stages of development, improved the standing of growing, peripheral areas. Interregional migration also accelerated the process of regional convergence of per capita incomes. Other demographic factors leading to increased inequality include a higher proportion of a region's population headed by single parents, the proportion of part-time workers, low labor force participation, and large minority populations.

4. *Technology.* Many analysts focus on technology and its relationship to levels of economic development. For example, Brian Berry, Edward Harpham, and Evel Elliott review "four great surges" of inequality in the United States, placing the debate over regional inequality in the context of "long waves" of economic devel-

opment, which increased incomes in the places experiencing faster economic development relative to others. They argue that there have been periods of increasing inequality and other periods of decreasing inequality that are related to technological change.[19] Regional change has accompanied technological shifts. At different times in American economic history, technological developments—such as the introduction of steam and coal power and railroads during the nineteenth century and petrochemicals and automobiles in the twentieth century—have been associated with increasing disparities. The first great increase in inequality came after 1816, when large-scale innovative industrial development took place and large-scale infrastructure (e.g., canals, roads) was built. The second surge came after the U.S. Civil War; again, there was substantial technological change in the form of steam engines, railroads, and steelmaking equipment. This period also saw substantial regional differences emerge, with the decline of the defeated South and the rise of manufacturing in the Northeast. The third increase in inequality came in the 1920s, a time of technological advances in automobiles, petrochemicals, and consumer goods. Spatial inequality also increased as modern manufacturing grew up primarily in metropolitan regions. Rural areas suffered in relative terms.

5. *Industry mix and industrial linkages.* The strength of regional development involves linkages among sectors that economic theory predicts will widen income inequalities. If increases in demand for a region's products are associated with strong backward linkages that increase local production, there will be more growth. For instance, an increased external demand for automobiles leads to an increase in the production of locally produced auto parts. Similarly, if there are strong forward linkages, an

increase in the production of goods at the primary end of the industrial spectrum becomes associated with production closer to the market. In theory, the strength or weaknesses of these linkages often play important roles in determining regional growth and, therefore, how income distribution changes over time. However, the data do not bear out the relationship between income distribution and industry mix. During the past thirty years, there has been a major decline in manufacturing, particularly in the northeastern states. If changes in industry mix were really important, then there should have been substantial inequality increases in manufacturing states. This did not take place. The Mountain states, with a relatively small and decreasing manufacturing presence, should have seen high inequality—but these areas were not particularly unequal. Therefore, the precise relationship between inequality and industrial structure remains unproved. However, as change takes place among regions, the distribution of industry among regions becomes more similar. Historically, the decline of agriculture, and its replacement with secondary and tertiary industries, meant that the former agricultural regions began to look increasingly like the rest of the nation. This "sameness" in industrial structure implies that regional income distributions will likely look more similar, too. Convergence of industrial structure, therefore, is really both a cause and effect of regional income distribution.

6. *International trade and investment.* The differential pushes and pulls of international corporations have had important effects on where investment takes place and, therefore, on regional development. Fan and Casetti show that the recent increase in inequality has largely been due to the spatial restructuring of the international economy and renewed growth of some traditional core cities and other areas. They hold that the flow of capital is a response to differences in regional competitiveness in the international marketplace.

7. *Education.* The role of education and investments in human capital by taxpayers has been cited as another factor in the development of regions. Scholars argue that education improves labor-force productivity and thus increases the attractiveness of the region. In the economic development literature, a better-educated labor force is seen as a generator of local growth. However, education is also associated with inequality. The growth in family income and employment increase income equality, while increases in property income and years of schooling decrease inequality. Expenditures on higher education represent income transfers from the poor to the middle class; the underrepresentation of poor people in universities contributes to inequality in the long term, since the benefits of higher education are only captured by those receiving it. Thus, although higher education may be good for local growth, it is associated with high levels of inequality.[20] As in the previous discussion of personal income distribution, it is evident that each of these "suspects" plays a role in changes in regional income distribution. Many of these factors also have ramifications for public policy.

The Future of Regional Differences in Prosperity

As we look toward 2045, what does the future hold for regional income inequality? Will there be a return to the years of declining inequality, or will the increasing inequality of the past twenty years continue? In order to answer these questions, it is important to understand that complete convergence is not guaranteed, although many scholars argue that migration and trade tend to promote convergence. Several dynamic factors may preclude convergence of regional per capita incomes and other measures of income dispersion predicted by neoclassical economic theory. Differences in labor productivity, industry mix, family size and composition, amenities, differences in living costs, and other factors will cause income differences to remain even if migration of people and capital to high-return regions lessens interregional inequality.

Moreover, some of the divergences of the past two decades can be attributed to shocks to regional economies emanating from changes in the national and international economies. For example, in the 1980s, New England received a boost in the real estate and financial services sectors that affected both incomes and their distribution; similarly, the decline in the energy sector influenced the Southwest. These shocks to regional systems take time to work through and can result in changes in income distribution that last a considerable period of time. In the longer term, there may be a return to less interregional inequality, but the process of convergence, if it does reoccur, will be slow. Robert Barro and Xavier Sala-i-Martin forecast that convergence will take at least forty years at a rate of about 2 percent per year.[21] Since there are forces pulling in different directions and little way to confidently predict what, if any, changes could occur in technology, world trade, demographics, or other variables, the future direction of inequality is difficult to predict. The research in this field seems to hold that it is most likely that some intermediate set of trends will dominate the future, with some decline in interregional inequality in the offing. This suggests that the increase in interregional inequality during the last two decades may be reversed and that there might well be continued equaliza-

tion of income differences—as indicated by movements toward the ranges of points C, C', or C'' in Figure 38.1.

My calculations of future Gini coefficients for regions, based on U.S. Department of Commerce projections, show a small decline in inequality (Figure 38.3). However, these forecasts are based on the assumption that regional industrial structures will not change greatly over time along with several other assumptions about a relatively stable economic structure. All predictions about the future of regional dispersions depend, of course, on changes in the overall distribution of personal income, and no one has produced indisputable estimates of those numbers. As a result, we have very rough estimates based upon assumptions about the future that remain debatable.

We are also left with a number of conclusions concerning regional inequality. First, changes in inequality come slowly and over long periods. Second, the long-term pattern has been toward a lessening of inequality over time, among both people and regions. The recent swing toward greater inequality runs counter to the overall course of the last century's economic history; however, there have been medium-term periods of increasing inequality within long-term declines, including the past twenty years. Third, and finally, it is very difficult to say with precision what the future holds regarding inequality. No one can forecast with any great accuracy what changes will take place in technology, industry mix, and interpersonal patterns of income to say what will happen at either national or regional levels.

Notes

1. Simon Kuznets, "Economic Growth and Income Inequality," *American Economic Review* 45, 1955, pp. 1–28.

Figure 38.3 **Weighted Gini Coefficients: 1969–2045** (weighted by the share of the state in the total U.S. population)

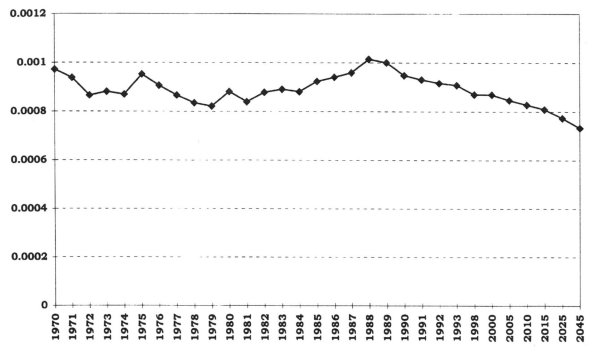

2. Jeffrey Williamson, "Regional Inequalities and the Process of National Development," *Economic Development and Cultural Change* 13, 1965, pp. 3–45.

3. Rebecca Blank and Alan Blinder, "Macroeconomics, Income Distribution and Poverty," in Sheldon Danziger and Daniel Weinberg (eds.), *Fighting Poverty: What Works and What Doesn't* (Cambridge, MA: Harvard University Press, 1986).

4. Jeffrey Williamson and Peter Lindert, *American Inequality: A Macroeconomic History,* Institute for Research on Poverty Monograph Series (New York: Academic Press, 1980).

5. Lawrence Mishel and Jared Bernstein, *The State of Working America, 1992–93* (Washington, DC: Economic Policy Institute, 1993).

6. Katherine Bradbury, "The Growing Inequality of Family Incomes: Changing Families and Changing Wages," *New England Economic Review,* July–August 1996.

7. Edward Gramlich, Richard Kasten, and Frank Sammartino, "Growing Inequality in the 1980s: The Role of Federal Taxes and Cash Transfers," in Sheldon Danziger and Peter Gottschalk (eds.), *Uneven Tides: Rising Inequality in America* (New York: Russell Sage Foundation,

1993), pp. 225–49.

8. Frank Levy and Richard J. Murnane, "U.S. Earning Levels and Earnings Inequality: A Review of Recent Trends and Proposed Explanations," *Journal of Economic Literature* 30, 1992, pp. 1333–81.

9. Sheldon Danziger and Peter Gottschalk, "Introduction," in Sheldon Danziger and Peter Gottschalk (eds.), *Uneven Tides: Rising Inequality in America* (New York, NY: Russell Sage Foundation, 1993), pp. 3–17.

10. Barry Bluestone, "The Inequality Express," *The American Prospect* 20, Winter 1995, pp. 81–93.

11. Ibid., p. 87.

12. Norman Glickman, *Does Economic Development "Cause" Regional Inequality?* Working Paper No. 101, Center for Urban Policy Research, 1996.

13. Amy Glasmeier and Robin Leichenko, *From Free Market Rhetoric to Free Market Reality: The Future of the U.S. South in an Era of Globalization,* Pennsylvania State University, Department of Geography, 1995, unpublished.

14. Luis Suarez Villa and Juan R. Cuadrado Roura, "Regional Economic Integration and the Evolution of Disparities," *Papers in Regional Science* 4, 1993, pp. 369–387.

15. Cindy Fan and Emilio Casetti, "The Spatial and Temporal Dynamics of U.S. Regional Income Inequality,

"Regional Economic Integration and the Evolution of Disparities," *Papers in Regional Science* 4, 1993, pp. 369–387.

15. Cindy Fan and Emilio Casetti, "The Spatial and Temporal Dynamics of U.S. Regional Income Inequality, 1950–1989," *Annals of Regional Science* 28, 1994, pp. 177–98.

16. Katherine Bradbury, "The Growing Inequality of Family Incomes: Changing Families and Changing Wages," *New England Economic Review,* Federal Reserve Bank of New England, July–August 1996.

17. John Kasarda, "Industrial Restructuring and the Consequences of Changing Job Locations," Report for the 1990 Census Project Committee of the Russell Sage Foundation, University of North Carolina at Chapel Hill, 1994.

18. Norman Glickman, Michael Lahr, and Elvin Wyly, *State of the Nation's Cities: America's Changing Urban Life* (Washington, DC: U.S. Department of Housing and Urban Development, 1996).

19. Brian Berry, Edward Harpham, and Euel Elliott, "Long Swings in American Inequality: The Kuznets' Conjecture Revisited," *Papers in Regional Science* 74, no. 2, 1995, pp. '53–74.

20. John Bishop, John Formby, and Paul Thistle, "Explaining Interstate Variations in Income Inequality," *Review of Economics and Statistics* 74, 1992, pp. 553–57.

21. Robert Barro and Xavier Sala-i-Martin, "Convergence Across States and Regions," *Brookings Papers on Economic Activity* 1, 1991, pp. 107–58.

List of Contributors

Ray Marshall (editor) holds the Audre and Bernard Rapoport Centennial Chair in Economics and Public Affairs at the University of Texas at Austin. He served as U.S. Secretary of Labor under Jimmy Carter from 1977–81.

Avner Ahituv is an assistant professor at the Hebrew University at Jerusalem.

Eileen Appelbaum is the associate research director of the Economic Policy Institute, Washington, D.C.

Dean Baker is a senior research fellow for the Preamble Center and the Century Foundation, Washington, D.C.

Peter Berg is an assistant professor at Michigan State University, East Lansing, Michigan.

Daniel F. Burton, Jr., is the vice president for government relations at Novell, Washington, D.C.

Anthony P. Carnevale is the vice president for public leadership at the Educational Testing Service, Washington, D.C.

Jorge Chapa is director and professor of Latino Studies, Indiana University, Bloomington.

Ernesto Cortes, Jr., is the director of the Southwest Region of the Industrial Areas Foundation, Austin, Texas.

Jane D'Arista is a lecturer at the Boston University School of Law.

Karen Davis is the president of the Commonwealth Fund, New York City.

Donna Desrochers is a senior economist with the Educational Testing Service, Washington, D.C.

Gary A. Dymski is an associate professor of economics at the University of California at Riverside.

Robert Eisner, before his death, was the William R. Kenan Professor Emeritus at Northwestern University, Evanston, Illinois.

Jeff Faux is the president of the Economic Policy Institute, Washington, D.C.

Richard Fowles is an associate professor at the University of Utah, Salt Lake City.

William A. Galston is a professor at the University of Maryland School of Public Affairs, College Park, Maryland.

Teresa Ghilarducci is an associate professor of economics at the University of Notre Dame, Notre Dame.

Eli Ginzberg is the director of the Eisenhower Center for the Conservation of Human Resources at Columbia University, New York City.

Norman J. Glickman is the director of the Center for Urban Policy Research of Rutgers University, New Jersey.

Heidi Hartmann is the director of the Institute for Women's Policy Research, Washington, D.C.

Harry J. Holzer is a professor of economics at Michigan State University, East Lansing.

V. Joseph Hotz is a professor of economics at the University of California, Los Angeles.

Christopher T. King is the director of the Ray Marshall Center for the Study of Human Resources at the University of Texas at Austin.

Thomas A. Kochan is the George M. Bunker Professor of Management at MIT, Cambridge, Massachusetts.

Thea Lee is the assistant director of public policy of the AFL-CIO, Washington, D.C.

Donald W. Long is a program specialist with the Texas Workforce Commission, Austin.

Diane J. Macunovich is an associate professor of economics at Williams College, Williamstown, Massachusetts.

Garth Mangum is the Max McGraw Professor of Economics and Management Emeritus, University of Utah, Salt Lake City.

Daniel P. McMurrer is a senior research officer at the American Society for Training and Development, Alexandria, Virginia.

Robert McPherson is a senior research associate at the Ray Marshall Center for the Study of Human Resources at the University of Texas at Austin.

Mary Merva is an associate professor at John Cabot University, Rome, Italy.

Richard P. Nathan is the director of the Nelson A. Rockefeller Institute of Government, Albany, New York.

Mark R. Rosenzweig is a professor of economics at the University of Pennsylvania, Philadelphia.

Isabel V. Sawhill is a senior fellow with the Brookings Institution, Washington, D.C.

Elliott Sclar is a professor of urban planning at Columbia University, New York City.

Robert M. Solow is an Institute Professor Emeritus at MIT, Cambridge, Massachusetts.

William Spelman is an associate professor at the Lyndon B. Johnson School of Public Affairs at the University of Texas at Austin.

Michael S. Teitelbaum is the program director of the Alfred P. Sloan Foundation, New York City.

Lester Thurow is the Lemelson Professor of Management and Economics at MIT, Cambridge, Massachusetts.

Marta Tienda is the director of the Office of Population Research and a professor of sociology and public affairs at Princeton University, Princeton, New Jersey.

Marc S. Tucker is president of the National Center on Education and the Economy, Washington, D.C.

Thomas J. Usher is chairman and CEO of the USX Corporation, Pittsburgh, Pennsylvania.

Paula B. Voos is a professor in the School of Management and Labor Relations at Rutgers University, New Brunswick, New Jersey.

Richard H. White is a project manager for the Institute for Defense Analysis, Alexandria, Virginia.

Robert M. White is president emeritus of the National Academy of Engineering, Washington, D.C.

William J. Wilson is the Lewis P. and Linda L. Geyser University Professor at the John F. Kennedy School of Government, Harvard University.

Edward N. Wolff is a professor of economics at New York University, New York City.

Index

411